Other Works by Drs. Comer and Poussaint

JAMES P. COMER, M.D.
Beyond Black and White

ALVIN F. POUSSAINT, M.D.
Why Blacks Kill Blacks

Black Child Care

HOW TO BRING UP A HEALTHY
BLACK CHILD IN AMERICA

A Guide to Emotional and Psychological Development

BY James P. Comer, M.D.
AND Alvin F. Poussaint, M.D.

 SIMON AND SCHUSTER | NEW YORK

Copyright © 1975 by Dr. James P. Comer and Dr. Alvin F. Poussaint
All rights reserved
including the right of reproduction
in whole or in part in any form
Published by Simon and Schuster
A Gulf + Western Company
Rockefeller Center, 630 Fifth Avenue
New York, New York 10020

Designed by Irving Perkins
Manufactured in the United States of America
By American Book–Stratford Press Inc.

4 5 6 7 8 9 10

Library of Congress Cataloging in Publication Data

Comer, James P.
  Black child care.
  Bibliography: p. 387
  Includes index.
  1. Children—Management. 2. Adolescence. 3. Negro
children—United States. 4. Education of children.
I. Poussaint, Alvin F., joint author. II. Title.
HQ769.C632   649'.1   74–28261
ISBN 0–671–21902–2

ACKNOWLEDGMENTS

We would like to thank the many people who helped us write this book. We owe a special thanks to Ms. Hattie Gossett and Ms. Audreen Ballard, two black women with vision and commitment who were our editors at *Redbook*. With their guidance and support, we wrote two articles for *Redbook,* one addressed to the questions that black parents most frequently ask about rearing a black child in a predominantly white society, and another addressed to what white parents must do to rear their children free of prejudice. These articles were well received, and follow-up stories appeared in other magazines—*Time*, the *New York Times Magazine*, and others. The *New York Times Magazine* story was entitled "Wanted: A Dr. Spock for Black Parents." These responses convinced us that both blacks and whites wanted to know about rearing black children, and thus the idea of this book emerged.

Along the way, many persons, black and white, both parents and professionals, have helped us bring this project to completion. Many read portions of the manuscript and contributed their ideas and criticisms. Among them were: Ms. Audreen Ballard; Dr. Leon Eisenberg, a Harvard psychiatrist; Dr. Irving Williams, a Harvard pediatrician; Derrick Bell, a Harvard law professor; Dr. Sally Provence, a Yale pediatrician and child development specialist; Dr. Joan Costello, a Yale psychologist and early childhood specialist; and Ms. Wendy Glasgow, a social worker at the Yale Child Study Center and a specialist in education; Ann Ashmore Poussaint, a psychiatric social worker; and Shirley Arnold Comer, a child development nurse and a concerned mother; Dolores Nethersole and Julia Prettyman, two concerned mothers; and Bobbie Poussaint.

A special expression of gratitude is owed Ms. Toye Brown Lewis, who spent many hours researching and collecting relevant information for this volume. In addition, Ms. Mariana Fitzpatrick and others at Simon and Schuster contributed invaluable editorial guidance and support.

We appreciate especially the assistance provided by our secretaries, Ms. Nancy Levoy, Ms. Janice Gore, and Ms. Deborah Weiner. Without the help of these and others, *Black Child Care* might have remained a bright but unfinished idea. However, we, the authors, remain solely responsible for its contents—its strengths and its weaknesses. We hope that you will experience the same joy and hope for the black child in reading this book as we did in writing it.

Contents

CHAPTER 1

About This Book

This book is for all people who are involved in the important job of helping black children develop in a healthy way . . . beautiful and black.

As black psychiatrists, we are constantly being asked questions about rearing black children—in the office, at schools, at social gatherings. Prior to the last few years these questions were almost never raised. Blacks and whites alike, for different reasons, pretended that all children—in fact, all people—were the same. Rearing a black child was just like rearing a white child. Some people still make that claim.

We believe there *is* a difference. Growing up black in America, where policy-making and attitudes are largely influenced and controlled by whites who are often antagonistic or indifferent to the needs of blacks, poses many special problems for black parents and their children. The black awareness movement of the past few years has brought these problems out into the open. Increasing numbers of people are now conscious of the need to prepare black children to deal with the questions and issues of race in a way which will be the most beneficial to their overall emotional, social, and psychological growth and development.

What is the basic problem that faces black parents? The responsibility of *all* parents is to help their children develop in a way that will equip them to function well as individuals, family members, and citizens. Parents are most able and willing to do this when they have a sense of belonging in the larger society. This sense of belonging can only be felt when the rights of parents are protected and obstacles to earning a living and respect are not placed in their way. Belonging to the whole provides individuals with a sense of security. A sense of belonging makes it easy and right for parents to accept the values and ways of the society and pass them on to their children.

In America, however, racist attitudes and actions deny blacks a oneness with society and the security that comes from this feeling. Racism forces blacks to fight for the respect that whites take for granted and often bars blacks from acquiring an adequate income. Hence many black parents question and have mixed feelings about passing on the values and ways of a society that says in so many ways, "We do not value black men and women, boys and girls, as much as we do whites."

As black parents, we generally don't spend much time thinking about this larger problem of alienation because we are so busy trying to answer and handle the day-to-day questions and problems that the situation creates. For example, should black children repeat the "Pledge of Allegiance" to the American flag? The question itself indicates our mixed feelings about our place in the nation. This same doubtfulness shows up when we challenge mainstream or middle-class, i.e., "white" ways. The need to preserve our culture and community springs from a desire to maintain a real and psychological place, belonging only to blacks, where we are accepted, respected, and protected. For this reason we are concerned about whether "white psychology and child-rearing approaches" will change us, hurt us, destroy our culture.

How to deal with our feelings of aggression and to what extent we should adapt white standards are further issues of great concern to black parents. Many blacks feel that in the past we have been too passive; that we are going to have to fight more aggressively for the rights, respect, and opportunity we want for ourselves and our children. We ask ourselves to what extent is adaptation compatible with black needs. These questions of aggression and adaptation and how to deal with them effectively in raising our children will be dealt with in several chapters in this book (see index).

Besides the above-mentioned concerns, black parents must also deal with all of the child-rearing issues that face every parent. At the same time, they must also take into account and be prepared to cope with the many new issues posed by rapidly changing attitudes and values within our society regarding such vital matters as family life, sex, and authority. As a result, the issues and questions facing black parents are many and varied. We also receive numerous questions from whites who in one way or another are involved with the development of black children—as teachers, social workers, parents, and friends.

Typical of the race-related questions we have been asked are the following:

"My fifteen-year-old daughter attends a high school that is about fifteen percent black. She was recently elected to the student council, but some of the black students called her 'Aunt Tomassina' for running for office. She is all mixed up about it. How can I help her?"

"My husband refers to all whites on television as 'honkies.' Can't that cause a problem for our children when they have contact with whites?"

"I read in a sex book that blacks are more susceptible to venereal disease and that the susceptibility is inherited. Is that true? If it is true, should I warn my teen-age children of that fact?"

"How can I, a white teacher, help a black child establish a positive black identity?"

In the area of general child care and child rearing, queries include:

"My child is two years of age and he still isn't toilet-trained. What should I do?"

"How do you help disadvantaged children develop self-confidence in school?"

"Can a mother who works outside of the home give a child adequate emotional support?"

"My daughter was a very happy child and a good student in elementary school. This year she went to junior high school and we have had nothing but trouble. There is no obvious problem. What do you think is going on?"

And in trying to deal with specific problems raised by our troubled society, parents and others involved with children ask us such things as:

"What should I tell my teen-agers about sex in this sex-crazy age?"

"How can I help my child stay away from drug addiction when it is so common in the neighborhood?"

"How does a teacher help a child become a good citizen when the teacher has no authority in the child's eyes?"

Where do we turn for answers to these and other questions? In spite of the fact that there are a large number of child-care books on the market, most of them are geared toward the middle-income white family. Few discuss race-related issues of child rearing. Few discuss low-income children and families. Because race-related and income-related issues *do* cause special problems, it is essential that an approach to child rearing that takes these important factors into consideration be available. That is why we decided to write this book.

It would be presumptuous of anyone to think that they could or should give absolute and final "answers." We are not going to try. We have a point of view, based on years of experience in the field, which we will present to you, but we believe in your right to rear your child as you see fit. We have confidence in the "good sense" of parents, and we don't want you to become dependent on this or any other book to the point that you don't think for yourself. An African proverb says, "If you catch fish for a man, he will be grateful to you and dependent on you forever. If you show him how to catch fish, he will catch his own and be proud of himself." "Answers" alone would be catching your fish.

On the other hand, it is possible to have good sense yet lack certain insights into how children grow or why we as adults react to them in certain ways—thus causing more trouble with our children than we need to have. For this reason we are going to talk about how children mature and how that growth affects their emotional, psychological, and social development. Our intent is to share with you some of the latest findings and thinking in the child-development field. We hope that you will select and use what appears appropriate for you and your child. We believe that the more you understand about the way you and your child tick, the better your chances of keeping things under control, of being the kind of parent you would like to be—the kind of parent your child needs and deserves.

We have designed this book to serve as a practical reference guide for parents. The bulk of it is devoted to a stage-by-stage study of the black child's development from infancy through adolescence, with special emphasis on the role of parents and teachers of school-age children. By way of background, we will begin with a brief summary of the historical experience of black youth in America.

The tendency to compare blacks with whites as if white behavior represented the norm still exists in the minds and writings of many, including many blacks. This is so because the white-controlled media have highlighted black problems but have seldom discussed the reasons for their existence. (In fact, the media have only recently begun to portray healthy and successful black families.) Yet knowing the causes of black family problems and what can be done about them, as well as having an awareness of black family and community strengths, can affect how black mothers and fathers think about themselves and, in turn, influence the kind of care they give their young. It can also affect how white teachers and others view black youth.

We will use the question-and-answer format throughout the book. In our daily work we are constantly receiving questions and giving answers, and we have found that parents generally find this approach the most useful. We, in turn, feel that this is the most simple and direct method by which to present you, the reader, with the facts. In addition, after you read the book, you may want to refer back to various sections as specific problems arise. The question-and-answer style should provide a convenient way to locate your query and our response.

CHAPTER 2

America and the Black Child

The Black Child and Slavery

How were black children treated during slavery?

Black children were abused and denied a happy childhood and the opportunity to develop to their fullest potential. During slavery, they were put to work at very early ages picking cotton in the fields. As house slaves, they cared for members of the mistress' family, including the children and adults with mental or physical disabilities.

These black children who served as helpmates and personal servants to white children were often assigned to them for twenty-four hours a day. Slave children slept on the floor beside the beds of white children and reported to the master if their charges were in distress. During play, white children often used the slave child to test objects of curiosity or go first into strange places. Slave children attended to every minor need of the white children. When other white children came to visit, the black children were at their command too. Black children were also used as playmates but were often sent away, depending on the occasion.

How did black parents handle this situation?

Black slaves did not have enough opportunity to rear their own children because they were assigned to work either in the fields or in the house of the slave master. Often they were responsible for the rearing of the white children. This meant giving very special attention to the physical and emotional needs of the white child, while one's own black child was either back at the cabin being attended by other children or, if older, helping the mother care for the white slave master's child, or tending a white child on his own.

How did black children manage to survive as well as they did up through the Civil War?

Black children survived because of the love, support, and struggle of the black family. However, many black children did not survive. Because of the poor health care provided for the slave parent and child, many suffered grave illnesses and injuries which resulted in physical impairments for life.

The Black Child Today

How have black children fared since Emancipation?

Even after slavery was legally abolished, black children were one of the most mistreated and neglected groups in American society. They have consistently borne the devastating effects of white racism. Many have shouldered the double burden of growing up both poor and black. Some have been damaged so severely early in life that their chances for a happy, productive adulthood have been small.

How early do social conditions begin to affect the development of the black child?

A child's life chances are to an extent determined before his birth. The health of the mother while she is pregnant affects the well-being of the child. Black women have often carried their babies without the benefit of a balanced diet and adequate medical care. Children born of malnourished women are often weak and sickly, running a high risk of mental retardation and delayed physical development. Black women have suffered more from anemia and other complications of pregnancy than have white women. The care received by the mother and infant at the time of birth also affects a child's development. Black women have consistently lacked adequate access to doctors and medical facilities at the time of delivery. In many parts of the country, their children have been delivered by untrained midwives. Prenatal complications and physical birth injuries have resulted in brain-damaged and otherwise handicapped children. As a result the infant mortality rate for black children has always been many times the white rate. Today, the black infant mortality rate is about twice that estimated for whites.

In material terms, how has the black child fared after birth?

From slave days on, the black child has experienced economic and social deprivation. The simple basics of food and a warm, comfortable home have not always been available. Children's physical and mental development lags when their diet is poor and the environment is harsh. Many black children have died from disease and infection because of these conditions. Lack of medical care has compounded the problem.

How else has the black child's welfare been influenced
by social and economic factors?

The economic hardships that traditionally plagued the black family have directly affected the black child in a number of ways. In some parts of America, blacks still live in shacks without running water or toilets. Some homes lack heat and have dirt floors. It is difficult, if not impossible, to maintain the necessary sanitary standards in caring for a baby. In many city ghettos, families are crowded together in dilapidated tenements infested with rats and cockroaches. Food, clothes, shoes, and other basic items are often scarce. Such aids to a child's motor and intellectual development as toys, books, and play areas are frequently unattainable. Black parents have been forced to teach their children games and activities that do not cost money . . . which may have been a blessing in disguise.

How true is the charge that black parents have
traditionally neglected their offspring?

Frequently both parents have had to work because black families have been overburdened with social hardships and because wages were low. Indeed, some black women still work in homes taking care of white children. This has meant that black children left at home usually have had to assume many responsibilities at a very early age. The black child at age five and six is often obliged to watch over the younger children, run errands, and help with housework. At age eight and nine, many have odd jobs—as field hands, newsboys, shoeshine boys—to supplement the family income. Often they earn their own money for candy and other pleasures. In many Southern towns, the children of black sharecroppers are exploited as a source of cheap or free labor. In the past, schedules of black elementary schools were so arranged that black children could be released to pick cotton and other crops during harvest seasons. Their education was secondary to meeting the labor needs of the plantation bosses. Similar patterns exist in certain parts of the country today.

*Do black children feel that their parents
are unable to protect them?*

Probably so. This was particularly true in the past when children quickly learned that authority lay in the hands of white men and women and that blacks had no protection against white violence and lawlessness. Even in his own home the black child saw evidence of the white man's control over the economic and social well-being of his family. The black child was likely to grow up regarding his parents as weak figures under the domination of the white man. Today, however, these patterns are slowly changing.

*How have black children been trained to cope
with white oppression?*

In the past, black children were taught the rituals of servitude and docility from the time they could talk. These included addressing all whites, adults and children alike, with a "yes sir" or "no sir." In turn they were called names like "tar baby" or "Little Black Sambo" and otherwise cruelly mocked and tormented by whites. Today the black child is still made to feel inferior to whites. From his earliest days he senses that his life is viewed cheaply by white society and that he enjoys little protection at its hands. For example, black youths are frequently the victims of racially motivated police abuse at an early age.

*How has the black child managed to adapt through the years
in a society that so profoundly threatens his self-esteem?*

The black child has been forced to learn to live in two cultures— his own minority culture and the majority one. He has had to teach himself to contain his aggression around whites while freely expressing it among blacks. Some people call this a survival technique.

Does the black child resort to other such tactics for self-preservation?

Yes. Over the years black children have become skilled in the use of a variety of techniques in their struggle for survival and well-being in a hostile and unjust society. They have had to learn to be practical as well as cunning. They have had to learn how to win some sort of acceptance from belligerent whites. Black children as a result have often assumed the responsibilities and burdens of adulthood at a far too early age. Many have had little of what we call a childhood. In the black world, adolescence starts early in life, and unlike most white youngsters, many black children do not enjoy the luxury of a period of playtime and learning which extends into their late teens.

Education and the Black Child

In view of the general situation, how have so many black children managed to get an education?

Thanks to sheer determination, black parents have sent their youngsters through school, college, and on to great achievement despite the fact that schools have deliberately educated black children to assume menial roles in society. Much of the credit is due, as well, to black children themselves, who through their internal strength have refused to accept forever being "boys" and "girls."

In the past, what happened to those black youngsters who were denied an education?

Many black boys denied a chance for an education developed athletic and physical prowess. Much of the heavy manual labor in this country has been carried out by young black men. The opening up of sports to blacks in the 1940's, however, acted as a signal to black youth. The muscle and stamina that has made them excellent workers could now be directed to sports. A whole new world was opening up before them. In a similar vein, fewer black women today are being forced to accept backbreaking domestic work. The horizons for black youth continue to expand, and as new opportunities arise in the professions, politics, and the skilled labor force, blacks will take advantage of them.

Isn't it fair to say then that things are much better now for black children than they were twenty years ago?

Yes. Recent social, political, and economic gains have opened horizons for the black child that were only dreamed of twenty years ago. It is possible now to project that there may be a black President or Vice-President of the United States in your young child's lifetime. Black children must be encouraged to enter and achieve in all fields.

But isn't it difficult for parents to keep up with our rapidly changing times?

Yes. However, black parents and friends must avoid at all costs teaching black children today the kinds of behavior and attitudes needed for survival in earlier periods of greater white oppression. There is no need any longer for docility. It should be replaced with an attitude of black pride, self-confidence, and assertiveness.

How can we best develop these new qualities in our youngsters?

In order to make the greatest use of our new opportunities, we must raise strong black children. Good child-rearing practices have become a crucial element in assuring the future of black Americans. Children raised in an atmosphere of love and security, even in the poorest homes, will be prepared to face the challenges of tomorrow.

Without family and community support, however, children cannot thrive. The family—mother, father, grandparents, cousins, uncles, and aunts—passes on to a growing child both the strengths of the old culture and the rules and techniques essential for successful adaptation in the modern world.

CHAPTER 3

The Infant

Establishing Your Infant's Identity

What is the age range of infancy?

About two years.

Is this period of life as important as later periods?

It is one of the most important. During this period the infant must establish a relationship with a caretaker, which becomes a blueprint for future relationships with other people. It is now that the biological, social, and emotional patterns are established which, with modification, will remain with the infant the rest of his or her life.

Should black children be brought up in the same way as white children?

Our basic child-rearing practices should be the same as those of others. There will always be some differences between groups, however, because we all bring our different cultures to bear in the job of child rearing.

Good child-rearing principles are fundamentally the same for all, because the basic needs of children are universal. Youngsters need food, clothing, shelter, and protection from physical and psychological damage. They need to be able to trust and feel affection for one or more adults from whom they can learn. They need to be taught to control their aggressive and impulsive energy in order to be able to learn, work, and play in gradually more mature ways. In providing for the psychological well-being of our children, we, as black parents, will occasionally need to act in special ways. (We will discuss such situations as they arise throughout the book.) But this is no different from what other groups have done through such means as religious schools and indoctrination of one kind or another.

Modern life forces groups of every kind to have the flexibility necessary to accept changes. As long as such changes protect and provide for the best interest of our children, there is little reason for concern. Black parents must realize that culture changes are normal and do not mean culture loss.

Does white psychology apply to black people?

There is no such thing as a black psychology or a white psychology. However, psychological practices in the U.S. have been white dominated and are often culturally biased and racist. Many psychological tests are inappropriately applied to blacks and cause them to appear less intelligent or deficient. These types of abuses must be corrected. Nonetheless, blacks and whites alike experience aggression, affection, independence, dependency. Everything that the black mind is capable of, the white mind is capable of. What appear as differences are the results of experience and training. When used *correctly*, existing psychological principles are applicable to all.

We blacks have a concern about the threat of training or "brainwashing" black children to be passive or nonaggressive. We fear this has or can lead to acceptance of and adjustment to an unjust society. This has led to some confusion about the value of certain psychological principles, particularly those of aggression control and adaptation referred to in Chapter 1. These principles do not mean "accept and adjust" to everything. Control of aggression means handling it so that it works for you rather than against you, in any way necessary for as long as necessary. Adaptation simply means coping with the world around you, and changing it if necessary, even by militant struggle if there is no other way.

*If the basic rearing of infants is similar everywhere,
why then is it important to include a discussion of
infants when discussing black child development?*

Infant care determines a child's primary core and most important identity. A child's first idea of herself or himself as a person depends upon the responses of others; the child will feel he or she is a positive or good person when relationships with important people—parents, caretakers, other family—around the child are good. These early positive feelings about the self help the child to learn and do one thing after another. Each success adds to the good feeling about the self. This good feeling makes it easier to keep on learning and doing despite an occasional failure. In time an unshakable core of good feeling about the self develops. The child has an inner feeling that says, "I am a person. I am an able person. I am a good person." At this point a primary positive identity has been established.

*How can black parents help their child develop
this feeling of identity?*

As the child grows older, learning black history and experiencing black culture can add to his pride and broaden his sense of identity. Helping a child learn strategies to deal with racism and the negative feelings about being black that racism incurs is very helpful. But nothing can substitute for the love, care, and training that the child needs from birth onward.

With such preparation black children are able to have positive feelings about themselves when growing up in very racist environments, while those without it often can't have a high level of self-esteem. That is why some cling to "blackness" as an end in itself—which may be better than nothing—but "blackness" alone cannot sustain them. That's why some people who claim great pride in being black at the same time do destructive things to themselves, other blacks, and the black community at large. Although they reason, "Black is beautiful, I am black, therefore I am beautiful," they can't make it work for them. A positive black identity (secondary identity) must be built on an inner core of pride and positive feelings (primary identity), or it may fade away under the harsh light of life's realities.

*Have black parents been successful in
handling identity problems in the past?*

Black parents, for the most part, have traditionally helped black children develop this positive inner core. That is why so many blacks in every walk of life function so well. As we mentioned in Chapter 1, however, we want to share some insights from our training and experiences to help black parents better shoulder a burden that they have already shouldered so well. We, as a people, will be able to lighten that burden only when enough black youngsters can resist becoming the victims of racism and force society to drop racist social policies and attitudes.

We are not saying give up the fight (whatever your methods) to change society now. We are saying that simultaneous with that fight, we must try and bring more black children through the obstacle course of racism today. That is why a close look at what we can do as parents, caretakers, and friends, from before birth onward, is very important.

How can I promote racial pride in my infant?

Although infants become aware of color and feature differences, these things have no meaning to them. Unless they are taught in a very direct and specific way, they have little or no interest in the question of skin color or racial variations until around three years of age. Race is a complicated concept which they learn over time. It does not help to try to explain the idea of race to the infant.

But you can discuss color and race-related issues in a natural way. For example, you can talk about parts and characteristics of the body to your child in a way that includes skin color. Thus, when you are helping your child learn colors—and after he has learned the meaning of "arm"—you can indicate "brown" or "black," pointing to his arm or at your arm. He will eventually learn that it is an arm of brown color.

Race is a subject you should discuss with your child in an easy and natural way. Providing your infant with black dolls and toy people as well as white ones helps to make black, brown, and white normal—like the real world. When the question of color comes up later, it will not be loaded with anxious feelings if you have not previously ignored it or overdramatized it.

You and Your Unborn Child

What can be done before birth?

There is much to be done even before pregnancy. The beauty of having a baby has been oversold. A child is a major responsibility which will be with you over the next twenty to twenty-five years of your life. Parents can receive great pleasure from helping their children grow. There are certain experiences and memories that only a parent can have. On the other hand, there will be places parents can't go and things they can't do because they have children. Unless they are ready to take on a major responsibility and make sacrifices, they should not have a baby.

Since having a baby will change a person's life in far-reaching ways, the decision to do so should not be made in haste or result from an "accident." It should not be based on such reasons as trying to save a shaky marriage, religious beliefs alone, or attempting to add future soldiers to the black cause. The only valid reason to have a baby is that you are ready, willing, and able to share yourself and your relationship with your partner with a child . . . and be prepared to help that child grow in a healthy way, *whatever* may be involved.

What can parents do to help their child before birth?

As an expectant mother, your good health is your child's good health. Your diet, blood pressure, weight, and exercise patterns can affect your baby. The better you feel about having a baby, the more likely you are to take good care of yourself—which is a good reason to be sure that babies are wanted and pregnancies are planned.

There is evidence now that when things are going well, the expectant mother need not see the doctor or nurse as often as was once thought necessary. But you should be under medical supervision. Even today, too many black mothers see the doctor for the first time at delivery. This increases the chances of birth injury, defect, and death.

It is important for fathers and other relatives to be supportive of expecting mothers—without making mother the baby! Give some time to your wife, father-to-be. It's your baby, too. If you are not willing to do your bit now as well as after the baby comes, you shouldn't be having a child.

The Problem of Postnatal Depression

We wanted and planned the baby. I had good support.
I still got depressed. Why?

Depression after childbirth under the best of circumstances is not too unusual. Doctors are not absolutely sure of the cause. The emotional buildup—anticipation, excitement, fear—and then the normal letdown when it finally happens is thought to be the major cause. Chemical changes also play a role. When all else is well, the depression soon passes.

With first babies, there is often an additional factor. The mother asks herself: "Can *I* be a good mother?" With the support of others and contact with your baby, your doubts will soon pass.

Helping Baby Grow

What does a baby inherit or receive from parents?

A baby inherits all physical characteristics plus mental and motor or movement capacities. The vast majority of human beings inherit mental and movement potentials that fall within a very narrow range. Many of the eventual differences in ability and performance between people depend on "what you do with what you got" or, more correctly, what a baby's environment—parents, school, society—help and permit him or her to do with what he or she inherited.

Only a very small amount of the known genetic material, maybe 1 to 2 percent, is responsible for the physical characteristics that distinguish one group from another or one person from another. In other words, only 1 to 2 percent of genetic material is involved in creating the physical differences between blacks, whites, browns, yellows, and reds.

What must I help my baby accomplish in the
first two years of life?

You must help your baby achieve increasing motor (muscle) control, language, and social development. In addition, the baby must become dependent, secure, and trusting enough to receive protection and learn from others. At the same time, he must become independent enough to explore himself and his environment. You must help your infant develop the desire to gain one new skill after another—to observe, listen, think, learn, remember, and generally develop both mind and body. It is important that fathers be involved—where circumstances permit—as much as possible.

What is there about the relationship between me and my baby that makes it possible for me to influence this development?

Because a baby is completely dependent at birth, you must meet his every need. As you feed, bathe, and diaper your infant, an attachment of great force normally develops between you and your baby. In fact, it need not be the mother who performs these particular functions. The baby soon comes to attach pleasure and security with whoever the caretaking person may be.

The child becomes extremely close to the mother, father, or caretaker by three months of age. It is not until about nine months that the baby begins to move toward separateness again, but even then maintains a close tie. He wants to please you. Because of this, you are in a position to help your baby gradually learn to control or delay the need to satisfy every urge or impulse immediately. This permits the baby to give time and attention to accomplishing increasingly difficult tasks . . . and also permits you to live with him! When the caretaker-child bond is not well established, physical, social, and emotional growth and general development are hampered.

What is the time schedule of this development in the first two years?

(A) *Motor development* (*muscle control*). The only well-developed motor activity a child is born with is the ability to suck. Obviously this makes feeding and growth possible. You must help develop all other motor functions. We will discuss ways to do this on pages 33–35.

Motor development (muscle control) proceeds from the head or neck down. By four weeks the baby is able to control eye movement and looks directly at nearby objects or people. By three months the baby is able to look around in all directions. At about the fourth month, or sixteen weeks, the baby is able to control movement of his head. His hands are now open rather than closed. About the seventh or eighth month, the baby can sit steadily. He can grasp and manipulate objects with his hands and makes raking motions toward objects out of reach. At about nine months, baby can crawl and, soon after, creep. He is able to pull himself to his feet by using the side of his playpen or other fixed objects by ten months. He can now release objects from his hands with some difficulty. By the end of a year, most babies begin to walk, and have much better control of their hands and upper body.

By eighteen months, the baby walks without falling, can sit down readily, and has improved eye-to-hand coordination, which makes stacking three or four blocks or other such activities possible. The two-year-old walks with greater control and is not "all over the place," walking for the sake of walking. When two walks, it's because he has someplace to go!

(B) *Speech development.* Speech development starts at birth, perhaps even before birth, although we have no way to be sure. Infants make and respond to sounds from the beginning. A baby listens to the voice of the caretaker in the first few weeks. By the fifth or sixth week your baby begins to make repetitive sounds called babbling. By the sixteenth week a baby is cooing and clearly making sounds in response to the words and presence of those interacting with him. The infant is now clearly imitating what he hears. By the twenty-eighth week a baby is using his voice with gusto. There is a clear desire to have others respond and to make others understand. By the tenth month your baby is able to say one or two words and will respond to his name. On request he will wave "bye-bye" and shows caution or stops what he is doing when told "no-no."

By twelve months a baby jabbers away and appears to enjoy hearing himself. This jabbering becomes increasingly expressive and takes on a conversational tone. By eighteen months a baby begins to use key words to express a need and obtain a desired response. For example: "Eat" will mean, "I am hungry. I would like to be fed." "Potty" will mean, "I am ready to have a bowel movement. Help me with my potty." The value of language becomes apparent to the child through these requests and the responses he receives. Language also helps the child become more and more a part of the people and the world around him. Thus he is motivated to learn more and more words, to name objects, to inquire about the names of unfamiliar things.

The two-year-old can say "I," and has mastered two or three sentences but generally uses phrases. Language, through adult-child interaction, gradually becomes a way to understand or have a concept. This ability leads to thinking and reasoning.

Just as with motor control, there are ways in which you can help your infant improve his language skills. We will discuss these on pages 37–39. In this and other areas of training, however, it must be stressed that the parent should not become discouraged if he meets with success one day and defeat the next. That's the way babies are. Calmly start your training all over. Too much "to-do" about the normal course of events may cause the baby to feel failure where none exists, except for a parent's frustration. It is particularly harmful to refer to your baby as stupid . . . even in jest and before he understands the meaning of the word. The tone and the manner send a harmful message.

(C) *Social and personal development.* Social and personal development begin with the child's discovery of an outside world as well as the discovery that he is a separate and distinct individual. Better control of the eyes and hands permits increased exploration of the self, other people, clothing, and crib toys. Language development increases the interaction with the caretaker and speeds social and personal development.

A baby recognizes and responds to a human face at about one or two months of age. About the same time the baby smiles in response to your smile. Your baby will attempt to reach your face, will appear surprised and frightened when it disappears, and will attempt to follow it. A "ham" from the beginning, he will smile at his reflection in a mirror. The baby imitates the movements of adults and loves to be tickled and bounced within reason, but can become frightened when physical play gets too rough.

After the first six months, he will show interest in games in which you hide small objects and he looks for them. He will try and repeat what an adult has just done while playing a game. He becomes more and more an "actor." During the ninth to eighteenth months, the baby comes into his own. He is now very much aware of himself as separate and distinct from other people. Even before he walks, he explores everything he can get his hands on. Once he is walking, exploration is the rule. He is everywhere and into everything. He wants to make decisions for himself and learns to say "no" quickly. At the same time he will cooperate to please you.

To gain attention and to establish his separateness, he begins to show his clothing and personal articles to everybody, as if to say, "This is me, right?" He continues to figure out who he is, where he fits in, and how he relates to the rest of the world—largely his family at this point.

Again, all of this may be delayed when the caretaker-child bond is not good.

The Absent Parent

*I must work. Will I harm my baby by leaving
him with a caretaker?*

Not if you have a good caretaker. In the past, it has been said that mothers should not work and should stay with their babies. It was believed that an exclusive relationship between mother and baby was necessary for good child development. There is now evidence that as long as there are not too many adults involved, or caretakers do not change too rapidly, babies will do very well. It is important, however, that you care for your child regularly during available time after work. Temporary separations and reunions between mother and child probably help the child learn to deal with strangers more easily.

*What about vacations or extended periods away
from the baby during the first year?*

Keep in mind that it is extremely important for your child to make an attachment to parents during the first year of life. Children who do not have this period of total attachment and dependency often show a longing for dependency and a desire to be cared for, as well as a higher level of anxiety, later in life. Although it is true that some children, particularly if they are cared for by a single, familiar caretaker during your absence, will not show any ill effects, we nevertheless advise you to avoid extended absences during the first year.

Illness requiring hospitalization forces some mothers to be away from their babies. Hopefully a single caretaker will be possible during this period to keep the baby's environment as predictable and secure as possible.

I often feel depressed. Can this harm my baby?

Depressed or overwhelmed mothers are "away" even when they are present. It is hard for you to keep your child feeling secure and able to relate to things and people if you are overwhelmed or depressed. This is a harmful situation.

It is best to try to avoid conditions that lead to depression. This is one reason why we mentioned earlier that having babies should be planned. They should come at a time when you're likely to have support of friends and relatives and you are not under a great deal of stress. It is important to have the support of relatives and friends so that an evening or day away from the baby from time to time is possible. Father can spare mother and vice versa, depending on who is involved most and in need of a break. This is particularly true if you have a very active baby.

Variations in Infant Development

The baby down the street, the same age as mine, is walking and my baby is not. Am I doing something wrong?

Probably not. Each baby appears to have a time clock of his or her own which is determined from within. In addition, personal differences in activity levels and temperament show up from the very beginning. Only extreme cases of malnutrition or serious mishandling slow the growth of a baby. Babies grow and develop in spurts, with rapid growth and change, then level off, only to take off again. Most of the time what you observe as slow growth is a period between spurts. If the baby down the street is ahead of yours in some way, don't worry about it. Your baby's time will come.

Are the babies who develop faster smarter than others?

Speed of development is no indication of the level of intelligence. With good care, slow developers will eventually move to the level of ability of which they are capable.

*Isn't there some evidence that black babies gain control
of their bodies faster than white babies?*

There are conflicting reports about this. Evidence does exist to
show that motor development takes place faster during the first
year among many African babies than among many European
babies. Some observers feel that this is due to the fact that African
babies are carried on the mother's back; some feel that it is due to
genetic differences. But since Africa and Europe are such vast
areas and only a few studies have been done, we shouldn't make
too much of these findings. Closer to home, some observers have
reported a better control of the neck of black American babies at
birth. It is almost impossible, however, to determine whether there
are inherited differences in body movement control between black
and white American babies.

*Does faster motor development mean a
lower degree of intelligence?*

Experts agree that advanced motor or physical development is *not*
a sign of lower mental ability. This outdated theory has been
thoroughly disproved. There are simply too many bright children
from all groups who have very rapid motor development. The old
physical-mental argument is probably a remnant of Western culture's tendency to value mental activity over physical activity. In
other cultures, those who were physically gifted were thought to
be gifted mentally. We feel that this latter theory is more likely.
If your child is active and develops body control faster than he
or she should according to the book, enjoy it.

Ways to Encourage Motor Development

*How can I help stimulate my infant's
motor or movement control?*

Much of this can be done in the normal course of playing with
your baby. Rocking the baby to your own singing or to recorded
music will aid motor development. Enticing toys just out of reach
will encourage movement. After the child's hand opens up in the
second or third month, place objects of different size, shape, con-
sistency and noisemaking ability in it. This will encourage use
of muscles in the hand. Playing with the bath cloth, your clothing,
his clothing, the crib rail, and other objects helps the child learn to

use his hands. Moving his legs and arms, pulling him up, and holding the baby in a standing position will help him find and try to use these muscles.

A cradle gym is an excellent toy for helping the baby develop eye muscle control and arm and hand coordination. Bright or noisemaking objects will attract the baby's interest, and he will try to grab them or follow them with his eyes. Changing the position of these objects and substituting new objects from time to time will keep up the baby's interest. If you make your own cradle gym out of household items, be certain that it is safe. Beware of sharp objects or materials small enough for the baby to swallow! Once the child is out of the crib, a baby walker permits him to move about in safety.

What about feeding himself?

When your baby makes reasonably good attempts to feed himself, encourage it. Not only does this support a feeling of independence, but it also permits him to develop greater skill in using his hands. Some mothers feel that babies are so messy that it's easier to feed them. This prevents the baby from developing independence and delays the development of movement control. In teaching all skills, it helps to show the child how to do it first and then let him practice. Put the spoon to his mouth first yourself and then let baby try it, helping only when necessary.

Is "destructive" behavior sometimes permissible?

Children love to tear up newspapers, magazines, and anything else they can get their hands on. Some mothers feel that this is messy and destructive, but it is really a very safe release of aggression, an exercise of hand muscles, and a learning experience. Let them sit on the floor and "go to town" on things you don't want. With your "no-no" as they approach your bookcase, they will learn what is fair game for the "tear mill" and what is not. Speaking of the floor and bookcases, be certain to remove dangerous objects from reach when your baby is out of the crib. Furniture that can be tipped over should be removed.

What about activities for the walking child?

The walking child will want more interesting things to do. The toy he can pull along, as if he's taking it someplace very important, is one he will like most. You can make your own toys out of empty ice-cream cartons, hair rollers, small boxes, or pots and pans—if you don't mind the noise. Perhaps of equal pleasure to pulling a toy is pounding a block. Pounding in a peg with a wooden hammer is also a favorite activity. It promotes arm and shoulder muscle development and eye-hand coordination. Rolling a ball back and forth is another beneficial and pleasurable pastime.

Outdoors, sand and water play is the runaway favorite of the eighteen-month-old set. Slopping around in the resulting mess is close to godliness . . . and good for the release of tensions. It also encourages the use of the hands and offers the possibility of creative building and learning.

Around eighteen months, the infant also gets a great deal of pleasure from drawing with large crayons. Do not look for great artistic achievements. The development of your child's muscle and nervous system, at this point, will not permit it. A child is able to copy a circle only after he is about two years of age, a cross at about three years of age, a square at about five years of age, and a diamond at about seven years of age. But scribbling is wonderful fun and good for developing the hand. The child enjoys the act of creation and it is important to applaud or clap—for the effort rather than the outcome. Clapping and showing signs of delight— smiling, hugging, and such—will encourage your child to try and try again in a number of areas.

Around eighteen months your child will want to walk up and down stairs and jump off. It helps to hold at least one hand at first. It is also important to discourage heroic efforts like jumping more stairs than he can handle. About the same time a baby will try to climb onto chairs, tables, or anything else he can reach. When you *must* rescue your explorer from a precarious position, swift action, little excitement, and afterwards a clear, short explanation of the danger is helpful. *Screams startle the child and can cause the fall you were afraid of.* Prolonged scoldings, usually reflecting your anxiety over "what could have happened," do not help at the moment nor do they prevent future possible disasters.

Protecting Your Infant: How Much and When

How can I keep my baby from harm?

Infants don't plan to get into trouble. They simply don't know what is dangerous or can become dangerous. If you can anticipate danger by putting harmful objects out of reach, for example, this will help. Once an infant has been exposed to danger he will need a simple explanation that relieves his fear and increases his knowledge so that he can gradually learn to avoid the dangerous. But because babies can't yet "remember," they can't always transfer their learning from one situation to another; you must help them to understand over and over again. Be gentle. Angry scoldings can shake their confidence and reduce the exploration. Exploration aids learning and motor development.

Can't too much concern about safety
hurt a child's development?

Safety should always be in the back of a parent's mind—something that we think about when the baby is in the crib and especially when he or she is not. We should anticipate such dangerous situations as those already mentioned—sharp objects and tipping furniture. When you "think safety" it is possible to help your child learn from the beginning that paint peelings, caustic cleaners, and other dangerous materials are a "no-no." But once you have done all you can to ensure safety, a relaxed attitude is best. Fear and overconcern can cause you to keep your child from taking the ordinary risks and suffering the ordinary frustration and pain a child needs.

Some people have argued that black children will face greater hardships in life than whites, and therefore that soothing and comforting them after falls, fights, or frustrations is not good for them. It has also been argued that many white children, particularly those from middle-class families, are not tough or independent enough because they receive too much soothing, comforting, care, and attention, and are not allowed enough chance taking. Some parents—black, white, upper- and lower-income groups—do overprotect their children. On the other hand, some parents are neglectful and cruel in the name of making their offspring tough.

There is a balance which must be struck. It is helpful for a child to experience danger, frustration, failure, and pain occasionally, but not to the point of being afraid to act. Don't get upset about every little danger or possible fall. Smile so that the child understands that falling is what happens when learning to walk, and she will pick herself up and keep going. Enduring extreme frustration and repeated negative experiences does not give a child a psychological inoculation against future hardship. The will to "keep on keeping on" starts with support, protection, and encouragement from important loved ones. This will to go on breaks down when nobody cares.

What about protection from teasing by older children?

The infant can be hurt by teasing. At this stage he has little self-confidence. We know of one case in which a teen-aged sister laughed at an eighteen-month-old child sitting on the potty. It was several months before anyone could get the child to use the potty again. In the meantime, he had his BMs in a corner of the room. You should help other children in the family understand that it is important to respect the child's early efforts to crawl, walk, learn, and use the potty. A child doesn't start developing a self-image when he is five, ten, or fifteen. It begins to develop from the moment of birth and can be easily damaged early in the game.

Encouraging Language Skills

How can I aid language development?

Like motor development, language development starts at birth. Your baby speaks to you with gurgles, coos, and ga-gas. Gurgling, cooing, and ga-ga-ing back in a pleased and enthusiastic way promotes more gurgles, coos, and ga-gas. When your baby starts to make sounds close to words, imitating the sound and later pronouncing the words slowly and distinctly will help him eventually pronounce the word. For example, "da da da da" becomes "dada" and, finally, "Daddy."

Should I use baby talk?

Imitating and modifying the child's words is helpful, but it is also important to talk to your child just as you would talk to anyone else. In this way the child is exposed to the rhythm and flow of speech. He comes to enjoy the sound of a pleasant conversational tone. He will enjoy listening to conversations between you and others. The baby enjoys your speaking to him and will babble back and smile as if he understands. In the process he learns new words and develops a conversation pattern.

Talking to your baby about what you're doing while you're doing it is very helpful. Understanding language comes, in part, through the activity with which it is associated. If you say "Lift up your arm" when nothing is going on, your child won't understand you. But if you say "Lift up your arm" in order to put the arm in a sleeve while you are dressing him, he will soon understand the words and idea or concept. The more he understands, the more he will want to use language to make *you* understand *him*. Such phrases as "Let me stand you up, Jimmy" when you're doing so, or "Let's take those clothes off" not only establish language as a way to communicate but involve the child in the activity in such a way that he will not feel that things are done to him and for him without any involvement on his part. In this regard, it is also helpful to name objects—"bottle," "ball"—when a child is involved with them. This enables the child to name and call for those objects, giving him a greater sense of control and power. It serves as a preparation for describing and classifying the world later on.

In what other ways can I encourage speech?

Singing or reading to the baby also helps promote language development. The thing that is most important here is the association of words with a pleasant experience. Your infant will want to snuggle up close to you and/or sit on your lap and let you read while he tries to turn the pages. He will enjoy his closeness to you and the pleasant sound of your voice. This will result in a sense of security. Large bright pictures are attractive to children as young as five or six months. Infants will listen to you pronounce the names of the objects in the picture and try to repeat the sound. Reading and language associated with such pleasant circumstances receive a positive emotional charge. We believe that much of the motivation to read and use language starts in, or close to, the cradle.

Whether reading or singing, the child should be the center of the activity. Looking at him, pointing out things to him, being pleased about his joining in the singing or successfully naming certain objects—all these give the child a sense of well-being and encourage the use of more language. Name and finger games like "This Little Piggy Went to Market" not only help your child learn language but explore the body. They also provide important, warm physical contact.

At what age will an infant "follow" orders?

Even before your baby learns to respond to directions, you can begin to encourage her to try things such as wave bye-bye or come to you in response to calling her name. Most children begin to respond to simple commands by nine months of age. Don't feel discouraged if yours does not, or responds one day but not the next. It takes a great deal of repetition for children to learn. Very often they will wave bye-bye consistently when you practice with them alone. Just when you want to show your neighbor how capable he or she is, your baby will look at you as if you're crazy when you ask him or her to wave bye-bye. Don't try to force him or make him feel that he is a failure. Simply start training him all over again.

And remember, while it helps to understand that your play and activities with your child promote his or her development, it is equally important not to become too "teachy" about it. Relax, have fun, and interact with your child as the spirit moves you—or the crying calls you—but don't get hung up on rigid time schedules for promoting motor and language development.

Stimulating the Infant Mind

What can I do to help my baby begin to think and learn?

Interest created by body movement or motor activity automatically puts your child's mind into gear. It starts almost accidentally. The baby's body, by chance, goes through motions, such as thumb-sucking, which are pleasurable, and the act is repeated. Exploration continues. Your baby will examine everything he gets his hands on. He is doing more than being a busybody. He is learning about how things feel, how they work, how they're put together. Give him objects to explore of different size, taste, color, texture, and sound. Changing the kinds of objects he is exposed to helps. Your baby will tire of familiar things. Putting toys or objects eight to twelve inches in front of the very young baby's face and moving them helps him to look all around.

How can I best use words to help baby learn?

Naming objects gives your child words. Words used in connection with activities lead to understanding concepts and learning to think. For example, the word "water" is stated as a child touches water. Wet, the characteristic of water, may also be stated. A spill can lead to the concept of water as something wet, which flows, which can get on you and make you uncomfortable, and which sometimes makes Mommy angry. Eventually all of these meanings are sorted out and the differences and best usage are understood. A child who hears a lot of language and who has a lot of feeling, touching, and seeing experiences to which she can relate the words (and you can help her) will develop more concepts and start to become a good thinker earlier than a child who is hearing, doing, and receiving less.

Using words which describe the characteristics of objects—tall, short, hard, soft, cold, wet, and so on—is useful. These concepts can be taught in play and during feeding or other everyday activities. You can point out that your coffee is hot. After the baby has learned that a toy car is a toy car, you can move the car quickly and label the activity "fast." If the baby goes under a chair, you can say "under." As the baby climbs over the chair you can say "over," thus helping the baby learn new words and new concepts.

Having your baby identify parts of his own body, the same parts of your body, and similar parts in pictures helps the baby learn similarity and how to transfer learning from one situation to another. Using words like "after" you do this, or "before" you do that, or we will have a cookie "now" helps the baby learn the concepts of time—the fact that there is a past, present, and future.

What about learning through play?

Through play your baby gradually learns that rattles, coins, and other objects are permanent. Peek-a-boo is an all-time favorite game with young children, and it helps them learn the concept of permanence. Hiding objects under sheets or guessing what hand the coin is in becomes great fun around a year to eighteen months of age. Having the child find the hidden object helps the child use his mind to make a mental picture of it and to understand that things exist even when they are out of sight.

There are numerous other concepts you can help your child develop through play and in the course of everyday activities. When you have three objects in your hand of different size, you can ask the child which one is big, which middle-sized, and which little. Two piles of paper on the table containing different numbers of sheets provides an opportunity to discuss the concept of more or less. The baby can learn his colors by naming the color of objects in a room. Small objects of the same color can be matched, thus teaching the concept of matching characteristics—color, size, and shape. Putting pictures or puzzles together and taking them apart teaches the concept of whole and part. Tapping on objects made of different materials creates different noises and stimulates interest while the child gains information about the objects in question.

What else can I teach my infant?

One of the most important things you must help your baby with is learning to wait or tolerate delay. Babies want what they want when they want it, often yesterday, and not a moment later. At the same time they love you deeply and your represent all the security they have in the world. They don't want to lose this safe feeling, and if you call on them to "wait just a minute" or say, "Let me get this for Johnny and then I will get the milk," they will learn not only words but the concept of waiting. They will begin to learn to cooperate and gain the all-important capacity to delay immediate gratification. This is necessary for continued and more complicated kinds of learning. Once your child learns to wait . . . a little . . . you are free of some of his tyranny. This is the first step in negotiations about your rights, his rights, your needs, his needs. You are laying the ground for similar negotiations with other people in the future. While it is important for you to stimulate the child to explore his environment, to learn to understand language and concepts and to think, it is also important for the child to use his own imagination. Encouraging your child to play alone permits him to use his own imagination and think and do his own thing.

In Chapter 6, in which we take up the matter of intelligence testing, we indicate that verbal, analytic, and conceptual (use of ideas) thinking can be learned. We believe that underdevelopment of language and conceptual, analytic thinking—largely because there has been little need for it by blacks or whites not in positions of authority—is partly responsible for differences in test scores (not true indicators of intelligence) between groups. More attention to the development of language and thinking in the infant stage can improve later scores and school achievement without harming creativity and intuitive abilities. We will discuss this in greater detail later.

Can baby be overstimulated or overencouraged?

Yes, but let's be clear on what we mean by stimulation. We mean the kinds of activities parents can engage in to "turn on" their babies and bring about good motor, language, and learning development. If you are too active or persist when a baby is tired, he will become irritable, cry in distress, or signal in one way or another that enough is enough! Overstimulation by a caretaking person who "reads" the baby well is unlikely. But a noisy street, extremely loud music, loud and harsh arguing voices, and much coming and going of people *can* overstimulate a baby. Babies don't fare well in chaos, conflict, and confusion. Inner organization of sights, sounds, and thought is difficult under these circumstances. On the other hand, they don't thrive without adequate stimulation.

Don't some child-development experts think that black babies are understimulated?

It is true that some people have discussed understimulation as a special problem among blacks. However, understimulation has nothing to do with race. Many parents, black or white, dealing with stress of one kind or another, are unable to feel warmth toward their children, or play with or adequately stimulate them. Because of social conditions in America, the black population may have more than its share of parents who live under stress.

Working mothers, while doing well from a psychological standpoint, may be too tired to interact frequently and pleasantly with the baby. A greater number of black mothers must work. In such cases, it is very important for the father and other relatives to help out. It is better for mothers or fathers to work less—if possible—when fatigue interferes with child care.

Some people, regardless of race or background, simply don't feel that it's important to do anything other than feed and clothe the infant in a loving way. They feel that you talk with babies only once they understand. The point is that the infant's understanding is improved by being talked to.

Can parents benefit from child-development programs?

Some groups have viewed programs to help parents acquire skills to aid in their children's development as an insult or an indictment of the parents' capabilities. It may be that some of the program directors involved have not had the appropriate attitudes. But— pardon the pun—we hope that the baby will not be thrown out with the bath water. To throw out programs such as these is to deny some black parents what middle-income, white (mostly) parents purchase regularly in books or from doctors. Get a trustworthy program director, but let's have black children use large crayons to develop small hand muscles at eighteen months rather than coming to kindergarten unable to do so. We see this situation much too often!

The Infant and His Environment

How can I help with my baby's social development?

Many of the things you do in promoting motor and language development at the same time promote self-awareness and social development. Calling the child by his name from the very beginning, even playing name games once he is old enough to respond, is very helpful. For example, "Where's Mary?" or "Where is Jessie?" Beaming with satisfaction, your child will identify himself as the person you are searching for. The first birthday offers a good opportunity to help the child establish a positive identity, to understand himself as somebody of worth and value. This is *his* day! He won't understand the full meaning of it all, but he'll know it's for him; he's an individual. He is very worthwhile.

At about twelve months of age children begin to make costumes out of anything available and act in front of a mirror. This aids self-identification. Creating a place in the room which is theirs and available for their possessions is also helpful in this regard. Many parents today are concerned about an undue stress on individualism and may worry about this practice. However, children need some privacy, some time and some place they can call their own, a place where they are separate and safe from others. In addition, children aren't really ready to share much until a bit later. They are still very much wrapped up in themselves. For the one-year-old, it is more important to help establish an initial positive identity and a sense of security than it is to promote sharing. Unless "mine" and "yours" is forced on him too soon, he will be ready and willing to share and cooperate later on.

How can I get my child to do things by himself?

Some children will have trouble getting interested in anything on certain days. Taking a moment to help him get started can save you a lot of trouble later. Frustrated and bored, he is likely to act up. When you want the child to work alone, after you have gotten him started, saying something like "Now I think you'll enjoy doing that by yourself" usually works. You may want to assure the child that you will be back.

What about good manners?

Helping your child learn what to say or do in certain social situations is important. This training begins with bye-bye, hello, please, thank you, and then gradually grows more complex. These responses, when properly used, will win your child approval and respect. Most parents help their children learn these responses as a matter of course. But we also see youngsters who have not learned these and other appropriate social responses even after they are in school. They are often thought to be rude and crude. These children are uncomfortable, aware that they aren't doing something "right," and have negative feelings about themselves. Because of their behavior adults sometimes respond to them badly, and they, in turn, respond badly. This can lead to learning and discipline problems.

It is sometimes argued that "good manners" are part of middle-class behavior; that poor people don't and shouldn't be expected to respond in the same way. This makes for an interesting argument. But if children do not have some sort of respectful ways of relating, a problem exists. More than ever before it is important to be able to function in a socially acceptable way in a variety of social settings. Job, personal, and family security often depend on it. Given the fact that modern life requires greater togetherness, physically if not spiritually, social skills have come to be extremely important. Parents and schools have a responsibility to help children develop these skills. Learning *another way* at the day-care center or in school, as long as his *home way* is not "put down," will not make it hard for a child to get along at home.

Common Problems and Their Solutions

*How will I know when my infant's overall
development is not going well?*

The newborn will have excessive feeding and digestive problems. Fretful sleeping is also an indication that there is something wrong. Excessive crying and irritability as well as a kind of overall body tenseness is another indication of problems. Such babies are difficult to comfort. Most of all, *you* will feel greatly anxious. A part of you will feel angry because you are not getting the satisfaction from your infant that you had hoped for.

Often—particularly with a firstborn—the mother just needs to relax. Sometimes the baby is not getting enough food. Sometimes mother is too tired and a little help from relatives will improve the situation. Sometimes you will need professional counseling. Your pediatrician, family or clinic doctor can be helpful in helping you sort out the trouble and advising you about what steps to take.

*My seven-month-old is afraid of strangers. Is that
an indication that he has a problem?*

No. In fact, be careful not to force your baby to respond to outsiders. He has become familiar with brother, sister, father, and other relatives whom he sees frequently. But the stranger represents danger. Most children develop some hesitancy in going to a stranger after six months of life. This is particularly true around eight months of life, when the child has a good mental image of the mother or caretaker and has associated this face with security. He still does not know much about the rest of the world and is frightened by it. Your reassurance that it is okay when meeting strangers will help.

Many babies will want to carry their "security blanket" or "teddy bear" with them as they explore their environment, meet strangers, or go into new situations. It's important not to ridicule them about this. These objects have been associated with secure times and security-giving people, and are helpful to them in new situations.

*Things were fine before my baby began to walk
but now everything seems to be going wrong. Why?*

Parents frequently feel this way when they don't adjust to the role change required when their baby begins to walk. It is important that this adjustment be made. It becomes a blueprint for later relationships.

Prior to the time that the child could get about on his own, you had to care for him. It was largely a giving relationship. You didn't have to do much to stop or limit the baby. As a matter of fact, it was just the opposite. You were constantly encouraging him to sit, to stand, to crawl. Once he begins to walk, things change. The walker is everywhere—into, under, and on top of everything. Now, in addition to giving, you must set limits and take away. "No, no" becomes the pattern.

The child doesn't know what is dangerous to himself and precious to others. You must now protect both him *and* your valued possessions. Time and time again you say, "No, no." "No, no" when he touches the glass vase with his clumsy little hands. "No, no" when he sits on your clean couch with food—and can't always find his mouth. He bangs his hand against the glass in the window and you say, "No, no." Just as you get tired of saying "no, no," he gets tired of hearing it from you! Yet you must help your child learn to handle his or her world.

How can I deal with this conflict?

It is important to "seize the time" to show your baby how to function capably within certain limits without frustrating his every activity and without destroying his budding sense of independence. His assertive, exploring behavior is his way of feeling, "I can do things for myself. I am a capable individual." This is exactly what we want him to feel. But we have to be able to live with him while he is "coming into his own."

Helping your baby learn to handle his world without trampling on yours helps your child begin to develop self-control and begin to accept responsibility for his behavior. If he or she doesn't get locked in a continual power struggle with you over limits, then motivation and direction from within can follow more quickly. Mutual good feelings between mother and child can continue. On the other hand, if you are in constant battle with your child you will soon feel worn out and unhappy. One part of your child enjoys the fight, but the other part of him is frightened and unhappy about it. Most important, he is developing a pattern of relationship that may cause him trouble later on.

What is the best way to avoid power struggles?

Remember that your baby can't anticipate very much. He doesn't understand the full effect of his behavior on others. He needs help in thinking up ways to act that are not so troublesome to him or to others. Giving explanations for "why" with your "no-no's," raising suggestive questions, and preparing your child for what you are going to demand of him are the best approaches. "No-no . . . glass break . . . cut baby," delivered with appropriate gestures, gives the baby information and motivation that is more useful and powerful than "no-no" alone. You may have to say the same thing on many different occasions, but eventually the baby will stop banging the glass because he understands the reason behind your demand. He learns to transfer this understanding to other situations. In this way he learns to think, learns to protect himself, and increases his ability to function without you. At the same time, you save yourself many future problems.

With the older infant, if you try to put the round block in the round hole rather than the square hole, he may get angry or at least be disappointed that he couldn't do it for himself. He may keep trying to put it in the square hole "just because you got in his business." But if you say, "Johnny, what about this one?" your help will be more easily accepted. He learns to study and analyze a problem. He will eventually learn to think before acting. With similar questions you can help him think about other ways to accomplish other goals. Most important, he is doing it for himself. It is one more proof of his ability and one more brick in his foundation of self-confidence, one more impetus to spend his time and energy acting on his own rather than resisting what you try to do for him or what you try to make him do. If this pattern can be established now, there will be less trouble later.

Preparation for the next activity cuts down on resistance and conflict. For example, you might say: "Pretty soon we'll stop and wash our hands," or "It's about time for crackers." Explanations cut down on anxiety and acting up. "I'm going across the way to get some sugar and I'll be right back." Suggestions rather than commands are useful. "The blocks go in the box" is less likely to provoke resistance than "Put the blocks away." You can always command when suggestion doesn't work.

What other methods can I use?

Getting your baby in the habit of cleaning up, washing hands, or whatever you consider necessary is important. He realizes that this is a way to please you and to be a capable person. Doing a task alongside your child in the beginning not only shows him how it is done, but it gets him started and into the habit.

Children learn from imitation. You might say, "Okay, let's pick up now," and then pick up scattered play material with her. Praise—"Beautiful" or "Great job!"—makes it an achievement worth doing the next day. Later, "I expect that pretty soon you can clean up by yourself." To reward her success, a big hug is in order.

Your undivided attention at the moment you want your child to respond is important. If you say, "Stop that, Johnny," from across the room while talking and drinking coffee with Mrs. Jones, chances are good that Johnny won't stop. If instead you put down your cup, address Johnny directly, and point out calmly why you want him to stop—or suggest another, more acceptable activity—he is more likely to respond as you requested. If he continues what he is doing or stops momentarily and then begins again, it will be necessary to go over and start Johnny on another activity. Be careful that you don't spend too much time with Mrs. Jones. The "trouble" Johnny is causing may be a question: "Who is more important, me or Mrs. Jones?" On the other hand, you need some time for friends.

It is important to act before you become frustrated and angry. Not only is your loss of control a victory for Johnny over "Goliath" but it is a situation in which you are likely to overreact and punish him severely when the matter could have been handled without any punishment. In saving a step, you may lose a mile. The way you say what you say makes a great deal of difference. Your calm confidence that Johnny is going to accept your suggestions and ideas is extremely important. A hesitant voice on the one hand or a harsh, commanding one on the other is an invitation to battle. But remember, these are not mechanical operations. Your interactions with your child will be the most successful if you approach them with enthusiasm and spontaneity.

Are there particular times that are likely to lead to conflict?

Yes. Mealtime and bedtime are among the most likely to lead to struggles. Toilet-training is *the* time when troublesome relationships between parent and child are most apparent. It is also an event which can worsen already troubled situations. When you or the baby are overtired, anxious, or frustrated, "war" is more likely.

(A) *Feeding.* Feeding, whether by breast or bottle, can and should be a relaxed time. The stomach of your baby at birth can take in enough milk to last for about four hours. This permits setting up a schedule of about six feedings a day. You need not be absolutely rigid about it, but a schedule permits you to plan and be ready for the call. You should set aside enough time for feeding so that it can be a time of quiet pleasure. Cuddling, singing, cooing, and burping afterwards all make for a pleasant experience. When the baby is on a bottle, fathers can help. Why not?

Your comfort increases the baby's comfort; therefore, as the baby can take in more, you will want to eliminate the feeding hours which disrupt your sleep. The usual schedule is 2 A.M., 6 A.M., 10 A.M., 2 P.M., 6 P.M., and 10 P.M. Yes, 2 A.M. must go! Usually at around four or five months your baby's stomach can take more and he can sleep through the night. When the time appears right you may want to delay your response to his stirring or crying at 2 A.M. If he falls back to sleep, you've got it made. If the demand is strong, feed your baby and try again another night. The next step, when possible, will be to adjust the 6 A.M. feeding to a later hour.

You need not worry about overeating at the infant stage. From the beginning your baby will turn away when he has had enough. Don't turn her head back, pry her mouth open, and jam in food. She doesn't need it. You need not worry about what looks like a loss of appetite between twelve and twenty-four months. The average birth weight is about seven pounds, and this is usually doubled during the first five months; the small babies usually gain more and the big ones usually gain less. Infants tend to gain about a pound a month for the next seven months and then about one-half pound a month in the second year. Thus less food is needed after a year.

At the age of about twelve months, your baby is likely to become highly selective about what he eats. It appears to be his or her way of saying, "I'll make up my own mind!" You may begin to worry about whether he or she is getting enough of "the right things." Keep up the vitamins, but don't panic. Babies have a way of getting what they need. If you don't get tense and upset about it, you won't get into a struggle in which your infant becomes afraid or refuses to eat. By the second or third year he will again be eating a wide variety of foods.

(B) *Sleep.* At first, your baby seems to be asleep whenever he is not eating. By nine or ten months the baby is down to morning and afternoon naps. By eighteen months your baby will only require one nap during daytime hours. Shortly thereafter your baby may develop some sleep problems.

A lot is going on with your baby at about eighteen months. You are probably toilet-training, setting limits on his increasing activities, and expecting more of him. He has fears and doubts in spite of his "front." His mind is working overtime without being equipped to understand all that is going on. At this stage he believes that his angry thoughts and actions can hurt you. This all contributes to a fear of falling asleep at night.

Sexual intercourse in the presence of a young infant adds to this problem. The six-month-old infant does not understand what's going on. But it looks dangerous and violent . . . and the source of his security appears to be getting hurt. If possible, it is a good idea to have your child's crib out of your bedroom by five months.

The infant who has trouble falling asleep should be comforted. Putting children to bed with a quiet song or story will prevent some sleep problems. Assurance that he is fine and you are fine and his daddy's fine and brother is fine and sister is fine is useful. Rubbing his back slowly and affectionately will relieve tension. Be certain that something as simple (but dangerous) as an open diaper pin is not the cause of the trouble. The cry of distress is different—more urgent—when this is the case.

If baby cries, avoid removing him from his crib or bed or picking him up for as long as possible. You are asking for trouble if you place him in your bed. Be confident in your ability as a "sandman." Your anxiety and fear that baby will not go to sleep may cause you to hug and squeeze too much. If you secretly feel that your efforts won't work, they probably won't. The baby will wake up and demand to be held again. Eventually you'll get tired and angry, and you and yours will soon be in a "sho' nuff" struggle.

When you must—because the demand is extreme—hold a wakeful baby, don't hold him too long. If you must allow him in your bed, remove him to his own as soon as he falls soundly asleep. Prepare and assure the infant: "Pretty soon you will be able to sleep in your own bed all night long. Isn't that nice . . . a big girl!" When sleep problems occur for the first time simultaneously with toilet-training, it is best to ease up on training . . . go slower, but don't stop.

Any change or threat—such as the mother away or a new baby—may cause sleep problems. Calm, gentle support and assurance is always the best approach. You may see a lot of lost-and-found play, "losing" items and finding them, during this period. You may see the child facing a lot of imaginary dangers, or falling down and recovering in his play. Don't stop such play. This is one of his ways of dealing with the fears of losing his mother and father.

(C) *Toilet-training.* Toilet-training can easily lead to conflict between you and your baby. One major problem is a frequent tendency to start training before the baby is able. The second is the fact that many of us adults consider urinating and bowel movements a kind of "nasty business," without being aware that we feel this way. We often want our babies to hurry up and get the whole business over with. As a result we press too hard, show fear of failure, or ignore the whole matter.

Most children do not have good control of the muscles of the bladder and bowel until eighteen months to two years. Pressure on an infant to perform well before he is able can lead to anger, disappointment, and loss of confidence in himself, a fear that you will be angry with him, punish him, or leave him. He may also fear that his anger will hurt you. In addition, the eighteen-month-old still is not absolutely clear about what belongs to his body. Some will wonder about whether the feces is not a part of them being flushed away. After all, "Mommy was upset and disappointed with me, and maybe she knows that I was angry with her, and now she is going to throw a part of me away."

If this is not the case, withholding those precious pellets (they must be precious, look how much Mommy wants them) is certainly a good way to "fix" that demanding parent. Confused, frightened, and angry, your baby may either hold back or just get wildly active and antagonistic about many things during this period.

It is best to wait until around eighteen months before you begin to try to toilet-train your child. Remember early achievement of this task does not indicate mental or physical excellence. A pleasant response when your child indicates that it is potty time tells him that it is an activity as normal and nice as any other. A calm, confident manner indicates that you have no doubt in his ability. Once he understands what he is supposed to do, continuing with some activity of your own a reasonable distance away shows your confidence. Praise for success—not too much, not too little—is helpful. When he doesn't quite make it to the potty, reassure him that he will get there next time.

Sometimes you can figure out the schedule of your child's BMs and put him on the potty before he soils. But the child himself has not gained control over his bowel functions. Help your child learn how to tell you the time is near, what to do, and how to let you know he's finished. Children often do troublesome things because they have not been told what to do in certain situations. It is best to treat the feces as neither "good stuff" nor "bad stuff." Approval should be for the way he handles himself and not for what he produces. Any mess or play with his BM should be responded to with an explanation and not with horror, a threat, or a put-down like, "Look what you did!" Calmly but firmly stated, "We don't play in the BM" is more to the point and more helpful.

Some psychiatrists have said that black children can have negative feelings about their skin color because their feces is brown. We think this is a misinterpretation of what occurs. Any apparent relationship is due more to whether toilet-time was a pleasant experience than to the color of the feces. African psychiatrists see no evidence of this attitude in areas where all the people are black. We believe this is one of those areas in which traditional theory is misapplied.

When training your boy to use the toilet, it is probably not a good idea to hold his penis (or organ of pleasure) and direct the stream. There is a tendency to do this to prevent his wetting himself and the floor, especially at night when he is half-asleep. You might, when necessary, want to hold a receptacle (urinal or bottle) up to the penis to avoid spillage. But first urge him to "hold his own."

"Organ of pleasure," how does he know about *that?* He doesn't know about "the real thing"—sexual intercourse. But he does know that from the very beginning he got a pleasant sensation around the penis when it was being washed. The same occurred when he played with it, or when stimulation caused an erection. It is a part of the body he will want to preserve. This does not mean that you must refrain from holding it at all costs, nor does it mean that you must be quick or timid in washing the area. Neither should you be upset if he plays with his penis occasionally.

But encouraging him from the beginning to hold his own penis is best. Washing the penis with no more or less concentration than on the rest of the body is also helpful. Later, because playing (masturbation) in public is not socially acceptable, you will want calmly but firmly to indicate the situations in which you don't want your son or your daughter playing with their genitals. This is usually not a real concern until a child is three or four. We will discuss masturbation in more detail within this age group.

The Question of Permissiveness

Is it wrong to show anger? You stress handling everything with calm confidence.

When the infant is very young, only extended crying is likely to cause you anger. The walking child has more opportunity to "get on your nerves." You will undoubtedly get angry from time to time. The right amount of anger will let your child know that you have reached your limit. However, too much anger too frequently expressed can frighten and confuse your baby, particularly when you express it in an inconsistent way. (By that we mean the same act that angered you an hour ago does not appear to anger you now.) Exposure to too much anger can reduce a baby's confidence and his willingness to explore, learn, and express himself.

Most of a child's frustrating behavior occurs because he has little memory, little ability to figure things out, and little ability to restrain himself from certain acts even when he knows he should. Getting angry at him accomplishes much less than reminding him of what you expect, giving him information, and helping him restrain his tendency to act. Most troublesome situations can be handled without angry responses. A calm approach decreases the possibility of struggles between parent and child which in turn can lead to even greater frustration and anger on your part. "Be cool." Yet a jam sandwich or a dirty hand on your clean laundry, or some similar problem, is going to get the better of you from time to time . . . and that's okay.

Is it harmful to spank a child?

Some well-behaved, well-balanced people were never, or rarely, spanked as children. Some well-behaved, well-balanced people were spanked reasonably often. Children who were spanked by thoughtful, loving parents rarely have problems as a result of spanking. But if your child can achieve good control and behave well without spanking, why spank? If you will take the time, come close and look directly at your child while making your displeasure and expectations known, you can motivate your child to take responsibility for his behavior in a way that spanking alone will never do. The idea is not to frighten with angry faces or dirty looks but to get across the notion that you mean what you say.

Many children are relieved and feel less guilty after a spanking. With a spanking, they "pay their debt" and often go right back to misbehaving. They have not been called upon to take any responsibility for controlling their troublesome impulses or acts. A better control of undesirable behavior, with a more beneficial long-range effect, can be achieved through talking to your child. Letting him know that you are unhappy with a particular act . . . that it is the act you consider bad, not him as a person . . . is the best approach. Let your child know that you think he can do better; that he can control himself; that he can avoid doing whatever it is he has done. Through these expectations, you are giving him a chance to be responsible for his conduct. You are saying, "I believe in you. You are capable." Reasonable behavior becomes something that your child will want to achieve for himself. It becomes a way to demonstrate his capabilities to himself. This is the beginning of the development of control from within.

Talking to himself about acceptable and unacceptable behavior is one way your two- or three-year-old avoids unacceptable behavior next time. The cutest sight in the world is the two-year-old in front of your flower vase, no adults around, arm and hand out,

saying, "No touch." Your words are helping him control himself
. . . and use words.

What are some of the problems involved with spanking?

The most troublesome situation is when a parent spanks a child
without just cause or "uses" a child. It often happens like this:
Father had a bad day at work, Mother is tired, and an argument
develops. One party is losing the argument or there is just no way
out of it without someone losing face. At this point, Johnny climbs
up on the "forbidden" table and he gets a solid beating. Often the
general tension is thus relieved and the argument stops. Johnny
may have acted as he did because children get frightened and
often become active and destructive when parents argue. They
sometimes feel that they caused the argument. They often learn
that they can stop the fighting by "being bad" and becoming the
focus of attention. At the same time, they understand that they
didn't deserve the whipping, yet they can't do anything about it.
They simply develop hurtful rage and anger toward their parents
and themselves. This is even more likely to be the case where there
is little trust or love between parent and child.

Another problem: by being hit by you when you are angry,
children learn to hit others when in turn they are angry. Later
when you try to help your child learn to talk out a problem
rather than fight, you will be trying to undo a response that you
helped establish in the first place.

Occasionally you will lose control and spank your child even
when you do not intend to. Some parents are able to apologize for
their loss of control, but at the same time point out to the child
how his behavior made them strike out in anger; the child need
not have acted as he did; that if he does not want to be spanked or
yelled at, he should not run up and down the steps or do whatever
it was that caused your display of temper. Again, however, when
there is love and trust between parents and children, spanking will
not have a negative effect.

Are you saying that parents should not be strict?

If strictness is your style or temperament and you feel most comfortable as a strict, stern person, that may be the best approach for
you. The important thing is that in some way your child be able to

feel and understand your love and concern for him. You can be strict and yet be relatively calm. You can even be strict and stern without spanking.

There is a difference between being strict and being excessively harsh, arbitrary, and unfair. It is these latter tendencies that are likely to create problems. They promote rage, anger, unfair and otherwise undesirable behavior in children. As mentioned above, inconsistent responses—strictness one time and permissiveness the next, for the same kind of offense—add confusion, doubt, and suspicion to the child's feelings of anger and rage.

New child-rearing approaches are designed to help children develop more internal control, discipline, direction, and motivation, rather than depending on others to direct their behavior. On the other hand, children who are permitted to do whatever they want to are not any more likely to develop effective life skills than those under too much adult control.

I was reared by strict parents. I feel I am too strict with my baby. How can I change?

The way you respond to your child has a lot to do with what you think your role as a parent should be. Parents tend to consider themselves as either the owners, the servants, or the developers of their children. "Owners" tend to command, demand, and control their children. They tend to feel that it is not easy for their children to learn to be cooperative; that children are naturally stubborn and resistant and you must *make* them do things. Responding to them as if this is the case often angers or enrages the child and causes the very behavior that you are trying to avoid.

The "servant" parents tend to be permissive. They take everything the child can "dish out." They permit their children to hold tyrannical reign over the entire family . . . often believing such behavior to be "cute." Such children often become selfish and abusive. They frequently remain impulsive, are unable to concentrate, settle down, learn, or accomplish very much. They are often very anxious and afraid that their behavior will get them into trouble.

The "developer" viewpoint is most beneficial. As a developer, you do not think of your child as your possession but as an individual with rights and needs of his or her own. As a developer, you view your child as a "ball of potential," ready to unfold and blossom with your assistance. You help your child gradually develop skills. You give children increased freedom, independence, and opportunity to function on their own as they demonstrate the understanding and ability to do so. You may occasionally have to back up and permit less when they demonstrate they can't handle a situation.

As a "developer," you don't want to *make* your child do anything. You don't want to *let* your child do everything. You want him to grow in a way that makes it comfortable for you and the rest of the family to live with him. You want him or her to develop in a way which he or she can live with and view with pride. You feel from the start that you can prepare your child for a worthwhile life if you provide the information and encouragement that he does not have. Your role remains the same throughout his childhood, changing only in a way that's appropriate for a particular age. If you keep the "developer" viewpoint in mind, you can examine your behavior as your child matures to see whether your handling of various situations is helping him learn something or whether you are just making something happen.

Isn't it true that some child-care experts feel that black parents tend to be too strict?

Yes. We believe that this is the case in too many families, although far from the majority. The stress black parents live under too often results in, "Get away from me, boy," "Shut up," or "Mind your manners." These instructions too often occur when the child truly needs attention or needs to protest. We will discuss this again as a special problem of the three- and four-year-olds.

Don't many black parents feel that middle-income white parents are too permissive?

Yes. We have heard this feeling expressed among black parents of all income groups. Black teachers are frequently critical of what they feel is permissive management of children by some white teachers, although this feeling is not typical of the vast majority of parents or teachers, black or white. But we ourselves believe that too many middle-income people—more often than not white— have carried less strictness, less sternness, less demand too far.

Why is internal control important?

It requires much more internal control to function well in today's world than it did in the past. In earlier times, people lived on farms and in small towns. Jobs did not require a great deal of independent thought or decision-making. Television didn't take you to far away places and bombard you with ideas that were different from those in your own community. There was relatively little travel and little communication between people of different lifestyles. Children did not have to be reared to handle strange and rapidly changing situations. Parents, teachers, preachers, and policemen had unquestioned authority.

Conditions are much different today. In a mobile, rapidly changing, and divided society, there is less "outside the family" pressure to accept responsibility and live by law alone. We must develop and maintain our attitudes, values, ways, and life direction much more on our own. Thus, it is important that children be brought up in ways which will teach them to accept responsibility and handle strange and changing situations by themselves—with few outside guidelines or pressures. It can be done.

For example, in some schoolrooms, when a teacher is absent, classroom activities and behavior break down almost completely. In other cases the class goes on almost as if the teacher were present. Some parents complain that if they leave their children home alone for fifteen minutes, their house becomes a shambles. Other parents can be gone longer and return to find the house in relatively good order. In both situations the children involved are better able to care for themselves if they have developed internal control, self-motivation, and self-direction. Where children have not developed these inner qualities, things fall apart when the parent, teacher, or other source of external control is absent. People who develop inner controls as children function better as adults.

The development of internal control, direction, and motivation does not start at five or at fifteen years. It begins with the way you help your child learn to wait for his bottle or stop taking the toy of the boy next door. We have already given examples of how you can call on your child to accept responsibility for his behavior. We will do so throughout this book.

CHAPTER 4

The Preschool Child:
Ages Two to Four

Special Problems of the Two-Year-Old

*Why does my two-year-old show so much
frustration, fear and anger?*

Your two-year-old is "the great pretender." He has just gotten his
legs together. He has a few words. He has begun to figure out that
he is an individual. Now he wants to be and act just like you—big,
strong, capable, knowledgeable. But the truth is that he is a
"David" without a slingshot or a rock, in a land of "Goliaths." He is
only now learning to feed and clothe himself, to control his bowels
and bladder. Every fall or mishap reminds him of how incapable
he is . . . and too much help from you reminds him as well.

You are helping him explore his environment and protecting him
from danger for his own good. But he doesn't like the fact that you
must. You are his personal giant, frustrating and "helping." He
resents this and gets angry with you from time to time. He attacks
you and sometimes tries to drive you away. At the same time he is
afraid that he may go too far. It's a case of not being able to do
with you or do without you. His mind permits him to think that he
can control the world . . . or that you can control the world.

Most of a child's thinking is magical and unrealistic. A stop light
turned red just as a father stepped off a curb and all the cars
stopped. His two-year-old daughter said, "Do that 'gin, Dad, do

59

that 'gin!" With such thinking it's easy to see why your child can think that his angry feelings can hurt people—including you. But you are his helpmate, the source of all his security. The "great pretender" knows that in spite of his come-on, he can't make it all by himself. He needs you, yet he thinks he can hurt and lose you. Thus fears and anxieties mark this age.

Is there any way to decrease these "around two"
feelings of fearfulness and frustration?

If you talk calmly to your child about what you expect rather than hitting out at him, he will more quickly learn that you are not retaliating for his bad wishes. Through your firm but tolerant management of his anger and temper tantrums, he will gradually learn that his thoughts can't hurt. But be careful to avoid over-protecting your child. If you respond anxiously to every fall and every cry, your behavior suggests that there is something to be afraid of. If he falls, gets up, survives a number of minor disasters, he learns that the world is not too dangerous.

No matter what I say to my two-year-old, his answer is "no."
How can I manage his feelings of aggression?

From the moment you begin to help your child to wait, to walk (in certain situations) rather than run, to borrow a toy instead of taking it, to ask another child to return a toy instead of punching him in the nose, you are bound to meet up with resistance. Your child will fight your attempt to modify and refine his raw, aggressive energy and make it available for positive use. This resistance will reach its peak with the two-year-old in the form of balky, negative, "no" behavior. He is breaking away from the dependency of the first year, taking his independent, let-me-do-it-for-myself stand, which often means doing whatever he wants to do, whenever he wants to do it, to whomever he wants to do it. And there you are trying to help him become a tolerable human being. Who needs you?

In dealing with your two-year-old, it helps to be firm but fair. Make sure your demands are reasonable. *Don't take his attacks (hitting, refusing, etcetera) personally.* Let him do what he can do without harming himself, you, others, or valuable property. Help him succeed at what he is trying to accomplish when he bites off more than he can chew. Stop him—with firmness, but whenever possible without undue anger—when enough is enough. A firm, no-nonsense voice and an eye-to-eye confrontation is better than a heavy hand and a lot of ranting and raving.

How do you handle "no! no! no! no!"? Banter or kidding often helps—not ridicule. You might try something like, "Johnny's name is Mr. No. No." Use your good sense and sense of humor to help your child see that you know that he knows he's playing a game . . . and it's not getting your goat. If he's involved in a task like washing up, helping him see that it's for himself and not for you will let you both off the hook. "Leroy sounds like he's cleaning up for Daddy, but let's see now, Daddy's not dirty, Leroy's dirty." He'll soon catch on. He should do his own thing for his own good . . . not others'.

Unfortunately, aggression and its control is not a problem limited to the two-year-old. It comes up again and again with your preschooler as he matures. Since it is something you will be dealing with for years, let's stop a moment and examine this important area of behavior more closely.

Aggression and the Preschooler

You said earlier that aggression can be healthy. How?

Aggression in everyday language is interpreted to mean an unjust attack of some kind, ranging from a personal fight to large-scale war. But at the same time aggression is really a kind of life energy. It is very much like gasoline. A spark put to gasoline on the ground can be very destructive to all around. But the gasoline in your fuel tank provides the energy to run your car. Human beings need this energy to make their way in the world. But it must be modified and channeled, much like crude oil is refined and put in the gas tank.

Whenever a young child is faced with an obstacle or problem, he attacks it with raw physical energy (aggression). If this response is not modified, conflict and chaos result. Parents, caretakers, teachers, and others must help the young child gradually turn raw aggressive energy into the fuel for curiosity, determination, learning, work, and play. They must help the child modify, refine, and control his energy so that it can be used at the child's will and in ways in keeping with the just rules of the society.

How far should physical aggression be allowed to go?

Some parents feel that it is okay for children to destroy furniture or to attack other children as a healthy expression of their aggression. A parent who feels this way must be prepared for other people not to find Walter's or Doris's expression of aggression too cute. In fact, they won't want to see him or her coming for a visit. You shouldn't be offended if a parent tells her Sam or Sally to hit Walter or Doris back. Who wants their children to be treated like punching bags, servants, or slaves?

Children will learn where and how and when to let their anger out as soon as you make your expectations clear. They will learn that it's okay to show their temper in the basement, outdoors, or their room, but not the living room. The point is they need an outlet for aggressive behavior, and you should provide this opportunity under conditions that are good for you and good for your child. But at the same time, they need guidelines, rules, and limits, provided without great anger and heavy preaching.

My child bangs up all our furniture. Should I permit this?

We don't believe that children should be allowed to destroy furniture. We discussed in Chapter 3 the fact that certain kinds of "destructive" behavior are permissible and that your child should have areas and things that he can destroy. But why should he destroy your valuables, even if you can afford to replace them? It is helpful for him to learn that some things can be destroyed and some things should be preserved. "There is a time and place for everything" is an important lesson for adult life. We also believe that aggressive acts should be stopped when they are dangerous to your child or to others. The two-year-old in particular will use the scissors, blocks, or anything else he can get his hands on as a weapon when frustrated or angry. He will be embarrassed, ashamed, and feel bad about himself if you do not prevent him from hurting himself or others.

A word of caution about handling aggression: Where there is no danger, even though aggressive behavior is excessive, rude, or mean, don't be too quick to jump in if several children are involved. Very often children can work conflicts out by themselves, particularly the three- and four-year-olds. They really don't want to hurt each other. Working it out themselves is good practice in learning to negotiate with others in order to obtain their own rights without compromising the needs and rights of others. Help them out after it is clear that they cannot handle the matter.

Can I make my child passive, a "Milquetoast,"
by controlling his aggression?

Not unless you are excessive and severe in controlling your child's aggression. (Although sometimes severe treatment increases rather than decreases aggressive, acting-up behavior, or causes a child to resist in other ways—not hear, not cooperate, or not do whatever the strong-arm parent wants.) Passivity is caused in a different way.

It is the parents who do everything for their children so that there is no need to do things for themselves who are more likely to cause a child to become passive. Parents who are passive or withdrawn themselves often have passive children.

Children who have not been helped to handle such feelings as jealousy and death fears and wishes often hold back their feelings and actions. This can reduce curiosity, exploration, and aggression to the point of passivity. Such children may become quiet, obedient, and undemanding, even when their rights and needs are being stepped on. If your child doesn't protest under these circumstances, you should be concerned. Such "holding in" and "holding back" can lead to failure in learning and school problems later on.

Looking back on black history, isn't this the age at which
black children, particularly males, were crushed into line?

Yes. In the past, because aggressive black males were likely to be in danger, some parents, knowingly and unknowingly, tried to crush normal aggressive behavior in their preschool children. In order to survive in a hostile world, youngsters were taught to obey authority figures, right or wrong, fair or unfair.

This approach not only produced too many black children and adults who were afraid to stand up for their rights and needs and even eventually learned to see no injustice and smile and comply with anybody in a position of authority, right or wrong, it often backfired and created or continued the very negative, excessively aggressive behavior it was supposed to destroy. As mentioned before, this is sometimes the outcome when children are whipped and scolded too often and abused without cause.

In these two reactions to strict, crushing discipline can be found the beginning of "Dumb Sambo," "Geraldine," "Bad Nigger," and "Uncle Tom"—all types and stereotypes that were products of slavery and oppression.

To equip our black children for the modern world, shouldn't we be training them to be more aggressive?

Permitting early negative behavior, anger, and aggression to be expressed without any check or effort to turn it into socially acceptable, useful energy is just as harmful as trying to crush it. A child handled in this manner will not develop the inner control discussed in Chapter 3. Eventually family, friends, strangers, blacks, and whites can all become victims of his or her anger and aggression. In fact, a child through harmful acts to himself or due to harmful reactions his behavior brings, can become the victim of his own anger and aggression. The records of too many angry people show that their families and their own racial groups are the first and most common victims of their rage.

Again, patient, firm, and fair management of a young child's angry, aggressive behavior is best. When properly managed, the child is still free and better able to choose his own value system, so that as an adult he will be better able to work toward the political and economic system he believes in, through the method he chooses. He will still have the ability to be violently aggressive when he needs to be. But it will be under his control. If development continues well, he will be more effective than he would have been otherwise.

But shouldn't black children be taught to be angry in order to fight racism?

We must help children become aware of their rights and opportunities. We must help them acquire the skills to take advantage of these rights and opportunities. We must help them learn to identify and fight racism. But we don't have to help them become angry. Anger is a healthy human emotion. When youngsters are denied their rights and opportunities, anger will come naturally . . . unless they are crushed into line. This is not the case for most black children today.

Making children supersensitive to all injustice in a world full of injustices will cause them to be indiscriminately reactive and angry . . . or reactive and angry whether it will help or not . . .

reactive and angry when, in fact, the offense was unintended or minor. Anger consumes energy that is needed for establishing and carrying out life plans. We see teen-agers aware and concerned about injustice and racism but with little or no knowledge of how to fight it. They are paralyzed, often to the point where they can't function. Constant reaction to racist acts leads to frustration, more anger, and then more than anger—hostility. Hostility is not like healthy anger. It is a fixed "mind set" rather than a healthy emotional reaction. It does not help in the fight against racism.

Race and the Preschooler

Why is the three- and four-year-old more
aware of race than the infant?

During their first two years of life, children are not quite sure that they are individuals, separate and distinct from other people. By three years of age, the child's ability to understand himself and his world is better. He becomes very conscious of himself and very conscious of others as separate from himself. Now is the time that he or she will want to know: "Who am I?" "What kind of person am I?" He will become greatly interested in how he is like or different from others. He will question and be concerned about such things as similarities and differences in skin color and hair.

Should I bring up the issue of race with my three-year-old?

You need not sit your child down to talk about race. Children see blacks and whites on television. They may, depending on where you live or go, see or play with people of different colors and races. They will hear your household conversations about race, your mention of "blacks" or "whites." Their sense of observation and interest in understanding what you are talking about will cause them to raise the questions, "What is black?" "Am I black?" "Am I white?" This provides an opportunity to give an answer in a natural, calm, and—most important—confident manner.

A simple answer to a three- or four-year-old, "You are black . . . like Mommy (or Daddy)," is best. You may prefer "Afro-American" or some other term. The "like Daddy" or "like Mommy" relates the issue of race to yourself. You are your child's source of pleasure and security and therefore somebody very positive. If you show enthusiasm about the fact that you are black, your child will sense that being black must be both positive and good.

Is there anything else I should say or do?

More than that in the beginning is not needed. A child of three or four still can't handle complicated explanations. In addition, if you give long answers, appear upset, ignore the question, or bring up the issue over and over again, your child may sense that you are anxious about the subject of race. As a result, he may either avoid the issue completely or use it as one more way to tease and control you. For example, he might play the game of saying he doesn't like being black to "get your goat."

The concept of race and an individual's feeling about it develops gradually. If your response, directly or indirectly, does not say, ALL TALK ABOUT RACE IS FORBIDDEN, a child will be back for more information on the subject from time to time. Speeding up knowledge and awareness in this area does not ensure that your child will develop a positive racial identity. In fact, either extreme preoccupation with or neglect of the issue of race can actually create anxiety and even a preoccupation with the danger of being black.

Being black in a country full of anti-black feeling and action presents real problems. These problems need not be discussed until your child is able to understand and handle such information. But whenever you do discuss the matter, it is important to strike a balance between too much and too little attention to the issue of race, or you can defeat your own purpose.

We know many black children who have a positive racial identity, whose parents responded only to natural openings to discuss race. These youngsters handle themselves well with all groups. They can discuss race issues easily. They show a very mature concern about racism and injustice by the age of ten years. On the other hand, we know children who have been bombarded with discussions about race, almost from birth, and who are insecure about being black—even in all-black settings.

My five-year-old has never
mentioned race to me. Why?

If you don't hear inquiries about race by four or five years, it is probably best to think about what you are doing to turn off your child's interest in the question. You can open up a discussion about race by talking about it when natural opportunities present themselves . . . blacks on television, news about black affairs, a new black teacher in the school or on the job. If this doesn't work—although it rarely fails—you might mention directly to a child of late four or five that you have not heard him mention the issue of race and wonder out loud whether it is a problem for him. Even here, a gradual opening of discussion, not bombardment, is best. Once it's clear that it is okay to talk about race, he will.

Are there ways a child can develop a negative racial identity, even with reasonable discussion and apparent parental enthusiasm?

Yes. You can send your child mixed messages. If you talk about the beauty of blackness on one hand and say derogatory things about blacks on the other, your child will see through your big, black "front." It is true, and helpful, that we laugh at ourselves as individuals and as a group from time to time. There is a difference, however, between this and consistent and deeply felt animosity toward our own race. The latter feelings create the problem.

Children can sense the difference between kidding and group depreciation. They can tell when their parents' true message is: "Black is not really good, but I am black; therefore, I must pretend it is good." They must protect themselves and their parents; therefore, they in turn may talk "black is good." But they will have a good deal of mixed feelings, anxiety, and anger—some directed at you—about being black.

The most troublesome situations arise when a child who has been told that black is beautiful is made aware of the fact that he is black and then has his rights and needs ignored or abused by his own black parents. Here a child will feel rage, rage, and triple rage!

The first time my four-year-old raised a question about race, he said, "I'm white." Does this mean that he doesn't like being black?

Maybe yes and maybe no. But don't panic. This is not an unusual first response among children who are in a small minority in a neighborhood or in school. Children often want to be like people they want to be friendly with. This reaction can also occur in a predominantly black community, since we are a minority in the nation as a whole. The television brings your child the nation. We have seen white children who want to be brown or black like their therapist. We have seen young school-age white children who want to be brown or black like their favorite football heroes.

A response to "I'm white" could be, "No, you are black . . . like Daddy and Mommy." If light-skinned, he is likely to offer you a hand or arm in evidence of his whiteness. You can point out that the skin is light brown (or whatever it is), but he is of the black or Afro-American group. You can explain that black is the name of the group. Color within the group ranges from white to black. Again your enthusiasm and your confidence—without being phony —will make it okay. Your child may not fully understand until older.

Even with three- or four-year-olds, it is occasionally important for adults to intervene to make certain that the rights and needs of all children are being respected when they are in a group situation. Otherwise, difference—sometimes racial and sometimes otherwise —does become a basis for abuse and exclusion. Four-year-olds become comfortable with two or three people, and can be cruel, without adult help, in their exclusion of others. In fact, you may have to help your child accept a more timid youngster into a play group. He might well be the one who is making life miserable for the newcomer, black or white. We will discuss this more fully in this chapter.

What if my child says she wants to be white
because someone is calling her "nigger"?

You should point out that nigger is a name that some people call black people when they want to make them feel bad. Urge her not to feel bad. Explain that she is not a nigger or anything else bad. The same explanation used above should follow, this time—because she is under attack—emphasizing that you feel good about being black. You should speak to the offending child's parents, if possible, and to the child, if the parents are unavailable or are not responsive. You might explain to your child that the white child is being bad in calling names.

If your child settles it on the playground in her own way, so be it.

What do I say if she says, "I want straight, blond hair"?

In a relaxed and unperturbed way, point out that she is black and most black people have nice curly black hair; that most white people have straight hair—brown, blond, black. At this age, what you get across in your voice and manner will make it either okay or a problem. You will hear the issue again at an older age, and an explanation suitable for that age should be given—still relaxed. You should keep your eyes open for other questions about race or belonging when a statement like this is made.

Sex and the Preschooler

When are children first interested in sex?
What do you tell them?

Children usually first become interested in the differences between boys and girls around three and one-half to four years of age. Recall that this is about the same time that they become interested in racial differences—and for the same reason. This is the age that a child becomes conscious of himself and others. This is a time of great curiosity about many things. A girl may ask (and maybe a boy), "What is that?" pointing to a penis. They may want to know why boys have them and girls do not. Answer such questions truthfully. "Because when they are grownups boys can give the seed to make a baby. Girls can receive the seed and keep it inside where the baby can grow." Under no circumstances should girls be told that they are lacking, missing, or deficient of genitals. They should understand that their genitals are different from and just as important as a boy's.

How should I deal with questions about sexual intercourse?

Children often become curious about sexual intercourse by observing animals, either dogs or cage-contained animals. It is best to respond to animal sex as normal and not as something shocking. You don't want to call children to observe nor do you want to drive them away or cover up the cage. Again, it is best to answer a specific question in a way best understood at the child's age and wait to explain more until he asks again. Answering the "tough" question "What are they doing?" is really very easy. "They are having sex," said without embarrassment, is a good reply. If the next question is, "What for?" you can explain that that is the way they have babies. In this way, you will not scare the child away from the subject through "overtalk" or "undertalk." He will come back to it when he is interested and able to understand different and more complex aspects of the subject.

Disciplining the Preschool Child

What kind of discipline is best?

We indicated in Chapter 3 that we don't think much of spanking children, although it won't hurt with concerned, loving parents. But talk and time are more useful.

Some black children are severely punished by parents and relatives for too little reason. The purpose of "discipline" or punishment is to help your child behave in a way which enables him to make it in the world; to get along with others without "dumping" on them and without being "dumped" on. Punishment, whether by denial of privilege, spanking, or other means, should take place only when it is necessary to achieve these purposes. The more your child can be helped to perform well without punishment, the better it will be for him.

When you must do more than scold, a denial of privilege is best. A common error here is what we call "overkill." A week's denial of privilege means almost nothing to preschool children. They will forget they are being punished. *Punishment is most effective when it closely follows the undesirable act and gets the child's full attention, but doesn't go on so long that he or she forgets what it is for.* If you forbid them to do something they need or something that you want to do, such as take a walk, you are denying yourself pleasure and denying them an important outlet of energy. You will be amazed at the effectiveness of a punishment as simple as having your child sit in another room—"until you can control yourself." Often if you suggest that they can come back when they feel they are ready, they will sit for a reasonable length of time and re-enter with, "I okay now, Mommy." This approach also enables them to be in control of their inaction. They are setttling themselves. It helps them take responsibility for their own behavior.

Should I try to shame my child when he misbehaves?

No. Please don't say, "Shame on you, you're a bad boy." Making your child feel bad about himself will not help him feel good about himself. Again, it helps to get across the message that you don't like or won't accept undesirable behavior, but you like and accept the child. "I like you but I don't like what you did." Nagging, scolding, and complaining are not very useful either. The most frequent comment we hear from children is that their parents nag too much. Nagging, scolding, and complaining still don't stop the undesired behavior . . . in fact, they can increase it.

I always seem to be punishing my child. Is something wrong?

Harsh and frequent punishment often produces hostility and frequent misbehavior. If you must punish the child frequently, something is not working right somewhere. It may be that the punishment has become a way to get attention from you rather than getting attention by performing in a desirable way. Perhaps you are not praising desirable behavior enough. Are you praising his scribbling, his setting the table, his or her many efforts to be able to do things; to be grown up? Attention, applause, a comment that you are glad that he was able to do this or that is an important reward. Make certain the message is clear. A reward, such as a special treat on a day a child has been particularly difficult, is not helpful. There is no reason to give up bad behavior if "crime pays."

Children will begin to behave and perform in an acceptable way when they sense that you believe that they will do so. For example, "Let's clean up your room," said with confidence, is more likely to get results than a hesitant request, as if you don't expect that it will happen, or standing with your arms folded with an angry expression on your face, or ruler in hand, to make it happen. In fact, helping your child clean up the room, or whatever the job, establishes the habit. Once started, the child will often do it by himself. When your relationship with your child is not a struggle around everything, you will not need to punish to get action. For example, after you clean the playroom together a few times, your child will often follow your model and begin cleaning up, or whatever task it is, by himself. Just the comment, "What do we do when we finish playing?" can produce a clean room once the habit is established.

*When I deny or punish my three-year-old, she appeals to her
father and usually gets her way. Isn't this harmful?*

Yes. Parents should present a united front to their children—but
not *against* their children. There should always be an effort to be
fair. But children of three and four are quite manipulative. They
want what they want and they'll do what they have to do to get it.
One three-year-old appealed to her father after a "no" response
from her mother. When Father agreed with Mother, our little lady
shot for the weak spot with this comment: "But Dad, you're the
boss!" Manipulation is normal at three but troublesome at seven. If
it is not checked at three, it will be in full bloom at seven and
twenty-seven. In addition, your child loses the opportunity to learn
to live with the normal and just denials we all face. After all, none
of us can have everything, and a child must learn to live with this
fact.

In addition, children who "get by" through manipulation often
do not develop the ability to take an honest look at themselves. It
then becomes hard for them to take criticism which would help
them do a better job next time. Parents who are not getting along
well together sometimes play "funny" (but harmful) games
around permission and punishment as a way of "hitting" each
other. To permit what the other parent would not without a discussion and an agreement beforehand can make the other parent
a "meany" . . . or worse. Your child will know what's going on
but will play the game to get what he wants. He or she will feel
good about getting his or her way and guilty about it at the same
time. It is best to keep children out of parent or adult conflicts.
Manipulating them for your purposes will encourage them to
manipulate you for their purposes . . . with an undesirable effect
on their development.

Again, banter and good humor about the efforts to "get by,"
without giving in unless it makes sense, is better than a harsh,
angry response.

*My wife yells at the children too much. Does it hurt to
disagree with her approach in front of the children?*

Disagreeing with your mate in front of your child should be a
"move of last resort." As mentioned above, a united front is
extremely important. It is best to talk over your differences in
private. When disagreement in front of your child is necessary,

you should talk about the situation afterwards. It is hard for us to look at ourselves and to be certain that we are not just claiming "necessary disagreement" as a way to put down the wife, husband, or whomever. You should look for ways to help each other avoid being too harsh, too punitive, unjust and unfair toward your child at times other than problem situations . . . and without open disagreement. Sometimes a parent who yells, scolds, beats, or is too tense with a child needs some assistance from the other parent, or relatives, in managing the home and the children. Sometimes he or she may need some counseling or psychological treatment.

There are times when I simply can't accept my mate's treatment of our child. What should I do?

If none of the above measures work, it is important to protect the rights and needs of the child. If you feel you *must* disagree with your mate in front of the child, you will also want to point out to your child at the same time that you do not excuse the undesirable behavior. If the child gloats because you stepped in, let it be very clearly known that you don't appreciate it. Express your disagreement in a calm fashion and in the spirit of being helpful rather than as an attack. By responding to both your child's behavior and your mate's overreaction, you become the mediator of fair play rather than setting up a situation in which more manipulation can take place. Again, this is a "move of last resort."

If my three-year-old hits me, should I hit back?

Until a child learns another way, he or she, when frustrated, will strike out in anger. Some few parents tolerate their children hitting them but we generally do not think this is a good idea. Hitting back, particularly with force, is not helpful. Some parents hit back very lightly to make the point that if you hit people, they will hit you back. Tapping is okay but it is not necessary. You want the child to begin to respond to language rather than action, and even tapping is action. Sometimes saying, "I know you're angry with me but I don't want you to hit me" relieves the child's anger and stops the hitting. Some parents prolong "fights" to get in the last lick. Why do you need it? It is helpful to direct the child's anger to a stuffed animal, a punching bag, a pounding board or so on . . . but not toward other people.

Directing anger toward others sets the stage for using religions and racial groups different from your own to let out anger. Directing (or diverting) your child to another activity is a helpful way to ease frustration and anger. Often a young child given a favorite toy or offered a favorite activity will forget all about his "mad." Your child's play is a place where he handles a great deal of fear, frustration, and anger. A word of caution: don't give him food every time he is frustrated or angry. That is why so many adults eat when frustrated . . . and get fat. The habit can start from the very beginning—even when your baby is still in the crib.

When my three-year-old can't have his own way, he has a temper tantrum. How can I avoid this situation?

If you decrease the causes of his frustration and anger your child will have fewer temper tantrums. If your child learns other ways to express anger, he will have fewer temper tantrums. You also want to avoid confining him within truly unreasonable limits.

A child of this age should have some temper tantrums. You can't and don't want to eliminate all frustration and anger. It is important for children to learn to tolerate disappointment and frustration because there are many disappointments in life. You just want to decrease the unnecessary disappointments, frustration, and temper tantrums. A child who does not learn to handle disappointment and frustration is more likely to become depressed or to "drop out" as an adult.

How should I handle tantrums when they occur?

The best way to handle it is not to pay it too much attention. If you look out of the corner of your eye, you may catch your little angel watching to see what kind of "rise" he is getting out of you. When that's the case, a little smile or a friendly wink will help. Preaching, lecturing, spanking, too much soothing all focus attention on the child, which will continue the tantrum. Why give up the tantrum if it is a good tool to get what you want? Go on with your usual activities. If the tantrum continues, it sometimes helps to have him or her go to the next room. Tell your child that he may play or talk to you or return to whatever he was doing—when he calms down and gets himself together. Rather than fight over this, you might leave the room yourself.

Children often paint themselves into a corner in a tantrum situation. If you give in, they feel they can control you, but that leaves them without anyone to protect them from their own unreasonable demands. If they give in, they have failed and you have won. It is important then that a tantrum situation not be a battle of wills. You want to make certain that what you are asking is fair. Then it is easier to be sympathetic, hold your ground, and yet let your little one out of his corner. How?

During the tantrum, you might say, "I know that you're mad, but if you have more candy you won't want your dinner," or whatever the demand is. A reason for your action expressed calmly but without apology indicates that you are being helpful rather than controlling. You might say, "I know that you would always like to have what you want but sometimes you can't." This is a message about the way the world is. You might later say, "I think you'll be able to stop crying pretty soon." This can make stopping an achievement and lets him off the failure hook. Timing, calmness, and the amount of talking is important here. Your several comments should be far enough apart and said with a confidence that all will soon be well. After the tantrum you might want to say, "I'm glad you were able to stop all by yourself." This gives your child a feeling of control and he will want to help control himself next time. If you don't know what the fuss was all about, it helps to find out the cause of the upset. You might then want to talk to him about a better way to handle his feelings. Talk is important but you don't want to talk too much. It comes across as nagging or lecturing, and that often causes more acting-up behavior.

Good humor helps. Naturally there will be times when he or she will take the humor out of you. But when you can, it pays to be light of spirit, without laughing at your child. If you view yourself as helping your child learn to handle normal, vigorous and healthy feelings you are less likely to get uptight. When enough is enough and nothing works, you may have to act more firmly, but give your child a chance to pull himself together first.

Play and How to Make It "Work"

What is a child's play all about?

Play is a child's work . . . and play. A child uses play to deal with his thoughts, fantasies, and feelings. Often the anger he wanted to express toward Mommy is taken out on his doggy, teddy bear, or doll. In addition, he uses it to develop body control, language, thought, and social skills. In play, he can repeat an experience he enjoyed—a trip to the store, a ride in the car. He can pretend his way through a dangerous event to take the danger out of it. For example, the four-year-old may be seen giving a shot to a doll or teddy bear before or after he goes to the doctor. A child often practices being a competent, independent person in play to make up for the times he is dependent and unable to do things in the big adult world.

What kind of play is best?

Art—drawing, painting, clay work—is a particularly helpful form of play activity. At two a child loves the feel of clay or paint. He enjoys breaking up clay and putting it back together. If you have the room or can put paper down to permit enthusiastic finger painting, this can be real fun and is good for hand muscles. Such play can release angry feelings. It's best not to ask her to copy from a model or ask him what he has drawn. Your child is trying to express his world and it doesn't matter in what form he does so. The fun is in the doing and not the finished product or the name.

By three a child is beginning to pay attention to the results of his handiwork. That's when the drawings become precious. Displays of his or her work promote pride and motivation for continued effort. Vertical, horizontal, and arc strokes replace simple scribbles.

The four-year-old makes snakes and cakes, people and cars, animals and everything in his world with his clay. If he makes it, he's controlling it, right? He will also make such toilet-related items as BMs or a penis. As long as there is no preoccupation with such creations, it's best not even to notice them.

Four is an artist of some note. By four you usually see pictures—not in perspective and not with detail, but pictures nonetheless. Unlike two- and three-year-olds, four figures he's doing something and wants to talk about it. If you ask him too many questions, however, he will dry up. Listen, learn, and praise the wondrous creation! If you do, you'll encourage him to keep on producing as well as giving him a sense of accomplishment.

Drawings by preschool children from various income, ethnic, and racial backgrounds are very similar. Only later do clothing, jewelry, and other items characteristic of a particular culture show up.

Very small drawings, persistently gloomy colors, "tight" or heavy angry overpainting can be an indication that things are not going well. If, along with the artwork, your child is generally unhappy or things are not going well, you might seek professional help.

How can I help my child gain body control through play?

Your early preschooler's climbing on every box, chair, or bench he can find is good for muscle development and control. He will climb in and out and over old boxes, under the stairs, and wherever else he can get to. Wheel toys with pedals, such as cars and fire engines, and rockers are good exercise for leg muscles. The two-year-old loves to kick, run after, and throw balls. Swinging on low parallel bars is great fun for the two-year-old, even though it often frightens his parents. The two-year-old loves to roughhouse with his mother and father. Swinging on a grownup's stiff, outstretched arm is a favorite, and also good for his muscles.

What about play for three-year-olds?

Using scissors and building with blocks, small boxes, and other items all serve to aid small-muscle development. Working with pegboards and puzzles and stringing beads improve your child's coordination between his eyes and hands. At three, with good previous development, he is well on his way to making his body do what he wants it to do.

You will have trouble keeping up with your three-year-old. He will want to run ahead of you on walks. He will need plenty of space indoors and outdoors to run, climb, and jump. If you live in an apartment, it is important to take your children downstairs to the playground, empty lot, or park at least once a day.

All children love to dance, and this form of body expression has long been encouraged by most black parents. Any kind of rhythmic music will get them started—records, radio, your drumbeat. This is an extremely valuable method of self-expression as well as a way of "letting off steam," developing muscles, and improving coordination. Today more middle-income parents, black and white, encourage rhythmic body expression through dancing.

How does play encourage language development?

Before two years of age your child couldn't express—in words— much of what he wanted. But hopefully you talked to him, even when he couldn't understand. This has prepared him to become a talker. Once he gains a few words, he discovers he can use them to make things happen for him. "Spoon, Mommy" and "Down, Daddy," bring action. It is understandable that language becomes important. But his desire to express himself can be turned off if nobody responds or listens.

If all goes well, by three, his vocabulary and ability to use language has greatly increased. Engaging him in "normal" conversation can now be very rewarding. Talking about the things and activities around you not only improves language but stimulates curiosity and helps the child become an observer. By four he is not only a talker but a "discusser." He will want to talk about the books you read together. He will want to talk about the store he just visited. He will rush in from outside with a story about a startling new discovery he has made. It will be old-hat to you but *listen* with interest anyway. Listening, discussing his interest, remarking about how well he has communicated his thoughts, applauding, and so on are all very useful in encouraging language development.

What other methods can I use?

Certain toys promote language development and provide a lot of amusement as well. Three- and four-year-olds love puppets. Using your voice to speak for the puppet is great fun. Your child can be encouraged to use his voice to speak for another puppet and carry on a conversation or put on a play. Three and four love funny voices and funny comments. Toy telephones are also a great favorite. Preschoolers will carry on great pretend conversations about all the things they hear you discussing on the telephone . . . ordering the groceries, getting babysitters, making plans for the weekend. This all aids in language development as well as social development.

You mentioned that reading to children is important. Why, and what kinds of stories are most useful at the preschool age?

Above all, stories should be entertaining—even if the child doesn't understand every word. Reading is a way of being close to your child in an enjoyable shared activity. Listening to the spoken language is preparation for learning to read. Aside from the words, children learn pronunciation and expression. They learn to follow a plot and comprehend a story. Slipping in a question about what's going on now and then will help you know whether they are "getting it" or not.

Nursery rhymes, books with pictures, and stories with familiar sounds—"ding, ding," "honk, honk," "chug-chug"—are favorites for a two-year-old. He will want to hear them over and over. Don't stop reading a child a story because he or she knows it word for word. It's more fun that way. The youngster can feel, "I'm reading." But stop when it's no longer a fun story for your child.

The three-year-old wants the facts—information stories. When you go to the store, the zoo, or the circus, a book about such activities before and after will increase anticipation and encourage recall and recounting of an experience. The four-year-old is a book lover—if started earlier. He loves facts and fantasy. Because a preschooler is relatively powerless and has few skills, mastery, or the ability to do and accomplish things, is of great concern to him. The train that huffs and puffs to climb the hill, the baby horse that struggles to stand, and other such themes are of interest. There are age guides to help you select books for your child. But it is best to scan them before you buy or borrow. You know your child best.

Shouldn't the books be about black children?

The number of good books for black children is growing. We believe that as long as a book presents blacks with dignity—be it set in the suburbs, inner city, or Africa—it is satisfactory reading. Books showing black American children as capable and competent with only average frustration and failure are best. We do not feel that presenting black children engaged in unlawful activity is at all helpful—even if it is the reality for some. We see no harm in some books using dialect. But we feel that most should utilize standard English, because your child will spend most of his life with people and in places where standard English is used.

Books about African ceremonies and customs can prevent your child from developing the negative attitudes about Africa with which our generation is still struggling. Stories about such things as birthday parties and family activities—in an African or American setting—can be of interest to the three- and four-year-old. But we do not advise you to use only books depicting black children exclusively, unless you expect your child to spend his entire life in a totally black setting. The world of tomorrow will be even smaller than it is today. Books depicting black, brown, yellow, red, and white children are one way of preparing your child for tomorrow. Books that present different cultures provide you with an opportunity to help your child understand that people are different . . . and that's fine.

What is my child's thinking like during this period?

This is the period in which the child's thinking should move from the feeling that he, she, or others can control all things around them to a more realistic understanding of how things operate. Your child should gain the ability to imagine what will happen in certain situations rather than have to act in order to find out. He will gradually learn to tell the difference between his own imagination and what is real. One of the interesting aspects of the thinking of children in this stage is their feeling that wrongdoing will be punished every time. They become very responsive to rules as a result of this. Another is giving living qualities to a doll or even a tree or a door. That's why talking to a doll can be so "real."

How can I help my child in this learning process?

One necessary requirement in learning to think is being able to concentrate on a single activity for more than a moment or two. This is brought about through helping your child learn to wait, by taking time to talk with him about various activities, and by listening to his conversations so that he will listen to yours. Reading to him helps. His inner self quiets down and becomes organized so that he can use it in exploring, learning, and playing in the world around him. All of this should help your child "learn how to learn," develop strategies for learning, and apply information gained in one situation to deal with another. Many bright people do not perform as well as possible in school and elsewhere when the situation requires more than memory, because they do not have a strategy for learning.

The development of language helps you and your child share experiences. Through your involvement in play or in other activities you help your child learn many concepts, such as under, over, above, and through. Explaining words or concepts that will help him get the point of a joke or a story is very helpful.

Are there special learning games we can play together?

You can play a number of games that will help your child learn to think. "Simon Says" helps a child learn to concentrate and to listen for directions. You might play your own "Direction Game," "Stand up . . . go to this corner . . . that corner . . . under the table and then put your shoes behind the door." There is no end to this particular game, and the task can be as hard or as easy as the child can handle. "What would happen if?" and "What happens next?"—games in which you set up conditions or start a story and then let your child give an answer or complete the story—stimulate the creative or inventive side of your child. You don't want him to lose this as he gives up fantasy for reality.

Matching "like" cards from a mixture, making and pronouncing words, making sentences, printing names—his own name in particular—reading signs, and a host of other homemade games can "jog" his mind. Let your imagination run wild. Being right or winning is not important in such games. It should be fun. You should not criticize or be disappointed if he doesn't "get" this or that. He will. Let him know that you realize this. But for the moment enjoy, enjoy.

Television: Pros and Cons

Does television harm development?

Television programs for children are being severely criticized. Many could be better. Most will improve. A more important problem is parents who use the television as a babysitter. Many children are allowed to sit too long and watch anything and everything that comes along on the set—as long as they are out of their parents' hair.

Children need a full range of activities—indoor, outdoor, working on puzzles, being read to, talked to, listening to conversation and music. Some of these activities permit the young child to learn by doing. They encourage mental invention or fantasy. Television is simply absorbed, often without being explained or "broken down" so that younger children can understand it or use it to understand their own feelings or thoughts. For poor children and many black children, much television fare—white people, fancy homes, cars, jobs, etcetera—doesn't match their own situation. This can make children feel that television is the way the world is supposed to be and their own world is not good.

In what ways is television beneficial?

There are still too few blacks on television. But many shows now have blacks, making it easier for black children to identify with the people, the action, and the world beyond the home and neighborhood. Television provides experiences that many children would not have otherwise. Several programs—"Sesame Street," "The Electric Company," and "Mister Rogers," in particular—help children develop thinking, reading, and social skills. The adult talking to and with children on television shows is helpful. You can help by watching with your child when you are able. You will find that helping her understand words or concepts in a particular sketch will increase her learning interest and appreciation.

It is particularly helpful during this stage to explain the difference between make-believe and real with regard to dangerous or violent activity. This is one of the problems of young children watching television without supervision. Daring acts, violence in the form of eye-poking or hitting people over the head should be called "make-believe" and understood as something you don't do in real life. More than one child has jumped from high places like his television hero. We have seen disturbed children mix up events in their home with television events.

How can I prevent "too much" television or inappropriate programs?

Encouraging a full range of activities—with television as only one part—is a way of avoiding too much television. You will want to avoid certain scary shows for preschool children, particularly just before bedtime. Even childhood favorites such as *The Wizard of Oz* can cause bad dreams for preschoolers. Many late evening and night shows also contain violence to an extreme that may be frightening.

If there is something you feel that you don't want your child to see, tell him so and why . . . for example, you think he is too young or you think he will be upset by it, or whatever you're feeling. With older children, you are likely to get some flak: "Sam's mother lets him see it!" You can explain that you feel differently about the matter and you are doing what you feel is best. While your Johnny may protest violently, he is also likely to feel protected . . . that you are acting in his behalf . . . "My mama watches over me." But not too much, Mama.

Can my child ruin her eyes by watching too much television?

There is no evidence that this can occur. If her eyes appear bloodshot, however, this may be an indication that she is suffering from eye strain. You would then want to reduce the time she watches television, but there is no need to stop it altogether. You can develop eye strain from reading a book for too long a period at a time. Children should sit at least four feet from the screen and there should be at least a dim light in the room. Glare from outside light being reflected off the screen should be avoided.

While we're on the subject of vision, however, it is important to be on the lookout for vision problems with your preschooler. Children, particularly the very young, won't tell you if they can't see well. They will try and get along—hold their head very close to the printed page, very far away, or get upset when you ask them to read. Clumsiness or poor coordination in feeding or learning to write may also be indications of vision problems. Alphabet letters turned the wrong way is normal for the young child but should disappear by late five and six. If you notice these problems, it's money well spent to have an optometrist or an ophthalmologist check your child's eyes. Poor vision can cause poor performance, which can lead to bad feelings about the self and emotional problems.

The Preschooler and Society

Can I aid in my child's social development?

Yes. Around three children are better able to play with each other rather than beside each other but alone. The favorite game is "playing house." Here they practice adult roles like Mother, Father, and Worker. In such play they learn to strike the acceptable balance between aggression and passivity. This is a very important lesson to learn. It will be needed throughout life.

Such play can be troublesome to parents. Some view the make-believe play as bizarre and even a sign of mental problems. Others view it as too real, particularly the mother-father love scenes. Some worry about play in which boys are dressed as girls or girls as boys. Parents opposed to interracial dating or marriage sometimes worry about love scenes in interracial play.

There is no need to worry. It is all quite healthy. The important thing here is the social skills the child is developing in play. The sex, racial, and religious roles and preferences involved are only incidental. For the most part, anything you hear or see in child's play that is undesirable or socially unacceptable should not have been heard or seen by the child in the first place. Don't feel guilty. You can't and don't want to control all a child sees and hears. Stop undesirable exposure, if possible, but not the fantasy play. Children need it. A real sexual identity problem is not caused by the play. You can help by providing the clothes or equipment for fantasy play. But coming too close or asking questions about what is going on is likely to spoil the fun. It's "their thing." They need some place and some time without you . . . indoors and outdoors.

How can I help my children to be watchful of strangers without making them feel that the whole world is dangerous?

This presents a problem, especially with friendly, outgoing children. Nevertheless, as soon as they are old enough to be out of your sight for just a minute they need to begin to know what situations are dangerous and which are not, how to avoid danger, and what to do in case of danger. They need to learn to protect themselves against people, places, and things.

By three years of age, children in many areas can be left outdoors unsupervised for at least a few minutes. By four years, it is for even longer periods. (Unfortunately, in some areas it is unsafe to leave your children outdoors unsupervised for even a minute.) You will want to tell your children to stay away from strangers, in cars or on foot. It helps to point out that most people are good people; that just a few people are bad people and might want to hurt little boys and little girls. It also helps to limit the distance they can wander while unsupervised. Having them repeat these boundaries to you from time to time will help them remember. Stating the way you expect your child to handle dangerous situations in a short, clear manner is best. Again, the key is calmness. This approach, rather than anxious, long, preachy warnings, is likely to avoid creating the notion that the world is full of dangerous people.

*My four-year-old plays well with two other boys in our
building, but they close out another youngster in a very
cruel way. Isn't that harmful both for my son and
for the excluded child?*

It can be if it is not managed well. Around four years of age,
children develop "very favorite friends, in the whole wide world,"
—even though they only play with a handful of children and have
only seen a very small part of the world. A new or "different" child
in the neighborhood can be in for some trouble. He may be excluded, talked about, or made into a scapegoat. This is not always
the case. Some four-year-olds will welcome a newcomer in as a
new member of the gang. Some children are confident and aggressive and will make their way in a new situation even when there
are efforts to exclude them. It is really a matter of chance. Just as
with adult relationships, some personalities gel and some don't.

Should I try to step in on behalf of the rejected child?

Children have less need to get along when personalities do not gel.
They are also less likely to hold long-standing antagonisms toward
people they don't like—or are told not to like. When exclusion is
taking place in play, you will want to be careful about getting
involved. Give the children enough time to try and handle the
matter themselves. If they do not, you might suggest specific ways
that they can play together. "Let's let Jimmy" (the excluded
child) "be the conductor" if they are playing train, co-pilot if they
are playing plane, and so on.

If your child comments, "I don't like Jimmy," it is helpful to
spell out why Jimmy should be allowed to enter the group and
why the rejecting child should give himself a chance to know
Jimmy—without being moralistic or heavy about it. "Oh, Jimmy
wants to play. I'll bet you'll like him when you get to know him."
This usually works, but if your child still resists, you may want to
help him explore his feelings about Jimmy. He may be afraid or
jealous, for real or imagined reasons. What Jimmy has done to
him, what there is about Jimmy that he dislikes, and how he can
handle his feelings should all be discussed.

If your attitude and manner indicate that all can be handled
satisfactorily, in time your child will come to feel that he can work
out all problems in relationships. Otherwise he can develop

stronger tendencies to attack and exclude outsiders or excessive uneasiness and withdrawal from people he does not know.

What should I do if my child is the rejected one?

When your child has been fair, cooperative, and gone halfway and Jimmy doesn't like him—for whatever reason—you should help your child understand that that is Jimmy's problem or weakness. You should help him learn not to be concerned about Jimmy, but it is not helpful to teach your child to dislike or hate Jimmy. That would be helping him learn to feel, "I dislike you because you dislike me and I need you to like me before I can like myself." This is the bind that too many black Americans are in with white America right now. Such a feeling learned now can lead to a lot of wasted energy and stress later on when the last seat to be taken on a bus is always the one next to you—because you are black. Your child is better off when he does not need to like or dislike anybody; when he can like or dislike anybody not because of who they are but because of how they behave. Being concerned about or hating people who don't like you is a waste of energy that could be applied toward doing or thinking about your own interests.

How can I tell if my child is being rejected for racial reasons?

The natural tendency of children around four to exclude or scapegoat others is particularly difficult in interracial situations. It is always difficult to know whether the exclusion is because two children just happen to get along well with each other but not with the third or whether it's because the third is black and the other two are white. In this age of racial awareness, we adults are, and should be, very much tuned in to this problem. But we should be careful not to overreact. For example, one black mother, whose daughter was playing the horse in make-believe play, broke up the play and took her child home. Her daughter was angry and the white children understood, because of the anger, that something was wrong, but they didn't know what. Where there is no derogatory feeling or intent, this reaction can cause confusion and difficulty for your child.

It helps to watch the situation for a while before acting. If your child is being asked to play the horse but never the rider, the cook but never the mother being served, the porter but never the traveler—you may want to withdraw your child from the play.

The children involved have been influenced by racist stereotypes. But you can be more helpful to all if you assist them with their play. Young children often mimic without understanding and are less committed to racist attitudes. They are usually willing to play fair and share the good roles when adults specifically suggest how they might: "Let's let Mary play the rider sometime and you play the horse and then you play the rider and Mary play the horse." When discussing this matter later with your child, a racial approach will have little meaning. The child's ability to handle such concepts is still very limited. It is more helpful to encourage your child to expect her fair share of the best of everything. Today more black youngsters do just that.

What if my child seems overly aggressive with white children?

Black parents who live in neighborhoods where racism is not extreme are sometimes surprised by the aggressiveness and expectation of fair play and justice that their children demonstrate. Parents who were taught to be nice so that they would be accepted by whites are at first uneasy when they hear their youngsters saying, "I don't want to play with you!" Or, "Go away," or "Stop that or I'll sock you" in play with white children. It is just as harmful to overreact and squelch such responses—unless they are extreme—as it is to encourage them. You will want to encourage a reasonable level of assertiveness and aggressiveness without promoting rudeness and cruelness. Again, wherever possible— where children are not hurt physically, psychologically, or socially —it is best to let them work out their feelings themselves. If they can't, then you'll want to step in and suggest solutions.

When there are no black children around, and it is important to you that your child have contact with blacks, you may want to arrange for your child to attend nursery schools, visit relatives or friends, or attend churches and social affairs where there are more black children.

Morality and the Preschooler

How can I promote my preschooler's moral development?

In the years from two through four your child begins to have increasing contact with other children and other people. Yet he or she still has trouble sharing. Early in this stage, he is still inclined to violate the rights and ignore the needs of other people. A toy that he wants is a toy that he wants and it doesn't matter that it belongs to somebody else. He wants it. He needs it. He'll take it!

At the same time he is willing to go along with a "you scratch my back and I'll scratch yours" kind of arrangement with you and others. "If you will be fair to me, I will be fair to you; if you let me play with your doll, I will let you play with mine; if you don't hit me, I won't hit you." Numerous situations between your Johnny, other family members, and other children will provide an opportunity to help your child develop the habit of being fair and sharing. At the same time you will want to help him learn to expect and teach him how to insist that others be fair and share with him. This can only occur, however, when you, the parent, serve as a just negotiator and mediator in conflicts between your child, other family members, and other children.

But isn't Johnny still too young to understand all this?

Some parents are inclined to take the side of their children, right or wrong. They sometimes argue that the two-, three-, or four-year-old is young and should be allowed to mistreat other people, "Oh, he's just a baby." We have seen parents scold and even spank other children for hitting their child, even though the latter created the problem in the first place. The seeds of manipulation, exploitation, and poor personal control are sown right here. Such children often become crooks—on the street, in business, in government. Parents do a disservice to their children when they take their side whether they are right of wrong.

Certainly you want to support your children. But you are supporting them better when you help them look at their part in creating or perpetuating any conflict and point out how they can avoid it. "You don't have to take Johnny's car. If you want to play with it, ask him. I'm sure that he'll share it. Maybe you can let him play with your bicycle." Or, "If you take his car without asking him, he will be mad at you." Your involvement at this stage sets the tone for future moral reasoning by your child without your help.

But blacks are so often treated in an immoral fashion.
Shouldn't we side with our children, right or wrong?

Defining what is "moral" becomes more difficult later on. Particularly when your group is the victim of immoral conditions within the society as is the case for blacks in America. Parents who feel "put upon" by husbands, wives, schools, welfare workers, or society-at-large are likely to have difficulty seeing the troublesome role of their child in a conflict. This is understandable. But you can harm your child's personal development at this stage if you permit him to be unfair and unjust in his relationships with others because "we have it hard." When he is right he is right and when he is wrong he is wrong. This position is most helpful to your child. It puts him and blacks in the best position to demand just treatment from others.

You said that a child may take something because
he doesn't have much of a conscience. How does he
develop a conscience if he is not born with it?

Because your child is strongly attached to you, what you think, feel, or say is good or bad becomes pretty much what he thinks is good or bad. Your praises, your reward and approval for certain kinds of behavior establish what is good and your punishment and disapproval for certain other kinds of behavior establish what is bad. Before about four years of age, your child will avoid doing certain undesirable things because he or she doesn't want to pay the price—your anger, punishment, or abandonment. Around the age of four, your child has absorbed your feelings and made them his own, and will experience guilt *on his own* for acts *he* considers "forbidden." He now has a conscience. At this point most children will experience some guilt about taking something that doesn't belong to them, even when a parent or an adult is not around.

Can guilt be harmful?

Too much guilt can be paralyzing. Too little guilt is harmful as well. Most people try to behave within the rules of acceptable social conduct because of training and to avoid feelings of guilt. Some people are able to commit brutal crimes without any guilt at all because their ability to feel guilt was never adequately developed. Without guilt and the need to achieve social approval, there would be little reason for not trying to get all that you can get for yourself without worrying about the rights and needs of others. There could be no trust among individuals and there could not be a society.

But can't an emphasis on morality and
guilt hold back racial progress?

As blacks, we need not be afraid that encouraging moral development, a conscience, and guilt will prevent social action. Black children without the ability to feel the proper amount of guilt will victimize their parents, relatives, and community first. They are the least likely to be involved in social action to improve the black community. Their personalities will lead them to look out for themselves without concern for others, black or white. Guilt need not be involved when blacks, or anybody else, act against injustice. Dr. Martin Luther King, Jr., and the church members who broke the back of segregation without a gun, probably had the best-developed consciences—and the ability to feel guilt—of any group in the country.

How can a child develop too much guilt?

Much is going on between three and six which can easily lead to guilt. Boys have romantic love feelings toward their mothers and girls toward their fathers. They are jealous of the relationship between the parents. They will sometimes insist that they are going to marry the parent of the opposite sex when they grow up. They will wish that their rival parent would go away or sometimes even be destroyed. At the same time they fear that their rival parent has the same jealous feelings toward them as they have toward the parent. They then fear that the parent will harm them in some way. This is believed to be the cause of bad dreams in which children are chased by frightening figures such as bears and giants.

These are very powerful guilt-producing forces. Parents who "shame" their child at this age as a way of getting them to behave increase the guilt problem. If you tease your preschooler or flaunt his helplessness or your adult love relationship in his face—showing how much more power you have—you can increase the problem. Kissing your wife or husband probably calls for a kiss for daughter or son of this age range—when they are around. Some children will insist on it—a kissing trio, even. That's fine as long as it's not carried too far. There is no need for parents to avoid showing displays of affection. It is not helpful for a mother to try to "make it up" to her son or a father to try to "make it up" to his daughter by being permissive, or by pretending that the child is a real competitor.

But isn't it "wrong" for children to feel
this way about their parents?

It is best not to respond in a shocked or angry way when you realize that your child is concerned about your marital relationship. That increases guilt. Love of boy for mother and girl for father is normal and healthy. When a boy indicates that he is going to marry his mother, or a girl indicates that she is going to marry her father, it's helpful to indicate that you are already married; that someday they're going to grow up and fall in love with and maybe marry a nice girl or boy of their own age. This will reduce the frustration, anger, fantasy, and guilt.

We have described above the most common and usual relationships. Children have many different affectionate attachments to adults—to older brothers or sisters, grandparents, neighbors, etcetera. They have jealousies and rivalrous feelings of different degrees toward their competitors for the affection, time, and attention of the adult they "love." The closer the relationship, the greater the jealous and rivalrous feelings—greater with parents than neighbors, for example. At this age, these are feelings of affection and not true sexual feelings.

Our son walked in on us having sexual intercourse.
We were so stunned we didn't know what to say.
How would you handle this?

Sexual intercourse, as mentioned earlier, should take place in private. Parents sometimes have sexual intercourse in front of very young children or fail to close the door on older children because "they don't know what's going on." This is troublesome precisely *because* they don't know what's going on. At this age, they will make up their own explanations. Usually they think that it is a violent act, which increases their fears, fantasies, and guilt. Even if they got over the fear, the stimulation they would receive from watching could make it hard for them to develop certain needed inner controls.

You might have said to your son, "Edward, Mommy and Daddy are making love. Go back to your room [or wherever] and I'll talk to you later." If necessary, it's better to stop and take him back rather than get into a struggle here. You are already irritated by the interruption and not likely to handle a struggle well. Later, one of you—or both—in a relaxed way should explain that parents show their love for each other in a different way than children love each other or love their parents. (Otherwise you may see him "playing house" in a way that upsets the parents of the little girl upstairs.) You might also explain that when they grow up they will make love like Mommy and Daddy.

My three-year-old is a liar. How can I break the habit early?

At three, it is not a habit. It is not even really a lie. The desires, wishes and imagination of a young child can get in the way of what is real. Sometimes a three-year-old will start to tell a story and you will hear it get out of hand as he adds bits and pieces to fit the wishes and ideas in his head. Left with a babysitter, he will point out with solemn face and hopeful eyes that his mother said that he could have all the cake that he wanted. A helpful response would not be, "You are a liar," but, "I'm sure you like cake but your mother would not like it if I gave you all that you want. You may have a piece," said in good humor with an understanding smile and with a firm will.

What about fibbing among slightly older children?

Around four or five years, children are more aware of what is truth and what is made up to achieve a particular end. Even here you may or may not get the truth if you ask for it directly. It still doesn't help to be outraged about less than the truth. It is not a crisis of morality that is involved here. It's the child's way to get what he wants, which is normal and healthy at this age. It doesn't help to investigate his story like a detective. This makes your child feel that he can't be trusted, is devious, that the act is *most* serious! Your child loses face. You may get "the truth" but you *made* him tell. After he admits that he licked the chocolate off your cake, what have you gained? You did not encourage or help him take responsibility for his own behavior. In fact, your pressure can cause him to tell less than the truth next time . . . and the next. Doing the opposite of what your parents want is a strong tendency at this age. This situation can lead to a "lying" problem.

How can I help my child to be truthful?

Some parents say, "It is not important whether you tell me the truth or not. It is important that you tell the truth to yourself." Most children don't want this burden and eventually "tell it like it is." You might point out that you will not know what to believe if he does not tell the truth. Children "distorting the truth" are very interested in the story of the boy who cried "wolf" so often that nobody paid any attention when the wolf really came and he needed help. When your child is able to change his story and tell you the truth, it is helpful to say that you are glad that he was able to do so. This will make it easier to tell the truth next time.

Remember that children are great imitators. If you lie—even tell little lies—the child this age will know. You are likely to hear your child doing the same thing. We know one youngster who was told to tell bill collectors and others in search of his mother that she was not at home while she hid in the house. This caused confusion, insecurity, and anger in the child. As could be expected, by nine years old, he was known in school as a liar and a cheat. In a group, his friends said, "Man, that dude lies! You can't pay no attention to what he says!" Thus a problem which began in the home eventually led to problems with other youngsters and adults.

My three-year-old stole a toy car from the child upstairs.
Does that mean he's going to be a thief?

The whole world belongs to the three-year-old. Taking the toy, the candy bar from the store, or any other item at this age is no indication at all that a child will become a thief. Stealing is not inborn. Even when a child under five has been told that he should not take an item, he may still take it quite innocently. Desires and wishes are bigger than his restraint. He does not yet have a fully developed conscience and does not feel guilty about it. He should be taught, however, that taking the belongings of others is not acceptable. Mild punishment may help as a reminder that he must not act this way. Returning an item and apologizing also helps the child remember that the behavior is unacceptable. Scolding, spanking, and making a fuss are not helpful. Taking time to calmly talk to your child about the matter is much more effective.

Children who must ask before they take things that belong to others in their own home are less likely to take things outside the home. Also, in homes where others must ask before they take the possessions of a child, the child is more likely to respect the rules of ownership and borrowing.

Again, outrage in such situations and harsh punishment are harmful. We sometimes overreact to lying or stealing because we fear these impulses in ourselves. If we have a relative or friend who has a real problem or is in jail, we are particularly anxious to destroy such habits early in our children. But calm, persistent help toward the development of inner control is more effective than outrage and harsh punishment.

Father-Oriented Problems

I am very busy. Can I still be a good father?

Dr. Martin Luther King, Jr., is quoted as having said, "It is not the quantity of time you spend with children that's important, it is the quality." We agree. Truly listening to your children, being reliable, warm and friendly, firm but flexible, predictable, calm, confident, reasonable and mature when present makes for good quality. You should try to be present during important times, such as birthdays and meetings with the teacher. Setting aside certain times for doing things together, such as attending ballgames or picnics is important . . . more important than being an ever-present "dud." Your work can wait during that special moment when your daughter *must* tell you that she won the special prize at Martha's birthday party. If you are busy saving the world, making money or doing good, a little interruption won't stop you. But several rebuffs will make your daughter feel that you don't care. After a few minutes or a few interruptions you can and should point out in a friendly way that you are busy. Let her know when you will be finished and ready to play or listen.

Don't fool yourself about the quality of your relationship. It is important to be present and helpfully involved with your family. One mother said of her husband, "He always points out that Dr. King said it's not the quantity but the quality, but he's so bad that when he's there my kids ain't gettin' quantity or quality."

I do all the work and my four-year-old prefers her father.
Does it mean she doesn't love me?

It is easy to feel unloved or less loved in this situation. Frequently this occurs when fathers must be away a great deal. It is a very serious problem when parents are separated or divorced. It also frequently occurs when one parent is the sole "disciplinarian" and the other is the "good guy." One cause for these feelings at this age is the "love affair" between your child and the parent of the opposite sex.

As long as you are not too harsh, too punitive, or unfair and unjust, you have no reason for concern. The love affair will give way to less possessive attachment to her father. If you are the sole disciplinarian or more often present, and therefore the usual source of control, protection and security, your child will look for you in times of real trouble rather than to the parent he or she appears to prefer in "good times." Don't take it personally or try and make your child or your mate feel guilty about it. Your child may sense your disappointment or sense a rejection and use this as a way to "fix" you for what you didn't let him have or do. Be cool. It will all balance out in time.

If you are separated or divorced there will be a great temptation to "put down" your mate when your child appears to like him or her a little too much. You don't want to do this. You don't want to build a false good guy either. It is best to answer questions about your situation in ways which do not hurt your former mate or spoil your child's chance of having a good relationship with both parents. We will say more about this when we discuss divorce (pp. 110–112).

Raising a Fatherless Child

Can a child grow up to be healthy without a father?

Yes. But whether a fatherless child grows up to be healthy or not depends a great deal on the mother's ability to handle the problems which exist when a male breadwinner is not present. Most women who work barely make enough money to care for their families. Women who do not work and must depend on public support do not receive enough money to adequately care for their families. As a result, mothers who care for children without working males spend a lot of energy in worry, working or not. This makes it difficult to be calm and confident, which is *so* important in bringing up children. Support and help from family and friends can be helpful. Better help from the government—adequate health, child care, and income programs—is needed.

Boys growing up in fatherless families often turn to other boys for advice and information which they would ordinarily receive from their father. Often the advice is not good or the price is high. Because they receive attention, advice, and a sense of belonging from other boys, they are more susceptible to pressure to do what the group does, right or wrong.

Some few mothers, in the absence of fathers, work too hard to make their sons masculine. At other times some "cut their sons down" because of feelings they have toward men who deserted or abused them. They sometimes use their male children as "little husbands"—without sex, but pretty close. And in some rare cases, probably related to anger toward men, they make them "little girls." We know of one mother who wrestled with her son to make him tough. She was also sexy and seductive—voice, manner, body exposure, "accidental" breast contact—toward him. This overstimulated the youngster and made it difficult for him to develop inner controls. This, and other factors, led to learning difficulties and juvenile delinquency. On the other hand, a mother without a husband should show her normal level of affection toward her son.

How can I help my son accept a new man in my life?

Children who are made "little husbands" become very jealous and angry when a boyfriend or a new husband is brought into the picture. The rage and anger, particularly in the three to seven age range, can be very intense when the child has had Mommy alone for a long while. A child is usually guilty and anxious about these feelings. We know of mothers who think it is cute and are very proud when their "little husbands" angrily attack a new boyfriend. It is important for the boyfriend and the mother to help the child handle his anger and jealousy. Teasing and acting as if it is a real man-against-man competition for Mommy can be very harmful. The child should be helped to understand that there's a difference between the parent-child and man-woman relationship. It helps when the boyfriend does things for and with the child in a responsible way.

When there are many males in the neighborhood, there will be many models of masculinity and less trouble for a male child in a fatherless family. Where this is not the case, male relatives who are mature and responsible can be helpful, if they are willing to spend some time with the male child. "Big brothers," male teachers, and other males willing to pitch in can also be helpful. In all cases, reliable, predictable, and mature persons are best. People who promise to visit and then don't appear, come one time but not the next, or take advantage of your child in one way or another are more trouble, and can be more harmful, than no one at all.

I am often told that I should get a husband for my child's sake. Do you agree with that?

No. We don't believe that a man (or a woman) "at any price" is helpful. This can lead to an unhappy relationship which would be harmful to your child's development. Irresponsible, immature fathers add little to the development of their children even when they are present. Fathers who spend all their time watching television, reading, or engaged in personal activities provide very little for their children. Even worse, a weak father who will not stand up for his rights in relationships with you and others is not a good model. A father who is a tyrant and abuses the rights and ignores the needs of others is not a good model. One reasonable choice when you can't find "Mr. Right" is to do without . . . a husband, that is.

Parental Roles and Attitudes

We argue in front of our child. Is that harmful?

When the arguments occur occasionally in a home in which the atmosphere is usually one of affection and good feelings, there is little problem. The children learn that the expression of anger is okay and will not destroy people. They learn to express their anger verbally rather than by hitting or acting in extreme, angry ways. If adult arguments lead to physical violence, slammed doors or thrown furniture, children will learn to handle their anger in the same way. This is undesirable.

Very often children will not want their parents to argue. They are afraid that they may harm each other or leave and abandon them. You can help them by pointing out that mommies and daddies sometimes get angry with each other just like brothers and sisters. When they have brothers and sisters they will know exactly what you're talking about! If they don't, remind them of an argument or angry feelings and words they had with a neighbor child.

*When two parents are present, is it important
for the male to be in control?*

No. Some people feel that the decline of the strong father-controlled family has led to difficulty in child development and family life. We disagree. We feel that the increased difficulty for families —black or white—is due to the increased complexity of society. The only real benefit of a father-controlled family is that the source of authority, and therefore expectations, is clear. The problem with this in the past, however, has been that this male authority was achieved at the expense of women and children. It created a great deal of rage and anger on the part of wives and youngsters. To "get back" they often acted in a way to frustrate the male . . . no sex, poor grades in school, doing the opposite of what he wanted.

This family arrangement also creates a rigidity of personality and thinking. From the notion that some single person in the home has the right to absolute authority, right or wrong, comes the notion that somebody in the school, in the city, and in the nation is entitled to exercise authority and make decisions regarding your life, right or wrong.

That's the way minorities got hurt, women got hurt, children got hurt, and in the end, males get hurt. The feeling that the male should not fail, should never be sick, and cannot show weakness on occasion is created by this "all-authority," all-powerful notion. These are superhuman demands and nobody can meet them. Male frustration and disappointment often leads to the scapegoating of wives and children. It can destroy the assertiveness and aggressiveness in a female child. It can lead to tremendous father and son conflict. As mentioned, it often leads to women "getting back" at their husbands in subtle—but oh-so-powerful—ways.

*If it's not by having the father all-supreme, how
should a family be run?*

It is important to make it possible for all members of the family to experience respect for their rights and concern for their needs; to expect each to show that same concern for others; to expect each to accept his responsibility by contributing to the well-being of the family. These expectations and ways of relating should be discussed around various incidents and worked out in boyfriend-girlfriend, husband-wife, parent-child relationships.

One child should be asked to wait until the one who spoke first has had his say. In this way children (and parents) learn to listen to each other. We remember a two-and-a-half-year-old who was ignored by her mother, her father and her four-year-old brother, until she pounded on the table saying, "Listen to me!" Everybody listened. Right on for her. But her parents also insist that she listen to others. In that same house the TV channel can't be changed without mutual agreement—be it mother, father, or children who would like to change it. There is, however, an unwritten law that certain programs—football, news reports, cartoon specials, and certain variety specials—are cause for change.

Children in a home which operates in this way learn how to work out ways to have their rights and needs met. They also learn fair play, to accept responsibility, cooperation, and to compromise when necessary. Children who grow up in such settings will be less rigid as adults, have less anger and rage, have less need to dominate or exploit others and will not stand for the abuse of their rights and neglect of their needs. Vigorous discussions can and should follow the violation of house rules. But extreme abuse, verbal or otherwise, should not be tolerated.

*We tend to favor our two-year-old boy over our
four-year-old. Why? What can we do about it?*

The "favorite age" and "favorite child" situation is a very real problem. Some parents like children best when they're babies, others when they are three- or four-year-olds, others when they are seven or eight, and so on. Some favor the first child and others, the last. Some favor one child for a particular characteristic—aggressiveness, sweetness, strength or physical ability. It is often a characteristic that the parent wanted but feels that he or she did not have in adequate supply. It can be a characteristic that a parent has and feels is very valuable.

In this case, comparing one child to another, "Susie is more aggressive than Billy," or "John is smarter than Diane," can cause trouble between the children and between the children and you. The favored child may seek even greater favor at the expense of a brother or sister. This is harmful to the social development of both. It often makes it easy for a favored child to "get by" or develop a false picture of his or her worth and unrealistic expectations from others. The world doesn't care whether a child was Mommy's or Daddy's A-plus, number-one son or daughter. A child so misled is likely to have troubles. Your awareness of your feelings is the first step toward preventing such problems. Try to understand why you feel as you do, be fair in managing conflict, in giving each child time, attention, reward, and privilege. When you tend to favor one child for whatever reason, you should make a conscious effort to control yourself. This doesn't mean "treat them all the same." Children have different needs. For example, one may not need as much help in going to bed as the other. He won't object to the time you spend helping the other as long as he is getting a little extra time with his own problem area.

Special Problems

I am expecting a new baby. How should
I prepare my two-year-old?

It is important to talk about the coming of the new baby. It is best to use the correct words about where the baby is located and where it will come out, even though your child may not be able to pronounce "uterus" or "vagina." Do not say that the baby is in the stomach. Children can get eating food and having babies all mixed up.

Helping your young child look forward to the new baby will reduce the jealousy. Let him feel that he will have a new, grownup role; that he will share in the pleasure of a new baby. At the birth of the new baby, it is important to involve the older child. If relatives and friends pay great attention to the new baby and forget about your two-year-old, it is important for you to bring her into the act with praise for her and her new role. When younger children can do real and helpful things for the baby, this should be encouraged. But keep relationships clear. Telling the child it's his baby can cause confusion. It is the baby of Mommy and Daddy and the sister or brother of your child.

Don't feel hurt or guilty if your two-year-old is angry, demanding, or unruly around the time of the coming of a new baby. This may happen even if you work hard to prevent it. Even when your child works hard to "be good about it," the jealousy and anger may break through every now and then. Here it is important to be understanding, *to talk to him about his feelings,* to reassure him that you still love him, to assure him that he is going to like and have fun with the baby.

An angry, harsh response at this time proves his fear that he will lose your love to the baby. Tolerating extreme acting-up because "I know he's upset about the baby" *proves* that you are going to neglect him for the baby. If you have a nine- or ten-month-old, don't make the mistake of believing that he is too young, that you don't have to prepare him. Talk to your infant about the coming event; let him feel your "bulge" and otherwise be involved in the excitement.

I plan to stay at home until my children are school age.
Is it important to send them to nursery school anyway?

Nursery school helps a child learn to leave his parents and begin to relate to others. It can help teach your child how to get along with other adults, how to function as a group member, how to deal with how others feel about him and how he feels about others. In nursery school he will have an opportunity to play games which require sharing and playing by the rules; these help him to think and learn.

A good nursery school experience paves the way for smooth entry to school. It also provides parents and younger children in the family with an important relief. With fewer children around, the younger ones get more attention and parents get a bit more helpful rest. Children are best able to handle the nursery school experience after three years of age. Two or three half-days a week are sufficient.

I must work. Is it harmful to send my
two-year-old to a day-care center?

Again, we believe that it is best not to send a child to nursery or day care until after three years, and even then on a part-time basis. But what you must do, you must do. Do your best to find a good program and send your child without feeling that you are not being a good parent.

What makes a good program? Good people. Enough space, toys which encourage play, a safe and interesting place are all important, but, we repeat . . . look for good people. By good people we mean people who want to work, who like children, and who truly understand them. Good people are more interested in helping children gain controls than punishing them for things they did because of underdeveloped controls. Look for people who respect the rights and needs of children without letting them do whatever they please. Good people know how to make nursery school a fun place and yet provide reasonable rules and expectations. In short, look for a program that can help your child continue growing in the same healthy way he has begun at home.

With infants hopefully there will be enough warm, friendly, capable caretakers who will stimulate motor, language, learning, social development and all the things we pointed out as being so important in Chapter 3.

My girlfriend works on the same job but she always
appears less tired and has more time for her family.
Does she know something that I don't?

Some people just have more energy than others. On the other hand, the key to success as a working parent—and in almost every other complex operation—is organization, planning, and good use of available help. If you plan your meals in advance, even cook in advance, or plan how you and your husband or wife or children will share the cooking, cleaning, etcetera, you will feel under less pressure. If you talk with your children about the importance of their "chipping in" and plan their tasks with them, they can be a big help. You want to let everybody help in one way or another and let everybody know what you need in order to make it. Let them know that you appreciate the help and they will feel like they are doing something of value and will want to keep helping.

Some people have very real trouble organizing. A list of "things to do" which you cross off as you do them can help. If you make a practice of doing the things you "must do"—high priority—first, you won't be too upset if less important things don't get done. The more you keep on top of things, the better you will feel and you and your family will benefit.

Dealing with Adoption

When should we tell our child that he is adopted?

There is disagreement among child-care specialists about this matter. It was formerly felt that the child should be told around two or three years of age. Recently it has been suggested that children this young do not understand the meaning of adoption and can develop fears about the "solidness" of their place in the family. Some people feel that they should be told at about seven or eight years of age when they can better understand.

Our feeling is that the matter should be handled like all complicated concepts and possibly anxiety-causing subjects such as race or sex . . . gradually, in the ways a child can understand at a particular age. The only difference here is that there is usually nothing to cause a child to raise the question. Therefore, you are likely to have to bring up the subject. Choose as natural a time as possible. A neighbor, a friend, or a relative who is adopting a child could be an opening. We feel that there is no potentially serious harm done when you talk about adoption or tell your two-and-one-half- to three-year-old child that he or she is adopted, if your manner conveys acceptance. A simple comment, free of long-winded discussions which convey anxiety, is best. A warm, relaxed manner as you discuss the matter is helpful.

At a later period, you will want to point out that it is the love, care, and concern that makes a mother a mother and a father a father and all of them a family, and *not* the fact that a child came from the father's "seeds" or the mother's body. That is only a biological technicality. In many traditional African cultures, a child is not considered "born" until a ritual designed to strengthen parent-child relationships has taken place . . . sometime after biological birth.

We think that having a child find out from someone else later on that he is adopted can be much more harmful than when the child is told by his or her adoptive parents in a warm, accepting setting, over a period of time. If he learns from the outside, the child can't help but wonder: "What was all the hiding and secrecy all about if you love and accept me?" It is best *not* to tell an adopted child that he was a "special child"; that he stood out among all the others; or that he is better than a natural child because you had a choice and could have picked others. Such a statement can create more doubt than relief.

What is the best age for a child to be
at the time of adoption?

It is best to adopt a child as soon after birth as possible. A number of problems are avoided when the child is yours from the beginning. On the other hand, there are many older children who could get along well in adoptive homes. There are many people who are very good with children and can handle even very serious psychological and social problems—more common with older, neglected and abused children. Know yourself and your motives, and adopt the child you want.

What should I tell my adopted child
about his natural parents?

It is best to tell your child that his mother and father were not able to care for him properly and gave him up so that someone in a position to care for him better could do so. You can point out that you wanted a child and were in a position to care for him. You should tell your child how the adoption was arranged in language understandable at his or her age. It is best not to say anything that suggests that the child was unwanted or rejected.

After your child fully understands the concept of adoption, he is likely to raise a question about whether his parents are living or not. There is disagreement on the best way to handle this, but we believe that you should give an honest answer . . . to the best of your knowledge. The question indicates a youngster's need to discuss his feelings about being adopted, about being given away, about what kind of person he is, about what kind of people his parents were. All of this should be done in a very calm, matter-of-fact way. You should not act as if you are hiding something from him. Don't put down the natural parents. Don't build them up. We believe that it is better if there is no contact between the natural parents and the adopted child and his family. Where a relationship must exist, there should be clear understandings between the adults involved so that the child cannot manipulate them.

Older adopted youngsters sometimes want to find their natural parents. Don't take it personally and don't stand in the way. It is a search for roots, for full identity. The quality of relationship will be different. Your relationship with your adopted child is not likely to be harmed unless it was very poor in the first place.

Is there such a thing as a "bad seed"?

Some people have the notion that a child of troubled parents is from a "bad seed" and, therefore, means trouble in turn. What an adopted child becomes, except where severe psychological damage has occurred, depends on relationships in your family, in your community and school, and—as with all children—a number of chance factors. The "seed," or his genetic makeup, has very little to do with it. It simply sets the boundaries, the limits of talent, temperament, and intelligence. But the "bad seed" notion is a handy excuse. When we see behavior that reflects badly on us, some of us don't want to take the responsibility for it. It is very easy to blame it on the natural parent—the original "bad seeds."

You can create a self-fulfilling prophecy in which you help your child become the "bad seed" that you feel his mother or father was. Your expectation that he will become bad can lead to your encouraging and tolerating troublesome behavior which produces —as you expected—the "bad seed." You can go to the other extreme in trying to beat out the badness, or prevent the badness from showing up. Normal aggressiveness can be either crushed or increased in this way. When an adopted child, whatever his background, is fortunate enough to escape early damage and is reared well, he is as likely to grow and develop as well as any other child.

Aren't many black adoptions informal?

Most black adoptions are informal—without going through official agencies. A relative or even a friend will "take" or "keep" a child for weeks or throughout childhood. This is often the case with an out-of-wedlock child, with a young or sick parent, or parents who are not able to care for all their children. The caretaker should make the same kind of explanations as in formal adoptions. The long-range plan for the child should be known.

We have seen some of the problems of foster home children in a few informal adoption situations. The children often test to see how much the caretakers will tolerate and then are afraid that the testing behavior will get them sent away. This is particularly troublesome if their guardians threaten to send them away in order to get them to behave. If they live near their parents, they may feel that one day they may get snatched away. They may wonder, "Why was I sent away—bad?—and not my brother Norman?" These circumstances, without explanations, can cause anxiety and behavior problems.

We are white and we have just adopted a black child. Are there some general guidelines you can suggest?

Hopefully your motives were not to rescue the child from his or her blackness. Attitudes of either white superiority or pity for blacks are likely to lead to difficulty. You and your husband *must* discuss racial difference and adoption in a calm and natural way from time to time. Relatives, friends, or neighbors should not be allowed to pick on your black child, nor should other children. On the other hand you don't want to overprotect him about a difference in race any more than you want to overprotect him about anything else. See how he fights back and help him only if he needs it. Exposure to black history, culture, and heroes (and everyday black people of similar and different lifestyles) as well as a matter-of-fact acceptance of the child will enable your child to establish a positive identity—black and white. If you are of a middle- or upper-income lifestyle and expose your black child only to black people of a lower-income lifestyle, troublesome identity problems—rejection of blackness, guilt, overidentification with the low-income style, etcetera—can result.

As white people, you hear and see white racist talk and acts even more than blacks do. When it touches your child you are likely to be outraged, lacking, as you do, the long experience that black people have in dealing with white racism. You must make an extra effort to help your child understand the incident as the problem of the "attacker"; that your child is okay, fine, and good. You don't want to brood, complain, and wring your hands excessively or you will transmit anxiety, fear, lack of control, and the notion that it is bad for your child to be black. He or she needs to hear, "You can climb every mountain. . . . You must keep on keeping on . . ." in spite of racist incidents here or there or everywhere. You must provide a model of constructive ways to fight racism—ways that don't hurt you or your child. Note our suggestions to black parents.

We are considering adopting a Vietnamese child. Should we?
What kind of problems will we have?

We believe very strongly in individual freedom. Therefore, the decision must be yours. We would like to point out, however, that there are a large number of black children in this country without homes, and they are more difficult to place. The same approach is advised as in the case of the black child with white adoptive parents.

There is no more evidence that black parents adopting nonblack children will have additional problems than there is evidence that white parents adopting nonwhite children will have difficulties. Your motives and your management are most important. If you adopt a nonblack child because you feel that he is "better," then you are likely to have management problems later on because of your attitude. If you adopt out of pity, you are likely to have difficulty. This is true in all trans-racial adoptions.

I have just remarried and my husband wants
to adopt my children. Is this wise?

You might want to test your marriage a year or so first. If it appears solid and the natural father has died or deserted the family for a year or more, then adoption probably makes sense. This is particularly true if the children are still very young. A child over seven or eight years of age is likely to have difficulty, particularly if he has strong feelings of loyalty to his natural father. This happens even when the natural father was not a good father. Where the natural father is living and seeing his child regularly, it is probably best not to have the stepfather adopt the child.

My oldest child had a different father and is the
only one in the family with a different name.
Do you think we should have it changed?

We have seen this situation be the source of a great deal of difficulty. The oldest child may feel rejected. In cases in which the father is dead, never lived with the family, or deserted for a long period of time, then it would be wise to have your present husband adopt your oldest child and change his name. This should be done after a great deal of discussion with your child. Again, adoption is *not* wise when the child's father is living and attentive to the child—even if he gives his permission.

Helping Your Child Handle Illness, Divorce, and Death

I must go into the hospital. What should I tell my child?

He will be worried about you, but he will also be worried about what's going to happen to him. When you are sure of the arrangements, you should tell him who will take care of him while you are gone and assure him that he will be okay. If possible, you should make the arrangements and discuss the matter with him about four days before you leave—no less than two days. This will give him enough time to ask questions. You will probably have to respond to a number of "why," "how," and "what" questions. It helps to answer these questions in a matter-of-fact way—not too solemn or serious and not too glowing and positive. Try and explain the problem in a language he will understand without giving all of the details. You should explain that no person causes an illness; that people are well most of the time but sometimes things can break down or not work right and they have to be repaired—like his brother's car or his truck that stopped working. This explanation is important because children this age can believe that they are responsible for things that happen to other people.

It will help if your child sees you making preparations to return home. You might point out, for example, that you will wear a certain dress or shirt home. You should give a rough estimate of when you will return, but don't make any definite promises. If the stay is long, your condition is not too frightening, and the hospital will permit it, regular but short visits should be arranged. Again, a calm, matter-of-fact feeling of confidence is the key and is even more important than what you say.

Anytime you are going to be separated from your child for more than a day, some explanation is needed. Otherwise, children will make up explanations of their own, and these can be very frightening. If you fail to tell them but they sense that you are leaving anyway, they may become restless, belligerent, and hard to manage and so on. Even with older children, it is important to discuss any extended separation or stay away from home.

My four-year-old is going to the hospital.
How can I prepare him for it?

Again, it's best to tell him about it around four days ahead of time and no less than two days . . . not enough time to cause excessive worry, yet time enough to ask questions. If he should find out that he is going by overhearing a conversation, don't deny it or be upset that he has heard. Your child will benefit from a simple explanation of what to expect and what not to expect. It is best to be as straightforward as possible. Some parents in an effort to make it easier on the child—and themselves—tell the child about the wonderful thing that will happen, such as ice cream after the tonsils are removed, without telling him that he will have a sore throat and it will be hard to talk. The child should be prepared to expect both situations—if that's what's going to happen. If you don't know what's going to happen, don't make promises. It is a bad idea to offer your child money or special privileges for his "hardship." Most important, don't tell him you're taking him out to buy a tricycle and wind up admitting him to the pediatric ward. We have seen this happen with a pretty nasty outcome.

Looking at pictures and reading books about hospitals can take the fear out of it all. You can also play a hospital game with your child or he or she can play it with other children. You can tell him about the routine of the hospital—when he will eat, what kind of bed he will have, who will take care of him, what he can do in his spare time. It is not a good idea to take a very young child to look at the ward before he is to be admitted. But you can tell the child that he is going to miss his parents and you're going to miss him, that he may be lonely, but this will only be for a short while, that he will meet other boys and girls in the hospital. This information should be given over a period of several days and not all in one frightening burst. Again, the matter-of-fact, calm manner is most helpful.

Suppose he needs an operation? What
should I tell him ahead of time?

You should explain the cause of the hospitalization in a way that your child can understand. If he is going to have anesthesia (sleeping gas or painkiller) be certain to explain that he will have a "special sleep" and wake up again after the operation is over. You can explain that the purpose of this is to prevent pain. When children don't understand this, they can sometimes feel that they are being attacked, even being put to death. It also helps to explain the extent of the operation. We know of a child who was terrified because he thought he was going to lose his entire leg, when only a small growth was going to be removed. You want to reassure him that you will visit and bring him home as soon as the doctor will permit. It helps to allow him to help pack his own bag. Most hospitals will permit children to bring their favorite stuffed animal. The animal, carrying memories of safety and security, will help your child feel more secure in the strange and frightening hospital.

If your child becomes restless or acts up before going to the hospital, don't let your anxiety and guilt about not being able to protect him prevent you from setting some limits and expectations. Tell him that you understand that he's scared and is misbehaving because of it but you are sure that he will be able to handle the whole business like a big boy. At the same time, don't be outraged. Hospitalization is an ordeal for a little person . . . for some big people, too. Even with older children, it is important to explain the hospitalization to them.

We are going to get a divorce. How should
we prepare our four-year-old?

It is hard for children of this age to understand the concept of divorce. All they know is that their father and mother no longer live together. They are hurt, lonely, and confused. They wonder about what's going to happen to them and to their parents. They sometimes believe that their angry and "bad" behavior caused the parent to go away. Their anger and confusion can sometimes cause them to act up more. At other times they may try to be extra good and quiet so that their anger will not cause any more trouble.

Explanations about what is involved will be of some help, but there is usually a rocky period around separation and divorce for most children until a new adjustment can be made. You should explain that sometimes mommies and daddies just can't get along and living together is bad for Mommy, bad for Daddy, and sometimes bad for the child. You should explain that there are a lot of reasons that you and your mate don't get along, but they are not the fault of the child. Whoever is going to care for the child should explain that they will be there to take care of him or her. If a mother goes to work after the divorce and has not been working before, she should assure the child that she will be coming home every day. When this is not the case, the child should be told in advance. If your child acts up during this period, you should let him know that you understand why he is angry, but don't allow yourself to tolerate excessive misbehavior because of your guilt. The child may understand this as "neglecting him already."

The people in the life of your child, and his way of life, often change after a divorce. Grandmother, a babysitter, or a housekeeper often come into the picture. Sometimes the child must go to a day-care center. It is important to explain to all of these caretakers that they must help the child to understand that he was *not* the cause of the parents' separation or divorce. They should also understand that the child may act up because of his anger about the separation and the change of people in his life. They should be advised to be understanding and indicate that they understand the feelings, but they should not tolerate extreme misbehavior any more than you do.

Children, particularly those two or three years older, are sometimes delighted by divorce. This is usually the case when the parent who leaves has been abusive or difficult. Even here it is important to explain along the lines mentioned above. Even children who experience relief and happiness can experience guilt and other confusing feelings.

What is the best way to handle "visits" to my child?

You should make arrangements to visit on a regular basis. You should not "re-fight" the marriage battle during these visits. It is also harmful to try to turn the child against the other parent or make him choose sides. Above all, a promise made must be a promise kept. Your child is already hurt. A promise to visit, send a letter, go for a walk, or whatever should be kept if at all possible.

If for some absolutely unavoidable reason your promise can't be kept, you should notify the other parent or caretaker and the child as soon as possible.

As we said before, separation and divorce is very difficult for a child in this age group. Only time and careful management of the situation will heal the wound. There is always some psychological damage done. But sometimes it is less than that which would have occurred had unhappy parents continued to live together and hurt each other and the child.

If separation and divorce is that difficult a problem,
what is death like for a child this age?

It is very much the same. Children this age don't really understand the concept of death any more than they understand the concept of divorce. Again, all they know is that the parent is away. In this case, the parent will not be back. Again they may feel that they caused the problem; therefore, the explanations needed here are very similar to those given in the case of divorce. A child should understand that he is not at fault. He should understand that he will be taken care of . . . by whom and how. Those who take care of your child should be made aware of what has happened and should be able to help the child with his or her feelings. In divorce or death, you can't *make* a child feel better. It is not helpful to scold him for his sadness or crying. It is helpful if he can feel less powerless. Try to find meaningful things for him to do. As soon as possible, help him return to the activities he enjoys the most.

The death of an animal—a bird, a cat, a gerbil—is good preparation in the handling of feelings of anger and sadness which occur around death. It is a good way to understand death . . . how it is different from sleep and that the dead do not return. Helping the child find a box or container to bury the animal and having some kind of ritual over the grave, such as saying loving things about the animal, can be useful.

You want to be careful about what you say happens to the body of the dead—animals or people. One youngster who lost two grandparents and a favorite aunt all within a year's time was told that they all went to heaven to live in God's garden. The youngster was furious with God for taking his loved ones away. Some religious people tell their children that the spirit of goodness in the dead ones goes to heaven, but the body remains in the earth. They also explain that there is no pain and the body will change and become like the earth. People who don't want their children to believe in God and heaven generally give only the last part of this explanation.

Some kind of explanation is important. Many children have sleeping problems associated with death, particularly where there has been more than one instance, coupled with illnesses of parents and relatives. Young children often confuse death with sleep and will be afraid to go to sleep. Some will want to return to the bedroom of their parents even though they had been able to sleep alone before this time. When they are extremely fearful, you may want to permit this very briefly, indicating that they will soon be able to return to their own beds. You want to be certain to help them do so within a short period of time—two or three days.

How should death be explained to the older child?

Children better understand the concept of death around seven, eight, or nine years of age. Even here it is important to explain how the death occurred and reassure the child that he is not at fault. But don't overdo the explanations. Children are frightened by all of the sadness in the house, the coming and going of relatives, the funeral parlor, the rituals. Unless a child asks to do so, you should not ask him or her to give the body a goodbye kiss. While you want to explain what is taking place, give them meaningful jobs to do when possible. You don't want to stop their normal activities if they feel like going out to play ball or visit friends. Finally, it is a matter of balance: either too much involvement or too little involvement in the whole process can be harmful.

My husband is away in the army. Is that a problem for our children?

Not necessarily. Of course the best possible situation is the one in which children can grow up in a home with two good parents present. Equally healthy children can come from many other kinds of homes when the existing parent or caretakers are able to do a good job. Regular visits, telephone calls, and letters help. Preparing things for and sending things to "away" relatives is helpful. Separation because of military service, college, or training or work programs is less of a problem than separation caused by imprisonment or even hospitalization for mental illness. What you tell your child about an "away" parent—particularly if the child is slightly older, say five to twelve—is crucial.

Jail and mental hospitals have a stigma attached to them. Yet you want your children to know and respect their father or mother or other friends and relatives even if other people do not. At the same time—most often—you don't want a child to feel that he or she must follow the same path. When you feel that the imprisonment is unjust, you must be very careful that your feelings do not tell your child that crime is okay.

You can explain mental illness as a problem in which the patient does not always know or cannot always keep from doing what he or she is doing at the present time. You can give more specific explanations as your child can understand them. In the *very rare* case of danger to children on home visits, you want to take reasonable precautions—for the good of patient and child. In the case of hospitalization and imprisonment, you want to help the child get a fairly realistic picture of the "away" person as a person. No "all roses" or "all devil" is a good rule. This will leave the child free to form his or her own opinion through experience in the future. You can explain crime as a mistake and prison as the price and a chance to change. When others tease, you should repeat your explanations; assure your child that the parent is or wants to be a good person; that the child is a good person and that the teasing child is unfair and wrong. Most of all, children should not carry shame or guilt for a problem not of their making.

You and your mate should discuss how you want to explain imprisonment, particularly when you feel an injustice has been done or that it is for a cause. In general, when this is the case, we think that you should say just that. You should also explain how you are working to bring about change and why. We think that it is unwise to force your cause on your child. It may well be rejected or may not be around when he or she is older. Besides, if your relationship is a good one, your children are likely to take it on anyway. Some of these suggestions apply largely to older children, although some kind of explanation should be given to a younger child. We have discussed the matter here as an issue of separation.

CHAPTER 5

The School-Age Child:
Ages Five to Eight

Importance of This Period

*I have been told that this is one of the less crucial stages
in my child's development. Do you agree?*

No. It has been said in the past that basic development is completed by the end of two years, and certainly by the end of five years—except for a later period involving a certain amount of teenage turmoil and adjustment. Today most people realize that some very significant things happen between the ages of five through eight. This is a time of important changes (maturation and growth) in thinking, understanding, feeling, and social relating.

The Young School-Ager and Race

*Is the five-through-eight-year period an
important time with regard to race?*

Yes it is . . . perhaps the most important period in your child's development. During this period children become sharply aware of the fact that they are separate and distinct from their parents. They become more aware of differences. At the same time they are moving beyond the family and into the world. This arouses self-doubt and fear. As a result, around six or seven they develop a great passion *to belong*. To meet this need and to feel important and competent, children of this age group develop groups of favorite people. They often close other children "out" so that they can feel "in." It is a much more conscious and more serious business than the excluding of others that we discussed in regard to the preschooler.

The average four-year-old barely understands racial difference and it is rarely the basis for group exclusion. The seven- or eight-year-old does understand. Some will express angry, hostile racial feelings to deal with the fact that they really feel small, fearful, uncertain, rejected, or insecure themselves. They learn to use race as a way to deal with their feelings in homes where family members do the same or are constantly putting each other down.

Five through eight is an important period with regard to race for another reason. This is the period during which the child does or does not "sign a contract" with society. The society expects parents, teachers, and other caretakers to help children accommodate themselves (adapt to) and "swear allegiance" to the desirable attitudes, values, and ways of the society. This is done by introducing youngsters to books, information, religious and political ritual, and other experiences which convey these attitudes, values, and ways. The process is called socialization. In return for their accommodation and allegiance, the society should provide the children and their families with a strong sense of belonging to a concerned, more powerful whole. This sense of belonging reduces a great deal of life's insecurity for individuals—whether this is a rational response or not.

The problem is that black parents have been forced to "swear allegiance" to and accommodate themselves to society without receiving in return the same sense of belonging and security that white families do. Furthermore they are expected to teach their children to do the same. There are too many ways—economic, social, and psychological—in which our society says that it values black children and families less than whites. As a result, many questions are being raised today about how much accommodation and how much allegiance to the rules, attitudes, values, and ways of the larger society are in the best interests of black children. Your child is now mature enough to sense these feelings of conflict in his parents, and this affects his own attitudes toward society.

What are some of the questions parents ask that
show their inner conflict regarding the society?

Should my child pledge allegiance to the flag of a country in which blacks are the victims of unfair competition? Should I teach my child to play the competition game even better than whites? Should I teach my child *not* to play the competition game? Should black children study American history with all its distortions? Isn't it better for black children to learn about African history and culture? Should black children learn ballet and classical music? Shouldn't I expose my child to black culture only? Should I teach my child to support a governmental system that allows racism? How can I counteract what my child learns in school every day in support of that system? Should young blacks join the police force or the army?

These are important questions. The answers you establish for yourself will affect the way you help your child relate to the black community and the larger society. What he or she learns and accepts now becomes his or her platform and will be difficult for your child or others to change ten, twenty, and fifty years from now. We will not try to answer these questions in the abstract. We will try to answer them in relationship to questions about what children are like and how you can help them grow.

Shouldn't black children learn the realities of life rather
than be indoctrinated by "white" ritual and fairy tales?

Let's separate the issue of ritual from that of fantasy and fairy tales. The latter help give your child a sense of security in an often dangerous world. They help a child handle failure and help him dream and plan success. They aid learning. They are fun. If common "fantasy figures" (for example, Santa Claus) are "too white," turn them black, as we discuss later. Fantasy and fairy tales will drop away or change to adult forms as your child grows. Don't worry about them. Ritual, including saying the pledge of allegiance to the flag, is a more complicated matter.

The purpose of ritual is to give a person or group a sense of belonging, purpose and value in the larger society . . . "with liberty and justice for all . . ." and thereby a sense of security. It is part of the contract a society makes with an individual: "You develop, take care of yourself, and meet your responsibilities as a citizen and human being and I, the society, will protect your rights and work to give you reasonable opportunities." In many ways the society has not lived up to its part of the contract with black people. Some blacks consider the contract null and void and will not participate in related rituals such as the pledge. Even worse, they fear that participation will blind children to the reality.

We understand the feeling and in this case you should involve your children in some kind of humane ritual—a pledge to humanity, community, etcetera. You also have an obligation to help them develop realistic ways to bring about a better society—their own personal skill development being the first. In other words, you don't want them to be only against something and without obligation.

We want our children to say the pledge.
Is that wrong as black people?

No. Some black Americans see change, want to keep pushing toward a better America for blacks, and do not want to express rejection by not saying the pledge or not permitting their children to say it. You must make your own decision, and institutions should abide by the position of the majority. Some black parents handle this matter by permitting their children to say the pledge but explain that it is a statement of an ideal. (The wording probably should be changed to ackowledge this.) In addition, they explain the strengths and shortcomings of the nation. Here too you want to help your children understand that their own personal development is the first thing they can do to help bring about desired change.

Black people have many silent private protest rituals. Some will stand respectfully for the national anthem but won't sing, some won't stand, and so on. In all cases, you should give your child an explanation for your action suitable to his or her level of understanding. "'Liberty and justice for all' should mean you but it doesn't, etcetera." You should be involved in civil rights and other change activities when you feel so strongly—otherwise you teach protest without teaching constructive ways to bring about change . . . the cause of trouble for some black teens today.

In the above ways, black parents help their children recognize racist acts and help them learn how to handle them. That is why thoughtful blacks can often see injustice and imagine people in high and responsible jobs cheating, lying, and stealing when some middle-class white children, who aren't allowed to see and talk about things the way they really are, cannot. (This is also the reason some black people are afraid that black children who grow up in white homes will not be prepared to handle the realities of living black in a white-controlled America.) Helping your child see and understand the reality as he comes in contact with it, incident by incident, gradually puts all these matters in proper focus.

A white child recently bullied my seven-year-old son with racial slurs. I won't tell you what I told my son to do. But how would you suggest handling the situation?

You probably told him to knock his block off. Sometimes that's the only thing that gets a desired response. If the other child is too big or too strong, you may have to talk with the bully, his teacher, or his parents. But fighting is not the best solution to the problem— even if your child wins the fight. Win or lose, nothing has happened to change the other child's attitude about using racial slurs.

If you're against solving such problems with your fists, what do you suggest?

The problem can usually be dealt with in a way that helps the other child handle his feelings better and helps your child better understand what prejudice and racism are really all about—and how to handle it without fighting on a daily basis. If he must fight physically every time an act of racism occurs in America, he could become too busy to do anything else. Something close to that happens with a lot of us.

Remember that most seven-year-old white children are not diehard racists. They are often repeating what they have heard— sometimes from people other than their parents. They are usually trying to handle their own troublesome feelings as best they can. Without help in coping with their feelings, it is easier to become a diehard. Understanding this, one black father used this approach:

"Look, Joe, the next time Billy calls you a 'nigger top,' you tell him that he must have some problems if he has to call you names."

Joe did so. Billy was so confused and stunned that he just walked away. The next day he brought Joe some candy and never bothered him again; in fact, they became friends.

Joe learned to deal with the real problem (Billy's insecurity).

And Billy learned something about himself. Joe, with his parents' help, learned how to handle a difficult situation without his parents, teachers or friends getting directly into the act. This gave him a greater sense of control and self-confidence.

Your child can always threaten to fight—and fight—after talk doesn't work.

Is my young school-ager being exposed to attack only because he is black? Wouldn't there be problems between people of different lifestyles even if race were not an issue?

There would be some problems, but not as serious as the problem of racial prejudice. Because American leaders have not made it possible for most people to experience equal opportunity and acceptance, groups have scapegoated each other to gain opportunities and promote their own self-esteem. Too many leaders have encouraged such behavior for economic and political gain. Blacks have been the most vulnerable and have been scapegoated most. This creates a climate of suspicion and an intolerance for difference, rather than an appreciation of the richness that difference gives the country.

America has more difference between people and lifestyles than most countries. This means it has a greater need for a tolerance and appreciation of difference than other countries. In addition, change has been rapid in America and creates differences in lifestyles between people of the same group. Change is so rapid that nobody can really say what life will be like in the year 2000 or how best to rear children to be prepared for it. The only thing certain about tomorrow's world is that it will require a better ability to tolerate differences in others than most of us now have.

Tolerance is all well and good, but won't I be preparing my child to "sell out" our group if I teach him the ways of the outside . . . say, like taking his hat off in school?

This is an important question. Although it sounds unimportant, it gets right down to the nitty-gritty of the problem of different lifestyles. Such seemingly trivial issues may determine whether your child will do well or poorly in the society of tomorrow. Many middle-class youngsters, black and white, are downing such customs as taking off hats indoors. We want to point out that they can afford to because they know how to take their hats off in certain places and keep them on in others when they must; they know how to handle themselves at college teas; how to handle a job interview; how to handle themselves in a business office. We have seen youngsters wear beards and jeans and flout laws or customs during their teens and even twenties and then give up this attitude for what the larger society requires when they must earn a living for themselves. They can do so because they learn the rules and styles of the larger society somewhere between five and ten years of age. This is not the case for many youngsters from low-income backgrounds.

We don't think it's terribly important to make a child take his hat off. We *do* think that it is important for all children to learn how to handle themselves in situations that demand different behavior than that required in their home, community, or subculture. If the school expects a child to take his hat off, why not? Parents have a right to socialize a child as they see fit, as long as the way is humane. But if you socialize your child in a way that results in his or her being unable to tolerate the just ways of other people, to live by reasonably fair rules, or to tolerate people other than those in his or her group, then you will limit your child to successful functioning only within your group. Many people change their dress, speech patterns, and mannerisms daily in order to function successfully in different situations.

Getting Along with Others

How can I socialize my child in the ways of my group and yet be comfortable with difference and change?

In all our suggestions, we have been, and will be, talking about ways that you can help your child grow up to be a person able to cope with life, difference and change better than people of past generations. Let's take a specific example to illustrate what we mean.

We know of one set of parents who do not accept religious explanations about the world but were told by their seven-year-old that God puts stars in the sky. The child heard this from children in school. The parents pointed out that some people believe that that is how the stars got there but others do not; that they (the parents) did not. They explained that they believed that an act of Nature beyond human control put the stars in the sky. (A more detailed explanation, or giving your child a book which explains your point of view, can be useful at a later date. This is enough for a child in this age group.)

A child is likely to accept the explanation or belief of his parents. Yet, this explanation leaves the issue open enough so that the child can remain curious and perhaps search for a better explanation in the future. The parents' willingness to accept somebody else's explanations and beliefs as okay for that person, while they disagree with them, leaves their child free to do the same without a need to reject, put down, or not associate with someone who thinks differently. The fact that the parents were not upset by the fact that nobody knew the answer for certain makes it possible for children to accept the fact that there are unknowns in life and that's okay; that you can live without "the answer" to everything. You can see how a tolerant response, telling it like it is as you know it but being open to a position different from your own—over and over, incident after incident—can help your child become an open-minded, flexible person with his or her own beliefs, understandings, and ways, yet able to relate to different people and different ideas. Such an approach will make it easier for people of different lifestyles to get along together in school, at work, and at play.

I am trying to teach our five-year-old good manners. My teen-age son tells me that manners are a "middle-class thing." What do you think about this?

Many young people feel that good manners—good morning, thank you, please, that kind of thing—have been a way for many people to cover up bad motives and unfair and unjust behavior. But bad manners and bad behavior are just as undesirable as good manners and bad behavior. A different style is one thing and bad manners are something else. Nothing is gained by being rude and ill-mannered. Much can be lost. As mentioned earlier, if your child doesn't learn to express respect to people around him—and respect is what manners are all about—your family and his or her future family are more likely to suffer than anybody else. Also, good manners are a part of something larger—good social skills. Good social skills (the way you relate) will help your child at school, at work, and at play.

We have found that children who do not have good social skills receive a less good response from important people they must relate to, such as teachers and employers, than those who do. In fact, if an employer has to choose between two people of equal ability, he will most likely hire the one who has the best manners and/or social skills. A person with around average intelligence can handle most of the jobs in this and future societies. Whether a person will function well or not depends a great deal on his social skills.

Again, the way you raise your child is up to you. But we can tell you that his chances of getting along well are best when he can "make it" on the street corner, playground, the board room of Johnson Publications or IBM, and in the halls of Congress. Helping your child to be comfortable with people of different styles and free to have his own preferences will help him find his way in the complex modern world. There may be greater tolerance for all styles if this is ever the case for most people.

Competition: Pros and Cons

*Traditional African culture valued cooperation and opposed
competition for individual gain. Shouldn't we teach young
black school-agers to be less competitive and more cooperative?*

There is nothing wrong with competition or being a good competitor. There is nothing wrong with reasonable personal gain. Every social system promotes personal excellence through some form of competition and personal gain for individuals . . . even if it's the competition to be the most giving. The important thing is that competition not be angry, hostile, destructive, or primarily selfish. It is *also* important that children learn to value cooperation, fair play, and respect for the rights and needs of all people. We suggest that black children learn to be good competitors as well as be cooperative and respectful to the rights and needs of others. Even in Africa, traditional values are breaking down as people move out of villages and an agricultural economy into a cash economy—paying for what they need. You can drown trying to swim against the tide.

It is important to help your young school-ager appreciate the importance of cooperation with other black people and white people to improve conditions for *all* people. Obviously you will have a particular interest in blacks. But again, example and not words alone establish this attitude. If you belong to your particular black liberation organization—be it black college alumnae, black militant group, Urban League, or NAACP—and you give your time, financial contributions, and talents, your seven- or eight-year-old child will come to understand that this is important.

The reason that blacks don't adequately support black organizations as adults is that they don't establish the necessary value and habits as children often enough. We would like to see a United Black Appeal where each black child in America gave at least one penny once a year as a way of understanding that he and she can and should play a cooperative and constructive role in the liberation of all black people.

Because blacks have been the victims of unfair competition and exploitation, shouldn't black children learn to be more competitive and better exploiters than anybody else?

We have observed eight-year-olds allowed to fight to the point of seriously hurting each other in order to learn to be tough enough for the cruel world they will have to face. We know parents who refuse to tell their children stories in which "everybody lives happily ever after." We know parents who teach their children to cheat and beat the system (use the bus ticket both ways, for example) before the system beats them through such means as poor jobs and inadequate housing.

We understand the concerns and motives. But it is dangerous. As we pointed out earlier, such children are more likely to develop habits which make it difficult to live with each other and their families than they are to develop habits which enable them to improve conditions for blacks in America. In the real world you can't always play by the rules. But it's important to help children learn to try to be fair whenever possible.

Helping Your Child to Think

What is a child's thinking like at the ages of five and six?

The minds of five- and six-year-olds are still controlled very much by their desires, fears, and fantasies. Dreams are real; Santa Claus, Easter Bunny, and the Tooth Fairy live. Make-believe play is *almost* real. Rules and "the way" to behave are still absolute and given from some supreme but vague authority out there somewhere. You are in trouble with your child if you step into the street before the light is green. On the other hand, you will catch your five-year-old daughter with her hand in the forbidden cookie jar because her desire overwhelmed her ability to obey the rule. Children in this age group do not appear to understand the contradiction in what they say or do, or what they tell you to do and what they do themselves. This, of course, makes it difficult for them to reason logically at this stage in their development.

Their important play over the first four years has given them concrete experiences on which to build some abstract concepts. Your command, "Jump down," your warning, "Watch the door above your head," and other such clues should have given them over fifty basic concepts, such as "above," "below," "open," "stop," and "start." The five- and six-year-old still likes to imitate adults and this remains an important way of learning to think and understand. Five- and six-year-olds are still learning through "touch" investigations—picking up, pulling out, and checking out whatever they can get their hands on that's new or different.

In what ways will my child's thinking develop
between the ages of six and eight?

By six or seven, your calling peaches, pears, and pineapples "fruit," and a hammer, saw, and screwdriver "tools," has helped your child learn to classify objects. Your six-year-old may be able to count, "one, two, three, four, five" dolls, pointing to each, but if you then ask her how many dolls are there altogether, she may not be able to tell you. She can count, but she may not yet understand the meaning of numbers. Before eight a child will usually tell you that a tall, slender glass holds more water than a short, wide one. What comes before "twenty-two" and after when counting by twos (20-22-24) may be a stopper for a six- or a seven-year-old.

By seven or eight, even six, some dramatic things have happened. Dreams are no longer real. Santa Claus, Easter Bunny, and the Tooth Fairy are dead . . . or live for suspect reasons. (We know of one little girl who "knew" by six but kept them alive until nine because she loved fantasy, make-believe, and presents.) By six, with good training, most children know that Batman can jump off the roof without risk of injury, but they can't. Your child's wishes and desires about all things slowly yield to reality. "The ball I want belongs to Mary and I must ask to play with it, not take it."

What other advances in thinking will my child have made by the age of eight?

By seven or eight, youngsters begin to understand that rules exist to keep order, protect people, and to permit certain things to be accomplished; that rules can be changed through discussion and mutual agreement. Children of this age become greatly interested in rules—in games, at home, school, and everywhere. "Why?" or "Why do I have to?" becomes a big thing. Challenging and debating the rules is now a way of life. Yet in the interest of getting along well, they are generally interested in living by rules.

The memory of the six- and seven-year-old is longer. His ability to sit and involve himself in something of interest—or something he must do even when he has little interest—is longer. But time is relative. A short time is three hours in the swimming pool when she likes it and five minutes at the piano when she doesn't like it. The time is now. The past and the future are only beginning to have meaning. The same for space. You will have a hard time explaining that you are in Chicago and Illinois at the same time until your child is around seven. Even when he can repeat what you explain at an earlier age, he really doesn't quite understand it. Probe a bit more and you'll see.

We want to repeat a point made before. Your child's ability to think can be improved or hindered by what you and others do. What he or she inherits only limits thinking ability at both extremes. A child can have the natural ability to become a very good thinker but may not do so if this talent is not developed.

How can I help my child learn to think well?

You will want to continue doing much of what you've been doing—helping your child learn the names of things, talk about them, and generally understand the world around him or her. More complex learning is possible now because your child has a better memory, can put events together to explain or understand things, and can get interested in an activity or a thought for more than a few seconds.

Now when you are going to take a trip, your five-year-old can really participate fully. He or she can anticipate the trip, enjoy the experience, and think back on it in ways that younger children cannot do. On a trip—let's say, to the zoo—you can help your youngster learn to learn and enjoy both the trip and the learning experience by what you do. It helps to talk about what your child will see, describing it as best you can before the trip. A book with pictures of the animals will whet his "seeing and learning" appetite.

Being somewhat familiar with the animals will make it all the more fun to see them, hear them, and imitate their sounds. Asking your child questions about the animals which cause him to think is helpful. Answering his questions and clearing up confusion, such as, "Where is the grass?"—shown in the book of the animal in a natural environment but not in a cage—is very helpful. The same is true of follow-up discussions.

We heard a prekindergarten teacher say that there was nothing gained by discussing a visit to a park after the trip because most of the children would never go there again. Whether they will go again or not is unimportant. Forming the habit of anticipating an experience, having the experience, thinking back or reflecting on that experience is important. An important integration of knowledge takes place.

*Will it hurt my child's way of thinking if I "invent"
from time to time to get him to obey me?*

It is very important at this stage in your child's development to give logical reasons for rules or actions of any kind. Let's say you are at the zoo and your six-year-old wants to walk far ahead of you in a crowd. One mother, when asked "Why not?" by her six-year-old, said, "Because there are tigers in the zoo and they can get out and eat you up." Another said, "Because you can get lost in the crowd and I don't want that to happen." The latter approach does not create unnecessary fears, helps your child learn to size up a situation and respond favorably to reasons and logic, and it is not an insult to your child's intelligence. Unlike the "Santa Claus" situation, where you were protecting a pleasure, a child will resent your lying to maintain control.

While we're speaking of getting lost, will your five-year-old know what to do if he *does* get lost? Should he just stand there and cry? Go to any stranger? Go to the park policeman? Anticipating problems and suggesting ways to handle them can help your child learn how to think in a problem-solving way, to consider the possible approaches and act in the most beneficial way. Explaining why certain things happen will help your child learn to think in a cause-and-effect way. Helping him decide what he wants to see at the zoo out of all the many possibilities—because you have only an hour to stay there when it would take three days to see everything—is a way your child learns to establish priorities.

My child is constantly asking questions.
Is he trying to get my goat?

The seven- or eight-year-old loves to show off his knowledge and understanding. He loves to quiz parents about interesting things he has just learned himself. Such questions make learning fun when you treat it as fun. It helps to take an interest, treat the question seriously, and not be a know-it-all. You can make your child feel inadequate if you know everything. Besides, knowing how to find information or investigate a problem is as important as having the information. Having your youngster look up the answers to questions he doesn't know, with your help and assistance, can be more helpful than always telling him the answer. It also helps for a child to learn early that nobody knows everything.

My husband turns every experience into a "lesson."
Is this good for our child?

Some parents go too far with their quizzing and teaching. We watched a parent at a concert explaining every move of the musicians to her youngster—asking one question after another as if the child was on a quiz show—being frustrated and angry when the child didn't understand and didn't show sufficient interest. We wanted to say, "Leave that kid alone and let him enjoy the show!" There *is* a happy medium. Too much teaching and questioning can turn a child off or make thinking and learning a chore, and too little can lead to an underdevelopment of his ability to think about and understand the things around him.

Providing toys and materials that stimulate thought and learning is helpful. Building blocks for the five- and six-year-old, soft wood for cutting, model planes, rockets, and boats for the seven- or eight-year-old, mixes for easy-to-make cakes, all these are very useful in helping children learn to learn. They also permit them to have a finished product quickly. "Look what I made!" The sense of accomplishment is motivation to achieve more. A toy microscope or a cheap magnifying glass will enable them to play "scientists," "hospital," "detectives" or other make-believe games.

*That's all well and good. But what about
those of us who can't afford such toys?*

You can! Popsicle sticks, packing material, string, paper cartons, you name it, can become anything you want them to be with scissors and paste. Toys are just props or things to encourage the imagination. If the thing you or your child cut out is called an airplane, it will fly to Nigeria or China just as well as one that costs ten dollars or more. It'll crash on takeoff or landing and your child can do the whole rescue scene at a bargain price. (Just be careful of pins and sharp edges and other hazards with the toys you make—just as you must be with the toys you buy on many occasions.)

Such play deepens understanding of the words, concepts and roles involved. Don't ignore a little milkman or doctor or allow your older children to discourage your five- or six-year-old by calling the way he plays stupid or dumb. Detective-like games—involving such things as unscrambling letters, words, and sentences, following clues, and correcting errors—are interesting and helpful to the seven- and eight-year-old. They help develop reasoning powers.

*Won't letting my child indulge in "make-believe"
hold back his ability to learn reality?*

Some parents feel that it aids learning to speed up reality training. Such parents tell their three-, four-, or five-year-old children that there is no such thing as Santa Claus, Easter Bunny, or the Tooth Fairy. There is no need to do this. Fantasy is fun. Having fun or being happy is as important to learning as having information or knowing the difference between reality and fantasies six months earlier than the kid next door. If you don't like the fact that these symbols of goodness and good fortune are represented as white, make them black. Magazines, newspaper, and television ads as well as stores now have both a black and a white Santa Claus. This can be confusing. But it can be handled easily:

"But Daddy, how can Santa Claus be black and white?"

"Santa Claus is the spirit of goodness and giving and can be either black or white."

You have given an answer a young child will accept without destroying the fun. You have laid the groundwork for understanding the real meaning of Christmas.

Isn't it true that some people believe that black children have trouble with abstract (nonconcrete) thinking?

This has been said, but we do not think there is a racial factor here. Abstract thinking grows out of concrete experiences which are given meaning and understanding by parents, teachers, and others. For example, when your child picked up your Jackson Five record and asked what it was, you said, "record." Later through your input, the record was understood as a "record by the Jackson Five." Eventually it became—in the black vernacular—"a 'bad' record by the Jackson Five." This includes an understanding of the abstract concepts of a group, music, a quality of music—all given meaning to a child by others. Whenever parents or others, black or white, for whatever reason, are not present or cannot give meaning and understanding of this kind, a child remains a concrete thinker.

Again, we stress it is important to talk, talk, talk, explain, explain, explain to your child—especially at times other than when you are scolding or punishing. Encourage him to talk, talk, talk, question, question, question things with you.

The Importance of Creativity

I believe that black people are especially creative. This is a trait I don't want my five-year-old to lose. Can too much emphasis on logical thinking, cause-and-effect thinking and priority-setting destroy her creativity?

We see no conflict. Creativity is the quality of being able to produce something original. But creative people are usually quite logical and well disciplined. Helping a child become a logical, disciplined thinker need not dampen creativity. Forcing a child into rigid thought, belief, and behavior patterns can dampen creative thinking. Modern child-care approaches—the methods and attitudes we are describing—support creative thinking and activity as well as the development of logical, disciplined thinking.

Your concern may be with the claim that has been made that

black culture supports creativity and Western (largely white culture) does not . . . or less so. It has also been suggested that Western culture promotes problem-solving thinking more than other cultures. Such notions are dangerous generalizations. Children have been forced into rigid thought and behavior patterns everywhere. All cultures appear to include some form of art, storytelling, and poetry as well as some type of problem-solving training and behavior.

How can I help my child keep his creativity and
yet become a logical thinker?

Most children will come to understand what is real and not real and become logical thinkers through learning about the environment around them at home and at school. The inventive and creative side is more fragile. You can best encourage and protect creativity through showing the appropriate amount of interest and pleasure in your child's original work or ideas.

It has often been said that blacks are good dancers and singers. There may be some physical reason that many blacks are good in these areas. But more important, singing, dancing, and other forms of creativity have been, and are now, important, expressive methods in black culture. It is not uncommon to see black parents beaming proudly as their two- or three-year-olds, barely able to control their bodies, begin to try certain dance steps. This approval encourages children to develop these talents. The things that a particular culture values will receive repeated encouragement, causing more members of that group to excel in that area . . . unless it is deliberately avoided. Unfortunately, a few black parents, more often middle-class parents with strong scholarly interests, have discouraged early body freedom, music, and dance. This is distressing. People from all groups are rediscovering the value of these activities.

My seven-year-old's drawings look so babyish. Would
it help if he copied some of mine?

With regard to drawing, we suggest that you not encourage your child to copy or use other aids to get "good results." Copying limits inventive or creative expression. It is also frustrating for a child who can copy somebody else's "good" work and can't produce the same himself. Letters of the alphabet or numbers are the only copying we think useful. Even then you shouldn't push a child to copy accurately until his arm and hand control is fairly good, around seven or eight years of age.

How should we react to our children's creative work?

We do not think it is helpful to reward the creative work of children with money. If this habit is established, the creative work may not go on unless there is an outside reward. The pleasure and the reward should be in the doing.

Too much criticism, correcting, or improving your child's artwork, dance, or singing, especially among the five- or six-year-olds, can cause them to stop. A lot of questions and suggestions can be understood as a criticism or ridicule and turn off the creative urge. Do not allow older brothers or sisters to laugh or ridicule. Your young artist may fear that his work is not "right" or not good. On the other hand, some children appreciate the interest. You will be able to "read" his reaction. Some children are inspired by and learn from parents' doing their own creative thing—dancing, painting, singing. Many love to join their parents and do things together. This is very helpful.

All this talk about creativity is well and good, but all blacks can make music and dance. There aren't enough black scientists and scholars. My seven-year-old is very bright and could become a scientist. Shouldn't I be emphasizing books and learning rather than music and play?

It is best to offer a child an opportunity to find pleasure and satisfaction in the many different areas of life. This not only helps youngsters become well-rounded, but it provides them with the opportunity of finding the areas which will be most gratifying to them over the long run. It is true that listening to the Jackson Five or playing ball all day, *day after day,* with *no* interest in books or learning, is not likely to produce a scholar. But an interest in books and learning *only* is not likely to produce a healthy scholar. A scientist who makes music and dances is a thing of beauty. Most important, your child should not have to carry the "burden of the race" or fulfill the goals of parents. As the folk song says, "Give him room and let him grow." Don't try to force your interest and goals down his throat. Besides, this generation will produce large numbers of talented blacks in every area.

Developing Speech and Language Skills

How can I help my young school-ager improve his speaking and use of words?

At five or six years of age, your child's speaking becomes clearer and conversing with him is easier and more fun than ever. You should continue to talk about ideas, feelings, and the things you are doing just as you did when he was very small.

The six- or seven-year-old is beginning to use speech as a way to think, plan, act, and figure out the outcome of his actions rather than acting on every possibility. For example, a very young child viewing a wagon near the stairs might simply hop right on, take a ride, crash, and get hurt. A child of five or six can use words and language to think through the possible results of such a move. The wagon could provide a ride, but it could cause a crash; therefore, it should be pulled back from the stairs before you try to ride it. While he wouldn't use these same words, he could tell you the problem and solution.

You don't want to laugh or discourage your child from walking around the house talking to himself, talking to nonexistent people, or making up stories and conversations. He has learned that talking is fun, that you can use it to get things done, to say how you feel, to get questions answered, to be in contact with others. He can see that it's a great talent to have. He has also learned that it pays to be good at it. So, like every other talent, you practice it. You don't want everybody around at your practice sessions, so you talk to yourself. Nothing crazy about that!

Hasn't it been said that blacks are nonverbal?

Yes. But those who say so obviously don't know many blacks. Most blacks are "talkers." The next time you go to the barbershop or go to choir rehearsal, think about it. Many blacks turn off in nonblack, hostile, or uncertain situations. Overwhelmed people, black or white, sometimes become depressed and don't talk much. The people who make the above claims must have studied blacks who were living under difficult conditions.

Another point here is the fact that some people express themselves very well with very few words. Joe Louis was once asked how he would handle a punch-and-run fighter. His answer, "He can run but he can't hide." A three-page answer could not have made the point better. It also points up the image-producing nature of some black language styles. Some people talk and talk and say little. Some people talk and talk to cover up fear and anxiety and to avoid real communication. It is true, however, that people who can express themselves well in school and in the world of work tend to do well and are considered bright even when they are no more intelligent than some less verbal people.

My five-year-old still stutters. Should I be concerned?

Many children occasionally stutter, mispronounce words, lisp, or have other speech imperfections around two or three years of age. Calm, friendly correction—and help in slowing down and pronouncing clearly, not uptight and naggy help—usually solves the problem by the time your child is four or five years old. If your youngster becomes self-conscious, stop slowing him down and helping him pronounce and just listen patiently and calmly, conveying the notion that you are sure he will get it. Hearing may be a problem where mispronunciations continue at this age. Speech therapists can help identify the problem and work out corrective training programs. If the problem is tenseness, they will advise and refer you for help.

You mentioned children talking about feelings. My eight-year-old is very close-mouthed, even when he is troubled about something. Should I make him talk?

We know what you mean. After seven or eight, children want more privacy and less intrusion into their affairs. Some eight-year-olds will put a sign on their bedroom door saying "Keep Out." As they get older, it may read, "Anyone entering this room prepare to be sorry!!!" Or in this modern day, "This room is rated X. No adults permitted!"

This is only part of the story. They also have some very troublesome feelings during this period and want to talk about them. Language becomes all the more important when it can be used to manage troublesome feelings. If your child won't talk about such feelings, possibly you have made it known, without realizing it, that you don't want to talk about anything "tough," matters like race, sex, anger, and conflict. We all do this from time to time, but the damage can be corrected.

What can I do to get my child to confide in me?

When your child is obviously troubled about something, you can open the door for conversation by pointing out that you can see that he is upset about something and that you will be glad to talk with him about it when he wants to. Then, give him time, hours . . . a day before repeating your offer. If you try to force your child to talk, you are likely to get nowhere. When he does come to talk with you, it is best to be a good listener, and not an alarmist or a judge. Young children are not saints or criminals.

Very seldom can a little child do something that is so serious as to cause parents alarm. Even if he has been playing with matches near gasoline, for example, it doesn't help to panic. A short, to-the-point, discussion about safety and your support and understanding and belief that he'll be able to handle the situation better next time is the most helpful approach. When your child has been able to talk about something that is very difficult, let it be known that you know how difficult it was for him to talk about that, but you're glad he was able to do so. In this way, you have made his being able to discuss a difficult matter an achievement to be repeated the next time . . . it will be if you were helpful the first time.

Moral Development

What should I look for in the way of moral development in the five-to-eight-year-old period?

Five- and six-year-olds know right from wrong. Your rules—do's and don'ts—have been taken in and are becoming their own. Their own budding conscience now guides their behavior without your constant praise or punishment. But the "goodies of the world"—things like your money, jewelry, and cookies—are sometimes just too much for the young conscience to handle. If you leave your shiny bracelet on the dresser, it may disappear. When asked about it, your son or daughter may "lie" just as he or she did at three, although the story is now more grownup—maybe the neighbor stole your jewelry rather than a big monster.

Because the five- and six-year-old conscience is just barely working, your child can't bear to see anybody "get away with murder." You may hear your six-year-old talking in a disapproving way about "the boys who had their names put on the board for being

bad," while barely hiding his enjoyment of their behavior . . .
doing things he would like to do, and occasionally does. They are
beginning to develop respect for the rights and needs of others in
return for respect for their own rights and needs. Other kids acting
up is a kind of violation of the contract—if you can, why can't I?
He tells you about their misbehavior to get your support for his
doing right. The tattletale is asking for the same help. That is why
five- and six-year-olds are big tattletales.

What can I do to help my child's moral growth?

Beating the badness out doesn't help. Just as with your preschool
child, going to great lengths to make your child confess to a crime,
admit that he lied about it (and the several other lies he told while
you were holding your criminal investigation) won't help much
either. In most cases you both know what happened. You are not
the district attorney getting a record of convictions which will help
you become governor. You simply want to help your child develop
responsibility and good inner control of his behavior.

You might say something like this: "I can't know for sure
whether you took my money or not. Only you know. It's up to you
to be honest with yourself." You can point out that if he took your
money, you know it was only because it was so tempting and if he
can give it back you will be proud of him. You can point out that
anything on your dresser belongs to you; that if he wants something, he should ask you. Given the responsibility of being honest
with themselves and not attacked and strongly accused by the
parent, many children will acknowledge their misbehavior and
develop a greater commitment to self-control. The money may just
reappear or be given back to you directly. When it is given back,
you might say, "I'm glad that you were able to give the money
back to me." With this approach you have indicated that you
believe in him and you expect him to be able to control himself.
You have given him a chance to turn a failure of control and
embarrassment into good feelings and achievement.

By seven or eight the conscience is not only fairly strong, it is
strict. Yet many children are still unable to control their desires
and break the rules from time to time. They are hard on themselves and others when they do so. Adults sometimes have to help
children of this age be less hard on each other when they break
minor regulations. They want the rule breaker spanked and

"boiled alive." A lot of fussing, hard feelings, and attacks on each other are because of the strict conscience of the seven- and eight-year-old period. Some children, once they admit to misbehavior, will overapologize.

It is important to help them learn to discuss rule-breaking and make commitments to live by the rules better the next time rather than calling for extreme, harsh punishment or demanding apologies. Discussions about what's fair for all are much more useful.

Isn't the strict conscience a particular problem among young black children?

The strict conscience, angry feelings toward violators, and harsh punishment are a problem wherever parents, black or white, set hard and fast or rigid rules and give hard punishment. Because blacks have had to "toe the line" or be in trouble, child rearing had to be more strict and rigid more often. While a period of strict conscience occurs among all children at this age, it's probably more of a problem among black children where rearing has been rigid, strict, and harsh. We have listened to black seven- and eight-year-old schoolchildren from such backgrounds who expect and demand harsh treatment for minor misbehavior. Yet the punishment often does not stop the behavior, resulting in anger and negative feelings about themselves and each other.

Are there ways that parents can encourage "right" and "wrong" at the same time?

Yes. We can say all the "right" things and do the opposite. We can say the "right" things but our voice and manner will indicate that we don't believe it or that "these words are for the public—not for real." We can repeatedly see but not see misbehavior that we don't really object to. For example, if the lady next door doesn't want our Matthew to cut through her yard, we can say, "Matthew, don't cut through that old Battle Axe's yard." "Battle Axe" tells him where you really stand and gives him permission to disregard your words. In addition, you can just see and "not see" him do it time after time.

All of these things can lead to a conscience with a hole (or many holes) in it. Well-trained children of dedicated, caring parents sometimes have trouble living by the rules because they have been given permission by parents not to in a way in which the parents were not aware. This behavior, without help, can carry through to adulthood. We can remember a pathetic extreme in which uncontrolled aggression and conflicting attitudes toward rules and laws stood side by side. A driver turned into a one-way street and wanted to drive into the nearby alley to turn around. But two men drinking wine in the alley—in violation of the law—threatened to break his neck for driving the wrong way.

You mentioned five and six as years when many children tattletale. How can I help my young tattler to break the habit?

Let's take the following example as an illustration of what you might do. Your six-year-old Thelma tattles on her eight-year-old brother Charles repeatedly. Charles gets furious. You might say something like this on an occasion where she tattles: "Thelma, I'm glad to see that you know what is right to do, but Charles is going to be mad with you if you always tattle on him. You'd better let me help Charles learn to control himself." With this approach you have given them both support for doing the acceptable thing without putting either one of them down. It is important to watch your tone of voice in this case. There is a little lawlessness in all of us, and we sometimes appreciate the acting-up child more than we do the tattler. Our irritation with the tattling can cause us to put the tattler down in a way that makes him or her unhappy. On the other hand, if we are particularly fearful that the acting-up child will get into great difficulty, we may put him or her down too hard. If we understand that our job is to help children gradually develop control—and not expect them to have it already—then we can support desirable behavior without putting down the tattler or the child who is acting up.

Sexual Development of the Young School-Ager

When my seven-year-old was three, I was worried about his great interest in his penis, where babies come from, and so on. Now that he is seven, I'm worried because he doesn't appear to have any interest in anything related to sex. Is that normal?

The behavior you described is normal for the three-year-old as well as the seven-year-old. Children in the six-to-early-teen-age period tend to show less active interest in their bodies than at an earlier age. If development is going along okay, they have learned to separate their sexual feelings from other body feelings, and there is less confusion and concern about sex. They have learned—though they usually will not talk about it openly—that parents have a private sexual life of their own.

But while there is usually less open interest and curiosity about sex, the seven- or eight-year-old interest does show from time to time. You may overhear seven- or eight-year-olds telling sex jokes or using sex words. In groups they may even poke fingers at bottoms or breasts. There is often chasing and great excitement with such activity.

Unless the play goes too far, it is best to keep an eye on it but not stop it right off the bat. It can be a kind of release of sexual energy. You must determine for yourself when too much is too much and when it's time to call a halt to such play. When you stop the play, it is not necessary to deal with the issue of sex . . . you can't always be sure that's what's going on. You can simply tell the children that they are becoming too excited by the play; that it's time to stop. Providing them with ideas for other activities is helpful. They will be relieved by your stepping in and not letting things get out of hand. Lectures at the time won't help, but keep your eyes and ears open for questions and natural opportunities to clear up questions and confusions about sex, or to enlarge on your child's understanding, based on these incidents.

My eight-year-old hates girls. Will he be okay?

Your son's "hate" for girls at this period (and girls for boys) is not uncommon under present conditions. It is one of the ways that children firmly establish their own sexual identity—by being with their own, by doing things that a girl or boy does; by being against the other sex. Disliking the opposite sex is a way of protecting themselves against interests they feel they shouldn't have as a boy or as a girl. A seven- or eight-year-old boy's dislike for a girl is a good way to protect himself from his interest in cuddling a doll. The "hate" is likely to be less "needed" as it becomes more okay for boys to have "girl" interests and feelings and girls to have "boy" interests and feelings. We've always had these feelings but up until now we, particularly men, have just denied them. As attitudes toward women change and women's roles change, some of the "need" to "hate" girls will be eliminated.

Won't such play lead to homosexuality?

No. It should free men to express more real warmth and affection toward girls and women. Much male "design" on women or supermaleness today is to prove manhood and to disprove the lurking suspicion of softness caused by normal feelings of attraction to both men and women. What a young boy who plays with dolls or plays house can learn is that he can do that and still kick, run, fight, be aggressive and assertive—in short, be a boy and man. Girls, more and more, will learn the same. Masculinity and femininity can be maintained without the absurd extremes of the past.

There may be a problem when boys do *only* soft, warm, domestic things and girls do only aggressive, masculine things, though even here it may only be a phase. The parent or adult model, or what the parent encourages, determines sexual roles most. You can encourage both warmth and affection and reasonable aggression and assertion. Actually, female parents can encourage traits said to be male and male parents sometimes encourage traits said to be female. The truth is that nobody really knows the causes of homosexuality.

On several occasions, I have found my eight-year-old masturbating. I spanked him and told him to stop it but it didn't seem to do any good. What should I do?

First, we hope that your concern is not because you feel that masturbating is abnormal, bad, or nasty. Masturbating, in one way or another, is normal for boys and girls. A little girl may do so by rubbing her vagina against her father's or mother's leg or squeezing her own legs together. Boys' masturbation techniques are more detectable. Masturbating is a problem when it becomes the *only* way to relieve everyday anxieties and tension. You should make certain that he or she is sufficiently occupied with various activities. You should also make certain that your child isn't burdened with disturbing or worrisome concerns.

Spanking is not helpful in this situation. It is best to talk to your child about what is going on. Rather than trying to force him to stop, you might point out that you know that he has sexual feelings; that all boys and girls have sexual feelings just like grownup mothers and fathers do. You will want to remind him that it can be embarrassing for him to play with his penis in places where others will see him; that other people will not want to be around him if he has such habits. If your child appears to need to show you or others that he is masturbating—or appears to do so in preference to many other activities—you should talk with your doctor, the school nurse or social worker, or child guidance workers in your community.

Special Difficulties of the Young School-Ager

What kinds of problems am I likely to come up against with children of this age?

Let's take a hard one where the usual issues—race, sexual attraction to parents, anger, and guilt—all get tied up together. A five-year-old black girl living in a predominantly white neighborhood told her mother that she liked her (the mother) more than Daddy because he was not as light-skinned as the mother. The fact was that he was as light as or lighter than the mother. In any situation where the facts don't add up, the question must be, "What else is going on?"

Actually the girl was angry with her father, and "downing" the father to get some emotional distance from her strong attraction to him and getting closer to her mother was part of what was going on.

You do hear a negative feeling about being black in this case. But it is not fixed or hardened. In fact, it is more of a question than a statement. The child has attractions to both parents and guilt and confusion about the feelings. In this predominantly white neighborhood, she wanted to be like the other children in order to feel a sense of belonging. Her question is, "How *should* I feel about Dad, Mom, and my skin color?" These are not complicated things that only a psychiatrist can determine. We have found that when parents "keep cool" and listen, most can find the problem behind what is stated as the problem but obviously is not. In this case, grave concern about the child's feelings about being black could have made it hard to hear what else was going on.

Don't feel that if you live in an interracial neighborhood your child will not have racial pride; that you must live in a black neighborhood to appreciate blackness or that, "Oh, my goodness, I have failed my child." Such thoughts and feelings will cause you to respond anxiously to questions about race. Your uptight manner and not your words will say, "Yes, there is something wrong with being black." If you do, you are adding your own fears, uncertainties, and confusion to those of your child.

How would you handle the above situation?

We'd say something like: "Honey, you must be angry with your daddy. Sometimes little girls get angry with their daddies. That's okay. And dark skin is okay, too. Some nice people have dark [or black] skin and some nice people have light [or white] skin."

It is a simple but powerful response. You identified the emotion in question (anger), which is helpful. (Helping your child identify these emotions is good training. A lot of adults get into trouble because they are not close to or aware of their feelings or emotions.) You have said with words and a calm manner that angry feelings are okay and not a cause for guilt. Your child will notice that the feelings didn't harm or destroy Daddy. That helps her understand that angry wishes and what happens in reality are not the same thing. You said that skin color does not make a person a nice person; that the way a person behaves is more important. The message over time will lead to calm, positive acceptance of skin color and race.

When you look for and understand the real issue, you are less likely to get alarmed. Growing, searching, learning children are bound to ask questions which upset us if we give them adult meaning rather than trying to figure out what is going on within the child. It is important to develop the habit: "Stop . . . think . . . identify and address the real issue." Alarm and overreaction are our own feelings and self-doubt "talking." If you act disturbed it will also tell your child that he or she can't come to you with the tough one because you go to pieces.

My seven-year-old son is very aggressive. He is often in fights. I am afraid he is going to hurt himself or someone else needlessly. Is this just a stage he is going through?

Fighting at this age is not necessarily cause for concern. The seven-year-old is a fighter, and some children are just more physically aggressive than others. You will just have to stick in there with your management of his aggression and fighting. You want to help him be fair and not fight without a cause. You want to gradually help him learn to develop ways to talk and get others to be fair with him rather than fight it out all the time.

Be sure to provide enough other outlets for the child's energy. Running, swimming, and team sports in the community and at school can be helpful. As long as your child is a fair competitor, a good winner, and a good loser, there is nothing to be concerned about here. Children with a great deal of aggression often tend to be impulsive and do things on the spur of the moment. Some of their impulsive acts, like darting into the street, striking matches, and throwing things, can be dangerous to themselves and others. You will want to remind them again and again to think before they act, that if they throw while angry they may hurt someone and will feel bad about it. You also want to help an impulsive child learn to enjoy himself without getting overly excited.

I caught my seven-year-old playing with matches.
How would you handle this?

One father noticed his eight-year-old son hiding matches. Rather than showing alarm, he said, "I see you are interested in matches. Come here and let me tell you about them." He gave the youngster a demonstration on how to use them safely. He explained the possible danger to himself, the house, and others. He explained that because they could be dangerous, he didn't want him to play with them. He added that if the youngster had cause to use them (barbecue fire, toys, etcetera), an adult would be glad to help him.

The discussion took the mystery and attraction out of fire and out of a forbidden act—using matches. Many an apartment and home in the city and suburb alike has gone up in smoke from the tiny torch of a curious, impulsive seven- or eight-year-old. Matches should be locked away from somewhat younger children. Even before you catch youngsters playing with matches, you should discuss the matter with them. A natural time—when you're using matches, for example—is best.

Are there other problem areas during the
five-through-eight-year period?

Yes, competition is a major problem. Your child has been in competition with you since he or she was "knee-high to a duck."

Not only are you better at everything, but you have a lot of privileges and can order him around. In addition, he can now look beyond himself and can compare himself with others. He notices that in some things he's not as good as Sam and Bertha. Finally, five- and six-year-olds in particular start more projects than they can successfully bring off . . . or bite off more than they can chew. All of these situations are normal, yet result in disappointment and failure for your child from time to time. Anger and frustration can result. When this is the case, they need help in dealing with their feelings.

What can I do to help my child cope
with these competitive feelings?

You can help in several ways. You can assure your child that he or she will one day be able to catch the ball or read the book as well as you do. You can point out that he's doing fine for his age and size.

It is not helpful to compare your child with other children. He is already doing that. You want to help him learn to be satisfied with his best effort; to have personal standards of excellence but not to feel that he *must* do what he *can't do*. You can help by praising your child for a good try at whatever he is doing. When there is a prize for winning, there should be some recognition for "doing your best." In this way your child learns to take pride in a job well done—win or lose, best or not. Without telling your child what to do or nagging, you can help him learn to set up work and play goals which he can bring to completion. Raising questions which will help him adjust the "job" to the time he has to do it in and helping him learn to organize himself so that he can complete the job can cut down on frustration and failure.

You might also look for an area in which your seven- or eight-year-old has knowledge or talent but you are relatively uninformed. One father noticed that his eight-year-old son was very interested in outer space. He bought the youngster a telescope and the son learned a number of things which his father knew very little about. The youngster took great pride in "laying the facts" on his old man. He felt less inadequate in relationship to his father as a result.

Should I let my child win when we play games together
so that he won't always feel so powerless?

In games of skill, you can help him plan his moves—but don't play his whole game for him. Hopefully he can sometimes play with people of about his own skill. You don't always want to play as if you are playing for the world championship either. Unless he or she is very unusual, they won't always be best in everything and need to learn how to compete in work and play, do their best and learn to enjoy things without being first or winning all the time. If your child can tolerate losing without extreme frustration, with-drawing from competition, or giving up, you need not let him win at all. On the other hand, if the above reactions do or are about to occur, you can "help" him win. It's phony. He knows it. You know it. You don't want it to happen too often. Watch your child's reaction and "play it by ear."

I know what you mean about competition at this age.
My eight-year-old is so competitive he will cheat
to win. How can I help him?

First be certain of your own feelings about the importance of winning. Sometimes we criticize cheating to win in government and business and cheating to get higher grades in school yet, at the same time, make winning or being the best so important at home that children are encouraged to cheat. Watch parents "kill the umpire" for calling little Johnny out on strikes at the Little League game, and you will know why some children have to do any-thing—lie, cheat, steal—to win. Some children come to feel that they will not be loved or valued by their parents unless they win or are the best—by any means necessary. We parents do this because our children are our last chance to live out our unfulfilled dreams —whether it's to be a major league baseball player, a singer, or a lawyer. That's unfair! Your child should have a chance to carve out and live his own life. In addition, if he senses that success means so much to you, not doing well can become a very good way to frustrate and irritate you, his powerful, controlling parents. Many teen-age "drop-outs" or "runaways" are doing just that.

It helps to say very directly that you believe that the way you play or compete is as important as winning. You must be satisfied when your child makes his *best effort* and enjoys himself but loses. One eight-year-old cautiously told his father how he dropped a pop fly with the bases loaded. They laughed about it together. The father, in a matter-of-fact way, told the youngster that he was sure that he was embarrassed and his teammates were upset. When the youngster acknowledged that this was the case, his father went on to say something like, "Some days you win and some days you lose, but it's fun to keep trying." A few days later the boy won the ballgame with a hit.

This attitude, and not "kill the umpire," helps the child become a good competitor, yet able to operate under less pressure with less need to win at all costs. Had the father gotten uptight about the error, not only would the child have been under great pressure, but he would have been less likely to talk to his father about such a situation next time.

Speaking of competition, my four-year-old
tries to keep up with my eight-year-old.
Isn't that bad for them both?

The eight-year-old is bigger, stronger, and knows more about the world. He will tease and attack the younger child . . . often verbally, sometimes physically. At the same time he is often a teacher, helper, and a protector of the younger child. Unless it is too much of the former and too little of the latter, trying to keep up with big brother is helpful for your younger child. Big brother helps the young child with motor and physical development, language and thinking, social and moral development. It is less frustrating to your youngest to have a model who is not as big, strong, and able as his parents but more able than himself. The teasing and attack is one way the eight-year-old handles his own feelings of fear, anger, and frustration. The teaching and taking care of "little brother" helps the older child feel better about himself because he's able to help somebody else.

Though it is sometimes hard to take, the teasing, competition, and fights between your children can be quite healthy. Children want your affection and attention, and they want to be successful and able. They compete with each other and are jealous of the success of each other in their relations with you, the world, and others. They put each other down to feel good about themselves, and yet, most children in a reasonably well-functioning family—at this age—love each other dearly. Child-development specialists call this competitive behavior sibling rivalry.

With your help in not letting things go too far, calling for fairness, and helping them discuss and resolve their differences, your children will develop socially acceptable ways of handling conflict. In the meantime they let out anger, handle frustration, and compete with people who—in the long run—will be more tolerant than nonfamily members and parents. In fact, a certain amount of sparring is excitement and fun, and they will do "little things" to each other to keep conflict going. You can clamp down and stop the fussing and fighting altogether if you really want to, but that can create some other problems. We think it is better to permit disputes within limits that you and the children can tolerate.

It is important to protect the younger child, particularly when there is a wide age difference and the children are not of the same size or strength. On the other hand, the younger child should not be "allowed to get away with murder" because he is younger. Helping your younger child understand that he will be able to do the same things as older children when he gets to be their age will cut down on some of his frustration and disappointment, sense of failure, and inadequacy.

My children only fight when I'm around. Why is this?

It is very interesting that the same two children who fuss and fight when parents are home—when things are going well overall—often turn into adorable angels and helpmates when the babysitter arrives. Or the oldest, when left as a sitter at twelve or thirteen years, is very responsible for the younger child. The presence of the parents provides the security which allows it "to all hang out." When they are not there, it is better to band together in mutual support.

My eight-year-old son is a good reader, but he brags and calls the other kids dummies. How should I handle this?

Boasting is quite common at this age, but you should quietly but persistently discourage putting down losers or less able people as well as excessive bragging, although there is nothing wrong with reasonable pride. A helpful approach would be something like, "Freddy, I'm glad that you are a good reader and you should be proud. But if you brag and make other people feel bad about themselves, they won't like you very much." You can remind him of the time he was irritated by Joe's bragging or his brother's teasing for things he couldn't do. You can explain that some people are good in one thing and not so good in another.

When there are physical or mental reasons that one child will never do as well as your child or most other children, you should explain that they are different and that is okay . . . as long as they are doing the best they can. You want to help a talented and successful child develop an attitude of respect for the less able . . . even to assist them when it is not condescending or harmful to do so.

Let him do his bragging or talking about his success with you or other family members with whom he is not in immediate competition. He *should* be able to feel good about his accomplishment. Don't deflate his pride. We have seen gifted black children hide their talents because their classmates made them feel they shouldn't have them—especially in areas as "far out" as poetry or ballet, not to mention math and reading. The classmates were victims of society's brainwashing. You may have to protect your child's freedom to be good whenever and wherever he has the ability by explaining his classmates' behavior to him in words that he will understand, such as "Some people have made black children feel that they should not be good in math, but you have the right to do whatever you can do . . . as long as you don't hurt other people for no reason."

*Won't such attitudes make my child
too nice for the real world?*

No, but we understand your concern. An honored professional football coach has said, "Winning isn't everything, it's the only thing." An ex-attorney general of the United States has said that it is so important to win that lying, stealing, and cheating to do so is okay. People in business and government too often illustrate this point. An attitude of "They're all doing it" has developed among too many people in this country. In this climate it is understandable why a youngster rigged his soapbox derby car in order to have a better chance of winning. Such attitudes are fast making the country a jungle. It is in this kind of climate that the rights and needs of so many vulnerable people—minorities, women, children, the elderly—get trampled on.

Because the scandals get the headlines we forget that most people prefer fair play—even when they grow cynical about competitive excesses and engage in them themselves. As long as you permit and encourage vigorous, aggressive, competitive thought and action, but discourage cheating, lying, stealing, hurting others or looking down on the less successful, your child will become a healthy competitor and a fair person.

But it *is* important to help your child learn how to handle a cheater, liar, and thief. One of the reasons that wrongdoers can get away with so much is that too many people, as children, are not allowed to see "bad" or are not taught how to handle it. A child who is not allowed to play with a child who cheats does not learn how to handle a cheater. An adult who as a child was told that cheaters don't win or don't go to heaven can become disillusioned or can have a need not to see the truth. It is particularly difficult for him when the wrongdoer turns out to be someone in a position of trust. That is why so many people can't imagine a President or a minister lying, and have so much trouble taking action against them.

How should I teach my child to cope with wrongdoing?

It is best to wait for your child's natural response to a cheater or wrongdoer of any kind. If she tells him that she's not going to play with him if he cheats, great! But in some life situations it would be to the cheaters' advantage and her disadvantage if she quits. Because of this, we suggest that if the first approach doesn't work that she deliberately cheat back with an offer to play fair if the cheater promises to play fair. And we don't tell children that only good people are successful and go to heaven! We don't know about heaven, but we sure know that a great number of successful people down here are wrongdoers. In the real-life fairy tale, sometimes Cinderella is never found . . . her pumpkin never becomes a carriage and her clothes remain in rags.

Children have to come to understand this about adult life without becoming disillusioned or upset. Again, we don't need to drop the fairy tales or fantasy or children's books, but we need to help children learn to deal with the world the way it really is, incident by incident.

The Question of Work and Rewards

What kinds of chores are helpful for children in this age group?

Finding work for the young child in this age of automation is difficult. At one time, children were helping to bring in water, taking care of the chickens, and picking cotton by six or seven years of age. A few still do. Their contributions help keep the family going. The work of such children was real and needed, and they could feel good about themselves because they were contributing to the well-being of the family. We are not suggesting that there is a need to return to picking cotton, but we are suggesting that you look very carefully for real jobs and ways that your child can contribute to the family's welfare.

Regular responsibilities such as carrying out the garbage and helping make the beds are useful yet not critical, and they do provide an opportunity for the child to contribute in some way. Again, this is a place where children of working parents may have "one up" on other children. If they are not overburdened by responsibilities for younger brothers and sisters, taking care of the house and preparing meals, they can have a real sense of making a vital contribution to the welfare of the family. If you are a working parent, it helps to explain to your child why you are asking him to take on certain responsibilities that other children in the community might not have. It also helps to recognize and express your appreciation for the ability he displays and the contribution he is making.

For most children, however, their real work today is in school. We will discuss the child-school relationship in detail in Chapter 6.

Should I reward my child for his help? If so, how?

Some parents believe that giving children money for good performances makes money or other material reward too important. We agree. You want to help your child become a good performer because of his or her own personal pride primarily. Reward from the outside should be of less importance. Help your child understand that he is working, writing, reading, painting for *his* benefit and pleasure more than yours, working to do *his* part, not yours. Sure you are happy about his good work, but because he is able to do it for himself, not you. But a child is a child and an occasional treat for a job well done won't hurt your training and makes childhood a lot more fun. When they are able to do work that you would pay others to do, such as mowing the lawn, then paying your children for their work makes sense.

How about a regular weekly allowance?

This can be a helpful way to help your children establish good savings and spending habits which can follow them the rest of their lives. The amount you give should depend on what you can afford and what you consider a reasonable amount to spend. Even when you can afford to give your children a great deal, you should help them learn that "money doesn't grow on trees."

We have seen a number of middle- and upper-middle-income black families have trouble here. Most of us in this group just made it "running scared all the way." We want our children to have all the things that money can buy. But most of us don't have enormous wealth that will be passed on. More than providing three TV's and three weeks in Bermuda in February, we must pass on knowledge and habits which will help Junior make it as we were fortunate enough to do.

Junior must learn, like everybody else, that money doesn't grow on trees; that it is good work that most often leads to achievement and a reasonable income. He must be taught to "save some" and "spend some" and not to buy a toy or treat every time he goes in a store. This is the age—not twelve, fifteen, or twenty-five years— when these lessons must be learned. It's not easy. The children of a physician we know periodically respond to this message with a friendly "cheap, cheap" noise. Their father's friendly response back was, "That's right, I'm Mr. Cheap Cheap and I still say that 'money doesn't grow on trees!' " We are not suggesting that you be stingy . . . just reasonable. But it's all out the window if you are conspicuous consumers. The message is what you do more than what you say.

Don't be embarrassed if you can't give your child what the people down the street can give, or give even if they can't afford it. If you can't afford to give as much as you would like, you should explain this to your child. They may protest but will not love you less because of this. You can give in other ways. Special treats, favorite meals, family trips to favorite places all can be better and more important ways of saying to your child "We care a great deal about you" than giving them money.

Helping Your Young School-Ager Manage

It is a struggle to get my seven-year-old boy to do anything.
He is late for the school bus. He won't do his chores without
a fuss. He stays up late. Everything is a hassle. Then he
complains about my picking on him. What should I do?

You are not alone in this situation. These reactions are usually a part of the independence-dependence struggle which most children go through. One part of them wants to be independent and responsible for themselves and not ordered around by adults. Another part of them wants to be taken care of and dependent just as they were as younger children. Having things done for them which they could do for themselves makes them feel inadequate, weak, and powerless. On the other hand, it means that somebody is looking after them and they have a feeling of safety and security.

They can't acknowledge that they are having trouble giving up their dependency. They don't even know that's what's going on. They try to have their cake and eat it, too. They demand independence and less interference from adults and at the same time do things which bring adults into their lives to make them do what they're supposed to do. To avoid serious problems of this nature later on, it is important to avoid getting locked into struggles with your children about the things they should do as early as possible.

The best approach here—though never instantly or permanently successful—is to help your child go to bed for his own good and not as a favor to you; to help him catch the school bus so that he will have a good record at school for himself and not for you; to help him do his chores so that he can meet his responsibilities to the family and not just as a favor to you. In everything he or she does, you are encouraging your child to establish and meet his or her own standards—unless these standards are unacceptable to you, in which case that needs to be discussed and worked out with your child. If you don't jam your standards down your youngster's throat, for the most part, his or her standards are going to look pretty much like your own.

Now you may be saying, "That's an awful lot of work. It's easier to make him do what he's supposed to do." When a child is young, you can simply force him to do what you want him to. That is easier in the short run but more troublesome in the long run. By the time most children are ten and twelve and certainly by fifteen or sixteen (and remember by then you are ten to twelve years older) it is very difficult to control them physically. Even when the physical problems aren't that serious, the verbal fights can be *very* unpleasant. It is much better to take a little more time and help your child develop inner responsibility and ways of doing things that you both can live with at a later age than to get instant control through "making him do things" at an earlier age.

How would you handle a child who needs to
go to bed but wants to watch television?

We would suggest something like this:

> "Okay, John, it's our time to turn off the television and go to bed."
> "Aww, I don't want to go to bed. I want to watch television."
> "We agreed that you need to be in bed by ten o'clock in order to feel good enough to get up in the morning."

. . . or to feel good in school, or whatever your agreement was. The tone of your voice and your manner must show that you really expect him to do as he promised. If you are too strong you will sound like you're making him do it, which will not help him feel that he's taking responsibility for his own behavior.

If it turns out that there are five more minutes to go on a television program or he will finish his puzzle or model or whatever he's doing in a few more minutes, it's best to give him the extra time, then expect him to go right to bed. It helps to agree on how much more time will be needed and set the new finishing time. If he doesn't want to go after you have been reasonable, "making him go" is now justified, but it helps to point out that you would prefer that he lived up to his agreement. When there is a special program on, you might want to do more than extend the time a few minutes and make an exception to the rule. In all of this, you help your child learn to live up to basic agreements, yet be reasonable and able to make exceptions to the rule when that makes sense. On occasions where your child is particularly re-sistant, you might want to point out to him that if he doesn't want you nagging him about everything, then he should do what he has agreed to do without your having to push him. Don't use this one too often or it will lose its effectiveness.

So far I'm with you. But what if he
won't settle down in his bed?

Then you've got a real procrastinator (in one way or another, he puts things off) on your hands. Children like this will move from the television to their bedroom at your insistence, but once there will start to read a book or get involved in some other activity rather than go to bed. Here it is important simply to state the same expectation that he go to bed all over again without getting terribly upset . . . although you want to be a little more firm this time. You may have to eventually set the time that you're going to give him, and turn off the light yourself if he doesn't make it in that period. Even here, it is best not to get terribly upset . . . to understand it as a struggle the child is having in himself, but wants to draw you into. It helps to think, as in the spiritual, "I shall not be moved"—or in this case, be drawn into a fight. When you turn out the light you might want to indicate that you hope he'll be able to do it himself without your getting involved the next time.

On some occasions—but again, not too often—when he really tries very hard to start a fight or a struggle, you might say very directly, "John, you're trying to get me into a fight, and I don't want to fight with you. I can see you're having trouble taking responsibility for going to bed on time yourself, but you'll be able to do so later on."

Frustrating. Children can get you very angry. But that's what they're trying to do and it's best if you can avoid it much of the time. Sometimes you won't be able to, and that's all right, too. They *need* to know when you have reached your limit. You are a human being and not a machine, and they need to know that, too. But again, you want to try and handle touchy situations through talk which helps them develop inner control rather than use talk or actions that simply attempt to control them.

No matter how much I shout and threaten,
my child still won't obey. Why is this?

One parental habit that leads to trouble very often is what we call "long distance communication." Once you sense real resistance and your child has had a reasonable time to turn off the TV, yelling for him to do so from the upstairs bedroom when he is in the basement is an invitation to be ignored. Stop . . . take a few minutes to talk close up . . . and it will usually save you more energy than you thought you were saving by calling. Where there is real resistance and you must call again it is especially important to be close up . . . still friendly . . . more firm . . . certain that you can handle the situation without fantastic threats . . . but close up.

Fantastic threats, now *there* is another problem. Some parents go to town: "I'll kill you. I'll knock your block off. I'll beat you to within one inch of your life." When such parents deny privileges they do it like this: "You won't get your allowance for three months" or "You can't go to Bob's house for three weeks." Children figure out very quickly that you can't and won't follow through on fantastic threats. You and your threats can be ignored. Threats of punishment, when used, should be in line with the way you actually punish. The approach to punishment we suggested in Chapter 4 is good for all ages.

Once you have the pattern of expecting your child to do things and meet his own responsibilities fairly well established, he will take pride in meeting these commitments—although he won't admit it to you. From time to time he will still procrastinate and try to draw you into a fight. Sometimes you can shortcut a struggle over control by doing whatever you've asked him to do yourself. Again, you don't want to do this too often, but when you really don't want a fight and he's working hard to get one, it's better to dump the garbage yourself, or turn out the cellar light, or whatever minor thing it is, than to spend hours and even days in conflict. Children who have developed pride in taking care of their own chores will usually run to do the job before you can do it. After all, what is turning out the light or dumping the garbage yourself anyway? Your action of doing it simply says, "I'm disappointed that you weren't able to do this minor thing yourself. I'll do it." You might want to say this. Again, don't do this too often. When it seems necessary, you will want to suggest that they will be able to do their own chores themselves next time.

Much of what you suggest won't work for me. What can I do?

True, where parent-child struggles have become a way of life, some of these approaches won't work. If you get up to carry out the garbage your son was supposed to carry out when he hasn't accepted responsibility, he might say, "Fine, and when you get through with that you can polish my shoes." Other children locked in a battle will resist parental control by not hearing. We have had parents bring children for treatment who have said, "Maybe we ought to check his ears first because I can stand right over him and yell and he won't budge. At other times his hearing is okay."

Other parents report that their children do just the opposite of what they say. "Stop running" causes more running and "hurry up" brings a slowdown. This problem can become extreme and may need professional treatment. It is called "the oppositional child syndrome" by doctors.

All of these problems are a part of the independence-dependence struggle which goes on inside a child and between parent and child. You will see some of this in all children and between all parents and children. If you are caught in this struggle to the point where nothing seems to work, you need to try and get out of it and help your child accept independence and responsibility more gracefully.

First, you should think about the ways and reasons you are demanding certain kinds of behavior. Do they make sense? Are they really necessary? Is it really necessary to scream and yell repeatedly to get your child to do something? Why can't you just talk to him and expect him to do it? You might then calmly talk about it with your child and explain that you are unhappy about having to yell and scream at him all the time, and that you are sure that he's unhappy about being yelled and screamed at. You might suggest that the two of you together work out some way to avoid such struggle.

There are usually three or four problem times in every house (like bedtime, bath time, and taking-out-the-dog time) which repeatedly cause difficulty. When the moment comes to do these things, you might discuss them together and decide what is a reasonable time to be in bed, a reasonable time to take the dog out, and so on. Once you have made these agreements and established a kind of contract or understanding of what your child's responsibilities are, you should then try to encourage the independent and responsible side of your child just as we suggested for the procrastinating child. It will take *a great deal of time and patience* because the problem is more difficult now. Your child will try to see if you are "for real" about this. If you continue to respond in the new way—calmly, firmly, with reasonable expectations—your child will gradually become less oppositional and take pride in meeting his responsibility. But again, with a serious problem, you may need professional help.

*Can you encourage your child to give you
trouble while asking him not to?*

Yes. Ranting and raving as if you are powerless, or throwing up your hands as if to say that your child is hopeless, are both good ways. Comments like, "This girl is going to drive me to drink" or "This boy is impossible!" are very encouraging to your child. Calling in your spouse for minor problems, "Paul" or "Louise," "You're going to have to do something about this boy, I can't do a thing with him" is another goodie. In a struggle it means you're on the ropes and about to go down. Your child is winning and will often sit there with a pleased look on his seven-year-old "killer" face. But most important that part of you that enjoys getting beaten up—and as strange as it seems we all have a little of that—enjoys his behavior . . . and he knows it.

Back up. Admit to yourself that there is no way in the world that the vast majority of children in this age group can't be managed. Drop the dramatics. Work out clear expectations with your child. Be firm but flexible enough to make exceptions to the rules when they make sense. Calmly follow through until Junior completes his job. He will gradually come to realize that you really mean business.

The Importance of Games, Activities, and Family Fun

My seven-year-old is frequently bored. How can I help him?

First, think about whether he is actually bored and unhappy or just a loner. If a child appears to be happy while alone and is also capable of getting along well with other children when they are around, then don't worry about it. On the other hand, bored children or children who are *always* alone, even when they don't appear unhappy, need some help.

First you want to make certain that there is enough to do around your house—games to play, cookies to make, that kind of thing. Second, you want to encourage your child to visit friends and to have friends in. Five- and six-year-olds love company. It is an opportunity to have others on *their* turf. If the distance to a friend's house is long or the way is dangerous—even if it's the apartment three floors down—you need to take the time, even if you are busy, to take them there. It *is* that important!

You should also think about whether your seven- or eight-year-old feels free to bring his friends home. You don't want to tolerate chaos and disorder in your house, but if you are uptight, fussing, and scolding a great deal, your child might not want his friends to see you in action. It helps to have a place in your house—even a time, if it's not a big house—where your child and their friends can "mess around." Much fussing and scolding is centered around the disorder caused by active young hands. It is best to permit some disorder at some time and place. A certain amount of messiness is normal and healthy. It will not lead to disordered thinking or behavior if you help your child to learn to clean up after his play.

What can I do to make the time my child and I spend together as stimulating for her as possible?

Like all of us, children can get in a rut, do the same things, and get less pleasure from them each time. Your questions and specific suggestions about activities that would be a nice change can be helpful. You may need to help the five- or six-year-old plan her day. You will also want to plan yours to permit her to have outside activities, indoor activities, a little reading, a little rest, a shopping trip, a little music—at times that are convenient to your schedule. If your child appears bored all the time, and no amount of effort to get her involved with other children or different activities seems to help, you may need to get some professional help.

Finally, you might take a look at how much time you spend doing things with your child other than telling her what to do and what not to do. She spends a lot of time with you during which she is nothing more than an unimportant part of adult business. She needs, and you need, some time together which is playtime. Modern life keeps us busy and often away from home so much that some of us simply do not take the time to enjoy our families. It is important to seize the time and make the occasion to enjoy and do things together.

*Boredom often leads to moodiness. I can see this all too well
in the case of my child but nothing I do seems to help.
What is the best way to handle this situation?*

Most children are moody at one time or another. When they are
moody they are cross and difficult and hard to get along with.
They will accuse you of being bad parents. They will accuse you
of favoring the other children. They will accuse you of not caring
about them. Nothing you can do or say will help during this
period . . . particularly reminding them of all the good things
you've done for them. That only makes things worse. They know
that.

Moods are natural and normal. We all have them. The best way
to help is to avoid being provoked by your youngsters' accusations
and insults. If you get angry and attack them, they will "read" this
as proof of their rejection. You can point out that you understand
they're in a bad mood and you would like to help whenever they
will let you. Your show of concern says, "I'm with you but I
respect your feelings." All of us get angry with the person who
wants to joke when we're down. You are also demonstrating that
you can accept their bad moods as well as their good ones. This is
reassuring and part of the motivation for the return of their spirit
and confidence. Often if you can get them into a game or situation
which they have enjoyed and had great success with in the past,
the bad mood, like a cloud, will move on and a bright mood, like
the sun, will soon shine in.

*We would like to spend more time with our children, but
we can't stand those five- and six-year-old games. Should
we play when we're bored and the children know it?*

A few minutes of checkers, dominoes, or other games can be terribly important to your child. Try and play the games that you can
tolerate best. Don't play to the point of total boredom. Your child
may want to play until he wins, or play over and over to keep you
with him. It can be helpful to set a limit on game time . . . without being rigid about it. Some people put aside a regular time, ten
or fifteen minutes after dinner, for game-playing. The regularity
reduces the need of your child to have you play for long periods of
time.

Some parents love to play children's games and can really let go
and laugh and shout and be thrilled just like the children. If this is

not true in your case, it's nothing to feel guilty about. Whether or not you have the ability both to feel like a child and to be a mature adult at the appropriate times is a matter of luck. Family fun is just as important a way to provide the training, learning, and sense of security that your child needs as the information you give and the limits you set.

*I have seen parents playing marbles and "street games"
with their children. Isn't that a bit much?*

No. To each his own—as long as parents don't force themselves on the children and *their* play. Many children enjoy a game of marbles, a little stickball, hopscotch, baseball, bike riding, and other activities with their parents. Sometimes they will want you. Sometimes they won't. (Don't pout when they don't.) You don't want to dominate the game, play too hard, or play too long. This is particularly true for older parents and with older children—twelve or so. There is a great temptation, as you approach forty and your youngster approaches the peak of physical excellence, to win at all costs. Your play should be more fun and togetherness than competition. It is easier to play indoors together than outdoors . . . particularly if it means leaving an apartment on the twentieth floor. But outdoor togetherness is important and you should push yourself to arrange it.

Why is family fun important?

Family fun is the best relief and protection we have against the stress of the world: wars and rumors of war, racism, trouble on the job, or on the street. It can even be helpful as a way to deal with conflict and trouble in the family. We can't really control religious, civil rights, labor, political party, or government agencies that are supposed to protect us and give us a sense of well-being. We *can* work to make our family a place of fun more often than it is a place of conflict and trouble.

*What are some important things for parents and
children in the five-to-eight-year-old age group
to do together, other than play games?*

Special days like birthdays and holidays, and special events, including trips and bicycle riding, are important. We were once amazed by the story of a teen-ager from the Harlem section of New York City whose whole life took a turn for the better because of a birthday party—not one he was given, but one he gave. A mother asked him to help give a party for her seven-year-old son, whose father didn't live at home. She felt that the involvement of a male would make the event mean more to her male son.

The importance, the pride, the sense of "I'm somebody" the seven-year-old felt—and his appreciation to the giver—was shared and felt by the teen-ager. It became an important event in shaping his own future. Parents and children feel a strengthening of the bond between them when they give and receive in this way. Holidays—particularly Mother's Day, Father's Day and Valentine's Day—offer the same opportunity to give, receive, and strengthen the bond of affection.

An exchange of cards, making your own cards or notes, a special meal at home, dinner by candlelight, dinner out or any other way you can think of to say, "I care. I love you. I appreciate. You are important," will help your child have good feelings about himself or herself. This will lead to a positive self-image as much as repeating "Black is Beautiful." When it's not *his* day, the seven- or eight-year-old, even the five- or six-year-old, will still get a special kick out of helping Mom or Dad pick out the cards, plan the party, or however you mark each other's birthdays. This kind of participation helps teach a child to show respect and affection in specific ways.

Suppose we don't make a big fuss about holidays in our house. What then?

Some people have gotten away from marking special days in special ways—Christmas, Thanksgiving, Fourth of July, occasions like that. If you don't mark these days, it would probably help to mark something—important dates of your own religion or belief for example. Pausing to mark things that we believe in, things we hope for and accomplishments that have been made, give purpose, direction and meaning to life. Some of our warmest memories as grownups—upon which we draw for much of our sense of security and well-being in adult life—include the barbecued ribs on the Fourth of July, the New Year's Eve prayer watch at the Baptist Church, and decorating a Christmas tree. Even if you no longer choose to observe these occasions, you do want to give your child *some* experience tree on which he can hang his emotions . . . Martin Luther King Day, African Liberation Day, etcetera.

Why are family trips important?

The family trip is an important way to introduce your young child to new things, to stimulate his thinking; it is an important opportunity to be together; it's an important way to play together. It's a chance—particularly for the seven- and eight-year-old—to be useful helpers preparing for the outing. A picnic offers the best opportunity. Don't do all the planning and work and then tell your children a few minutes or even hours before that you are going on a picnic. Let them know far enough in advance so that they can help choose the time and place, and the menu. They can also help prepare the food and have their say in what games to take along. Trips to the museum, to hear the Jackson Five, the zoo, all require this kind of planning.

We have found that including your child in the planning is important to the success of the trip. Children act up less when they are not "shuttled" from one place to another with no say and no part in what's going on. It is difficult for them to have positive feelings about themselves when they are treated like baggage. This does not mean that you must do what your children say. For a number of reasons—including money and time—this may be impossible, and you will want to explain to your youngsters the whys and why nots of what you do. But hopefully you are open to their suggestions. Children, particularly when they are encouraged often to contribute, can come up with some good ideas, remember things you forgot, and be generally helpful in a number of ways.

Children can learn to organize and plan if you can organize and plan and give assignments to them which they can handle and will make them truly useful to you. Make certain that you have what you need and give yourself plenty of time so that you won't be anxious about being late and, therefore, irritable toward your children. The better you can plan ahead without being obsessed with planning, the more fun you can have together. You will be less likely to "dump" on each other. Learning to plan and organize is one of the most important skills that exists in this modern world, where almost everything must be planned and organized. This early experience of planning with you helps your child learn to plan and organize in school, at work and in every situation where things are not planned and organized for him.

Do black children have greater trouble planning and organizing than children from other groups?

Many people—black, white, middle-income and low-income—have trouble planning and organizing. They have trouble doing first things first and second things second and the least important thing last. The housewife who has two hours to get ready for a party and decides to clean the insides of her cabinets is an example. But there does appear to be more trouble in planning among people who have had little experience, or little reason to plan for long-range activities. Children who grow up in chaotic and disorganized families often have trouble planning and organizing. You can see, then, that blacks, closed out of the larger society and suffering from more stress, might have more families and children with this problem. On the other hand, blacks involved in church and other social programs are likely to have as much training in organization and planning as anyone else . . . or more.

Because we as a group do perhaps have more children who have difficulties in these areas, we will discuss this matter further in Chapter 6.

We seem to do fine planning and organizing local trips, but our vacation trips are a disaster. My husband and I argued and were unhappy most of our last vacation, and we said we'll never take the children with us again until they are teen-agers. What happened?

Vacations can be more trouble than fun, but they don't have to be. All that we have said about local outings is even more important on vacations . . . regardless of how you travel. Familiar things, people, and activities give us a sense of security and well-being without our even being aware of it. When we are suddenly separated from these things and faced with new situations one after another, we can become upset without even knowing why. We just know that we're irritated with the children, with each other, and that the children are fussing more than usual. Some of their acting up is a response to parental uneasiness and fighting, plus their own uneasiness.

The first thing to do to avoid such situations is to realize they often occur, and why. Planning and organizing your trip well in advance—especially how much you're going to spend—can help. But the day to day planning of where to go and how to get there should be the subject of family conversation. Getting enough rest is also important on vacations. We generally do more than we ordinarily do in trying to "see it all." Fatigue can lead to irritation and conflict. It is also important to plan so that you can see some of the things that are important to you and the children can see some of the things that are important to them. Vacation trips provide a good opportunity to learn to give and take or compromise in a way that's fair to all.

Vacations—wherever they may lead you—can be a source of great mind stimulation. Talking about the trip afterwards, looking at your photographs, and writing stories about what happens during the vacation period can be particularly rewarding to your seven- or eight-year-old. You might suggest—but don't force this—that he keep a log or draw pictures during the trip itself. This is a good way to use the unplanned hours. Just as at home, your child will need some leisure time that doesn't include you.

*Some of my eight-year-old's leisure-time activities seem
so worthless—like reading comic books.
Shouldn't I discourage this?*

Comics have great appeal to children in this age group, particularly seven- and eight-year-olds, for very good reasons. Inside your child a struggle is going on between good and evil—your rules and regulations are slowly becoming his against his desires to have anything he wants, do anything he wants. It certainly simplifies things to have Mr. America, Superman, the Globetrotters—all the "good guys"—triumphant over evil. But evil needs its moments. Youngsters also like to see children like themselves getting away with the kind of bad behavior they'd like to be getting away with—thus the popularity of Dennis the Menace and others who drive their parents up the wall. (And you must read it to them, yet!) No wonder most parents want their children to read as soon as possible.

Superman also takes care of something else that goes on in a child. We mentioned earlier that children in this age group often bite off more than they can chew. They are often faced with not being able to do what you and other grownups can manage—this makes them feel like failures. It sure is nice to have "Mr. Good" be "Mr. Bad" who can "do it all"!

Comics won't decrease your child's interest in reading other stories. Comics take care of one set of needs. Other books take care of other needs. You want to make certain that your eight-year-old gets to the library and other places where he'll be in contact with other kinds of books. Comics are ordinarily not hateful or vicious. But you want to take a look at them from time to time. You don't want to let some adult "humorist" take care of his own anger and hate feelings at your child's expense. Children have enough angry, hostile feelings of their own to learn how to control without taking on those of adults.

By the time your child becomes an adult, there will probably be more nonwork time for everybody. It is important to help your youngster learn how to use his leisure now—both with others and alone. Give some thought to hobbies . . . things like model building and painting. Many adults who have never learned how to use nonwork time are miserable on long weekends, fussing and fighting with relatives and friends . . . and worse.

CHAPTER 6

The Black Child in School— An Overview

Before moving on to discuss the nine- through twelve-year-old, let's pause for a moment and take a look at a very important development in your child's life. His days are no longer centered around his family and his home—by now he is deeply involved in a whole new world, the world of school. What problems does his new environment present to him? What is the most effective way for you to help him cope with them? How can his teachers best aid him to fulfill his potential?

Many factors are involved in the all-important question of education, and one of these is the interaction between you and your youngster's teachers—between home and school. Your child's development is no longer in your hands alone but has been entrusted in part to specialists in the field of education. It is by working together that parents and teachers alike can best achieve their common goal.

With an eye toward furthering home-school interaction, we are dividing this chapter, devoted to the black child in school, into three sections. The first deals with questions parents ask, the second with questions asked by teachers, and the third with queries from parents, teachers, and friends (all those who affect the life of black children in one way or another). We hope that by studying each other's questions, each group will gain a greater awareness of the other's problems and think about ways they can help to solve them for the good of the children involved.

FOR PARENTS

Home-School Interaction

*I am busy and my child is doing well. Is it still important
for me to be involved with the school program?*

Many parents must work, and it is difficult to be involved with the
school program at the same time. But if it is at all possible, you
should do so. It is important not to let other activities—such as
politics, social clubs and volunteer work—keep you from involvement with your youngster's education. Your child should come
first. This is particularly true in the early elementary school years.
Your youngster will want you to be less involved at a later period.
But even then, he or she will want evidence of your interest.

It is sometimes difficult for parents to see the importance and
the effect of their involvement in the school program. But an
important transfer of attitudes and feelings must take place as
your child moves from the home to the school. You and your
family have been the important developers and motivators of your
youngster up until now. Your relationship has helped your child
develop a sense of security and competence. The teacher and staff
of the school must now do the same thing. Your presence and
interest gives a stamp of approval to the staff and the work of the
school in a way which makes it possible for your child to identify
with school work and school people.

If a parent is not involved in the school program and shows no
interest in the work and performance of a child, the school program may not be as highly valued by a child as it should be. If you
are highly critical of the school program and the school staff, you
can send a double message to your child: "The school is your
friend and hope for the future," and, "The school is your enemy."
This can cause your child to do poorly in school—in work and in
relationships with staff and other children.

*Suppose I disapprove strongly of something
the school is doing? What then?*

In cases where you disagree with the school, it is important to
work this out with the staff rather than involve your child in the

conflict. This problem is similar to the problem which exists when two parents disagree. Children will play one adult against another —as a way of dealing with their own fears and feelings of powerlessness—if we permit them to do so. This does not mean that you should teach your child to tolerate anything the teacher "puts down." On the other hand, it does not help your child to believe everything he or she has to say about a teacher or school until you have investigated the situation with an open mind. When you believe someone has been unfair to your young child, it is up to you to act in his behalf. As your youngster gets older, should such situations develop, you should try to have three-way discussions—you, the teacher, and the child—around any given problem. We believe that it is as important for children to learn to work out conflicts—to learn to hear how they come across to other people and what other people expect from them—as it is for them to learn their ABC's.

Why should I bother to go to school? I asked the
teacher, "How is Donald doing?" She said, "Fine."
I still don't know how he's doing.

When you want to know how your child is doing in school, go armed with specific questions. Know what courses he's taking. Find out how he's doing in each. Can he concentrate? Is he able to complete assignments? Is he capable of organizing his work and developing a strategy to complete it? Does he understand concepts? This is more important than getting the correct answer. For example, we watched a bright youngster miss nine out of sixteen problems on a math test. When we took a close look at the paper, we saw that he had made the same kind of subtraction error every time. Once the concept was explained to him, he got all of the problems correct.

Is he able to explain what he understands? Is he able to express his understanding in writing? Does he participate in class discussions? Does he appear to work up to his ability? What are the teacher's goals for the class and for your child? Is your youngster meeting these goals? If not, why not and what can be done? You can get some evidence of progress by looking at the written work starting back at the beginning of the year and observing the changes as the year progresses. If such work is not on hand you might indicate to the teacher that it would be helpful to you if she could find it. Finally, you should ask how you can help the school help your child.

Our daughter is unhappy in her classroom because the teacher shouts at the students all day long and we seldom shout at home. Can this be harmful, and how can I help?

Just as there are too many parents who routinely yell and scream at their children, there are too many teachers who do the same. Younger children, and particularly sensitive children, often feel uneasy in such a situation. They frequently imagine that the teacher does not like them, even when the yelling is not directed toward them. You should make certain that the situation is not extreme and is not directed toward your child. When you have assured yourself of this, you want to help your child learn to understand that that's simply the teacher's style and not to take it too seriously. Sooner or later children have to learn to deal with a full range of personalities in a way which does not badly affect their own performance. With your help now, they will be better able to handle such situations later.

On the other hand, should you find that the situation is extreme, you should try to help the teacher function in a better way. You might observe in the classroom and then discuss your child's unhappiness with the teacher. If you are tactful in pointing out the cause for your concern, the teacher may well reduce the yelling or make an effort to make it clear that she does not dislike your child. If this is not successful, you may have to discuss the problem with the school principal, or someone else in charge. The more closely you are involved with the school, the easier it is to deal with such problems.

We have always found it more helpful to state the problem and ask how you can help rather than to go into the classroom and raise the roof. Teachers don't want to hurt children. But for many reasons—problems caused by the society, school problems, their own problems, the nature of the growing child—they sometimes do. If you can see their side of a problem, it will increase the chance that they will see your side and make an extra effort to make an adjustment. In addition, it is important not to expect miracles. All schools have problems from time to time. At the same time, you don't want to tolerate bad conditions without letting your dissatisfaction be known. But you are much more likely to get the outcome you desire when the teacher does not feel "attacked." It is best to try to create a situation in which you and the teacher are working together for the good of your child.

Some members of the school staff are not good models for our children. What should we do about it?

We have heard parents who wanted their children to learn to be neat complain about a principal who threw his leather jacket on the floor in the corner of his office rather than hang it up; about messy classrooms; about teachers who left the building with the children at the end of the day without giving any time to preparation and organization for tomorrow. Such behavior indicates a disrespect for the community and often indicates an underlying belief that the parents don't care and the children aren't capable; that it is not worth making an extra effort. Many teachers in such settings would like to do better but are simply not allowed to by others. New teachers who come into such situations are often quickly crushed into line.

Many parents are reluctant to do anything about these conditions for fear that their children will pay the price. If this is a possibility, you should organize a number of parents to make your needs and wishes known. Ministers or other responsible community people, including your alderman, can be enlisted to change conditions in your school. But again we caution you not to go after "the enemy." Many people can be helped to function better if you call on their good side rather than putting on the squeeze. Some can't, and the squeeze will be necessary in such cases.

My nine-year-old told me that his white teacher slapped him and called him a nigger. After I got to school and made a screaming fool of myself, he told me it was not true. What was going on?

We must be careful that our own strong emotions about racism and our strong desire to protect our children and prepare them to protect themselves from white racism do not get "used." The fact that there is a good deal of racism around makes this difficult. We know children who have done similar things because they felt they weren't getting enough attention and appreciation from their teacher. They simply played adults against each other in order to get what they wanted. Until children are more mature, they don't confront parents, teachers, or other authority figures and let it be known that they feel they're not being noticed. They often use the immature method you have described here.

Children can sense circumstances that will cause trouble or enable them to manipulate people to get their own way. In most cases they don't see, and in some cases they don't care about, the consequences of their acts as long as they achieve their goal. This can be very troublesome for your child in the future. It can lead to serious personality problems. On the other hand, some people with such personalities become very successful in business and government because they are manipulators. But such personalities often get involved in the kinds of "dirty tricks" in business and government that have been so troublesome in this country—recently revealed so dramatically around the Watergate scandal. You can reduce your child's need to manipulate you and others by helping him learn more healthy ways of dealing with problems.

One black parent, aware that the young mind sometimes handles problems in troublesome ways, responded to a charge of racial injustice in this way:

> "Is that right? That doesn't sound like Miss Smith." [That's why it's important to visit the school or the adults wherever your children are involved. Then you know the likelihood of such events occurring or not occurring.] The mother went on, "That would be mean and unfair if she said that . . . Of course, it would be mean and unfair of you to say that about your teacher if it's not true." [The child hesitated but did not change the story.] The mother went on, "Well, I'll just have to go to school and hear her side of the story. If she did that, she's going to have to apologize to you. If she didn't you'll have to apologize to her."
> With that, the child said, "No she didn't, no she didn't!"

The mother was calm during the discussion. She did not accuse her child of lying. She did not deny the possibility that the teacher had been unfair in a racist way. After the child acknowledged that the incident did not occur, the mother indicated that the child must be upset about something if she made up that kind of story. The child then went on to indicate that she was upset because her mother had started working recently. What the child's behavior was all about was an attempt to ask the question, "Do you still care enough for me that if I'm in trouble you would take time off to come and help me out?" The mother's response not only answered the question—that she would take time out—but it also established the fact that she was not a pushover, gave the child a lesson in fair play, and encouraged direct discussion of the matter rather than setting up a test that would have been troublesome to everybody.

The mother did go to the school shortly thereafter just to make certain that everything was A-OK. In fact that child was getting along very well in a racially integrated classroom with a white teacher.

What do you think the mother should have done if the teacher had called the child a nigger or hit her?

Even if the child provoked the teacher, such a response is inexcusable. Teachers should not permit annoying situations to get to the point that they respond in a verbally or physically abusive way. Where the response is racist, black parents have a responsibility to see that such teachers do not teach their children. Even in situations where a parent doesn't have the power to make changes, a responsible confrontation with the teacher involved or his superior is very likely to cause the teacher to be more careful and responsible in the future. Certainly the teacher—or anybody else responding in a racist way to your child—needs an experience which will change his or her racist attitude. But we know the limitations here, and all we can really do is insist that people be responsible and fair in their relationships with us and our children—even if they maintain racist viewpoints and attitudes. That's their problem. Our job is to make certain that their racist attitudes and behavior do not interfere with our opportunities and performance.

Such confrontations, when handled well, preserve our sense of dignity and can force racists to develop less racist ways of responding to blacks. Angry, hostile attacks, while relieving us of feelings of justified or unjustified anger, often reinforce racist attitudes and hostility toward our children.

My son's teacher says he is hyperactive and should be put on drugs. Do black children tend to be more hyperactive or is this a racial put-down on the part of the school? What should I do?

Several school systems have used drugs to control children who were too active in school. A large number of these children were black. There is no good evidence however that there are more hyperactive (and hyperkinetic) black children than any other group of children. Very often, poor conditions at school and at home are responsible for what is said to be hyperkinetic or hyperactive behavior. In these situations, it is better to work to improve the relationship between the child and the adults than to put the child on a drug.

On the other hand, there are some rare situations in which neurological problems make children too active. Certain kinds of medication can be helpful in these cases. You should talk this over with your doctor and the school very carefully before you permit anyone to use medication to control your child's behavior. Once done, there should be at least two or three evaluations a year to decide whether the medication is needed or not. Ask about these.

Questions of Curriculum and Method

My seven-year-old doesn't bring schoolwork home. Don't you think there is too little emphasis on reading, writing, and arithmetic and too much on fun—art, music, dance, and physical education—in the schools today?

School learning need not be a painful experience. We shouldn't look back to our own school experience to evaluate modern education. The test should be whether your child is learning well and is reasonably relaxed and happy with school. Art, music, dance, and physical education aid body development and expression. These areas can provide a climate in a school which aids in the teaching of basic educational skills. Certain organizing skills which are used in these areas are helpful in reading, writing, and arithmetic.

Sometimes the arts and physical education provide children with a success experience when they are not feeling good about themselves because of difficulty with the "3 R's." We think that every teacher should be trained to use the arts to aid in the academic areas. It is a serious mistake to drop art and physical education—as is being done in many financially pressed areas—when they offer so many benefits. Also they are so basic a part of black culture!

*My son is in an open classroom. Is this kind of
learning good or bad for the black child?*

The open education classroom—with less rigid seating, more
individualized learning programs, more student choice—can be a
useful approach for black children—in fact, for most children. It
can be a particularly helpful approach for children who have not
developed good organization and planning skills. It can also be a
very good way to help children learn to cooperate and talk out
problems that crop up in work and play. The approach lends itself
very well to helping children develop inner controls, self-direction,
and responsible independent action. All of this can lead to a less
stormy adolescence. On the other hand, a poorly functioning open
classroom can be more troublesome than the traditional class. We
will discuss this matter more below.

*My child is in a predominantly white school system, yet
I would like for him to appreciate black culture, know
black history, and develop concern about the black
cause. Is this possible under the circumstances?*

Yes, although it may require more activity on your part than otherwise. This is not necessarily the case, however, since unfortunately
many schools serving predominantly black areas do very little to
achieve these ends either.

With young children, you will want to help them understand
American history as it is rather than the way it is presented in many
schools and texts. You should provide them with information and
books which help them learn about the black experience, achievement, and obstacles to achievement. You should take every opportunity to expose them to black art, literature, and cultural
programs of all kinds. Your participation in and contribution to the
activities of civil rights organizations will impress upon them the
importance of being involved. Most important, you should help
them understand that their own personal development—educational, social, and moral—is the most important contribution that
they can make to the black cause. As the society becomes more
complex, it will be increasingly difficult to maintain and make new
black gains without many more *very* skilled people.

It is possible and important for predominantly white schools to
do more to give all children an honest education. We have seen

enlightened white school districts make an effort to do so. It's interesting to watch the seriousness of eight- or nine-year-old white children putting on plays about the life of Martin Luther King, Jr., or doing research projects on Africa. This is important for their development. You might suggest that your child and his white classmates would benefit from such study and programs if they are not now available. Many school districts are making an effort to develop multiethnic education programs. This makes sense in a multiethnic society.

Why is it important for my child to be on time
and have a good attendance record?

Wherever people work together and depend on each other, being on time and being present, except when there is a good reason not to be, is very important. It is unfair to a classroom or to a work group when someone disrupts or slows down the progress of the group by being late or absent without good cause. People who are late and absent from school as children are likely to be late and absent from work as adults. Such patterns often make it difficult for people to hold a job and keep their friends!

We have heard people say that black culture is more spontaneous than some others and less time-bound, and that that's a good thing. But a person doesn't have to be late or absent, especially without letting you know, to be spontaneous. Such behavior in blacks, when it exists, is a carryover from slavery—a reaction to powerlessness and forced dependency. It was a way to "fix" the all-powerful master. Poor jobs and harsh treatment have maintained such habits among too many blacks. Oppressed white workers have shown the same patterns. These habits make it difficult to develop well-managed institutions. We believe that parents and schools should help children establish the habits of being on time and attending regularly. If relationships with the employer or teacher are not satisfactory, they should be talked out rather than acted out through lateness or no show.

Again, parents are models. If you make appointments with others, arrive late, postpone without good cause, or don't show without cause, your children will put little value on doing otherwise. Such behavior is really a sign of disrespect for ourselves and others. It is less likely to exist where good relationships have been established.

Teacher-Pupil Interaction

My son comes from a fatherless home. Wouldn't it be better for him to have male teachers?

Maybe yes and maybe no. The quality of the relationship between a child and an adult, parent or teacher, is more important than the sex of the adult. When there are good male teachers available in the community or in school, it is helpful if boys from fatherless families can be exposed to them. Ineffective male models, as fathers or teachers, may do more harm than good. Where effective models are not available, it is important for mothers and women teachers to permit the boys to identify with and play male roles— which should not include sexist attitudes toward females. For example, there is no reason that they should not play with dolls, as male children preparing to become helpful fathers. But we would not suggest sacrificing quality for sex any more than we would suggest sacrificing quality for race—black teachers for the sake of blackness, male teachers for the sake of maleness.

Be cautious about making assumptions about the cause of fatherless families in black communities. Whitney Young, the late executive director of the National Urban League, once told the story of the teacher who pointed out to a youngster that he did not give his father's name on a questionnaire. When the youngster said, "I don't have a father," the teacher apologized and said knowingly, "Oh, yes, I understand." She understood that it was one of those fatherless black families, but in fact, the youngster's father was killed in a car accident when the child was three years of age. The point here is that although we talk and think from time to time in terms of groups, we must work hard to remember that children—people, for that matter—are individuals and should be treated as such.

I feel that white teachers don't have high enough expectations for black children. What's your impression about this?

We must be careful not to generalize here. We know many white teachers who have had reasonable expectations and have had a good deal of success with black children. On the other hand, when white teachers have outright racist assumptions—that blacks are lazy, crazy, dangerous, and dumb—they are likely to have lower expectations and less success. Such teachers should not work with black children. It is the responsibility of administrators to help them improve their attitudes and behavior or to help them transfer to another setting.

The other side of the coin is that some white teachers feel that some black teachers concentrate too much on manners, dress, and behavior. We have seen such things as "shirt tails tucked in," "hats off" in the building, and "gum out" considered major problems. Again it is dangerous to generalize. We have seen this kind of concern on the part of teachers in both racial groups. But it is more pronounced among blacks.

A difference in background and age group leads to these differences in concern. Many black teachers had to overcome great hardships to get an education. They know that certain kinds of behavior and performance will be harmful to a black child when it may not be for whites. They also know that some black children, because of harsh social conditions, do not have the support and guidance of parents that they will need for the long haul in education and in life. They are acquainted with the pitfalls and temptation in the community that may lure a youngster from the educational pathway. As a result there is often passionate concern and strong demands to "straighten up and fly right."

Questions of dress and behavior should be worked out by teachers and parents (and children when they are old enough) and reviewed from time to time. The decisions should be based on what will help youngsters function well as adults rather than what somebody was taught as a child thirty years ago or what somebody is rebelling against as a young adult today. Children function best when they know the time and place for everything—to laugh, to cry, to compromise, to rebel, to run, to fight, to hold your ground, to be neat, to "tog down," to be casual, to use street language, to use black English, to use standard English or whatever it may be. This is the kind of person who will function best in our multistyled, fast-changing society.

In a school where the rules are worked out by all, there is less likelihood of mixed feelings, disruptive arguments, and fights over any particular rule.

Problems of Public Education

*As the mother of school-age children I get terribly upset
when I hear people say there is no hope for the
public schools. What do you think?*

It's easy to give up on the public schools, but we see no alternative
to public education. It costs money to run private schools. Even
with the wealth of the Catholic church, they are having difficulty
supporting their school system. Private schools can educate only a
very few children. In our opinion, the only solution is to help
public school systems work better. This can be done. There are
many public schools that do function well. It is our impression that
it depends a great deal on the quality of the leadership . . .
parents and school staff.

We are in agreement with those who say that social change is
necessary to dramatically improve conditions in the society and in
school. But in the meantime the school is shaping the lives of
people who must bring about the social change. Therefore, we
must help the public school systems do a more effective job *now*.
You should start with your school.

*Do you think that "slow" children in the public school
will hurt the education of my child?*

We believe that children of different ability levels can be together
without hindering anyone's progress. We don't believe that rigid
grouping of children by ability (tracking) is necessary. This
appears to be a phony issue used to avoid facing the real issue.
Children from different backgrounds often don't get along well
unless the school staff actively helps all children develop adequate
social skills and helps them manage their feelings about difference.
Ability-tracking frequently separates children according to their
social development and sometimes . . . race alone.

Such tracking often means that if a child in the lower-ability
track shows promise, he must "leave his own." It also means that
children in the higher tracks are denied the opportunity to get to
know and learn to respect different people. In addition, it has been
shown that you can affect the quality and level of work of children
by giving them a label. Children quickly learn whether they are in
the smart, "dumb," or average tracks.

More and more school programs are being designed to allow children to move at their own rate of speed. Flexible groupings can be used where skills must be taught at different levels—particularly with young children—without separating children of different abilities for all activities. A wise teacher will have children helping children. When working with young children this way, the teacher can help them learn to accept differences in ability levels without putting each other down or feeling bad about not being the best. This can decrease antagonisms between different groups. It is also a way to promote cooperation and fair play as important values. It is in chaotic schools and classrooms that mixed-ability groupings don't work. But here your child is less likely to do well under any circumstances.

How can I help at home?

You can help most by making schoolwork worth doing and making it possible to do. Your interest in projects and papers, and questions like "How did it go in reading today?" can be helpful. It is not wise to be too eager to help your son or daughter do *his* or *her* homework. If your child is having specific problems and wants your help, help. "Let me know if I can help" is supportive without interfering. Praise for interest in doing the work, started early, is an important incentive for young children. Don't criticize the teacher for too much work, too little work: "Why did he tell you to do it this stupid way?" This makes the work seem less worth doing and the teacher less worth learning from. Talk to the teacher if you have a disagreement, not to your child.

Protect your child from too much Stevie Wonder, too much basketball, too much television and too much fun, games, and noise from brothers, sisters, and whoever. Some of all of this is cool. But you should give "doing your schoolwork" top priority and consideration. Have your child or children plan their schedules so that they can do it all without interfering with each other. You may have to help work it out in the beginning, but they can learn to budget their time and do their work so as not to interfere with each other or need you to force them to do it. We know parents of well rounded teen-agers who have never had to make them do their homework. Such acceptance of responsibility, planning, and organization is important preparation for the future.

Noise? Find or make a quiet room or a quiet corner for a child who needs it in order to work. You should miss your favorite TV show if that's the only room available. What better way to say schoolwork is most important!

FOR TEACHERS

Teacher-Parent Interaction

If black parents are really interested in education,
why aren't more of my students' mothers and fathers
involved in the school program?

It will surprise even black professionals to find out how many black parents feel uncomfortable with professional people. This is the case in spite of the fact that many of the professional people have come from backgrounds similar to those of the parents. In some cases parents feel that they have very little to offer the professional school staff. In others, they feel bad because they did not achieve professional status. In some cases, they have somehow received a message from the staff that they have little to offer and are unwanted in the school. Finally, many black parents work two jobs, or both adults are working. Often they are too tired to get involved in the program of the school unless it is particularly inviting, although, as we have mentioned, it is very important that they try to make the time.

I have noticed that whenever there is a problem in my
classroom, many black parents automatically assume that
the school is against their child. Why is this the case?

Blacks experience antagonism at the hands of so many service agencies, in their dealings with welfare workers, policemen, and clerks at the license bureau, to name a few, that it is natural to assume antagonism in the case of the school. Differences in income and training between the staff and the community can also lead to a feeling of alienation. In this case, it is the responsibility of the staff, as individuals and as a group, to make adequate efforts to break down the distrust between the parents and the staff.

You as a teacher, particularly if you are involved with early elementary school children, should make an effort to get to know the parents of the youngsters in your classroom in situations other than conferences about a child's problems. This can be done through communication by notes, telephone, and face-to-face conversations at home and at school. The school as a whole should develop programs that reduce the social distance between home and school. These programs—whether they are banquets, parties, the church choir singing at a school program, or workshops about the school programs—would enable parents to get to know the teachers and staff as people and vice versa. Parents and staff could then respond to actual human beings rather than stereotypes. When this is the case, parents are less likely to come to school assuming that the teacher and the staff are against their child, and more likely to come in to be helpful in managing problems or simply to help out in the school.

As a teacher I get the runaround about home visits.
I am not sure that parents want me in their homes.
What is your thought about this?

For reasons mentioned above, some parents assume that teachers will think badly of them if they see their homes and living conditions. If you go into a home, you should be very careful not to pass judgment on the lifestyle of the family in question. Negative attitudes, facial expressions, and comments will be picked up in one way or another, and you would defeat your purpose for going to a child's home in the first place.

It may be easier all around, under some circumstances, to invite parents to the school. Again, your attitude is very important. Parents who have experienced discrimination or abuse of one kind or another are particularly perceptive. If they feel that you don't respect them as people, they are likely to stay away from school or be critical or abusive toward you when a problem develops.

I have invited parents to school, but they don't come
or they break appointments. What else can I do?

First, you should explain why an appointment is important even when there is no problem. When a parent does not show up for an appointment, don't take it personally. You should make a follow-up effort to have the parents make a visit. If "no show" becomes a chronic problem, you might want to send reminders the day before or the same day by telephone or by letter. *Most* important, you should have something to say when you call parents to school—such as explaining the school program to them, explaining how they can be helpful at home, explaining how you motivate children. Otherwise it is not worth their taking the time out to come to see you. In the case of people who simply refuse to come or make appointments and fail to show, don't assume that they are simply irresponsible. Because of various insecurities discussed earlier, some parents will test your interest through a "no show."

Certain parents, fearing bad news about their children, use avoidance of the teacher and school as a way of dealing with their fear. Some simply lack the confidence to sit down and talk with a teacher. In these cases you must reassure parents of your interest and concern and at the same time, particularly when the problem is chronic, you can point out in a friendly way how it makes you feel when you are disappointed by "no show" and how you lose time in preparing to help their children and other children when appointments are missed. In short, without using these words, you will be saying, "I will respect you and treat you fairly if you will respect me and treat me fairly."

Why are homework and the report card so important to black parents?

This is really not a racial issue. Most of us were educated in traditional and competitive school programs. In addition, blacks from the traditional culture believe that hard work is the key to success. Homework and hard work are almost the same thing. Some parents forget that the same "seat work" and homework that turned them off as kids is what they are asking their children to swallow.

Report cards enable parents to know at a glance where their children stand . . . largely in relationship to other children. As we pointed out, such information is not very helpful. But if a school, or the educational establishment, in general, wants to reduce this tendency to compare, then we must put less stress on being number one and more on doing your best. In addition the goal of development in the social, emotional, and psychological areas should be made as clear to parents as those in the academic skill achievement area. The objectives and program of the school in these areas should be clearly spelled out to parents. Some statement of achievement in these areas should be given.

More and more teachers are now evaluating children in this way rather than giving report cards . . . or in addition to giving report cards. We hope that many more will do so. Report cards tell one very little. What does an "A" mean in a school where children are two years behind in grade level? A "C" means one thing when a child is working at the top of his ability and something else when a child is capable of making an "A." Letter grades are quick and easy, but they tell very little about the objectives of the classroom or course and often tell little about the performance of one's child. Letter grades give parents little indication of how they can help. Unfortunately, some teachers do not evaluate children along the lines we have mentioned. But if you raise questions in these areas with your colleagues, this may help them to do so.

I am a white teacher in a predominantly black school.
I want to be fair, but some black parents doubt my
intentions without giving me a chance. What can I do?

You must first examine your own feelings and actions to be certain that you are not doing something that causes the parents to distrust you. Open racist comments lead to trouble but are rare in a teacher who wants to survive in a predominantly black school. More often, problems are created in indirect ways—by frequently proclaiming that you are free of prejudice, by proclaiming a love for all blacks, by leaning over backwards to please everybody, by overexcusing shortcomings of a youngster because he is black, by expecting too much or expecting too little from black youngsters. You should try to be fair and respectful and expect the same in return.

We have found that except in areas of extreme racial antagonism, black parents and children are fair with white teachers when they feel that the teachers are respectful and fair with them. Close contact can destroy stereotypes. In one instance, in Washington, D.C., during the riots of 1968, black children escorted their white teacher out of the danger area and returned to throw rocks at cars of white people whom they did not know. A number of educators have pointed out that white teachers who claim to have trouble with black children are often the same ones who have trouble with all children, but are less aware of their difficulty with white children.

Incidentally, you might also point out to the college where you trained that not all people are going to teach in middle-class white schools. It is their responsibility to prepare people to teach anywhere. One black history course won't do it. Child development dealing with social problems, teaching by objectives, and a host of other things which are not yet being widely taught are sorely needed.

I have different ideas and approaches to discipline
and motivation than my students' parents do. Won't
this confuse the youngsters in my class?

Not necessarily. Children, particularly young children, are very good at adjusting to the demands of a given situation. This is particularly true if they feel respected and comfortable in these situations. But . . . here is a situation in which a child can play teacher against parent, and vice versa, if he so desires. It is very helpful—even in cases where problems are unlikely—to discuss your differences of ideas and approaches to discipline and motivation with parents. It also helps to share ideas with other teachers. Most of us would prefer not to shout, scream, and punish our children, yet we often feel it's the only solution. But when we are adult enough and sure enough of ourselves to look at how someone else does it, we may find another way.

Questions of Discipline

I'm in my first year of teaching and I have a great deal
of trouble setting limits. I don't want to be a harsh,
mean person. What can I do?

Setting limits need not make you a harsh, mean person. You are probably suffering from the problem of many young people—mixed feelings about having authority. When you are just out of adolescence and young adulthood—and for some of us, even as adults—having authority is a real problem. We ourselves sometimes still have trouble with people who have greater authority than we do.

Authority in itself is not bad. It is the misuse of authority that is troublesome. Your authority helps you set the mood and the tone for your classroom. It helps you establish the notion with your students, through your own behavior, that cooperation, fair play, and good work efforts are desirable. Your authority brings order and safety to the classroom. It helps you protect the withdrawn and frightened child. It permits you to help the aggressive child bring his aggression under his own control so that he is not the victim of it—acting up, being punished, and then feeling bad about himself. When you don't exert authority, chaos and confusion are likely to develop.

We watched one teacher like the one who asked the above question having some difficulty in this regard. She had real trouble saying "no." She wanted to be a friend of the children. A youngster walked into her classroom after school and asked if he could play her violin. She wanted to say "no" because she was busy talking with someone. Her voice said, "No, not now, I'm busy talking to someone." But her face, her eyes, her manner, all said, "If you bother me enough, I'll let you do it." The child continued to ask and then demand and finally acted up. He had to be physically forced from the room.

Because of her reluctance to be friendly but firm, exercise her authority, and work out some other time that the youngster could come and play, she created a problem. She finally had to deal with it in the very way she had wanted to avoid in the first place. We have seen this happen many times with young people who talk about all of the right things to do with children, then fail to set limits and eventually end up yelling, screaming, hitting, and being angry with children in ways that they are very much against. As a result they are not only furious but extremely annoyed and disappointed in themselves.

The trick is to be fair, warm, firm but flexible without being a "patsy." You have rights and you don't want the children to forget it—or you'll be trampled on. Part of your job is to help them learn to respect the rights of other people. They learn, in part, from the way they interact with you. In the same breath, we want to say again that children have rights. One of the ways that they learn to respect and stand up for their rights and respect the rights of others is to have a teacher who respects their rights.

How can we control the classroom when there are rules which will not allow us to spank bad children, people frown on our yelling at them, and we have no authority in the eyes of children?

Children sometimes behave in bad or disturbing ways because they are fearful, frustrated, angry, and abused. But children are not naturally bad—or good. It helps to think less of discipline and punishment as means of control and more about how to help a child solve a problem, develop inner controls, and learn better ways of handling his feelings. Having children work out problems between themselves, with your help as needed, is a good approach. We know one teacher who handles conflict in her first-grade class like this:

"Henry hit me." "She tore up my paper first." "No I didn't." "That was because . . ."

The teacher's response was "Okay, I can see that you and Henry have something going. I don't want to hear what he did and she did. Why don't you go to the back of the room and talk things out quietly. I expect you to have everything settled in five minutes."

In the beginning you may have to help children learn how to talk things out and come to a solution that is fair for everyone concerned. But even then you want to let them try it on their own first. Even very young children are amazingly good at the art of compromise. This approach helps them learn to negotiate, to stand up for their rights, and to communicate. It helps them learn another way than fighting. Learning to solve a problem in a way that allows him or her to maintain his or her rights and dignity but still get along with others is one of the most valuable skills a child can learn in this day and age.

Sometimes I feel a child really must be punished. What should I do?

When punishment is necessary, it should not be major and traumatic for minor incidents. For example, you don't want to keep a child who has been looking forward to going on the class outing to the zoo for a month from doing so because he got into a fight. It is the quality of your response that has an effect and not the severity.

In a case where it is clearly one child who is responsible for the trouble, it is best to find out what is upsetting him. Even if you can't find out exactly what is wrong, indicating that you know that something is the matter because of his behavior will help him to feel understood and will also let him know that you know he is capable of a more desirable kind of behavior. You should then let him know what he can do when he feels angry or disappointed. Some teachers have pounding boards, painting corners, and other frustration- and anger-handling equipment and approaches.

Even when a problem must go beyond the classroom and to the parent, counselor, or principal, it should still be handled in the spirit of problem-solving rather than punishment. You may have to help others, including parents, develop this attitude. We know of situations in which parents have come into classrooms and whipped children, or done so at home when they were told that there was a problem at school. This either kills a child's spirit, or has no effect at all, or worsens the problem, or makes it more difficult for you to work with the child in school . . . he no longer trusts you.

Everyone involved with an acting-up child should work out ways to help him or her develop the kinds of controls they will need to function in the classroom. When parents, teachers, principals, and others convey to the child that we want you, like you, and would like to have you in this school and this classroom, but there are certain things we expect of you, the response is often miraculous. The provocative and troublesome behavior is sometimes a way of testing whether you care . . . whether you want him or her in the classroom or not.

My students keep saying I'm not fair. How should I handle this?

Asking a child to be fair and responsible is going to work best when you are fair and don't play favorites. Incidentally, what do you do when you are wrong? Secure teachers permit children to correct them when they make an error in classroom work, conversation, or other areas. For example, a child returns late from the playground and you reprimand him. Then you find out that he was stopped by the principal, or had some other good reason for being late. We believe that it is best to apologize in this kind of situation.

One of the subjects young children we deal with are concerned about most in regard to parents and teachers is the issue of fairness . . . or the lack of it. Six- and seven-year-olds in particular are "sticklers" about fairness, and this is understandable. They are developing a conscience, learning and understanding rules that will help them govern their own lives. The teacher provides a bad model if he cannot be wrong and apologize when, in fact, he is wrong. There will be no loss of authority and control because you apologize. Children will simply appreciate the fact that you have been fair with them. They are then much more likely to be fair with you. Your fair behavior strengthens their developing inner controls.

What should I do when I have tried, nothing works,
and my patience is growing thin?

If you can make an arrangement for handling difficult situations *before* you lose control, you can often avoid a lot trouble. Many schools are geared to help you out in such cases. The principal, an aide, volunteer, or someone is prepared to work with the child during this period. When you are under good control and the child is out of control, you can handle the situation in a way which will help the youngster improve his self-control. We have seen this work very successfully.

One third-grade teacher, after other efforts failed, said to a youngster, "Hugh, you are having a real problem handling yourself today. Let's give you a chance to pull yourself together. I want you to take this material and work on it in the principal's office. Let's see . . . it's one-fifteen now. I want you to get yourself together by two o'clock and then you can come back to the classroom." At two, Hugh was back, without being called for, ready to work, and did so without further difficulty. If he had stayed in the classroom, he would have acted up to the point where he embarrassed himself and received punishment which would embarrass him more and possibly bring out more acting-up behavior. By giving him room, but at the same time setting definite limits, the teacher was able to allow him to save face, and feel good about himself for being able to bring things under control on his own. By the same token, when you lose your cool, leaving the situation temporarily helps to give you a chance to calm down without a head-on collision. This is not running away. It is a strategic retreat which allows you to handle the situation better. After all, it isn't war . . . or at least it shouldn't be.

A final word here. We must all handle behavior problems or disorder sometimes, but the majority of these difficult situations can be avoided by a good instructional program and careful classroom management.

My second-graders talk all the time when they are supposed to
be doing their work. Should they be punished?

Friendship and conversation are very important. Children develop communication skills and enjoyment from being with and talking to each other. Much school work can be done while children talk at a reasonable noise level. No talking—at any time—is an old and bad habit. There is a classroom noise level that means chaos and confusion. There is another level of sound that is the noise of production and satisfaction. It has a hum and a ring of warmth and enthusiasm. You can hear the difference between the two.

You want to help your children keep at this second level of conversation, understanding that going beyond it will interfere with work—their own and that of others. There are times and places that you will want near silence and you should help them understand why this is necessary during a particular period. The same is true of order and neatness. Too much disorder is chaotic; too little usually indicates that the classroom is oppressive and that the spontaneity and creativity of the children are being smothered. Some children who talk a lot need more physical activity. We are distressed that some schools do not have a physical education program, and some teachers punish children for talking by not letting them go to P.E.

How would you handle fighting in school when children have been told to fight by their parents?

Parents teach their children to fight in neighborhoods where they must fight to keep from being constant victims. Some children are told that, "If he beats you, you are going to get another beating when you get home!" But when the school is safe and your classroom is peaceful, most parents are happy to have their children solve problems in some way other than fighting.

At PTA meetings, during home visits or whenever you meet and talk with parents, you should inform them about what you and your school are trying to do with regard to fighting. You should let them know that you understand that sometimes their children may have to fight, that fighting to solve a problem occurs very often among young children. At the same time, point out that your job is to try to help them learn ways to work out their problems through talk and compromise rather than stomping on each other. You can explain that an offer *not* to fight but a willingness to fight if you must can "save face" and cut down on the number of black children who victimize each other.

If you point out that children who learn a better way to handle disagreements are less likely to fight each other as teen-agers and adults—in gangs, with knives and other weapons—most parents will be willing to go along with your approach. The majority of people in troubled black communities are sick and tired of assaults and living in fear. We all know that making our neighborhoods safe is going to take more than the way we teach our children to handle conflict—but that's one part of it.

Sometimes I feel as if I spend so much time struggling with a few disruptive students that there's no time left to teach. How can I cut down on these battles?

It is important to help the youngsters understand that you do not want to struggle or fight. If you *need* to fight—verbally or physically—with a young school-age child, you are in the wrong business. In your own way, you will want to direct a student's provocative, challenging behavior into classroom achievement, success on the athletic field, in art or in music, or into improving his relationships with other children. You should let it be known that that is what wins points with you. But you can't do it by saying, "Look, Billy, if you keep fooling around you're going to grow up to be as dumb as your mama." (We have heard this approach.) Again, you help best by praising the positive, the constructive, the direction that you would like the child to go, or the direction that will bring him success in his relationships with others without a loss of dignity and self-respect. Your response to negative behavior should be to try and direct it into a positive area, ignore it when it is minor, and stop it head-on when other approaches don't work . . . enough is enough.

Often the disruptive child has not thought about the needs of others and how his or her behavior interferes with these needs. A screaming child prevents another from reading or concentrating. A strong, aggressive child can intimidate all the other children and prevent them from wanting to be his friends—unless he forces them to be. A provocative child can make you so angry that you won't want to have anything to do with him. Pointing these things out from time to time—but not too often—will help a youngster understand what it takes to get along in the classroom and elsewhere. When he begins to change for the better, it helps to point out that you're pleased that he is able to do this or that . . . but not too often or to the point that it becomes phony. When other children respond to him better because he is handling himself better, again you can point out what is happening . . . but again, not too often.

This approach is more powerful than it seems on the surface, particularly with young children before they've given up on the human race. What most people want, particularly children, is to belong, to be accepted and respected. Your responses help the child learn how to achieve these goals. He appreciates your aid and this gives you a better chance to influence his behavior in a positive direction. Getting along better with others will give the child a greater chance to succeed at his schoolwork. Scholastic success can change a troubled child. In fact, your classroom and school can become an oasis of security and good feelings in the overall insecure and difficult life of a child.

Be careful not to look for too much too soon. A child in trouble at five has usually had four and even five difficult years. (But it is also important not to hide behind the fact that he's only in your classroom three to six hours a day.) We have seen children, and even their families, change dramatically because of breakthroughs made in the classroom during those few hours. But it takes time. There are those few unfortunate cases where little will happen regardless of what you do. But even here, sometimes way down the road—in jail, after a few failures at work and in marriage—people pull themselves together thanks to the advice, values, or training they received from a handful of teachers or people they "heard" but couldn't respond to at the time.

Creating Effective Classrooms

What kind of a classroom atmosphere should I try to provide for children who come from a home environment very different from that of their school?

It is important for the teacher to make his or her expectations for the classroom known in a friendly, calm, and confident way. Most of us, without thinking much about it, make the assumption that children know why they come to school and what they are to do. But usually they are there because they are brought or told to go. Often there has been no discussion about learning and how they will learn or what to expect. If they have been told anything, they have probably been told, "Mind the teacher." If children are in-volved in doing the opposite of what their parents want them to do, an order to mind the teacher can be a challenge to do the opposite.

We believe that in areas where the ways of the home and the ways of the school are different, it is important for children entering school for the very first time to move into a highly structured setting—whether it's a traditional or an open classroom. By structured, we mean that the children are told where to sit, how they are expected to line up for the bell, how to go to the washroom without running. Schedules and ritual also give structure and order—an opening classroom exercise at the same time every morning, a specific time for reading, a set period for artwork, and so on. All of this can be accomplished in a warm, friendly manner. As the children begin to understand what is expected of them, they can start to work toward these expectations. By learning to work together without hurting each other, being destructive or disruptive, they make it possible to move gradually to a more open classroom, with more choices, more free time, more self-direction. Often this can be done in a few weeks.

Both children of authoritarian (all-powerful) parents and neglected children are better able to handle a more structured situation than an immediate open classroom.

*Why do so many black educators raise questions
about open education classrooms?*

Unfortunately, the open education classroom approach was promoted as a cure-all much in the fashion of many patent medicines. It became a sign and symbol of "progressive education." Teaching in such classrooms was thought of as a "happening" by too many teachers. It is the opposite. Open classrooms require more planning and constant evaluation of progress than traditional classrooms. "Happenings" occur without chaos *because* there is solid planning and management underneath. We recall an open education classroom in England, where the idea was developed, in which children were all over the place, apparently "doing their own thing." The teacher then showed us a massive record book in which she kept up with the academic skill and social progress of every child.

A retired district superintendent in London told us that he was afraid Americans would adopt the system without fully understanding it or preparing teachers. He was right! Too little planning and too many inexperienced teachers can be found in open classroom situations today. In addition, in adopting the open classroom, Americans failed to consider very important differences between British and American culture and social conditions—there is less sense of alienation from the larger society among most Britons than is the case in the United States.

Black educators and parents, perhaps more than white, have raised serious questions about indiscriminate, unmodified use of the open classroom approach. Because of difficult social conditions, too many black children grow up in homes and communities where they must struggle for survival by any means necessary. Sometimes the ways of the school are different than the ways of the home and community. There is sometimes open or unspoken alienation and conflict between parents and school staff. Moving directly into an open classroom before these relationships are improved and before children understand the expectation of the school can lead to chaos. This is even more likely when teachers are inexperienced and do not value planning.

Many black educators have cause for concern. Too many black children come through the educational system without developing the discipline necessary to achieve in school, at work, and even at play. Moreover, a number of successful parents, teachers, and black school programs are highly authoritarian and structured—but not oppressive. Some of the Muslim schools, black nationalist schools, the Summer Study-Skills Program, and some public schools are cases in point. We suspect that any approach or method which gives children a sense of belonging, worth, comfort, direction, and purpose—and includes good instruction—will work. While we lean toward an approach which gives children more responsibility, we are not against any approach which produces the above results.

What kind of classroom provides the best climate for learning?

The best climate for learning is one in which children get along with each other and with their teacher and vice versa. That is not to say that differences of opinion or unpleasantness will not arise in such situations. But it does mean that such problems can be worked out in a way that is not too disruptive. Some people look at this kind of classroom and imagine that it is the charisma of the teacher, the background or the intelligence of the children, or just plain magic that makes it possible. But organization is the key.

When we're working in a group, and nobody knows exactly what to do, how to do it, or when to do it, we tend to get restless, irritated, and even angry, sometimes striking out at other people. That is exactly what happens with young children, who have even less control and less experience in handling such situations. That is why it is important for teachers to have classroom goals and well-thought-out ways for children to accomplish these goals. It is even better when a teacher helps the children establish goals themselves. Children should know exactly what you and they are trying to accomplish during your lesson period—for a morning, for a day, for tomorrow, for the week.

What classroom techniques can I use to help my students work toward goals?

It is helpful for children to keep a record in their notebooks of their individual progress toward goals which have been established for them or by them. This helps a child learn to think in terms of long-range achievement instead of only in terms of the here and now. It helps him and her begin to see the connection between yesterday's work, today's work, and tomorrow's work. It creates a kind of relationship and connectedness between things that many children from "here and now" homes do not automatically bring to school. Yet understanding the relationship of yesterday's work to today's and how the work leads toward a goal is what helps a child become goal-oriented and motivated. As children learn to work toward goals, they discover that there is more fun in achievement than there is in acting up and other disruptive activities such as "punching George" or "controlling teacher."

With young children, two elements of organization are particularly important. The first is movement from one activity to the next, and the second is providing activities which are within the child's ability range. For example, we have seen teachers present lessons which were exciting and helpful, but watched the classroom fall apart after the lesson because they did not give clear instructions or establish routine ways to help the children move to the next activity.

We watched a group of children play a new game designed to

improve their arithmetic skills. Unfortunately the teacher did not look at the game ahead of time and did not realize that it was beyond the ability of his class. The children tried very hard to play the game but were not able to do so. They knew they were supposed to be quiet because other children were working. But they were unsuccessful at the game and eventually bored. They became talkative and the teacher yelled across the room several times without asking about the cause of the problem. Finally, Ernie hit Maggie and a full-scale disruption was on. Such problems will occur from time to time with all children. They are even more likely to occur with children unfamiliar with the style and expectations of the school and among those who lack inner control.

Educating the Very Young

I believe that it's important for black children to learn to read, and I work on reading more than anything else in my first-grade class. What are your thoughts about this approach?

Reading *is* important. But there is a near-hysteria about reading which can be harmful. We have seen teachers work on boring drills in barren, joyless rooms because, "They must learn to read!" Most children will learn to read if we don't overreact. In fact, we have seen children who could not read learn to do so during the summer vacation, without their teacher . . . not that prior help wasn't important. But a relaxed atmosphere will probably do more to help children learn to read than an uptight approach.

Of course, good instruction is the key, relaxed or uptight. It is not enough for children to read more. A careful evaluation of specific reading skill weaknesses and training and practice in these areas is needed.

What kind of prekindergarten and early elementary experiences are the best for my black students?

All children should have a curriculum program which enables them to prepare to learn the basic skills of reading, arithmetic, spelling, and writing. But even at this early age, attention can be paid to providing black children with materials which will give them a sense of self and racial pride. Books, magazines, films, and other materials showing black children and black adults having success experiences in all walks of life should be available in classrooms. Success experiences should run the gamut from rock-and-roll singers to ballplayers to professional people and families.

All children are not at the same stage of development when they enter school. Children from backgrounds where talking was not as much for conversation or sharing information and experiences as it was for control—"sit down," "shut up," "don't bother your brother," and so on—have had less experience in hearing the language used for conversations. Hearing conversational language is good preparation for learning to read. It can be very helpful to set up classroom situations in which such children can use language for conversation and hear it used in that way by others. Talking to each other, reporting on personal experiences or television programs, play-acting as newscasters, playing house, store, town, and a host of other experiences provide this opportunity. You as teacher might also want to lead conversations with groups of children so that they get to hear and use language for sharing information and feelings.

It is also helpful to read to children who have not had books read to them. They will need a familiarity with words and the rhythm of words, sentences, and paragraphs to learn to read. When you take school outings, discussions before, during, and after the trip help children learn to use language more and more in a conversational way and helps them to learn to organize, rethink, and reorganize their thoughts and expressions. Once they learn to write, having them write about a trip before and after helps them learn to anticipate, observe, and recall—all important skills to develop. Making drawings and later making cut-outs and reconstructing certain scenes helps to do the same thing.

An additional advantage of observing and describing things in the child's school and community is that it indicates that such things are worth observing. Children learn best in the early school period from the things around them, just as they first began to learn by exploring their own bodies. Once they are "hung up on" or addicted to learning, more distant and less immediately stimulating things will turn them on.

What other experiences besides book learning
are good for this age group?

Hopefully every teacher of young children will use the arts and physical education to provide additional ways for children to learn. Through such means as painting, model-making, and drama, children can express their feelings about the things they are doing and things they have observed. The arts, movement, and physical education help children channel energies into activities that help them learn. They bring rhythm and control to the body. Some children who are less good or "slow bloomers" at academic learning are more successful in the arts and physical education. Sometimes they turn off to school learning—and we suspect some never return—if they are not able to have success as early as some other children. The arts and physical education sometimes make it possible for them to have this success.

The arts and physical education can be used to take advantage of the physical and rhythmic excellence of some black children. As we said earlier, some middle-income black parents favor "head" things over "body" things; for example, learning to read, write, and do arithmetic as opposed to clapping, dancing, and singing. Such parents may be cutting off important ways of learning and expression. One is as valuable as the other, and physical and body expression can aid learning and written expression. Certainly no harm is done if both receive sufficient attention.

Should children in this age group be "graded"?

We believe that careful and consistent study or assessment of the work of children is what is important at this age. What reading skills has Martha mastered? What does she need to work on? We feel this is particularly important in cases where parents, for whatever reason, do not follow the progress of the children. Not only does your following the work give it added value, but it should enable you to do educational programming which identifies obstacles to skill development and permits you to develop exercises which will enable children to overcome these obstacles. Without such programming it is possible to miss confusion in a child's mind . . . confusion that can lead to an unnecessary feeling of failure which in time can cause children to lose their confidence and turn off to learning.

We observed a youngster doing addition problems. He had missed nine out of twelve problems. A big "X" marked each wrong answer. He added 12 and 4 and got an answer of 56; 10 and 7 and got an answer of 87; 11 and 3 and an answer of 44. He was badly discouraged and hid his paper from his classmates. Once the mechanical error he was making was pointed out to him, he got all of the problems correct. The moral of this story is that it is not how many are right or wrong but how much is understood that counts. Hopefully teachers will look for this rather than simply "grade" papers. Understanding and learning to learn is far more important at this stage of the game than the number right or wrong. You are best able to keep up with the level of understanding and the level of skills a child has if you make some kind of consistent, periodic assessment of skill development.

Racism and Racial Pride

I am a teacher in a predominantly white school. I sometimes have a lot of trouble handling my anger when white parents, teachers, and children say and do racist things. Is it best to try to control myself, or should I let it all hang out?

Such a decision must be up to you. But as we pointed out earlier, you can spend all of your time responding to racism without necessarily decreasing your frustration and anger. If you can keep your cool—most of the time—and handle racial incidents without losing your self-respect, you may be able to help whites, particularly children, become less racist, or at least more responsible in their behavior toward their fellow citizens. Your question brings to mind an incident told to us by a black teacher in a similar situation.

A ten-year-old youngster who was quite insecure frequently bullied a black youngster on the school bus. The black youngster finally reported the situation to the black teacher. She promptly put a stop to it without getting greatly upset or putting the white youngster down for his "racist views." Several months later, after two other teachers had given up on him, the black teacher was asked to try the white child in her class. They got along fine. On the last day of school, she asked the youngster to remain after class just a minute.

She said, "Michael, I am glad we were able to make it together. I wondered whether we could. You remember the incident with Bobby Jones?" He indicated that he did remember and beamed with pride that he had been able to do well in the class. While his emotional problems might not be solved, his black teacher had helped him have two successes—one in school and one in race relations. The chances of his using race as a way of dealing with his own insecurities were reduced by his experience with his black teacher. As we indicated earlier, children of this age group understand the concept of race but are still learning how to handle their feelings about it. If you can handle yours, you can better help them handle theirs.

The same is true in dealing with parents and your colleagues. We sometimes resent being "teachers" in predominately white settings. But many white people have severe misconceptions about blacks. Some can directly, and many can indirectly, affect the lives of black children and people in general. We think it pays to clear up some of these misconceptions both through what you say and through your performance. Where you find whites who are really interested, you might point out literature and other information which will help them better understand and interpret the black experience.

In some situations, you simply won't be able to contain your anger—and that's all right too. This response will say, "Enough is enough."

As a white teacher, I worry about putting children down when I correct their errors, particularly their English when it is the style of their community. Won't they take it as a racial slur?

It is not so much *that* you correct, but *how* you correct that is important. It's your voice, facial, and body expressions and attitudes that count. If a child says, "That's number fo'," and you respond, "The word is not fo'! It is four!" you have sent a message. You have said that the child is wrong. The language of his community is wrong. You have shown disdain for his way of talking. But if you explain that that's one way of saying it, or that may be the way he's heard it pronounced, but at school the word is pronounced "four," you will be giving him information without putting him down. The words "at school" really mean standard English. The tone of voice, choice of words, and attitude do not convey error, disdain, or a racial put-down. You now have a child learning standard English without having to reject his dialect. Eventually you will be able to give the standard English form without giving an "at school" explanation.

There are formal and informal school papers, and some of the unimportant, rough work of children need not be corrected. But when youngsters are doing serious assignments it is helpful to correct spelling and grammar. How else will they learn the standard form? It is important to praise what is praiseworthy while pointing out the errors here and there. It pays to make more of a point of helping than finding fault. Again, it is the way you do it and not what you do that counts.

Some of the children in my first-grade class call each other names when they are angry—"black nigger," "black pig," and so on. How should I handle this?

In young children, such expressions are not always an indication of a deep-seated negative feeling about being black. Sometimes the children have simply heard the words used at a time of anger and are repeating them. You can often end such name-calling by saying something like this, "Black people who feel good about themselves do not call each other names." The major task is to reduce the cause of anger and help the youngsters learn to handle it in a better way. You should think about whether the youngsters are having success in class—and ways to help them do so if they are not. Hostile and aggressive anger toward each other is often related to failure and frustration in learning. Helping them learn to talk out their differences is the best way to reduce anger, but there are others—from writing to running to pounding on a bag made for such purposes.

A black seven-year-old and one of his white classmates called each other racial names in my schoolroom. I stopped them and made them apologize to each other. Do you think I should have punished them as well?

Punishment helps little. Racial attacks by young children are simply the repeating of expressions which they have heard used in anger or fear or at any time of insecurity. Stopping the name-calling and making the youngsters apologize is okay, but a discussion can be even more useful here. You will probably find that the real issue is that Mary had a ball Joan wanted to play with or Peter wanted Paul to be in his group. By the second or third grade, the problem probably goes deeper. At this age, it is important to indicate that racial attacks will not be tolerated. An eight-

or nine-year-old who repeatedly makes racial attacks is usually a frustrated and insecure child . . . except when he has been carefully taught to act this way by older people. You will want to help such a child with the underlying problem.

As a white teacher in a predominantly black school, how can I help black children develop racial pride?

Some people have said that it is not possible for a white teacher to help black children establish a positive black identity. We do not think this is true. For example, we remember one situation in which a white teacher left her predominantly black class at the end of the year to get married. The children drew a picture of the teacher and her husband-to-be as a going-away present for her. The color of the teacher was brown and her groom was white. This was an indication that they recognized the difference but accepted her. It also indicated that they valued brown or dark skin.

We have heard white teachers express concern just as we have heard black parents express concern when their four-year-olds try to wash away their skin color or indicate that they want to be white. Again, in children of this age this is not always an indication that they dislike being black. Children like to be like the people around them. A white physician, whose child was in a predominantly black school, told us of visiting school and seeing his child's self-portrait on the school board. The skin was colored brown like that of the children around her. We have worked with white children who color their drawings brown as an indication that they like their therapist or want the therapist to be like them.

There is cause for concern here only where this incident is not isolated or limited to a three- or four-month period. When your child repeatedly makes negative statements about being black or makes extreme efforts to be white, there is a problem. Remember . . . you can be the one to create it by overreacting to his race statements rather than discussing the matter in a calm, confident way. Efforts to expose such a child, in a relaxed and natural way, to successful black figures as well as black culture and experiences should be made.

As we indicated earlier, a sense of worth and value and pride grow first from the way one is treated by adults. If a white teacher is fair, respectful, and, at the same time, has expectations for learning and behavior that are reasonable, black students will succeed and feel good about themselves. Using materials that show blacks having successful experiences can also be helpful. Your respect for black art, literature, dance, and music will be observed by the children. Your interaction with black staff and black parents will also be observed by the children. Your respect for black people will prevent the child from having any doubt about the value of his blackness. At the same time, it is important for black children to see blacks in positions of authority, upon whom they can model themselves. Where there are a significant number of black children in a school, there should be some black teachers and administrators.

A black youngster in my nursery school class slapped her black doll, and said, "Shut up, you black bitch." I know I should have said something, but I was horrified and turned away. How would you have handled this?

Brutality fascinates and then horrifies most people. This is particularly true of the majority of people in the "helping" professions—teachers, doctors, social workers. It is even more horrifying when you realize that the child was repeating an act that she probably learned at home. In fact, she was just "playing house." As a white teacher this could well have caused you to feel some guilt. But the child doesn't need your guilt. She needs your help in learning how to handle a frustrating situation. The baby was crying and frustrating her. In a case like this you could say, "Nadine, I'm sure the baby will stop crying if you hold her [or give her milk, or whatever you do to comfort her] rather than hit her or call her names." At the same time you might want to put your arm around Nadine (*if* you feel real compassion).

A lecture or discussion about black pride would mean almost nothing here. That is too "intellectual" at this point. The issue is "feelings." You can help best by providing her with a better model of behavior and a little warmth. Hopefully children who live in abusive situations can learn to respond in school and other places in ways which will enable them to receive nonabusive treatment from other people. This, in time, could make it possible for them to respond in nonabusive ways. At some natural time—story time, cutting out pictures, on a trip, a spontaneous question about blacks—you will want to help the child experience her blackness in a prideful way.

Violence and Other Problem Areas

*I work in a school where you lock the doors or risk attack
from somebody off the street, and there is a buzzer to
call for help if you are attacked by the students. The
kind of control measures you have mentioned so far
are not going to help me. What can I do?*

Most elementary schools are manageable, but it is sad but true
that many junior high schools and high schools, both black and
white, throughout the country are troubled and dangerous. The
solution to the problems here very often goes beyond the individual classroom or school, beyond change through management,
instructional, and relationship improvements. Troubled homes and
troubled communities—a product of inadequate social policies for
all and negative attitudes toward poor people and minority groups
—are the real problems. Social change to improve the quality of
community life and home life is needed in such cases.

But let's be careful here. We are all too quick to put the blame
outside of ourselves. We have seen good leadership "turn around"
some tough, tough schools.

One teacher, in response to an article about how teachers fail in
inner city schools, wrote, "No teacher has ever failed in an inner
city school!" She went on to point out that City Hall fails, the City
Council fails, administrators fail, but not the teachers.

Nonsense!

It is interesting that in some of the most troubled schools, some
teachers are successful. We have seen chaotic schools change to
safe and successful schools through the cooperation of parents,
teachers, students, and administrators. Yes, there are dangerous
schools. Much needs to be done beyond the schools. But much can
be done with the schools in these difficult areas, even in high
schools.

*That's all well and good, but in the meantime how do I cope
with a child who's about to knife another child or me?*

You should do the best you can to see that nobody, including
yourself, gets hurt and to prevent a youngster from hurting himself and his own future. Calmness—to the extent possible under
the circumstances—and allowing the two combatants to save face

and maintain their self-respect is the best way to survive in such a case.

We recall a situation in which a young black man moved to stop a fight between two snarling, furious eleven-year-old black youngsters at a shopping center. He parted them only to find himself, a second later, between two cocked arms holding bricks. A crowd of amused white adults had gathered. The black man pointed out that the crowd was thinking, "See, that's the way 'they' are." He also pointed out that if they threw those bricks they were going to hurt him and themselves—when they had previously been and could again be friends. He also indicated that the problem could be solved without hurting each other. The arms slowly dropped. If you are a fair and respectful teacher, you have the leverage of being someone the youngster really doesn't want to hurt.

Although the above approach is the best way to handle an extreme and dangerous situation in principle, in reality it doesn't always work. You are the expert when such situations arise because only you can "read" the intensity of rage. You must decide what to do. Again, don't get yourself hurt.

When your school is in trouble—be it dangerous fights, drugs, or other difficulties—the staff must look for new approaches. Have you involved and given support to the parents who want more for their children? Even troubled parents want more. Does your staff treat each other in a way that is a good example to the students? Does the staff treat the youngsters in a fair, firm yet reasonable way? Have you developed programs and activities which give the youngsters skills they did not receive at home, which focus on problems around them, which give them direction, purpose, and hope for the future?

Easier said than done? Right on! Teachers in such situations have the toughest jobs in this country. You also have the best chance to "turn around" confused black youngsters, and we need all the "turn arounds" we can get—if our communities are ever to be safe places to live and good places to rear children. We know it will take more than better schools—but better schools are one part of what is needed. Better schools can produce more people capable of taking effective political and social action . . . to the degree and in any way necessary.

Let us say once more, loud and clear: if it's going to take a militant struggle, remember that it's the disciplined, dedicated and, in this day and age, well-trained people who can bring off a militant struggle, not irresponsible thugs exploiting other people for self-gain in the name of some greater cause. We are highly suspicious of proclaimed revolutionaries wearing expensive clothes, driving flashy cars, "digging" jazz on expensive stereos. We suspect inner trouble—even suicidal intent—when a person's acts appear designed more to bring the roof down on his head than to bring about lasting improvement.

A six-year-old threw our classroom pet, a gerbil, against the wall. Is that an indication of a serious psychological problem?

Not necessarily. Children who have been neglected, rejected, or brutalized in one way or another often show a brutality and harshness which is beyond the ordinary. Sometimes this is a sign that psychological problems exist which will require professional help. On the other hand, if teachers understand that there are reasons for this behavior and do not simply consider the child "bad," they can be very helpful . . . although you don't want to tolerate such behavior.

Youngsters who are cruel or rough usually have had difficult experiences with powerful adults. Their reaction is to try and control adults through provocative, negative, even threatening behavior—or to take their anger out on a building, animals, or children who don't fight as well as they do. They often are distrustful of adults and need evidence that they can trust you. Such trust comes through your being fair and respectful to everyone in the classroom. This includes the teacher aide, parents, and the custodian who comes in from time to time. A distrustful child will often provoke and test you to see if you are for real . . . whether you honestly care and are really concerned about him and others. If you make an effort to help the youngster but become provoked by his behavior, shout, and punish, your response will enable him to say, "See, I knew it all the time," even though he will probably not say so out loud.

If you do lose control, it's not the end of the world. Gather your cool and say that you're sorry. But then calmly but firmly point out that there are certain things you expect in the classroom. You can also use a situation like this to help the youngster see *what he does to you* and other people to cause what he considers mistreatment to himself. Such incidents provide the opportunity for "verbal contracts"—you play fair with me and I'll play fair with you; you live by the reasonable rules of this classroom and I will be better able to be fair with you.

Some black children seem to have a chip on their shoulders.
One of my students rolls her eyes at me whenever I ask her to
do something. What does this mean and what can I do about it?

Abused children, black or white, are likely to have a chip on their shoulders. Such a child expects you to be unfair and unreasonable like other adults he has come in contact with at home and in the community, or like the society at large that dislikes blacks. Don't let the rolling eyes throw you. It is the expression of the questions, "Who are you? Where do you stand? What right do you have to tell me what to do?"

Distrust, testing, and questioning will disappear as you demonstrate, time and time again, that you are fair and working in the best interest of each child. Directly challenging the eye-rolling or the hostility generally gets you nowhere. Banter or kidding, rolling your eyes back—after you have a fair relationship and if you are comfortable doing it—generally lessens the tension, but still doesn't answer the question the child has on his or her mind. The important thing is to be able to tolerate a certain amount of hostility without using your power and authority to crush it. "Stop rolling your eyes at me" may stop the eye-rolling, but not the "mind-rolling"—anger and hostility.

Most of us have our own ways of handling hostility. If you do not overreact because the hostility is coming from a black child, your usual methods will probably work. If there is an *irrational* feeling that blacks are dangerous and the hostility and anger may get out of hand, you may be fearful and ineffective in handling a hostile response. There are some dangerous black children just as there are some dangerous white children. But most young children can't do much harm, and you must learn to be able to separate the real danger from irrational fear.

I have the impression that many black children lack
confidence and avoid difficult academic work. Is this true?

The problem is not race but the preparation for learning and the quality of instruction. We have seen children who were not adequately prepared to learn use all kinds of avoidance methods. We have observed this most in relation to beginning reading, where children have not heard the language used very much in the giving, receiving, and sharing of information; have not been read to; and have not come to appreciate reading as an enjoyable experience.

It can also be a question of comfort—is it safe to risk trying to solve a problem and perhaps be wrong? A sharp word, a facial expression, a body movement, may tell a child that he's "a dummy" for missing a problem or answering a question wrong. A classroom where children are permitted to tease each other for making errors can be an uncomfortable place to make a mistake. Where teasing has been permitted at home, some children have learned to avoid any situation in which they can make an error. We indicated before that because of difficult social circumstances, too many black children are "put down" by too many people, at home and away from home. We recall black children in a hostile, predominantly white classroom setting who did not respond to classroom questions at all. At church and on the playground, they were quite expressive and obviously bright.

Avoidance occurs less when children feel safe and accepted enough to make an error, try again, and eventually learn. Teachers of young children, particularly those who have been put down and made to feel stupid, bad, or unwanted, should be particularly supportive. Such children will put each other down. Teachers should discourage this. But be careful not to be supportive to the point of producing dependency . . . a need for your presence in order to do anything.

My problem is that I favor bright children although I know this is harmful. How can I handle this?

We are less than good professionals if we favor any child, and it is *our* responsibility to police ourselves. It helps to think consciously from time to time about the way we treat children from different backgrounds, of different ability levels, of different sex and personality. Do we limit girls to passive play and encourage boys to be self-assertive and aggressive? Do we expect more from white children from middle-income backgrounds (or black children from middle-income backgrounds for that matter) than we do from black or white children from low-income backgrounds?

It is important to remember that all children are valuable and must be helped to develop, regardless of the level of their IQ or their achievement test scores. It is also helpful not to think of children as naturally good or bad. We have pointed out in previous chapters that many factors can cause troublesome child behavior. Yet the behavior of children, particularly young children, can be modified. If we do not assume that he is what he is or she is what she is because of her race or his father's position, we have a better chance to modify the behavior of a child toward a more desirable direction.

As professional educators, we tend to favor children who are bright. On top of this, those of us who feel that the future of black America depends on the development of bright, aggressive blacks are likely to favor "the brightest and the best." We must be particularly careful to recognize and deal with this tendency, for only in a climate where *all* children feel valued can all achieve at their highest level.

Some of my students are terribly withdrawn and shy? Why is this?

Children are withdrawn and shy for different reasons. But they all generally lack confidence and are fearful of rejection and abuse—harsh criticism from adults or other children and occasional physical abuse. Sometimes children are simply shy because they've been cautioned to "be good" in school and are uncertain about what they can and can't do. The latter group come around very quickly when they understand the rules of the classroom and school. The problem is more complicated for other children. In some cases, black children are quiet and withdrawn in settings where white adults are in control. The children may be unsure of where you stand on race or of whether a white teacher or principal will be fair or not. Home visits or school visits by parents at good times—parties, special programs, etcetera—can be helpful . . . if you are a fair person.

This group generally fares very badly in chaotic classrooms with a great deal of confusion, scapegoating, and mutual abuse. These children fare best when a teacher is able to create an environment in which each child feels safe, believes that his rights and needs will be respected, and feels that he will not be ridiculed and put down. In such an environment you can work to help timid children develop more self-confidence and personal pride. When you are dealing with severely withdrawn and shy children, usually psychologically traumatized, do not move too quickly or expect too much too soon. We know of one situation where a child did not smile or show trust in her teacher for an entire year. But most withdrawn children will come around after a month or so—when they see that the coast is clear.

How can I best work with timid children to
help them become more assertive?

You might start out by encouraging them to participate in classroom discussions or activities . . . without waiting so long for them to answer a question or join in a game that you embarrass them. It helps after extending an invitation and waiting a reasonable length of time to indicate that you know that they will be able to join in later on. You might say very directly, particularly if you can say it in private, that you can see that he or she is a little bit embarrassed and uncomfortable, but that he will be all right . . . he'll come through . . . she'll gain her confidence, or whatever your way of soothing and reassuring happens to be. When they begin to participate, it helps to express your pleasure and delight that they are able to do so, again, without overpraising and embarrassing the child.

Withdrawn children often become the victims of more aggressive (but often just as insecure) children. You must protect the effort of the withdrawn child to come out of his shell just as you would protect a budding plant from too much sunlight, too much water, or whatever will kill it. For example, if you see a withdrawn child suddenly rise to defend himself from a bully or some kind of attack from others, you don't want to stop the fight too soon—unless there is a possibility of injury or it looks like the withdrawn child is going to get the kind of beating that will make him never want to fight again.

There are two problems to watch for here. Sometimes the withdrawn child will overshoot the mark and become aggressive beyond what is desirable. Sometimes he or she will become overdependent on you. We remember one situation in which a teacher placed a withdrawn child next to an aggressive, acting-up child, and in a short period of time you could not tell the difference between the two. A child who is functioning well—aggressive and assertive but not acting up—is the best model for a withdrawn child. You can avoid the overdependence situation by encouraging and protecting the withdrawn child without smothering him or her. In other words, as he gains confidence you will want to encourage him to stand on his own and fend for himself, just as you would any other child.

Some children will need professional help. When this is necessary and services are available, think of the withdrawn child as much as you do the acting-up child. The misbehaving child is more troublesome and disruptive in a classroom and therefore is the first to get help. But the withdrawn child has a problem which is just as serious—for him or her, if not for you—as the problem of the acting-up child.

What can I do when there are so many children who need help and so few psychologists and social workers in our schools?

It is unfortunate and unwise that schools in financial trouble cut back on social work and other support services, psychologists, counselors, etc., first. But it is also unfortunate that support service people stick so closely to a costly and less effective casework model, better for sick people than for basically healthy children and families. There will be more personnel to go around when parents, teachers and support personnel work together to change the atmosphere of a particular school rather than try to "fix" each child and family. Many of the conflicts between classroom teachers and people outside the classroom will be reduced when this is the case.

Take another look at your school and classroom. Children who do not ordinarily have problems often have them in chaotic and confused schools and classrooms. Often the individual teacher cannot do much about changing the school, but it *is* possible to do something in the classroom. But we have also seen chaotic schools brought under control and the number of children needing help for behavior problems cut almost eighty percent. Good classroom organization, careful management and praise for good performance (accentuating the positive while ignoring the negative, whenever possible) usually bring this about. But, as we have said, there are times when you must deal directly with misbehavior. It is easier to deal with when not *everybody* is misbehaving.

FOR PARENTS, TEACHERS, AND FRIENDS

The Role of Education in the Black Community

Many studies show that black parents from the low-income group, more than parents from other low-income groups, indicate that they want their children to get a college education. Why is this so?

Actually blacks from all income groups show a great interest in higher education. This is the case for two reasons. First, high-paying, high-prestige blue-collar jobs which do not require college training—electrician, bricklayer, etcetera—have been less available to blacks than to other low-income groups. Second, just as the Israelis have found that Jews from countries with oppressive conditions are less willing to work as waiters, delivery men, or in any other service capacity, the same is true of blacks. A college education provides the best opportunities for a high-prestige, white-collar job.

While everybody who can go to college and successfully compete should do so, the high-paying, high-prestige noncollege jobs should not be ignored. It is unfortunate that we "put down" any training but college training. Some people are not cut out for college, can't hack it, and won't make it. Yet they might do very well from a financial standpoint and from the standpoint of their own personal satisfaction if they became TV repairmen, mechanics, or technicians of one kind or another.

You have indicated that learning and education has its roots in the early childhood experience. Isn't the black community anti-intellectual, and doesn't that hurt the black child in school?

The black community, like most communities, is a combination of many different things. Some segments of it are anti-intellectual. In some segments, people read and debate the Bible as the scholars at Yale and Harvard debate the meaning of the works of great philosophers. In the poolrooms and barbershops, people debate and discuss the great issues of life—war, love, and the like—as thoughtful people everywhere and in all times have done. There is a tradition of scholarship and intellectual endeavor in the traditional sense of long-standing among some blacks. But there *is* a problem.

From the beginning, all elements of organization and control among the slaves were destroyed—families, government, business, traditional religion, and work. The only elements of traditional African cultures which were permitted were those which provided pleasure and prevented depression—music, dance, games, and other physical activities. But it is the need to establish understanding, order, and control in the environment—done through organizations such as business and government—which stimulates intellectual activity of the kind most useful in school and certain occupations. Blacks were closed out of such roles almost entirely until very, very recently, and still are today to a large extent.

While we have great appreciation for music, dance, and all the other spiritual and social aspects of black culture, it is unfortunate that too many blacks give more attention to these activities than the pursuit and application of knowledge. Not true? One look at any black newspaper or magazine will tell you that this *is* the case. It is not surprising, given this situation, that black children aspire to be athletes, entertainers, or civil rights leaders more than college professors, bankers, and businessmen. But it is the latter who are involved in the pursuit and application of knowledge, organization, and control. Schools, as well as other institutions in the black community, should work to balance this situation. After all, only a handful of people can play professional football.

Concern about knowledge and control of the environment is a white middle-class thing. The application of knowledge has been used to exploit people. Why would you urge that the black community go in that direction?

The fact that learning, schooling, and control through the political and economic institutions is even considered a white middle-class thing is part of the problem. These are necessary skills in every social system. Blacks had them prior to coming to America . . . and many have them now. Schooling and knowledge have been used positively as well as negatively to improve medical care, reduce hunger, and in many other ways. We should encourage black children to gain knowledge and develop their skills but to use them more humanely than has been the case among controlling groups in the past.

Middle-income people sometimes expect too much in the
way of school achievement from their children. I have
seen warm black parents in our community who expect
very little from their children, and the children are
much less frustrated and anxious. Why would
you urge otherwise?

We *must* train and encourage enough people to be leaders so that we are able to develop the kind of social policy which will not cause so many black people to be victimized. Leaders of business, industry, and educational institutions make decisions which influence and shape our lives and the lives of our children and their children. For every mother who is warm and accepting of children, because she is not involved in competitive education or in the process of trying to get a good job, there is another who is frustrated, depressed, powerless, and abusive because she is unable to provide for the needs of her children. (The same is true for fathers.) All people must be careful not to push children or anyone else beyond their capabilities. It is possible to be warm and accepting as well as competitive and achieving.

Curriculum and Skill Development

Do you think that black English should
be used in any black schools?

No. We think that standard English should be used in all schools. Black English appears to be a combination of African language forms and Euro-American language forms, brought together through the contact of slaves with whites in the Deep South. The fact that black English contains elements of legitimate language forms is not a reasonable justification for the routine use of this form in the classroom, except as an aid in learning standard English. On the other hand, we should not be disrespectful of black English, or push it aside without trying to learn something from it.

We believe that black English should be studied by scholars for academic and practical purposes—for example, to determine whether there is anything in this language form which could better help black children learn standard English and foreign languages. One of the strange paradoxes of the language-reading problem is the fact that black African children often speak two and three languages or more, and some black American children have trouble learning to speak and read standard English. Perhaps the study of black English and African languages will shed some light here.

But the purpose of education is to help children function well in the society in which they live. Children from many ethnic groups come to school with language forms or dialects different from that of standard English. As we mentioned earlier, teachers should respect the language of the home or community, but should help children learn the language which will help them function in the bank, at the university, at the computer programmer training program. If they learn standard English at school, they have a choice. If they use only black English or the language of their home, they will only be able to function successfully where that language is accepted.

How can the curriculum of the upper elementary and middle-school child help give a youngster a positive feeling of racial identity?

Biographies, filmstrips, and other material dealing with successful black people are particularly interesting to youngsters in the nine-through-twelve-year-old age group, because this is a period of becoming like or identifying with important role models. It is particularly important for children living under difficult circumstances to know about and be able to identify with black people who can help them feel good about being of the same group.

School projects which require research into traditional African village life or study the contributions of black Americans or black American organizations can also be helpful. These programs should be made a part of reading, social science, science, and other curricula. Skits and plays developed around black contributions to America and struggles against obstacles will sensitize children to the black experience. They can give youngsters a sense of blackness that goes beyond their immediate family, ties into the past, and helps point them toward a direction for the future. This is very much needed.

We recall a black child who, in 1966, looking at pictures of famous black Americans, did not know who Jackie Robinson was or what his contribution had been to America and to black Americans in particular. Not one black American of our generation would not know the story. It is a story which has both a far-reaching symbolic meaning and a direct impact on the life of all blacks. It is a tragedy that every black child does not know the story of Jackie Robinson and many other blacks who made important contributions that have made life somewhat more tolerable for all blacks.

Without such teaching, the works and contributions of each generation are lost, and each begins anew as if there were no past. In fact, the young are more critical of older blacks than they would be if they fully understood. More young people could respect and learn from the older generation—and vice versa. Young people could build on the past and learn from it as a way of gaining direction and purpose. Schools serving black children should dramatize these experiences and serve to link the past with the present and point toward the future.

*Can a child's immediate community contribute
anything in this regard?*

Yes. In reality, Jackie Robinson, Shirley Chisholm, Malcolm X, John B. Johnson, George Washington Carver, Frederick Douglass and others are far removed from the life of many black children. In fact, their lifestyles are and were often quite different. It is important to have people of the community—who have talents and skills, and are making important contributions now—recognized and involved in the school program. We have often felt that one of the problems of public schools in inner city communities is that the culture of the school is so very different from the culture of the community. This can be overcome by involving parents or people from the community who hunt, do needlework, sing (choirs, musicians), and are involved in other activities—in the school program. Such people, when they are good examples and support the goals of the school, can bridge the gap between the community and the school for many youngsters.

*What kinds of skills should schools
help black children develop?*

The schools must do more than teach basic educational skills. Black people have been consistently closed out of the political, economic and educational mainstream of this country. As a result, many of the skills that white children and a few black children gain because their families are involved in banking, education, administration, and politics are not automatically passed on to most black children. This could be done through classroom projects and programs.

It is absurd to have fourth- and fifth-grade students plodding through the "curriculum as usual" when a political election is going on—with black candidates yet! English, social science, math, and other courses could relate to the action. Essays, stories in the class newspaper, percentage of votes, a study of the campaign issues and a thousand and one other things could be made relevant. A visit to the polls would make it all even more significant.

Candidates, and others, could be invited to school. Teachers could help their classes learn how to invite guests, prepare programs and send thank-you notes. In make-believe projects, youngsters would learn to make all the arrangements to purchase land, save money, contribute to drives, and serve on boards. The need to be punctual, efficient, and organized in our modern world should be stressed. Such activities should help to teach children how our social system works, who makes the decisions which determine whether their parents work or not, and what kinds of organizational and work skills they will need to influence or control their lives and the society around them. Such programs could give black youngsters greater personal skills, direction and purpose.

As things now stand, we generally tell black youth that it's a racist society, sometimes tell them they will need an education to do something about it, but rarely direct their attention to the machinery of change—the operations of political and economic institutions. Can these institutions work for us? We don't know. But before anyone talks of overthrowing them, we had better help our youngsters thoroughly understand them. We rarely directly point out the personal skills they will need to influence institutions and the system. The same skills required to understand and run institutions would also be required to greatly change them in this day and age. In fact, these skills are needed to successfully function in a family.

The Pros and Cons of Busing

*We find that we have more problems with the children
who are bused into our school district than with the
black children who live here already. Is that true
because of the socioeconomic level?*

Most children can get along well when a school enables them to
feel valued, comfortable and capable. There are many subtle ways
in which the opposite attitudes can get across. We were told of a
situation in which a black child from the middle-income neighborhood gave a very advanced explanation for the cause of war. A
passing teacher said to the youngster's teacher in a knowing
fashion, "She must be one of ours." The point was that the bused-
in black children would not be that smart. (The fact is that many
of the children, black or white, who lived in the neighborhood
could not have given the same explanation, but that wouldn't be
held against them.) Such attitudes will be picked up by children.

The exposure, experience, and educational development of the
middle-income children is likely to be greater than that of the
lower-income children, regardless of race. Again, the important
point is not to make assumptions about the intelligence or motivation of the children bused in. It is important to provide the
opportunity for growth in the classroom. This is most likely to
happen when you reach a child where he is, demonstrate concern
and respect for him as a person and not as an IQ score, and move
him toward his highest capability without comparing him with or
judging him against others. There is less likely to be trouble for
children outside of a school district when this is the case.

It is unfortunate that so many school busing programs have
been accompanied by so much bad feeling. The success of such
programs depends on children feeling wanted and valued and
capable. Teachers and parents in the receiving school district are
less likely to be able to create this climate after being involved in
bitter opposition struggles.

Is school busing desirable?

Let's answer another question first. Was school integration desirable? We feel that school integration was necessary because
school segregation was the sign and symbol of black inferiority.

Education, after defense, is the single biggest business in America. In addition, it feeds people into the most powerful positions in other businesses—industry, government, and the like. The isolation of blacks in school made it difficult for blacks to become opinion- and decision-makers in these areas. This, in turn, made it easier to limit black opportunities. School desegregation destroyed the argument for limiting black participation anywhere.

Unfortunately, housing desegregation and the development of new towns did not accompany the school desegregation decision. Housing has always been the basic problem, not busing. With a spread of income, racial, ethnic and religious groups in most communities, we would not have the serious racial problems we have in many schools today. At the same time we could have retained and upgraded many of the black schools which are the carriers of black culture—particularly at the college level.

We do not believe that busing is undesirable where it is pos- sible. A mixture of people from different incomes and cultural backgrounds—when properly organized—can reduce the stereo- types they hold about each other and permit a sharing of values. In addition the victims of poverty and extreme racism will not all be in the same school or area. The danger here, of course, is that the problems of the victims can become the culture and climate of the school. The same is true with regard to affluence. This is not to say that there are no problems when schools are integrated, through busing or otherwise. But we have seen these problems greatly reduced with enlightened school leadership.

The reality of today, however, is that there are many schools that simply can't and won't be integrated. It is important here to make certain that the youngsters receive the best education pos- sible. We have seen Black Muslim schools, schools operated by civil rights activists and black nationalists, as well as some public schools in which the climate for learning is highly favorable. The principles used in these situations can be used in other places.

Intelligence and Testing

*It seems to me that black children are very verbal and
physically active in creative ways indicative of intelligence.
But some are less good at written expression and analysis.
Has this been your observation?*

Again, it is dangerous to make generalizations. There are wide
differences of ability and style within the black community just as
there are wide differences in the white community. The differences
within groups are greater than the differences *between* groups. On
the other hand, this is an area that deserves more attention and
research. *Ability in written expression and analysis is more a
matter of experience and training than it is an indication of intelligence.* Yet intelligence and achievement tests require these skills.
If what you have observed is true—and we think we see the same
things—blacks are being unfairly judged and often barred from
academic and work programs which evaluate people largely on
their ability at written expression and analysis.

We must remember that traditional black culture was an oral
culture. In addition, large numbers of blacks were closed out of
opportunities in the society which required the development of
written expression and even analytical thinking, planning, and
organizing. Finally because of difficult social conditions, some
black families developed a "control" language: "sit down," "shut
up," "mind your business," "be nice." Language used to explain and
share information and ideas helps to develop verbal and written
expression, the understanding of concepts, and analytical thinking.
We really don't know the effect of these factors on the black child's
abilities at this point, but they should be studied.

We do know that programs exist which have improved the
learning of black children through rhythmic exercises. We know of
black students who have been judged as bright as or brighter than
their black and white peers on verbal examinations who do far less
well on written examinations. These observations suggest that
there is much that we don't understand in this area; that there is a
real need for more research in the area of the learning style of
some black children. We suspect that it would be very easy to
improve written expression and analysis in cases where it is simply
underdeveloped in otherwise bright youngsters.

Aren't there some culture-free tests?

No, and even if there were, cultural difference is only one part of the problem. Most cultures in America are not that different, and tests could be made which cancelled out the middle-class white advantage if that was the only problem. (This should be done if we continue to use such tests to measure potential.) The real problem is that blacks and other minorities are unwanted and often despised groups confronted with deliberate obstacles. These factors—past and present—affect black performance on achievement and intelligence tests.

Deliberate segregation and inadequate educational and economic opportunities implied inferior ability when it was not stated directly. Exclusion from important decision-making and social roles created real knowledge deficiencies in certain areas. Limited future opportunities hurt the motivation to develop some skills measured on so-called intelligence tests; for example, the collection and storage of nonessential information. Limited achievement by too many blacks as a result of these circumstances has been used as "evidence" of limited intelligence.

In subtle and not so subtle ways, by omission and commission, the mass media—print (books, papers, and magazines) and electronic (TV and radio)—have spread the notion that blacks are less intelligent than others. Much of the white public is all too willing to buy this in order to justify their "right" to hold more than their share of the better jobs. Direct and indirect individual and institutional claims to this effect are everywhere. As a result, self-doubt becomes a tremendous problem and plays an even bigger role in affecting intelligence and achievement scores than cultural difference.

The loose use of psychological, achievement, and intelligence tests to judge and place black children is unfair and dangerous. The case of the boxer Muhammad Ali is a case in point. He was ridiculed by many sports writers for his "low intelligence" as shown by Army entrance examinations. But anybody with common sense who had listened to him field questions and give bright and clever answers should have known that he was a very intelligent man. Mistaken judgments of this kind are made every day in this country because of our overreliance on tests and figures which often don't tell the real story. We have seen Irish, Italian, Spanish-speaking, and other foreign-speaking youngsters judged "not too bright" because of their performance on intelligence and achievement tests when they couldn't even understand the language. Often they suffer serious consequences!

You're not suggesting that all black children could do better on IQ and achievement tests. Wouldn't that be a dangerous assumption?

We are not suggesting that all black children can do better on intelligence and achievement tests. Some black children, *like some white children,* cannot achieve at high academic and intellectual levels because they do not have the intelligence to do so. But they shouldn't have to. The fact that they cannot should not make them less important as human beings. Our job as educators is to help them develop to their highest potential, but not to frustrate them by trying to push them beyond their potential. Our concern is that existing tests and attitudes may cause some people to assume that black children don't have it when they do.

7

The Elementary-School-Age Child:
Ages Nine to Twelve

Importance of This Period

*Is it true that the personality of a nine-year-old
is the same one he'll have at ninety?*

There is some truth in this, but the notion is misleading. Certain
basic attitudes, values, and strategies for handling problems in life,
ways of working and relaxing gel (become the usual way of
responding) during this period. But important events in the lives
of people after this period—in college or at work, in marriage and
in the family—can and do modify a person's personality. Let's put
it this way: generally, the *basic* personality does not change much
from this point on. Yet much personality development takes place
during this period and in adolescence.

Dealing with Racial Attitudes

Are racial attitudes among those that gel during this period?

Yes. Children understand the concept of race quite well by this
stage. Attitudes about their race and that of others are fast becoming a permanent part of their personality. But changes in attitude
can still take place. The kinds of experiences children have and the
kinds of persons they become will determine the final racial atti-

tudes they develop. Again, fear and frustration are the underlying causes of racist attitudes in individuals. Children of this age group who have positive feelings about themselves, who are successfully coping with life—and do not have the racist attitudes of their parents forced on them—have no need to repeatedly put down other groups as a fixed way of building up their self-esteem. This is true of all children, regardless of race.

What can happen if parents express strong
racist feelings during this period?

A problem is created even when parents do this at an earlier age. But nine through twelve years, for most children, is in a sense their last chance to develop healthy ways to handle their fears, frustrations, and disappointments. Brian can still learn to accept the fact that he is not as good in spelling as Debra, and that's okay. Joe can learn that he isn't liked by the fellows because he brags too much, but that he can change. Matthew can learn that his family is on public welfare, but that's no mark on him as long as he is working and developing himself to be able to contribute his fair share. But if children in this age group are "given" blacks, Jews, poor people, white people, or any such "other group" to hate—by adult instruction or example—in order to make them feel better about themselves, we are cutting off their opportunity to develop more healthy and more helpful ways of arriving at a positive self-image. They can easily develop a low-level, Archie Bunker-type way of trying to "be somebody." Racist attitudes will end up limiting the success of most people in later life.

Since children are so sensitive to racial issues at this stage
I realize that my child will watch closely to see how I deal with
problems in this area. What's a general approach for handling
racial incidents in a way that will be helpful to him?

The important thing is to handle the incident in a way that does not consume too much of your energy. Otherwise such occurrences can prevent you and your child from functioning well. There is no such thing as "a" best way. It is really very much an individual approach. Your temperament, situation, mood at the time, and a number of other factors will determine how you respond. The blatant incidents are easier to deal with. The subtle incidents are more difficult to deal with, and probably the most troublesome in the long run.

Two examples of the latter type should be helpful here:

CASE A

One black father, accompanied by his son, asked to look at an expensive piece of camera equipment. He did not have on his business suit, nor was he carrying his attaché case, but he did have his black skin with him. The white clerk responded, "But that costs three hundred dollars!" With a steely voice, the man replied, "I didn't ask you the price, I said that I would like to see it." The clerk got the point and apologized. It is important here not to feel obliged to buy the equipment after such an incident . . . unless you want it. Some middle-class blacks overtip and overbuy under such circumstances just to prove that "We ain't all poor." Your child should learn from you that you don't have to prove anything.

Shouldn't you educate the clerk? You can, but for the most part, it's a waste of time. He was operating from an attitude that said, "All blacks are poor." The incident—his response and your response—does more to change his way of thinking than any amount of words could ever do.

CASE B

On this occasion, a black family was rushing to the airport and went through an intersection on a "late yellow" stoplight signal. A white policeman stopped them. It was truly a judgment call, that is, it could have been called either way. The driver explained that the light was still yellow when he entered the intersection, but acknowledged that he was rushing to the airport because they were late. The policeman indicated that it could have been yellow, but it appeared red to him. The policeman considered the situation for a few seconds and then told them to go ahead but to be careful.

This simple little incident is just loaded with all of the "stuff" which leads to black and white conflict: the issues of manhood, "Establishment power," and whether the policeman represents a just or unjust authority system. The father could have reacted in a way which might have caused the child to feel that every white person, all the time, is out to get "us!" That every authority figure, all the time, is out to get us! When a policeman, or any other kind of authority figure, has a valid question and is conducting himself or herself in a fair way, it is important to respond in a fair way as well as a way which does not cause you to lose your sense of dignity or self-respect. At the same time, it does not help to become unjustifiably belligerent.

We recognize all of the forces which might cause a belligerent reaction. But such a reaction is likely to cause you to lose your dignity rather than maintain it. We have seen an awful lot of "bad talk"—"what I'm gonna do"—followed by meekness and power-lessness. Nothing is a more troublesome model to your child. In this case, the father was "cool," lost no dignity in the eyes of his wife or son, and successfully resolved a problem.

Was the child watching and learning? While father and son were on the way home, after putting mother on the airplane, out of the blue came, "Black people don't like policemen, do they?" The father replied, sensing what the child was after, "Some black people don't like policemen." That kind of answer gave the child permission to go ahead and he asked, "That's because of the way policemen have treated black people, right?" The father answered, "Yes, some policemen, but I'll bet you're thinking about that policeman that stopped us on the way to the airport." The son replied, "Yes, he was nice, right?" The father replied, "Yes. I spoke nicely to him and he spoke nicely to me." A smile of relief spread across the child's face, probably for a couple of reasons.

First, the father's response permitted the child to see and hear what he saw and heard rather than be bound to a stereotyped response, "Black people don't like policemen." "All policemen mis-treat black people." Seeing and hearing what isn't there in a specific case, because that is the group response one is supposed to have, is the way a generalized paranoia develops. This is trouble-some, because a great deal of our sense of security comes from a feeling that authority figures or people with power can and will be fair with us if we are fair with them; can be *made* to be fair with us by higher authorities when they are not. Of course, you do just as much damage when you pretend that all is well when it is not. In short, we are not saying that you should never see a race prob-lem when you see it. We are saying that you should call it like it is.

Even if the child had not talked about this incident, as it was handled, it would have been helpful to him.

Suppose the policeman had said, "What's your hurry, nigger?"

As we all know, it has happened. Most of us cannot (and should not) walk away from such an incident without a confrontation. On the other hand, it is important to maintain your self-respect without paying a high price—physical harm, psychic energy, and social consequences (job, jail, etcetera). A policeman is an authority figure with a loaded gun. If you punch him or use a "bunch of dirty names"—and happen to be fairly isolated—he can beat or kill you and justify it. Some have done so with less cause.

Before suggesting a response, let us tell the "little girl and the cookie jar" story to show how people in the wrong react to protect themselves. A cookie jar was placed out of the reach of a daring two-year-old. She stacked books and chairs in a precarious fashion to reach it. Just as she stuck her hand in the jar, her father walked in. Frightened that she would fall, he yelled at her. With no excuse for her disobedience, she paused to think and said, "I'm mad at you, you yelled at me!" She neatly shifted her violation and any fault from herself to her father.

A policeman who calls you a nigger in a community with even marginal black political and social power can be in trouble. But if you punch or abuse him, he can justify whatever he does to you. With this in mind, we believe that it is better to take neither a "Tom" stance nor a "crazy nigger" stance (an aggressive response without fear or concern about consequences) in such situations. You can point out that nigger is not your name and that you plan to report the incident to the NAACP or whatever group is in a position to take action. Even here you must weigh the danger. You may want to say nothing but take action through black civil rights groups, white civil rights groups—or your alderman, councilman or mayor if they are concerned about the rights of blacks. The important thing here is to follow through. It is too easy to "forget it" after a time or in the face of roadblocks put in your way.

In most parts of the country now, you can do something effective in such situations. It is important to explain to a youngster involved exactly what you are doing and how. The more effective complaints are made and actions taken, the more policemen—and other authorities—will think twice before they show racial abuse. We don't deny that black anger and violence have already caused authority figures to be more cautious and respectful. On the other hand, abuse and violence in a specific, isolated situation is likely to bring you abuse and violence and other serious harm. Such action and outcome is not a helpful model for youngsters.

When the authority figure is not a policeman, such caution is not necessary, although physical attack and extreme abusiveness may cause you difficulty. Even here—with supervisors, public service workers, teachers—the most effective action is to bring pressure on them through civil rights groups. The problem of abuse because of race from people in authority is a greater problem than most of us realize. Authority figures—leaders, policemen, public service workers—should provide us with protection and opportunities. Their lack of fairness creates much of the rage, anger, and mixed feelings we often feel toward *our* country.

Can you make your child overreact to racism?

Yes. There is no need to go around looking for racism everywhere. Every black child in America today knows there is racism. Again, the important thing is to help youngsters learn to deal with it in an effective way that takes as little energy as possible, and permits them to maintain a sense of dignity and well-being. At the same time, black parents must not deny disrespect that stems from racial grounds. But we must be careful not to call disrespect based on other grounds—religion, income, occupation, lifestyle—racial prejudice. (Hopefully we are opposed to all disrespect.) Calling it all racism can make your child feel that he is drowning in a sea of ill-feeling with no allies or potential allies anywhere. It can cause black children to be fearful and uncomfortable, except in the company of a black group . . . and much friction within black groups suggests that even here they will not always find peace of mind. While it is important for blacks to be able to get along with each other, it is also important to be able to function as adults in important places where there are few blacks but where we need to be, in order to protect the rights of the group—such as school boards, finance boards, and bank boards.

If you call everybody a racist and every injustice racism, your child will learn to do the same. Your child may want to fight all injustices, but at least he ought to be aware of the fact that not everything is a question of race. It pays to study an incident or a situation before jumping to a conclusion and reacting. Is the store clerk cold and aloof with you because you're black or because that's his personality? Look around. How does he treat white people? Very often what you think is a racial response turns out to be something quite different.

But what if the white museum guide talks only to the whites in the tour group and it is clearly a conscious act of racism? You can leave, but you've paid your money like everybody else. You can leave any situation where you feel slighted or rejected, but why? You have the same right to enjoy every benefit in the country as anybody else. When you feel certain that the unfair response is due to your race, rather than calling the offending person a racist, a string of other names, or leaving in a huff, you can often gain your rights and due respect by calling the behavior in question to his or her attention. Such a confrontation when handled well will preserve your sense of dignity and force racists to develop less racist ways of responding to blacks.

*But don't you have to be more aggressive
about putting a racist down?*

Why? You're already operating from the morally superior or "right" position. Because racism is everywhere, it makes no more sense to spend all your time and energy putting racists down than it does to keep stomping out rain on a rainy day. It makes more sense to help your child learn to survive and thrive in a "race storm" in the same way you teach him not to get too wet in a rainstorm. If you develop ways to get your rights respected and your dignity preserved without always being in a fight with white folks, you and your child will have more energy to give to fulfilling your personal goals and aspirations. This is the age when black children will either learn how to do this and thrive, in spite of racism, or feel a growing insecurity which often hurts their future functioning.

Many blacks get trapped into asking and demanding that whites prove that they're not racists. So what if they are? That's their problem. All Americans are racist at some level, including blacks being anti-black. The important thing is not to let racism of any kind interfere with your life performance and to force racists to respect your rights and the rights of your children. This is part of their responsibility as citizens. Many whites today don't want their unconscious prejudice known. Many companies and government agencies won't tolerate an open display of racism. Your reasonable demand for respect will be heard in many instances. All people, black and white, make themselves vulnerable if they look beyond their family, close friends, and associates for more than this.

Of course, when people ignore the reasonable approach, you will have to be more forceful. But the forceful approach should be an approach of last resort. If you go that route, you are likely to pay a high price energy-wise and otherwise.

Is there any danger of children misusing the issue of racism?

Yes. Children this age will hide behind "stuff"—race or anything else—to excuse poor performance. It is just as important to help your child learn *not* to use race—or any other jive excuse—to get what he wants without "cutting the mustard" as it is to teach him to fight for respect as a black person. Some success in this life comes from luck. Most comes from good effort and performance. Your child *must* learn before he gets beyond this age that, cute as he is, aggressive as you are, as unfair as the society is, a good effort and a good performance are still his best chance. The job of blacks as a group is to make sure that this is indeed the case by changing the society rather than using its faults to excuse poor performance.

Many, many parents help their children become mediocre, irresponsible, dependent, and even criminal by allowing them to "get away with murder." In fact we heard a mother plead for her son, convicted of murder, saying, "But he's my baby!"—and he was twenty-seven years old! Racism is racism, and jive is jive, and it's up to you to help your child learn the difference . . . or you, your child, and his family and associates may be the victims down the line.

Black parents—and particularly black writers and social service people concerned about the race problem—must be particularly careful here. Because we are outraged—about the opportunities we are denied, about harmful myths still being developed, about the fact that the government has gone back on its promise of the 1960's, about the fact that the press and government are outraged about the deaths of whites at the hands of blacks but less concerned about the deaths of blacks at the hands of whites, about the fact that big business and industry are moving to the suburbs leaving blacks jobless in the city, about so many other things—it is sometimes easy to excuse black mistreatment of whites or "foolin' the man" when there is no just cause for doing so.

*What can happen to a child who is allowed to
"hide" behind race issues?*

Such children may have difficulty being honest with themselves
about the quality of their own performances. They may not
develop the ability to respond in a responsible and fair way
toward other people . . . including blacks. We recall the black
youngster who justified ripping off the stereo components from a
white student because, "He's just a rich white kid." When ques-
tioned further he admitted that he stole money from his father's
wallet regularly. He also made a practice of exploiting his girlfriend and friends.

A young black man in jail, when asked about the cause for his
imprisonment, indicated that he was a political prisoner. Asked the
specifics, he acknowledged that he'd killed his mother and father.
In other writings, we have shown why there is a wee bit of truth to
his argument. But his dead parents—and the jailed youngster—
did not and will not benefit from being allowed to hide behind the
racial issue.

Parents have the right to raise their children as they desire . . .
as long as they are not inhumane. That may be the most important
good thing left about this country. But . . . we must remember
that in spite of the fact that the society created most of the problems confronting blacks, it is mainly blacks—organizations, professionals, and the community at large—who can "save the children."
Helping a child learn to be responsible for his own behavior while
working toward the development of effective ways to fight injustice is more helpful to a youngster than allowing him to take out
his angry feelings on whitey or anybody else without specific
justification. Children who are permitted to "take it out on somebody else" are the very ones who make many black communities
unsafe and unhappy places to live.

How the Nine- to Twelve-Year-Old Thinks

*What is the thinking ability of children
in this age group like?*

As we mentioned in Chapter 5, the seven- and eight-year-old
begins to understand that rules are made by people and not
enforced from on high. Nine-, ten-, and eleven-year-olds fully

understand this. They may spend as much time working on—arguing, changing and agreeing on—the rules of a game as they spend playing it. While it may wear on your nerves, it is good practice in establishing orderly and organized thinking. Help them move on to the game only when they are helplessly bogged down in "rules."

Youngsters will improve their ability with math concepts during this period. Your child's memory will continue to improve as well as his ability to observe and remember. His reasoning and general information will sometimes amaze you. Late in this age period and in early teens is the period in which batting averages, rock group membership, the number of bolts in the Eiffel Tower—and 1001 other bits of "important" information—will be "laid" on you, if being knowledgeable is a good thing in your house.

How can I help my child improve his thinking ability?

Much will be learned in school and in books. Much can be learned from games. Naming singing groups, cities, famous people, the streets in town and any "brain game" you want to make up is good training. Observing the contents of a room for two minutes, leaving, and trying to recall what you have seen is helpful and fun. Puzzles, checkers, chess and many other games can sharpen your child's ability to think, reason, plan, organize, and develop strategies.

Most important, around eleven years of age, your child will begin a lot of "if . . . then" thinking. This makes it increasingly possible to understand "cause and effect" twice, thrice, and more removed from what is obvious. The good thinker is now full of questions, possibilities, and theories about the world. Again, raising questions which will help your child figure out how to solve a problem is helpful. Uncovering "frauds" in TV commercials is very helpful. For example, "if" the stomach is made to handle acid "then" the acid in the soda is not the problem the antacid people claim it to be. Building up your child's interest and enjoyment in thinking through a problem is more important than helping him acquire information. Information is in books and can be had.

Aspects of Emotional Growth

*My nine-year-old daughter acts twenty-seven one day
and three the next . . . even sometimes within
the same few minutes. What causes this?*

This is not unusual for a nine-year-old. Don't let the looks and
sounds of maturity fool you. Children today know more words,
hear more complex and interesting things than we heard at nine
years of age. But they still have the same nine-year-old emotions
and limits of understanding that we had. They still need a great
deal of help in handling their feelings and emotions.

We as adults sometimes feel we have "bitten off more than we
can chew," that we're in over our heads. We despair and we're
afraid that we are going to fail. The same is true for your nine-year-
old. Because she is trying to demonstrate her capabilities to you
and to herself, failure at something she considers important can be
humiliating and cause her to feel bad and react immaturely. Children often set their own standards for success, so that although
you may think they've made a good effort, they may feel they have
failed.

Nine-year-olds are often still quite fearful . . . and too often
we tell them they *must* be fearless. Bad dreams and trouble falling
asleep can be a problem at this age. Squeaking floors and doors
and rustling trees at night can mean danger. Illness, death, or
violence involving friends can increase the fear. All you can do is
"hang in there." Point out that, as real as it seems, the dream is not
real. The "prowler" is just the wind against the window—when
that's the case. See Chapter 4 for more about death and sleep
problems.

When a child acts twenty-seven one minute and three the next,
it's easy to be disgusted and angry that she can't act twenty-seven
all the time . . . or at least nine. Shaming your child because she's
acting like a baby is a great temptation, but it's not helpful. It's
best to try and find out what she's concerned about, be supportive,
and help her learn to accept a failure and work toward success
next time. If your child bites off more than she can chew, help her
chew it. It helps to praise her for her efforts, but at the same time,
aid her to learn to establish realistic goals—or at least to ask for
help when things are beyond her ability.

One little girl we know arranged a surprise birthday party for her mother. She invited guests, ordered the food, and made most of the arrangements before her father knew about it. When faced with the question of who was going to pay for it all and how to get the mother away from home in order to prepare for the festivities, she became frightened, moody, and irritable. Sensing a problem, the father inquired and was told the whole story. He helped her bring the affair off, praising her for her effort and accomplishment, but at the same time he indicated that next time it would be a good idea to let him in on her plans from the beginning. It is important to encourage and help children achieve things, but it is also important for them to learn to be realistic.

My nine-year-old has a "fit" when I say "no,"
and then he cools down quickly. Why?

The nine-year-old is on the verge of bringing his unreasonable desires and demands under control, but he hasn't quite made it yet. He needs help from time to time. Outrageous demands are meant to test your concern and ability. Even though he may put up a fuss, he respects a strong hand when it is reasonable and fair. This makes him feel protected from his own inner desires and demands, which he knows to be unreasonable but can't control. Your ability to say "no" indicates that you can protect him from threats from other people and other dangers in the world.

When you feel you *must* disapprove of some of his behavior—for example, riding his bicycle on busy streets—think carefully about the position you are taking. Are you being overprotective? Is the street really *that* busy? Is there a time when it's not busy and okay for riding? Is your child safety-conscious enough to handle at least the nonbusy hours? It helps to give your reasons for taking a certain position, without preaching and without being defensive. Discussions concerning such issues help your child become a logical thinker, a safety-conscious person who can learn to anticipate and solve problems, plan and organize in advance.

Regardless of the issue involved, don't take a stand because of "what the neighbors will think" or "my reputation." This can make your child feel that you care more about your reputation than about him. Most of all, don't take a stand because "I'm your father," which means "I have the power to make you do whatever I want you to do whether it's right or wrong." You should take a stand because *you* believe that the action he wants to take is in some way hurtful to him and others. The more you are seen as a reasonable and responsible being with the power of parenthood, able to *listen* and *change* your position when convinced that your child is right or not change it when not so convinced, the more likely your child is to accept your decision without extreme protest. "I'm your father (or mother)" is like waving a red flag at a bull.

My nine-year-old son frequently has "stomach trouble." The doctor says that he hasn't been able to find anything wrong with him . . . that the problem is psychosomatic. How can I help?

Most doctors are very careful before they suggest that problems such as asthma, diarrhea, vomiting, excessive perspiration, and allergies are psychosomatic. Other diseases can cause these problems, and they do not want to miss them. On the other hand, they *can* be caused by emotional tension alone, and then they are called psychosomatic illnesses.

Doctors are not in complete agreement about the cause. But it is generally agreed that a combination of a person's physical makeup and certain stressful or difficult situations cause emotional tension and psychosomatic illness. It is a very individual thing in that the kind of stress that would cause one child to develop an illness will not affect another. Some children will be bothered with a psychosomatic illness for perhaps one or two years and will never be bothered again. Others will have the problem for a while, with a long free period, only to fall ill again at a time of stress later in life.

The problem usually starts with a crisis in your child's life such as starting school, trouble in the family, a problem with a teacher or relative.

It is not helpful to tell a child who develops a stomachache, diarrhea, or another problem that it is "all in the head." It is best to look for and deal with the cause of the stress rather than pay a lot of attention to the symptoms. Problems at school or at home which could be the cause of the stress and upset should be talked about and solved by whatever means possible. As we mentioned earlier, where there is severe conflict between parents, children sometimes react in ways that make their parents focus on them instead of on their marital difficulties. In such a case you should try to help your child stay out of the situation, and you and your spouse should attempt to improve your relationship. If the health problem persists, you may want to get professional help from mental health workers. They are likely to want to make certain again that there is no underlying physical problem.

My eleven-year-old son was a fighter and a half at seven. But now he rarely fights. What's the change all about?

Seven-year-olds fight largely because they are out in the world of competition but have not yet learned the fine art of negotiation and compromise. The only way they know to handle problems and their feelings is to battle it out. If all disagreement and opposition from others had to be fought over, children would have little time to do anything else but fight—little time to accomplish a goal. In situations where others are not reasonable or fair, your child may have to fight . . . and should. But the child who is repeatedly fighting at this age generally has some kind of problem—feels insecure, has been excluded from the group, has poor inner controls, or has a need to "bully."

In some communities where there are a large number of children with problems of this kind, fighting at the "drop of a hat" or the "cross of an eye" becomes a way of life. This is the case with street gangs. Even here, street workers and others working with problem children have been able to turn these tendencies into constructive work and play efforts.

Less fighting generally does not represent a loss of healthy aggressiveness. The aggressiveness is simply no longer physical and now often shows itself in the desire and effort to learn, and in play. You need to be concerned about this change only if the child will not stand up for his rights and permits himself to be pushed around. Even in this case, it is best not to encourage your child to fight but to encourage him to speak up for his rights. If we don't encourage our children to be willing to fight if necessary, but to be more willing to "talk it out" first when possible, we may never see a decrease in attacks of black against black. It takes more of a man to talk and work out a problem than it does to fight it out. *Anybody* can fight.

Youngsters this age should also be encouraged to develop other ways to work off their angry feelings. These might include fake boxing, "big" and "bad" talk that comes to nothing, and teasing.

But again, above all they need to develop the skill to "talk it out" and compromise so that both contesting parties can feel that a fair solution was reached . . . and save face. If they are constantly fighting they have less chance to develop this most important art.

My eleven-year-old was very fearful at four, wild at seven, and now at eleven is calm and confident. What happened?

Your eleven-year-old now has a lot more information about the world than he had at four. Because you helped him think and talk about sex, violence, racial discrimination, death, and other troublesome things, he now has a number of things under control which were once frightening . . . not that he won't ask any more questions about these things. They simply are no longer so pressing, urgent, and ever-present. In addition, his inner controls are now stronger than his desires and impulses to act to get what he wants, when he wants it, regardless of the consequences. As a result, he is not always an inch away from trouble and punishment the way he was a few years ago.

Much of the energy that once went into "mischief" now goes into doing things that represent achievement of one kind or another. If development is going well, achievement has become pleasurable and important to your child—not in order to please you, but to meet his own developing standards. Again, because of this, he is less likely to do things for which he will be punished. At the same time he now fully understands that the punishment you give him cannot hurt him; that in fact it is a reminder and not designed to hurt. Also, he now knows that the angry feelings that he has toward you will not actually hurt you. All of these developments decrease fear and testing, acting-up behavior. But before you figure you have it "made in the shade," remember that the calmness of eleven and twelve years of age usually gives way to fear, confusion, and much testing and troublesome behavior in the early teens.

Ways and Means of Discipline

Will spanking be effective during this period?

From this age on, it's important to be able to encourage and work with your child through talk alone. As we pointed out above, it is absolutely clear to children by this point that your spanking or

hitting can't hurt them. We have seen children with bad relationships with parents who just laughed when their parents spanked
them. Certainly this situation is not good for the child or his
parents. Where the relationship is not good between the parent
and child, spanking as a method of discipline can lead to actual
physical violence between parents and children.

We recall an incident which reinforced one father's notion that
it made more sense to talk to his son than to use physical force.
From the time the boy was a tot, his father threw a football to the
youngster and the boy ran directly toward his father and the goal
and was playfully tackled. When the youngster was eleven, he
grabbed the ball, put his head down, and drove toward the goal.
The old man looked at that "huskie" and decided that it made
more sense for the youngster to score. In short, your children grow
bigger and stronger at a time when you are in less good physical
shape. By this age period, the quality of your relationship and
respect for you as a protector, provider, guidance counselor and,
most of all, friend, must be working for you rather than your
physical strength or title of "parent."

If I don't use physical force, what kind of discipline is best?

Again, we are not the masters or the servants of our children. We
are not here to rule and control them or let them rule or control us.
We want to help them learn to control themselves so that they can
accomplish their goals and accept their responsibilities. We want
to help them learn to do things in a cooperative, fair, and just way.
We do this best *not* through punishment first, but by putting our
emphasis on *praising* and *encouraging* the side of our children that
wants to be cooperative, responsible, and accomplished; by being
interested and involved in the things that our children do; by
doing things with them.

Your child, under the best of circumstances, will not live up to
your expectations and his expectations all the time. You *must* deal
with this. But again, you want to do this with as little outright
punishment as possible—spanking, yelling, or denying privileges.
When your child doesn't do what he is expected to do, then it
helps to tell him about your disappointment in the fact that he
wasn't able to do what he agreed to do or was expected to do. If
you have established this pattern over time, this in itself will be
enough to make most children accept their responsibilities better

in the future. Only with persistent misbehavior or failure to accept responsibility do you have to move to more direct forms of punishment, primarily denial of privileges. The denial should be reasonable in time and severity.

Again, you won't be perfect at this. Your child is going to "get your goat" and you're going to "explode" from time to time.

Dealing with Profanity

My nine-year-old comes out with the most horrible words.
But there are those who say that profanity is part
of the black language style.

Profanity is profanity, period, and not a part of the black language style. On the other hand, you should not let words like fuck, shit, ass, and motherfucker cause you to have seizures, see red, or run for the Bible. These and other words are used in "vigorous expression" by paupers and Presidents, black and white—but in the appropriate place and at the appropriate time . . . in the poolroom, on the street corner, on the ballfield, in the locker room. They are usually used in anger—when a team loses, when a statement in the press hurts one's image, that kind of thing. They should *not* be used in anger against someone—a teacher, parent, or another child. When improperly used—in the classroom, in the hallway, among strangers in public places—swear words are usually a sign of disrespect for others and the self.

True, some people do not use profanity at all. We should respect and try not to offend them. On the other hand, they should not consider people "bad" because they cuss. A youngster who says, "I don't like this fucking sandwich" or "That son-of-a-bitchin' Jimmy Jones hit me!" is not a menace to society, to be drummed out of the human race. What he needs to hear from a "cool" adult is how, when and where such language *may* be okay—if he needs to use it—and where it's not okay. When you forbid angry profanity, you can get to first base by starting with "I know you're angry, but . . ."

Are you saying that it is all right for a youngster to swear?

Some parents permit their children to use cuss words directed toward them as a way to release anger. This is not harmful when it is *controlled* anger and the parents point out that such words should not be used against other people, in the classroom, store, or church. If you don't approve and don't swear at your children, point this fact out and ask them to treat you in the same way. When parents talk to their children about their feelings and the reasons for certain actions the *need* to "cuss the parents out" is not there. When a youngster is using cuss words to try and shock you, a calm smile or the comment, "I'll bet you thought I never heard such words before" or some such response will usually make the "bad words" go away. Direct disapproval in a calm fashion will usually work also: "Come on now, you know I don't like that . . ." and so on.

If you forbid swearing completely, you won't do a child any great harm. That's your way. You should not think of yourself as a "square." You are not denying your child a basic right and you are friendly and respectful. The child should learn to adjust to your wishes. We will discuss profanity further in Chapter 8.

Family Fun Again

Is family fun still an important factor in this age range?

Yes, it is. Now, more than at earlier ages, friendship and mutual respect are needed to make it possible for you to influence your child's behavior in a desirable way. As mentioned above, physical control is less possible and the denial of privilege can create great bitterness. Family fun provides the storehouse of good feeling which makes the setting of limits less of a hassle.

Your daughter will want to sleep over at Dawn's house more often and your boy at Martin's. They will have more trips or places to go without you—school trips, outings with friends and the parents of friends. They will roam on their own more. Toward the end of this period they will not want to visit the Johnsons with you, as they have done for ten years before. But home and family, when it is usually a friendly place that tries to give children all the independence they can handle in a responsible way, is still important.

Including your youngsters' friends in trips, games, and other family fun is helpful. Don't insist that your children come with you to the Johnsons' when they can be under responsible supervision elsewhere. When you really want the Johnsons to see how much they have grown and what fine young people you have, tell your children that. They are often not "above" a few cheers, but don't use this too often.

Special dinner treats, homemade ice cream, popcorn, malted milks, and a number of other inexpensive treats can make home a relatively "hip" place to be. If you can tolerate the exuberance of eleven and twelve—loud *yeahs*, dig that blue racer! whoee! and so on—you are even more likely to provide a happy home. Too much is too much but call for reason rather than threatening to knock somebody's block off or close down the record playing, dancing, and car racing altogether. Enjoy it. You may never feel or be close to such exuberance again.

"Work" and the Nine- to Twelve-Year-Old

Some people call this period the "age of industry."
What do they mean?

Children of this age are workers . . . even at play. They are no longer the uncoordinated, uninformed tots of two and three, struggling with strange body feelings and a strange world. They are more than the fairly well-coordinated and learning little men and women of six and seven years of age. At nine and twelve, they are ready! They are usually healthy and full of energy and well-informed about the immediate world around them. They will be paying more and more attention to the world beyond their home, family, and schools during this period.

While they are still great explorers, satisfaction appears to come more now from finishing things than starting things . . . doing a job . . . bringing an assignment, or a project they start themselves, to completion. (They still often resist the things you tell them to do.) They want to do real things, like the things they see the adults around them doing. If not real, they want to do things as close to real as possible. They enjoy race cars, trucks, model making, and teaching school and detective play . . . *because* the play can be so much like the real thing. They want to test and demonstrate their abilities during this period. It is the proving ground for adulthood.

My ten-year-old is involved in so many things.
How can I help him get everything done?

This is usually the period when the amount of school homework increases. It is the time when organized sports and recreation present more of a challenge. If you have been successful in helping your child understand that achievement is for himself or herself and not for you, your child is likely to approach homework, sixth-grade basketball practice, and movement lessons with a dedication that amazes you. Now you only need to help them learn to do first things first and schedule their time in such a way that they can do the things they must or want to do. You might suggest a written schedule until they have scheduling "down pat." Some people are never able to achieve at their true level of ability because they never learn to organize and schedule well.

My eleven-year-old always has her nose in a book.
Isn't this harmful?

If you feel that your youngster spends too much time on her schoolwork, don't say so or imply it. Provide other exposure and activity opportunities. Help her slowly work out a balance of activities. But if children prefer the books, cool it—as long as they're not hiding from people. If they are, help them learn what to say and how to handle social situations in a way that will make them comfortable. In the generation to come, there are going to be more black "eggheads"—students first and foremost—and that's fine. We'll still have a lot of linebackers and singers.

What benefit do youngsters this age receive
from good work? How can I help?

Children who learn deep within "I can" from their work and play of this period develop a deep sense of adequacy, of being okay. Children who learn deep within that "I can't" can develop a deep sense of inferiority.

You can help your child during this period by not expecting performances far above his abilities, and not accepting performances far below his ability. Gentle encouragement, "Oh, come on, you can do better than that!" is in order when his or her effort is below par. Your interest and praise for good effort remains important during this period.

Talking about workers, I have just the opposite
problem. My eleven-year-old son is lazy. How is he
going to make it as an adult?

Laziness is not a simple matter. It can be due to boredom, apathy, and depression. It can be caused by a lack of direction, purpose, and inner discipline. It can be a way to "fix" you because you want your child to be active. It can be a way to remain dependent on you when he or she is fearful of failure in the world. In most cases, however, it occurs because taking responsibility for doing his or her part in work and play has not become, over time, your child's way, style, or habit.

Calling him lazy, telling him that he will come to no good end, pointing out "lazy people" and telling him he'll have the same problems generally doesn't work. Help, rather than criticism, is what he needs. First you want to identify the problem. Is he locked in a struggle with you? Is he afraid of failure? Is he afraid of taking responsibility for his own behavior and standing on his own two feet? Have you set routine chores and expectations?

There is another problem to look out for here. Sometimes adults fight each other in a way that can hurt a child without being aware of it. This can be a mother and father, a mother and grandmother, or any two people deeply involved in the care of a child. They can undercut each other by providing the child with excuses for not performing well or working hard when the other person expects him to do so and the expectations are reasonable. "You're too tired to rake the leaves today, aren't you?" "You had a hard day today, why don't you let your homework go tonight?" When this is the case, the two adults involved need to talk about what they are doing to each other . . . and stop it—or at least leave the child out of it.

We have already discussed approaches for handling the above-mentioned problems. Again, when you attempt to break a long-standing but harmful pattern, you are going to get great resistance. Your child has become comfortable in handling things in this way. He, like we, will be threatened by the possibility of change. It is important, however, to patiently, persistently but firmly establish chores, responsibilities, and expectations for your child. Again, this is a critical age. If not doing becomes your child's style, it will be more difficult to change from this point on.

I have chores and expectations for my child, but in school they let him do whatever he wants to do. Isn't that harmful?

If that's the case, it is. But in some modern schools, as we pointed out in Chapter 6, it may look as if they're doing whatever they want to do, when that is not the case. But we do know of cases where some whites and some blacks—such as schoolteachers, boy scout leaders, and coaches—do not expect or ask for good work performance and responsible behavior from black children. This is one of the most troublesome kinds of racism and classism there is.

Children will often see the permissive person—the one who does not expect them to do their schoolwork, who expects them to be late and disruptive—as easy, their friend. They may see people who expect a good effort as hard and mean. Years later, after they've missed an opportunity to enjoy a sense of achievement during this critical age period, they often realize that they were "had." But for some it will be too late. The same "friend" who had no expectations for them because they were black, poor, or on public welfare will often criticize them later on because they are "lazy" and unable to work or perform well.

This is another reason that it helps to know the teacher or the adults, and what they're about, wherever your child is involved. You should make your expectations known and insist that other adults working with your child have desirable expectations for him or her. Remember, however, that there is more than one way to skin a cat. If other adults working with your child are not doing exactly what you do and working in the way you work, you want to be open to their explanation of what their methods are all about. After all, achieving the goals is more important than the method—unless the method is unfair or unethical.

What's the point of encouraging my child to work and "be something" when I hear people say that black children lack confidence, are easily discouraged, and discourage each other?

This is less of a problem today than it has been. Less than twenty years ago, the model of a black child the society held up to a black child was "Little Eight Ball" or "Little Black Sambo." The message: stupid, incapable, inferior. There are many models of bright, successful, able black children around today—on television, the Jackson Five, youngsters like that. This is helpful, but it is still important to remember that for most children, what goes on with

important people around them—with parents, teachers, friends—
has more influence than what goes on at a distance.

There are still too many black children who are made to feel
that they are worthless and unable to accomplish anything of
value by their parents, teachers and friends. Self-doubt causes too
many to avoid making efforts to develop their abilities. Where this
negative feeling is widespread, any child who attempts to achieve
is a threat, and he must be ridiculed or discouraged to the point
that he gives up on the belief that "I can."

Many successful blacks indicate that their parents encouraged
them to keep on keeping on in spite of efforts to discourage them
made by "friends." We recall the twelve-year-old who was told by
classmates that he needn't bother to try to make the choral club
in his predominantly white school because the director was prejudiced and freshmen rarely made it anyway. His parents encouraged him to keep on singing, and said that if he was unfairly
judged, they would speak to the director. He did . . . and made it.

If you live in a community where black children and families
have been "beaten down," it is very important to stand strong
behind your child in this same way. Most of all you *must* be careful that your own comments generally support the notion "you can"
rather than "you can't." On the other hand, "you can" when, at the
moment, the child "can't" can be a harmful suggestion. Again, you
must carefully study the situation and respond in the most reasonable way.

You talk about workers. I think today's kids are quitters.
What do you think?

"Hanging in there"—undergoing a struggle, sacrifice, and hardship, even hard work—is a very great problem in this affluent,
push-button day and age. Too many children are given so much
with so little effort that they expect things to come easily or they
will quit. They receive little experience with struggle and hard
work as a way to make things pay off. This is less the case with
struggling black families working toward a goal. It is a very real
problem for middle-income black families and creates a dilemma
for families on public welfare.

As we mentioned earlier, many middle-income parents had to
struggle so hard themselves that they are too willing to give their
children too much for too little effort. This has been harmful to

many middle-income white children. We can make the same mistake. Parents on public welfare have an even more complicated problem. It is important that they do not feel ashamed of being on public welfare and that they do not pass feelings of shame on to their children. At the same time it is important not to cripple their children by making them feel they will be taken care of, whether they make their best effort or not. Once a child begins to think like this, there is no longer any need to compete, struggle, face hardship, or develop personal discipline. Youngsters are thus denied the sense of well-being that comes from achievement and the competence which grows out of sustained efforts or work.

Both welfare parents and middle-income parents, from the start, must set expectations for performance and give rewards and approval for a good, hard try even more than for success. Many parents do this and many young people have fight and determination. But there are still too many youngsters ready to quit when they trip over the first hurdle. Well-coached athletic teams, wilderness programs, and other such activities can provide young people with demanding experiences which help them develop "fight," determination, and stick-to-itiveness.

Aren't black parents accused of overburdening their children with work during this period?

It is often said that some black parents deny their children their childhood by loading them with too many "adult responsibilities." It is of interest that young children, seven and eight years of age, begin to take major responsibility for their brothers and sisters in many traditional cultures of Africa. Often young children carry younger children on their backs. It is impossible to say whether this is a carryover or not.

When parents use their children to do house and child-care work they could and should do themselves in order to have more social time, this is neglect and exploitation. When the whole family must pull together to survive, helping to take care of the other children and pitching in to cook, wash, iron and keep house at nine, ten, eleven, and twelve years of age makes sense. When parents are working or ill or unable to get along without the help of the child, there is a special reward for the child—he is a valuable and necessary contributor to the welfare of the household.

When children feel "used," they often act up and act out against their parents by doing just the opposite or less than what their parents want them to do. Parents who are neglectful or exploit their children do not build up a backlog or storehouse of respect. Without this respect, it is much more difficult to encourage or influence a child toward ways you consider desirable. The influence of the street, or any other outside influence—great at this point, anyway—becomes even greater. Frequently boys and girls in this situation act up in aggressive ways, with destruction of property and fighting. Later sexual acting up is added.

Neglect and exploitation of children is not the case in the great majority of black families. Because of limited opportunities in the past, low expectations and little demand for performance tend to be the rule in too many families—with overly demanding expectations in too many others.

Sports Versus Schoolwork

My son is crazy about sports but has no time for his studies. What can I do to get him to buckle down?

Organized play or sports are tough competition for anything. It requires thinking, judgment, and planning. It is a test for physical fitness, it provides competition, the thrill of victory, and the agony of defeat—thus touching and moving emotions wildly. Much of what is important or meaningful in life is involved in athletics. Unless your child has been exposed to music and painting or had the opportunity to be excited by science, reading, or other kinds of learning, these areas will have difficulty competing with organized athletics . . . that is, unless athletics is an area in which your child always experiences failure. In that case you would want to help him develop athletic skills.

You can force him to spend more time at his schoolwork and less time on the sports field . . . or even forbid athletics. This, however, is a poor, even harmful, way of handling the matter. This is another time when your best weapon is not the force or authority you can bring to bear, but the strength of your relationship and your willingness to talk directly to your child about the problem. You can explain why he enjoys athletics. At the same time you want to point out the importance of learning and developing skills in other areas. You might also point to the many people who enjoy athletics but have other interests and talents as well. You can point out the relationship between learning and getting a job in the future, but this is less meaningful to your child than most of us imagine. The future seems so far off to children in this age group, even though, in fact, it is right around the corner.

We know parents who fuss and fight with their children about this issue.

> You're not going to be anything but a basketball bum!
> Yeah, well only a handful of people make the pros and you're not big enough anyway.
> You play ball from sunup to sundown and you're not interested in anything else!
> Why don't you do something cultural or intelligent for a change!
> I don't like that gang you play ball with anyway.

And on and on and on.

These responses are irrational and harmful. A parent who does this is putting down the area in which his or her child is getting enjoyment, satisfaction, and a feeling of accomplishment and well-being. It is better that a youngster be involved in athletics than getting into trouble on the street . . . although it's possible to do both. Whether the interest in athletics pays off financially or not is unimportant. The discipline, the learning, the joy of achievement in athletics can be transferred to learning and even to a fuller appreciation of music, art, and dramatics. Notice how many professional athletes are also musicians, artists, and actors!

How can I get my child to appreciate these other things?

It is often possible to help your child transfer his enthusiasm for athletics into enthusiasm for accomplishment in other areas. Begin by asking your child to give himself a chance to enjoy other areas. Then look carefully to see if there isn't some area of school work that is at all interesting to him—what about reading books about athletes or athletics? Fulfilling school requirements by doing research projects or writing about athletics is a good way to get the interest transferred and associated with the skills of reading, writing, or expression in some form.

Think back. Have you really made it possible for your child to develop other interests? Have you gone to the museums, libraries, zoos, planetariums, art shows, drama presentations, or music shows? If not, now is the time . . . better late than never. It is your presence and your interest in these other areas that are needed to "turn a child on." The feedback or reward is so immediate and great in athletics that it frequently does not require an adult to get a child interested. Thus you must work harder to expose and involve your child in areas outside of athletics. Finally, it helps to help your child organize himself so that he'll have plenty of time for athletics and sufficient time for his schoolwork and other activities.

Don't be discouraged if gentle persuasion and more exposure to other activities don't work. Many a parent has lost the battle of the piano versus the football. You want to help your child give himself a chance with the piano, but if it doesn't work, no big deal. You want to be more insistent when it comes to schoolwork. You may have to insist that he play ball only after he does his schoolwork. When this is necessary, it is best to discuss the matter with your child and come to an agreement about the time and place for schoolwork and the time and place for athletics. You will want to try to stay out of the role of enforcer. Encourage your youngster to set up a schedule and make it his responsibility to stick to it. When he does this successfully, praise for his achievement goes a long way toward helping him keep it up.

The Question of Identity

*You said earlier that the nine-year-old's
personality is pretty well framed. What about
his sense of identity at this stage?*

A child establishes an identity by becoming like a particular person or group of people—mother, father, teacher, women, men, blacks, middle-income people, and so on. This process begins with the infant. Love and respect from the person or group being imitated enable the child to become like that person or group without mixed feelings about it. Sometimes a child must identify with rejecting persons and here there are often mixed (good and bad) feelings about becoming like that person or group. In addition, a child accepts the cause, problems, aspirations, and privileges of the group he identifies with.

Identification as a male or female, black person or white person, rich person or poor person, gives a child a sense of "I am." Such identification can provide direction, limits, and motivation to think and act in particular ways. People respond to his behavior in spoken and unspoken ways. They say, "You are smart, black, friendly, outspoken, tall, shrewd," or whatever the case may be. Attitudes and feelings about whether these qualities are good are also passed on to the child. Through a complicated method a child accepts and rejects some of the outside feedback, puts in his own impressions, and the mixture is his self-concept.

How does self-concept affect achievement?

If a child develops an overall good self-concept, he or she becomes free and confident enough to go where his or her skill, desires, and opportunities will take him or her. Success improves the self-concept and makes it easier to take on the next challenge or tolerate the occasional failure. On the other hand, people with low self-concepts may never fully develop their talents or pursue opportunities they desire because of self-doubt and the fear and pain of failure.

Although the identification process is going on and the self-concept is being developed from a very early point in the life of a child, the self-concept does not really gel until the nine-to-twelve (more or less) age period. "Who am I?" is the question teen-agers raise in many different ways. They wear different clothes, take to different fads, swear off fish or meat because killing is involved, and do a number of things to say "I am" or "This is me." But it is all a rearrangement of what became fairly firmly established during the nine-to-twelve-year age period. A child's self-concept and identity is simply moved to a higher level of consciousness during the adolescent period.

An established self-concept can create a sense of comfort within a person even when it is not a desirable self-image from the standpoint of other people. That is why there is so much resistance to change, even among people not faring well. Change means uncertainty, readjustment, and establishing new identities with no promise that conditions will be better. The suggestions we have made to help your children become more flexible people will also help them better handle change.

There is good evidence that children who have a positive self-concept and are accepting of themselves are more tolerant and accepting of others and of change. You can see then that a positive, personal and/or racial identity is a must in order for your child to better deal with other blacks and whites.

Speaking of self-concept, my twelve-year-old son
wants an Afro hairstyle because he says it's important
for his racial identity. Does the hairstyle help?

The business of establishing a positive racial identity is important. The society has sent and still sends many messages that indicate that it's not good to be black. Yet, his racial identity is a part of his personal identity and this influences his self-concept. As we indicated above, a person needs a positive self-concept in order to become free and confident enough to go where his skills, desires, and opportunities will take him. There has been some change in the society, and black excellence is too apparent now for the negative message to do as much damage as it did in the past. But your child's racial identity may need some support against the negative message even now. The Afro haircut is simply one more way of saying, "I'm black and that's a positive thing."

But don't permit your child to feel that being black or having an Afro haircut is enough. The good feeling that comes from accepting black as beautiful or even identifying with successful blacks or the beauty of the black culture or the rightness of the black cause cannot be sustained in the face of individual failure. We are sure that you have noticed that some of the people who yell "I'm black and I'm proud" the most do destructive things to themselves, their families and the black cause. This is because they are really "using" blackness to try and feel good about themselves when their overall self-concept is low. Usually an individual's overall self-concept is low because of the way he is treated by important people around him—parents, teachers, and others. It is low when poor treatment leads to poor performance. Blacks who have been well treated at home, at church, or in school have often been protected from the negative or racist message about blacks in the larger society. In fact, the notion of black self-hatred is an overstatement. People who have studied the problem and made such claims generally studied people who did not have this kind of protection. That is not to say that all blacks have not been affected to some degree by the racist message sent out by the society.

It would be helpful to your child if you would explain to him when there is an opening that lasting pride is a product of performance; that black talk without a determined effort to develop one's self, one's skills, and one's sense of responsibility is double-talk and nonsense. Then go on and warn him about what we call the "crabs in a basket" problem.

People at the bottom of a system which permits and encourages the exploitation of others will be the most destructive of each other—regardless of race, religion, or anything else. They will show jealousies and try and pull back anyone who tries to climb out of the basket—in this case, achieve or simply be different. Starved for success and attention, every crab will want to lead or be seen and will unfairly criticize and put down anybody who appears to be "getting ahead." Such behavior has destroyed all too many black groups. We can't even begin to talk about blacks working together until we help enough children—who learned from adults, or were not helped to unlearn what is really immature behavior—overcome such tendencies.

Can black children who did not have a positive experience at home or in their communities develop a positive self-concept by identifying with successful blacks and the black movement?

Many black children have gained direction and purpose by identifying with blacks in important positions and with the black cause. A youngster from a fatherless family drew a picture of a man and called him her father. When asked what kind of person she would like her father to be, she replied, "Like Mayor Washington" (then mayor of Washington, D.C.). But whether a child like this can use the mayor or the black movement as a source of strength will depend on a number of things—how harmful or helpful her home and early experience was and is, the kind of people and conditions that she is exposed to in her neighborhood or community, whether she is able to reach out and identify beyond harmful things in her immediate environment, and what aspects of the black movement she identifies with. If she is able to identify with excellence, fair play, and personal development, her chances of performing in a way in which she will receive a positive feedback is increased. This will increase her chances of developing a positive self-concept. But often this is not enough.

The ways to success—in society, at school, on the job—are

learned through contact with successful people. Children from troubled backgrounds lack continued and close contact with success models. They often feel that they are destined to be like the people around them or that it is "selling out" not to be. They often sense the rejection of outsiders.

In trying to help a youngster talk about his feelings about his father, a therapist said, "I'm sure it must be difficult for you to see your father drunk on the street corner as you go to school every day." The youngster exploded, slamming his hand against a wall. As troublesome as he was, the father was all he had. Such children often need professional help. In many cases you can help youngsters from troubled backgrounds understand that they are not destined to become like the adults around them, that they can take a different direction. At the same time, it is important to help them understand the problems of these adults—accepting them as relatives and friends while going in a direction which will permit the child to have greater success. But in some cases, it will be too difficult for such youngsters to reach out and even when they can, the "how to achieve" and the reward for trying will not be present on a day to day basis.

The Question of Sex Education

*What kind of information does a child need
about sex during this period?*

At the most natural time possible, when your child is ten or eleven years of age, you should discuss menstruation or ejaculation or discharge in a simple and straightforward way. Bleeding is associated with an accident, pain, or an unhappy experience. If your child is prepared in advance, she can think of menstruation as an important growth landmark. You should explain to your girl that fully developed girls and women have two ovaries in the lower part of their abdomen. The abdomen is the chamber or big room which holds many of the internal body parts. Every month an egg is freed from one of the ovaries and passes through tubes into the uterus. The uterus (usually called the womb) is like a small, oval room. It, too, lies in the abdomen. Because many people refer to the abdomen as the stomach, young children often become confused and think that a baby can come out of the stomach and can result from eating. To prevent confusion, you should explain that the womb and ovaries are separate from the stomach, which also lies in the abdomen.

If a man and woman have sexual intercourse during the time that the egg is released, the egg can join with the sperm from the man. The joined egg and sperm attaches itself to the wall of the uterus and begins to grow. It is then called a fetus. A cord develops between the fetus and the wall of the uterus. Nourishment passes from the mother to the baby by way of the blood vessels inside the cord. As the baby grows, the uterus expands to make room for it. After about nine months the baby is fully developed and pushed out of the uterus through the vagina.

If the egg does not become fertilized (joined with the sperm of a man) the egg and the lining or wall of the uterus peels off and passes through the vagina out of the body. This lining is a bloody, meshy mucus and does not contain any body tissue that is needed. This material is the blood of the monthly period.

The lining of the wall of the uterus is needed when a woman is going to have a baby. It does not peel off during pregnancy and that's why there is no menstrual period when a woman is expecting. Instead, the lining expands and becomes a solid disclike form called the placenta (or "afterbirth") which nourishes the growing fetus. It is expelled at the time of birth.

You want to put it in words your child will understand. Don't go on and on to the point that your youngster is made uneasy. It may help—as with all complicated or potentially touchy discussions— to talk about the matter at different times and in different ways and not "snow" your youngster all at once.

There are many false explanations given about how a woman has a baby. For this reason, you should explain that it only occurs when a woman has sexual intercourse with a mature boy or man.

Explain, but don't overexplain, that menstruation is normal and desirable. As with everything else, children will have doubts when you overexplain. You will want to explain that being able to grow up and have the *possibility* of having children is something that a girl should be proud and happy about. On the other hand, you don't want to indicate that it's her duty or her responsibility to grow up and have children. You also don't want to suggest that the woman's role in life is to have babies and rear children while their husbands follow careers. It is around the discussion of these issues that boys and girls begin to firmly establish their identities, and harmful or limiting suggestions that you make during this period can be very difficult for them to overcome later on.

Some parents talk about menstruation as if it's a woman's burden—unpleasant, indecent, and unnatural. Such attitudes can increase a child's likelihood of having problems about menstruation throughout life. Also, a mother complaining loudly and demanding sympathy at the time of her own menstruation can also have a harmful effect on a young girl. Negative feelings about menstruation can negatively affect one's attitude about sex or the sex act. Menstruation should be regarded as a normal, healthy body function. See Chapter 8 for additional discussion about menstruation.

Should I discuss sexual intercourse?

You mentioned it when you discussed how the sexual organs work. Generally it is best not to flood children with information or tell all at the same time. Discussions about sex should be ongoing and different aspects should be discussed at different and natural times. A book explaining sex, a pet having sex, or a television comment about sex may spark a question from your child which leads to a discussion about sexual intercourse.

You can acknowledge in a natural way that adults—young and old—have a sex life; that people have sex in order to have children and for pleasure, out of a closeness and good feeling for each other. You need not give the details or you may want to give them a book that explains. Most children won't want the details, but you won't create a problem if you explain that the male penis is placed in the female vagina. You can point out that one day when they are young adults, they may feel very strongly toward someone with whom they may have sex.

You should point out that sex is a private matter so that you don't ask people about their sex life. You should point out that youngsters are not ready to have sex until they have given themselves a chance to grow up some, to have good control over their feelings, and to be able to make good judgments about what they want in life.

I can't talk to my child about sex. What should I do?

You should try again. It is best that parents themselves discuss sex with their children. This takes the mystery, intrigue, and unnaturalness out of the whole matter. But if you can't, you can't. Most of us were reared to think of and treat sex in a hush-hush way. One thing you can do in this case is provide your children with books that discuss sex in a calm, nonstimulating but straightforward manner. Even when you are able to talk to your children about sex, it will help to provide them with a well-written book explaining the essential facts. We advise you to read the book first, to make certain that it is helpful but does not try to excite or stimulate your child.

Some mothers can't talk to their sons and some fathers can't talk to their daughters about sex. If you can't and there is only one parent, again a book can be helpful. Or you might call upon close relatives or friends to do the job. Be careful here. You should have a talk beforehand with whoever discusses sex with your child, agreeing on how the matter should be handled. Make certain that the person you ask will not take advantage of your child—stimulating or even assaulting. Even you, yourself, must be careful not to overstimulate your child. But don't worry about the fleeting sexual thought or feeling you have about your child. We all have them. The mature adult does not act on them . . . although frequent, extreme, harsh physical punishment is sometimes a parent's way to avoid facing these feelings or acting on them. For more information on sexual development, see Chapter 8 on adolescence and young adulthood.

Morality and Religion

Where is moral development during this period?

For many children of this age, good behavior still means being fair so that others will be fair with you. For many others, "right" is that which pleases or helps other people. For still others, doing right comes out of a respect for authority and a sense of a need to maintain law and the social order—whether that order is the school, the home, or the society. Some children—capable of and allowed to develop theories about themselves, life, and society— begin to think of right in terms of personal values and opinions. This last group, around eleven and twelve years of age, will generally go along with authority figures—you, the teacher, the President—but they will begin to consider and raise challenging questions about the way the society is run, the way they are treated, and the way others are treated. Some of this is a challenge of your right to authority. Some of it is an effort to be less dependent and beholden to you. Some of it is a real search for a code of ethics or a way to behave that makes sense to them. Many, if not most, people operate at the "I'll be good if you'll be good" and the "law and order" stages throughout life.

Children who grow up in a climate of fairness but who are permitted to challenge and question the rules and the rule-makers of society and are encouraged to work out the best ways of handling or solving problems with you, with teachers and with other children are most likely to reach the stage of having a set of ethical values which are personal and flexible, yet generally in keeping with the rules of the society. Such children, as adults, do not say, "My country, right or wrong." They are more likely to say, "My country, and if it's wrong, I'm going to try to help make it right." Children who are forced to do what you or other authority figures tell them to do are more likely to become strong law and order people, even when the laws are unjust and the order is through force.

Bucking the law or going against *just* authority figures *without a cause* can also be harmful to your child's development and lead to future problems.

*We are a religious family. Won't that take care
of moral development in our children?*

There certainly is nothing wrong with going to church or being religious. Any method that a person can use to find dignity and respect and find encouragement for treating others the same way is fine. But just going to church alone won't do the job. Some people go to church regularly and still behave in an immoral way— inside and outside of the church. It is possible to be a moral, fair, or just person without religious training. A child's deepest sense of morality comes from the way he or she is treated—whether or not concern is given to his or her rights and needs. In fact, going to church and talking Christianity and mistreating your husband or wife, children, and other people in one way or another can confuse or anger your children. They may see you as a hypocrite. This can make the usual teen rebellion against your beliefs and teachings more extreme and difficult.

*We send our children to church so they'll have good moral
training, but we don't go anymore. Does this do any harm?*

If we were your children, we'd probably ask, "If going to church is
so important, why don't you go?" On the other hand, if your children want to go because other children in the neighborhood are
going, there is no reason why they should not. But they are most
likely to value and take in the teaching of the church when they
see that it is important to you.

*My eleven-year-old daughter was listening to television
reports of government scandal in Washington and out
of the clear blue sky said, "I hate the
government." What was that all about?*

Most children this age are still very interested in the things that
happen to people and in places close around them. On the other
hand, when parents have a great interest in outside events, youngsters are likely to develop an interest as well. But they tend to see
the outside world in a very personal way. Who can they count on
if they can't trust and gain strength from parents, teachers, ministers, and Presidents? Many children in this age group are very
aware of a contradiction when you tell them to be fair and honest
and many leaders are shown to be crooks.

The reporting of crime and wrongdoing by high government
officials and other important authority figures can be confusing
and frightening to children. Your child's statement, "I hate the
government," was quite probably an expression of disappointment
and anger in having the bargain broken ("I'll be good if you'll be
good"). Television, more than the newspapers and radio, has given
public officials a kind of presence and importance as models of
morality that did not exist before. But again, you are your child's
most important model of morality. You will have much more effect
on the kind of person your child is than Watergate or anything else
that goes on in the society.

On the other hand, you must be careful how you respond to
such situations. You don't want your child to be naïve, but you
don't want her to be cynical and have a sense of hopelessness
about the future of blacks, the country, or the world. Again, such
feelings often lead to apathy, depression, and "dropping out."
There have always been hypocrites, thieves, and liars in the world.
There always will be. You want to help your child understand that

the vast majority of people would prefer to be good and honest; that many people in important positions are responsible, fair, and just. Besides, the only protection against "Doomsday"—be it black genocide or the use of the bomb—is the development of enough people who are spirited and talented enough to keep fighting for fair play and justice.

How can I help my child understand adult shortcomings?

You don't want to justify undesirable behavior. But you can help your child learn that people aren't simply good or bad, that they are subject to certain pressures to deceive, cheat, and lie. Reminding your youngster of what he has done occasionally to get his own way—half-truths and manipulations (such as telling your husband that you said he could buy a game when you didn't)—is a good way to help your child understand why adults lie and steal to get money and power. You want to point out how this kind of behavior hurts people and is bad for a country. You might want to talk about how you spot and stop the con man whether he is your neighbor, a businessman, or in government. This is a good opportunity to point out the importance of using your vote and how to write letters to consumer protection agencies, legislators, and other groups working to promote fair and just government and business. Such discussions will give your child a beginning understanding of how his country works. Most important, a discussion of this kind about what can be done prevents your child from feeling powerless.

It doesn't pay to "lip" about the world unless you are doing something to make it a better place. Aside from spreading depression and hopelessness, your child may decide that you are all mouth and no substance. What great "ammunition" for the teen-age put-down of parents which is coming up next.

The Role of "Outside Activities" and Hobbies

My eleven-year-old daughter is in school clubs, on the
girls' basketball team, loves games, dancing, reading,
and is ready to go whenever we propose a trip
anywhere. How much is too much?

This is really a very individual thing. Children in this age group seem to have more energy than the law allows. They are joiners.

They are goers, and they like to make and do things. If your daughter is not worn out, I would not worry about it, just enjoy her enthusiasm . . . if you're not too worn out to keep up with her.

If she does overschedule herself to the point of exhaustion, help her learn to limit her activities and do the things she wants most without "overdo." If necessary, step in and rule out certain activities yourself. Simply make certain that the reasons you give make sense. Aside from being overtired, an overscheduled child may become irritable, anxious, and troublesome.

The opposite of your situation also presents a problem. Some parents push their youngsters into more activities than the child wants. These parents often expect too much. We know youngsters who were forced into Little League baseball to live out their parents' dreams and they tired of baseball and quit as soon as they could. On the other hand, we know of parents who were very interested in their son's playing sports, but did not push him because he appeared more interested in his schoolwork and other hobbies. Without participating in organized sports, we have seen such youngsters later become very well-coordinated, fine athletes, through an interest that developed largely on their own. Certainly, the parents' interest had some influence, but when parents don't jam their interests down their youngsters' throats, children are more likely to develop a lasting interest with less need to rebel against the parents' interest.

My daughter develops one interest after another.
We bought her an expensive piano, and she started
piano lessons. Two months later, she stopped. How
can I help her stick to one thing?

Every parent is familiar with this problem in one way or another. If it's not piano lessons, it's bicycle riding, photography, or dancing lessons. This is normal for this period. Before you put a lot of money into something your child swears on a stack of Bibles he or she will be interested in forever and ever, you ought to make certain that they show a sustained interest . . . even if you can afford to buy it.

First, you want to make certain that you are not strongly suggesting to your child to develop a hobby or activity area that you want for him or her. This does *not* mean that you should not discuss the relative advantages of one activity over another. You should not buy a piano or push football in the hope that you will someday see your youngster's name in lights or that he will be receiving a fat bonus contract. As we have said before, children should not have to live out the dreams of parents. If your child has unusual talent, you will know it without pushing. Even if he does turn out to be very gifted, you can kill the motivation by pushing too hard. Only if your child shows continued interest do you want to try and help him get the lessons he needs to develop a talent.

If your child has given something a fair try but then lost interest, it's better to let her drop out for a while. There is a good chance that she will want to come back to the activity later on. Before she drops out, however, you might ask her to give herself a final chance to enjoy it, perhaps setting a time limit. You might also discuss the problem with the teacher and your child, and see whether there is any specific problem that can be worked on to improve the situation. Sometimes, for example, children think teachers are too demanding. If this can be talked out, they very often can go on and enjoy themselves. It helps to find a teacher who stresses playing the piano, dancing, taking photographs, or whatever the activity may be for sheer enjoyment and transmits that feeling to the child. At the same time, the teacher should emphasize the need to develop basic skills.

It is important to stay out of struggles with children about taking lessons. Again, you want to encourage them, praise their success, support the notion that if they weren't successful with this lesson, they can be with the next. But remember that you can't make them learn. Struggles will make you unhappy and will make your child unhappy. In this case, after a reasonable try, it is better to quit than fight.

My eleven-year-old son is interested in photography, and sometimes wants me to help him develop pictures. I don't want to get in the way of "his thing." What do you think about it?

If your child asks you for help, you are not invading his privacy. If you help without taking over and doing things your way, you will not make him dependent on you. He may simply want to spend some time with you or show you how competent he is. On the other hand, he may feel that he is a little bit over his head, and may need a little help to be able to do a good job.

If he is asking for help, you can help best by raising questions which will help him see the problem involved. Have him give you explanations of how he would solve a particular problem. Very often when children are involved in complicated activities, they need help with organization. Developing pictures is a good case-in-point. Here you have to get your solutions prepared and lined up to meet time and lighting schedules. If a child needs and receives help, this can become a helpful lesson in organization. Without help he might drop the hobby and experience an unnecessary failure.

But isn't it best to let children learn by trial and error?

Some people feel that you should let children this age explore, make mistakes, and develop their own interests. We feel that that's fine before they have found an interest which they would really like to develop. Once they have really settled down to an activity, however, it is important to try and help them achieve competence. We remember a situation in which youngsters took cameras without instructions, and went out and took pictures with a great deal of excitement. They came back and developed their work only to find that they had made a thousand and one errors. They were turned off and "through" with picture-taking. We observed another situation in which the teacher gave the youngsters a great deal of instruction in the use of cameras, how to identify a good shot and how to take it, before they went out to take their first picture. Some of the youngsters got very good shots, and it was a rewarding experience—not only in picture-taking but in how to approach a problem and achieve a goal.

We can't afford an expensive hobby like photography.
Do you have any other suggestions?

Children don't need brand-new materials or kits to develop a hobby. Most of us feel that we are fortunate that we can afford to buy manufactured items. We might actually be better off if we knew how to make our own furniture and repair our cars. By the time our children are adults, people will probably be working fewer hours with more free time. If they know how to work with tools, there is no end to what they can do . . . as a hobby or in providing goods and services necessary to the maintenance of their homes. Old and damaged materials like old motors, wires, and broken utensils can provide much of what is needed for an inexpensive hobby. Hopefully you have helped your child learn to think and work safely by now!

Collecting anything from old Christmas cards and postcards to baseball cards can also make an interesting hobby. Weaving, needlepoint, making model cities out of cardboard, leatherwork, and a whole host of inexpensive leisure-time activities can be enjoyed. There are some good books on leisure-time activities for children. You might want to check at your library for some of these rather than buy them.

Films, Books, and Outings

I went with my twelve-year-old son to one of the
black movies for what I thought would be good shared
recreation. But I was horrified by the message of the film.
What are your thoughts about the black film?

Several have been quite good. But we are as concerned as you are about most of them. If there were more films which depicted the full spectrum of black life, the films which glorify pimps, prostitutes, drug addicts, con men, and sexual exploitation of women would be less troublesome. But that is not the case. Many black children from troubled communities don't even know the full spectrum of black life.

One black youngster from such a background got up and left after a tender, powerful love scene in the film *Sounder* and commented, "That ain't black!" We know too many black youngsters whose notion of blackness is the trouble within their home, housing project, and neighborhood. Most of the black films confirm their impression. This is the message that the white media—movies, newspapers, magazines, radio—have long conveyed. As a group, we have complained that they were not presenting us with desirable models and good representation. Now too many black movies are doing the same thing or perhaps worse.

Certainly there is some value simply in seeing blacks on the screen rather than always observing whites in action. Certainly observing aggressive blacks on the screen is helpful. But the message of "rip off whitey" as long as you don't "rip off blacks" is first of all just plain inhuman and racist, and second, calls for a very fine line of distinction which many young people can't and won't make. Even more unfortunate is the fact that the children who have had less care and concern from parents will have the most problem making that distinction, and they are the ones most in need of developing controls and styles which can lead them to success—success as people, if not financial success.

We don't think most of the films are very helpful overall, but neither are they quite as harmful as everybody claims . . . particularly if your child does not have fantasy and reality mixed up and already has good moral development.

Isn't seeing anti-white films a way for blacks to work off their feelings of frustration and rage?

If we believe that getting rid of our anger toward whites in the society through fantasy is a valuable thing then many black films can be recommended for giving blacks a chance to do so. But that's not much different from what many black churches have provided and been criticized for. In fact, these films offer even less. Churches provided community, comradeship, and skill development. The films provide only a few minutes of release.

Aren't these films helpful in teaching black youngsters to be aggressive and assertive toward whites?

The above traits and their management are best learned at home with parents who can teach a child realistic and effective ways to operate. Besides, the films show none of the nitty-gritty but essential aspects of organization needed for aggressive group action. They show a lot of youngsters just enough to get them into trouble.

My twelve-year-old son likes to read. Are there any books that might be particularly helpful for a black youngster of this age?

First, let's pause a moment to say that reading is a great leisure-time activity. Second, we don't believe that black families read enough. Usually this is true of poorly educated families but too many middle-income, educated blacks don't read either. As blacks, we have an urgent need to change this society, and reading can be helpful in this regard.

The biographies of successful blacks—King, Carver, DuBois, Robinson, etcetera—can be very helpful to youngsters in this age group. They provide a child with an opportunity to read about some of the factors which lead to success without having a parent constantly "pounding them into his head." Books can also give much more information about the complexities of problems and the way that one must organize and plan to solve them than can any other medium. Books are less likely to be as one-sided when dealing with blacks than are films, television, and radio.

Finally, we encourage you to have your child read a wide range of material. It does not help to read only people with whom you agree. There is much to learn from people with whom you disagree. You are limiting yourself if you read about your culture only. There is much to learn in reading about other cultures and other groups. Children this age enjoy reading about children their age in other places and cultures. The time has come (young though he is) for your child to be dipping into a variety of reading matter which will open his mind to new possibilities, prepare the way for future interests, and perhaps eventually guide him toward a career.

When a child does not have an interest in reading, it is important to try to find an area of interest that might attract him or her. Look for books about the things your child likes to do—train books for the avid subway rider, sports for your athlete, detective books for your John Shaft or detective comics reader. Reading is a valuable skill—for pleasure and for learning. Encourage it. Books on your shelves and in your hands speak louder than a thousand words.

What are some good trips for children this age?

You've been to museums, zoos, art exhibitions, and dance exhibitions. Keep right on going. But also, think about taking your nine- or ten-year-old youngster with you when you go to vote. This is a meaningful experience for a child. Youngsters have a pretty good idea what's going on at this point. If they are introduced to the practice of voting by their parents at this age, they are much more likely to attach an importance to such things than other children. After all, we need all the voters we can get . . . and then some.

The same is true when going to the bank, when going to buy furniture, when going to do any number of matters which amount to "taking care of business." You might want to take your twelve-year-old to an Urban League fashion show or to a fund-raising banquet for black colleges, explaining the underlying objectives. Children should have plenty of fun but they should also be introduced to the decision-making, problem-solving organizations in society. This is where white children from upper-middle-income families have a tremendous advantage over black and other white youngsters. Their interests in the stock market, board decisions, and government action which affect our lives as much as theirs, are developed early by listening to and being with their parents who *are* the decision-makers. Because of this, they see the importance of developing (and so develop) certain kinds of skills—leadership and social grace for example—sooner than many other children.

My twelve-year-old daughter's idea of a trip is to hitchhike around town, although I have told her it is dangerous and forbidden her to do so. What more can I do? Why do children sometimes do obviously dangerous things?

Some of a child's attraction to danger is tied up with the struggle for independence. Some of it reflects a child's effort to demonstrate to himself or herself that he or she is not vulnerable. Or it can be a statement of both concerns: "See, I am apart from and independent of you and I cannot be melted down or destroyed." Sometimes it is an effort to prove that the world is not dangerous so that children don't have to be afraid of moving out into it. You can't be with your child every minute so that forbidding him to do dangerous things often doesn't work. If he's in the business of defying you, he will do just what you forbid him to do because you forbade him to do it.

If you have had good communication all along, your child is much more likely to stop doing extremely dangerous things when you discuss the matter in a concerned and reasonable way. You can let it be known that you consider hitchhiking dangerous, that you are concerned about your daughter's safety, and that you don't want her to do it. The important thing is that you help her understand that doing dangerous things is no indication that she is stronger or better than people who are more cautious. You want to help her learn that there are real dangers in the world; that she and all people risk harm from these dangers; that she should take reasonable precautions to avoid danger, without stopping everything because there are dangers in the world. In other words, you want to help her learn to live with the reality of her vulnerability. Of course, if you are a great risk-taker or do things that you know to be dangerous—like driving very fast—your child is likely to do the same thing.

While we're on the subject of hitchhiking, my twelve-year-old daughter says that it's all right to hitchhike in our neighborhood because it's black and blacks will do her no harm. I want her to have racial pride, but . . . ! How should I handle this?

Late in this age period and in adolescence, young people establishing their own identity identify strongly with causes—in this case, the black cause and the need for black unity and trust. They go all out and everything black becomes good. You should help your daughter understand that there are individuals among all groups who are capable of doing harm. There is little reason to believe that blacks who have lived under extremely difficult circumstances would produce fewer people capable of doing harm than whites who have lived under less difficult circumstances. We have seen young people be harmed believing that black is beautiful and all blacks are capable of only beautiful deeds . . . ignoring and denying the reality of the "not so beautiful" deeds they observe.

Friends and Friendships

My ten-year-old spends a lot of time at the home of a friend. Could there be something wrong with our house?

Friendships are very important to children of this age group. As a rule the boys are with boys and girls are with girls. Their favorite friends are usually children who are very much like themselves in interest and personality . . . though "odd couples" do occur.

With friends who are more or less equal, they can share hobbies and play games without the threat to their self-image and self-concept that your ability constantly presents. Until around ten or twelve, you can beat them at everything. They develop ways of handling competitive feelings and jealousies with "their own." They argue, tease, support and put down each other in an important give-and-take way. Sometimes they fall out, starting off friends in the morning, enemies by noon, and friends again after dinner. They bounce off each other and get to know and feel themselves as people in these close relationships. They begin to understand a lot about themselves as they notice what they like and dislike in others.

At this stage youngsters develop their ability to "read" or understand people and situations. You may hear a nine-year-old say, "Well, you can't always pay attention to what Ben says," or, "That Jimmy is some character, anything I have, he claims he has a better one. He sure has a problem." They remain friends in spite of these and other observations because of certain positive attractions. Learning to understand and tolerate shortcomings in others, and having others understand and tolerate your own shortcomings, is an important skill to have. It prepares a child for close relationships later on in life.

Being away from you, yet being in the home of someone much like you, the buddy's parents, enables your child to feel some independence and freedom while still feeling protected. When they're not at the house of another friend or at best buddy's, they are often traveling around the neighborhood together. Together they are braver and can go places and do things they might not do if they were alone.

Chances are there's nothing wrong with your house. If you stop to think about it, you'll probably realize that the buddy is over to your house a great deal as well. But you might want to think about whether you're doing something which makes it unpleasant at your house. Again, setting limits—even if it makes children unhappy temporarily—is important and should not be changed just to get them to come to your house. If there *is* a problem, it may be the *way* you're setting limits rather than the fact that you're setting them.

My child often talks about what goes on in his friend's house as if it's better than ours. I probably shouldn't feel jealous, but I do. Why?

You're probably concerned about whether you are a good parent or not . . . whether your house is as good a home for your child as someone else's. You shouldn't feel jealous. What your child has to say about someone else's house is not a good test of your parenting. The test is how your child functions. He talks about what goes on in other homes because he is dealing with difference. The way things are done in another house—the time for meals, who cleans off the table, the way the house is arranged—all of this is quite an eye-opener for your child, who has only had your home and your way of doing things as a model. The enthusiasm with which your child makes certain reports—Al's father washed the dishes! or Tiffany's mother painted the hallway!—is usually a statement of surprise and not a judgment one way or the other.

You can help your child learn to appreciate and be comfortable with differences by accepting them without condemnation or ridicule as reasonable other ways of doing things—unless they are unreasonable or inhumane. If your child insists that something is wrong because it's different from the way you do it at home, you can be helpful by pointing out the right of people to do things in different ways, as long as it is not unfair or harmful. On the other hand, don't apologize for your own way. But remember that reports from the outside world, if listened to with an open mind, can sometimes help us to change for the better.

If you are tolerant of differences during this period, your child is less likely to angrily attack your ways of life during his own adolescence. He will not feel so rigidly trapped into a mold or way of life from which he can't deviate because you have said it's "the only way." By noticing differences and talking about them you are saying that it's okay to be different, and that your child has the right to decide his own way of life.

But what if I really disapprove of how
the friend's family does things?

We are not saying that you should approve of everything that goes on in the homes of others. Where others are dishonest or unfair or extremely permissive, you will want to point out where and why your family disagrees with these approaches—without putting the other family down, and without having your child going back and reporting your opinion. Making it known that you don't want your opinion reported can be a little lesson in diplomacy your child needs to learn. Dishonest? . . . no. Tactful? . . . yes. We will never forget the "honest" young teacher who, when asked by a troublesome eight-year-old child whether she liked her or not, told the truth, "I don't like you." The child was crushed and the teacher was devastated in turn by the child's reaction. There are times to speak up, regardless of the consequences, but not when it serves no useful purpose and only hurts someone.

My daughter seems to be as friendly toward grownups as she is toward children her own age. Should I be concerned about this?

If she likes grownups because she has difficulty getting along with groups of children her own age, this is a reason for concern. In a case like this you would want to help her learn to relate to children her own age without discouraging adult friends. But relatives and neighborhood friends can be good "other parents" for a child. The "other parents" can be friends without having the major responsibility for the child's behavior. This can make visits with such friends quite relaxing. After all, children have enough places where they must "measure up."

What should I do about bad company?

When you *must* talk to your child about the behavior of another child, be careful not to simply call the other child "bad." Nor should you blame all the problems that have come up on the other child. All of us have a little lawlessness and mischief in our hearts, and so does your youngster. You will want to help your child to understand that a child who repeatedly does undesirable things has problems, and can create bigger problems for himself and your child. It is probably not a good idea to try and force your child to stay away from a child you don't approve of. Except in extreme cases, the "bad influence child" is not likely to do great harm to your child's development. One benefit of such a relationship is that, if you talk with your child from time to time about the problem, you can help your child learn to handle undesirable influences . . . observe undesirable behavior but not put down the person displaying it and yet not get mixed up in it. This is an *extremely* important lesson to learn during this age period, and children who learn it can better resist peer pressures to act up during the teens and throughout life.

Why would my child, who is doing well, get tied up with a troublemaker?

Sometimes it's because there aren't that many other children around to choose from. But most of the time, it's because your child is attracted to some aspect of the other child. If your child is a little bit on the timid and goody-goody side, a more aggressive, acting-up youngster, with your supervision, may bring your child out to the point of being aggressive enough but not too aggressive. Children who are in trouble or neglected often seek out the parents of friends for the guidance, praise, and attention they do not receive at home. If you give them respect and establish expectations of behavior in your home, some children with problems can use this to go on and develop well.

If you try to break up the friendship, you may have two children acting up against you—your child and the other child—when you might have been able to help them both. When you are concerned about your child's friend, it helps to have the child around your house fairly often, and do things with him or her as much as possible. In this way you can build a relationship which will enable you to influence the friend . . . and keep an eye on their activities. In cases where the development of your child is going well and the development of the other child worsens, the friendship is not likely to last. There is the rare case where nothing works and you must help your child break the tie. When you talk to him about why and how, you may be surprised to find that he was ready but needed your help.

Coping with Peer Pressure

My son stopped playing tennis because his friends told him that it was a white man's game. I think he should be able to play whatever he likes. What do you think?

We're with you. But the pressure of peers is great. You might point out to your son that there are good black tennis players. (The same is true of golf, hockey, skating, gymnastics, swimming, and other sports where there are few visible blacks.) Blacks are not in these sports because they require a great deal of money, equipment, facilities, and coaching personnel. If you can afford to pay for your son or daughter's participation in any of these areas, by all means encourage entering into them. We believe that black children should have the freedom to go in any direction their intelligence and skills will take them. They must be helped to understand that there is no such thing as a white man's sport or a black man's sport. You can also help them understand that their friends may be jealous that they are doing something different, or that perhaps they simply do not know any blacks in these sports and therefore cannot identify with them.

Maybe it has nothing to do with tennis. Could it be that
they are asking my youngster to apologize because
he is from a middle-income family?

Yes, and just as we don't want our children to apologize or feel bad about being black or different from the majority, we don't want them to apologize or feel bad about being from a middle-income family. Both the black and white media have equated blackness with poverty and romanticized the black poor. This has put a number of black teen-agers from middle-income black families under a great amount of needless and harmful stress— being middle-income is "not black," less black, or even "Uncle Tom." This is the age period during which you will want to help your child prepare to handle the pressure he or she will feel more keenly as a teen.

It is important that your youngster understand that as long as he is fair in his relationships with all people, he has no reason for guilt. It helps if you can point out how you are supporting improved conditions for all people. You should help your youngster understand that much of the pressure put on him is due to jealousy and is often defensive on the part of the attacker.

We recall the situation of a low-income black youngster who teased a middle-income black youngster about his "Uncle Tom" job in a school office. But who was the first one in trying to get the job when the middle-income youngster graduated? . . . You guessed it!

Parent-Child Interaction

I feel jealous when my child talks about other adults as
if they're perfect and I am his enemy . . . when I do
all the work! Should I have such feelings?

We all do. Your child will talk about other adults as if they're perfect, but he will come to you when he needs help. This means that he has confidence and trust in you. Children often express angry feelings toward parents and positive feelings toward other adults as a way of showing some sense of independence from you. The angry feelings, while often exaggerated for dramatic effect, are real . . . and understandably so. You must set limits, express disapproval, and deny your child things that are not in his best interest. But as long as you are fair and often fun, you need not worry . . . you're the one, the one most loved and respected.

Is there a way to avoid some of the problems and difficulties of the teen-age period by the way I respond to my child during this age period?

Yes. All of childhood is movement from complete dependence toward a condition in which a person can care for the self—independence. The effort reaches its peak during the teen-age period. The degree of the problem you and your child have during the teens can be reduced through the approach you use right now. In fact, as we have stressed all along, hopefully you have been giving your child as much opportunity for independent action and expression from the beginning as he or she was able to handle in a responsible way. This is the last age—before your child is fully caught up in a more open struggle for independence—for your child to realize that you are pleased about and support his striving for responsible independence. This can reduce but will not eliminate teen-age turmoil.

There are many ways to offer your child a chance to make independent but reasonable decisions, without giving up your responsibilities. She can work out the time to do her chores. He can select his own school clothes. She can decide what she will do with the part of her allowance which she is not required to save. You will be able to think of many other such ways for your child to learn to think for herself, if you are truly ready to help her to achieve responsible independence. But don't just "go away" or dump *all* the decisions into her lap.

It is very important to help your son remember that if all of his allowance is spent on rockets, he will not be able to go to "the show" this weekend. You can help your daughter understand that certain clothing or fads are commercial "rip offs" . . . maybe okay after you have what you need, but not before. It helps to do this through matter-of-fact questions which help youngsters establish priorities and reason well rather than through criticism and ridicule. Too often we don't teach children how to reason and achieve their goals and then criticize them when they make "dumb decisions" or "get taken."

Not all fads and frills should be considered unreasonable. Funny-looking little hats, shoes, insignias, and so on may be important to your child. They are forms of self-expression. The same is true of your youngster's tastes in things like music. Where you disapprove, say so. At the same time help your child to see that he will have to live with any undesirable outcome of "his choice." You can and should reserve the right to veto a choice when it can be dangerous or harmful or just too, too far out. But try, try, try to help him and let him become a good thinker and doer, making decisions in his best interest and not against you. When it is made clear during this period that you support your child's strivings for independence, the teen-age period is likely to be less stormy.

*I have been told it is important for my child to see me
actively handling problems in the society during
this age period. Why?*

In the four-to-eight-year-old period, your child was a passive learner about the ways of our society or your culture—going to church, celebrating Christmas—with you and in your way. He was also busy trying to get control over himself, learning how to handle his feelings and making it in his group. With much of this under his belt and a greater ability to understand and learn, he can now turn away from personal concerns from time to time and look at the larger society.

Hearing you talk about the issues—the need for clean alleys, honest government, better schools, less crime and better black jobs—helps your child identify with these causes. But, more important, watching you helps him understand how he can do something about these problems. You are the model on which your child's response pattern will be built.

If you insist on seeing the airlines manager when your flight is oversold, instead of knocking the clerk down, your child will learn an effective way of handling the problem. If you write a letter to the company who failed to deliver your couch in good condition and send a carbon copy to the State Commissioner of Consumer

Affairs or to your Congressman, again, your child will learn an effective way of handling a problem rather than just feeling "had" and powerless. When you vote, or if you don't vote, it is observed. If you contribute to your favorite civil rights group or if you don't contribute, this is likely to be noticed too during this period when we actively socialize our children through what we say and do. If you don't talk to them about these actions, they will miss an important part of their education.

Sometimes I'm so discouraged by personal problems and racial conditions I find it difficult to be optimistic and encouraging. Can this be harmful to my child?

All of us go up and down in the degree of hope and confidence we have in ourselves, our family and friends, our people and our country. Moderate changes in mood from time to time are not harmful. Persistent and unrealistic optimism or persistent and unrealistic feelings of doom *can* be harmful. This is the age when a child should learn to reach for the stars. Through your despairing words and your actions, you can say, "There ain't no stars and there's no need to reach."

We hear many young black parents repeatedly despairing about the condition of blacks in America. While there are many very real problems and dangers, if you overstate the case or despair beyond reason, your child can develop a crippling cynicism and hopelessness about people, America, and the world. This can lead to apathy, depression, and "dropping out" by the middle or late teens. The ugliness of the world, racism being of particular concern to us, can become the excuse for not going out and facing life. A sense of hopelessness can also cause your child to remain dependent on you. This will lead him to attack your ideas, your way of life, and even your personality, in a way which a child who is moving to become less dependent on his parents during the late teens would not. It can also cause children to isolate themselves from all but those who think and feel exactly like them. Youngsters who do this often argue that they are "getting themselves together" or "preserving their culture." Where this is actually the case, they should eventually be able to associate fairly comfortably with people who are not the same or who do not think the same. When they can't, the truth is that they are hiding from the troubles of the world.

Are you trying to say that I shouldn't face the facts?

No, we don't mean that you should deny reality. You should identify and discuss injustice, on racial grounds or any other grounds. But you can help your child most by helping him work out ways to overcome injustice . . . to keep on keeping on. This has been the approach that has sustained black Americans throughout our history against overwhelming obstacles. If we give up the fight now—because the preacher isn't reminding us every Sunday anymore—we and our children are going to be in a lot of trouble.

My twelve-year-old wanted to go to camp and I didn't want him to go. I realized later that I was really trying to hold on to my last "baby." I won't know what to do without children to raise. What can I do about this?

This is a very common problem. Many parents—particularly mothers—devote some of their most vigorous and healthy years, between twenty and forty, to bringing up their children. As the children become more and more independent, the parents begin to feel cheated. This can be even more of a problem when a husband and wife do not have a very good relationship and the wife does not have a career or a social program—friends and activities—independent of those of her husband.

It is undesirable in this day and age for parents to put *all* of their time and energy into rearing their children. It is best for both children and parents that, as the development of the child permits it, parents enjoy a healthy mixture of activities, with and without the children. Clubs, hobbies, volunteer work, and part-time jobs all permit parents to have a life that goes beyond that of rearing children. Parents who are not otherwise occupied may, in conscious and unconscious ways, try to keep their children from leaving home or becoming independent. This interferes with a child's growing up and can lead to real trouble in adolescence. It can also lead to boredom and depression for mothers who no longer see themselves as valuable people with an important task—rearing children.

CHAPTER 8

Adolescence

Definition and Characteristics of Adolescence

What is adolescence?

Adolescence is the time between puberty (ages eleven to thirteen) and young adulthood (ages eighteen to twenty-one). It is a period in which critical sexual development and social and emotional growth take place. Puberty is the beginning of biological adulthood—the capability to reproduce. Secondary sexual characteristics (pubic and underarm hair, increase in size of penis and testicles, growth of breasts in girls, beard and deep voice in boys) appear, and there is a spurt in growth. Girls begin to menstruate and boys usually begin to ejaculate during this time. Because these bodily changes occur rapidly, teen-agers go through a period of physical awkwardness which should eventually disappear. Early and late adolescence are quite different.

What is the difference between the two stages?

Early adolescence is generally the time from puberty to age fifteen or sixteen. Late adolescence is the time thereafter to young adulthood. The beginning of puberty is marked by a rapid growth spurt, and sexual hormonal changes. There is usually psychological turmoil and a periodic return to less mature behavior and awkwardness. Early adolescents are particularly drawn to group relations with members of the same sex. Later, most develop strong attractions to the opposite sex.

After about sixteen years of age, the adolescent may feel more settled and sure of himself. He may be less self-concerned and devote more time to vocational plans and social and philosophical issues. Parental influence is greatest in early adolescence. As the teen-ager matures, the influence of parents decreases and peer influence increases.

Do girls reach puberty before boys?

Yes, girls are about two years ahead of boys on the average, but boys catch up by age twenty-one. Remember, however, that there is much individual variation. Some girls are fully developed at age fourteen and others are just starting.

Is it true that adolescence begins earlier for black children than for white children?

No, not in the physical sense. Sexual development and growth begin at similar times among blacks and whites. Occasionally puberty is delayed when a youngster has suffered from chronically poor nutrition. However, some black children who are reared in an environment of poverty may be given adult responsibilities earlier and so may be socially advanced for their age. Overloading a child with adult tasks may prevent him or her from passing through the usual stages of childhood. Sometimes such children may return to behavior that they did not have a proper opportunity to experience.

Why is adolescence such a problem period for parent-child relations?

There is a very important struggle going on during adolescence. Most youngsters move to give up much of their dependency on parents and become more independent. Although close emotional family ties are usually maintained, there is movement toward closer ties with people outside the home—fired by social and sexual needs. This is not without much fear. A number of questions run through the minds of teens without their being fully aware of them: "Can I be as able a person as my parents?" "Will I be able to succeed in further education and training?" "Look at me, Joe is taller and better-looking; Mary is smarter and her father is an engineer. How can I possibly compete with them?" "Will I be able to get a job, a husband, or wife, take care of a family?" "How shall I handle my sexual feelings?"

We should be available to help our teens handle all these questions and issues, but we often botch the opportunity. We are often at the peak of our own achievement and success, and therefore threatening to an adolescent, or floundering and frightened ourselves and threatened by the teen-ager. We are often past the peak of our physical excellence. We can be jealous of and frightened by the energy, beauty, and opportunity of adolescents. We fear losing control over our youngster's views and behavior. We see in them *our* last chance to be another Lena Horne or a Constance Baker Motley, Henry Aaron or Andrew Brimmer. We can see our children missing the boat, just as we missed the boat, in his or her every uncertainty or questionable move. As a result, we are too often inclined to push and nag, on the one hand, and throw up our hands or flap open our mouths in despair and criticism on the other.

Most important, we too often misread a teen tactic designed to make him feel more independent as a lack of appreciation for "all that we've done for you." Because it is a time of self-assertion and a concern about personal rights, teens often turn on parents. Adolescents are often critical of and hostile toward their parents—rejecting their views, ways, goals and so on. They say, through action and words, "Go away from me." But if you listen closely, you'll also hear, "Don't get mad and don't go too far. Who else is going to tolerate all of my 'stuff'?" "Who else can I count on for sure to help me answer all of these questions?" Thus, our problems and reactions and their problems and reactions interact to create the conflicts of adolescence.

How can parents be most helpful?

As we pointed out before, adolescence is less troublesome if all along you permitted your child to have as much independence as he or she could handle; helped him or her learn to be realistic, plan, organize, and carry various activities to completion; and made it possible for him or her to be able to call for help in words rather than act up in order for you to come to the rescue. With the calm knowledge that you support their independence and accept their limitations, there is less need to test you to find out where you stand. There is less chance that they will hide their fear behind claims that you are deliberately trying to block their freedom, make them your slaves, or whatever their rhetoric.

Be aware of how you are a threat. Be aware of your child's right to independent thoughts and actions, only raising questions to provide useful information or challenge things you consider inhumane or unjust. Be aware that your fears may be your problem, based on your experiences and aspirations, strengths and shortcomings, and not relevant to your child's situation at all. You should remind yourself and continue to inform your child, as you have been doing since he or she was knee-high to a grasshopper, that he or she is going to school, working, loving, and so on, for *himself* and *herself* and not for *you;* that you can try and help them, try and protect them, but you can't and don't want to live their lives for them.

Adolescents often pick quarrels and fights. Be aware that a television program snapped off in your face may be the old blues song, "Help me, somebody," and not an attack on your parenthood. If it happens, one of the first ways you can help is to say, "Joan, I can see that you want to get my attention. Let's talk about whatever is bothering you. But you know, I'm going to be better able to talk if I am not mad because you snapped off the television in my face." Then be cool. Don't expect an immediate apology or an immediate effort to find and discuss the problem—though you may get both. Be alert for an opening and a cue that says, "Now I can talk."

Be especially aware of the fact that you can crush the aggression, anger, and self-assertion. Instead of rebellion, you can get an apparently compliant child, but one who has turned the aggression inside and against the self. Here a child is sometimes silently angry and may be highly rebellious later on. Other youngsters become self-destructive—poor learning, poor work efforts, the use of drugs and alcohol, sexual promiscuity, dating people you don't approve of, or having a baby just to hurt you.

I know that I am at fault, but the approach you have described won't work with my youngster. We have been at war too long. What can I do?

Make peace. We mentioned earlier that the longer a pattern of relationship exists, the more difficult it is to change. But nothing beats a failure but a try. If things are really bad, you have nothing to lose. Again, the approach is to point out your unhappiness with the relationship, ackowledging your part in the difficulties as well as pointing out your child's contribution to the conflict. Call for a better way and spell out what you will try and do to improve the situation. Try to have a discussion about how you can be more helpful as well as how your youngster can be more helpful. If it works, you now have a new contract.

You will be tested. Are you really going to relate differently? You will want to hold up your end of the bargain and call on your child to hold up his or her end. Again, it is fragile, but oh so powerful. The glue is the fact that you need and receive so much from each other. It works less well where the problem is parents who not only don't care but also display their lack of concern in harmful ways—where there is real neglect and abuse. Where the latter is the case, many youngsters develop serious social and psychological problems during adolescence. Unfortunately, because of chance and life's complexity, it is possible for youngsters from the best social circumstances—love, guidance, and support— to have psychological and social problems. In this case, they will need you more than ever.

Are there other causes for the turmoil of adolescence?

Yes. The adolescent is in search of his or her identity. Sexual, religious and racial issues, fairly settled at eleven and twelve, come up again for reevaluation, new understanding, and rearrangement. In this regard adolescents ask themselves, again without being fully aware of it, several critical questions. "Who am I?" "What do I believe in?" "When should I take a stand for what I believe in?" "Where am I going?" "How am I going to get there . . . and with whom?" They ask and answer these questions through the clothes they wear; their hairstyles; the heroes, friends, and enemies they select; the cliques they form; the fads they follow; and the causes they support.

*Could this be why there is so much fuss about where
a person sits in the school cafeteria?*

It is a good part of the reason. Even where most youngsters are of the same racial and religious groups, certain similarities and differences cause the formation of "in-groups" and "out-groups" and for-and-against attitudes. "My group" is a way of narrowing the possibilities of who one is and what he or she stands for. Because adolescence is also a time of proving one's adequacy, it can be a time of scapegoating or putting down the most vulnerable out-group. It can be a time of serious racial and religious conflict. It is a time when young people ask each other to prove their loyalty to their group by living up to group norms—moral or immoral, reasonable or unreasonable, humane or inhumane.

There are groups and groups and groups. We have seen black and white youngsters who are friends in a neighborhood be friends and play together on the school team but not sit or talk together in the school cafeteria—where black-white group membership is the dominant issue. Some youngsters successfully defy such group-prescribed arrangements. This is usually a youngster whose parents have supported his or her independence from the beginning, a youngster who is clearly adequate by important standards—good student, good athlete, personable, and a person whose self-esteem comes more from within than from what other people think or say.

The community climate with regard to race or religion at a given time is also important. Minority-majority ratios can be important.

Is fighting a big problem of adolescence?

Yes and no, depending on conditions. Adolescents functioning well have largely channeled aggressive energy into satisfying work and play—school learning, hobbies, sports. They feel adequate enough, view themselves as getting better in many areas, and are receiving good "vibes" about who they are. They have learned to tolerate the average frustrations and discharge anger through joking, teasing, physical activities, and so on. Such youngsters are likely to fight only if attacked or in the extreme heat of competitive athletics. Youngsters not making it as well—particularly in an environment of strangers or "vulnerable others," without mature adult involvement—are more likely to fight. Youngsters not making it often band together and make it as an out-group, intimidating, disrupting, and fighting individuals and groups they consider to be making it and rejecting them. Their form of making it may include purse snatching and other antisocial behavior as well as fighting.

Parent, teacher, friend, youth worker: try to help a fighting teen learn to handle frustration, threats to his or her manhood or womanhood (adequacy) in some way other than a fight. Help them learn what they should have learned earlier—that it is okay to talk or negotiate, that manhood and fighting are not the same. This is the last chance for many. Too many violent acts in the black community are over insignificant manhood issues—"he stepped on my shoes," and so on.

How do the forces you described interact?

An example should be helpful. The racial climate of 1970 and 1971 was particularly ripe to call adolescents to racial causes. In that climate, a 15-year-old white male "loser"—poor student, no athletic ability or other special talent and so on—sought to feel good or adequate by insulting a black female student. The latter, bright but with little use for academic work, had a school history of minor conflicts with blacks and whites. The incident gave blacks and whites "a cause" . . . something to throw themselves into and prove their group loyalty. A full-scale riot of several days erupted. Both ringleaders were removed from the regular school program and put in a special, one-teacher, small-class, low-pressure class-room—together. In this less threatening situation they got along okay and the school social problems gradually decreased.

Don't the identity and adequacy struggles sometimes lead to more troublesome outcomes?

Yes. We are particularly concerned about the difficult racial iden-tity struggles we are seeing in some black youngsters completely isolated from whites and in those being told that it is okay, even desirable, to "get whitey." At the other end, the black youngster of mixed racial parentage, those with white features, those living in predominantly white communities or those with white families can have some very difficult identity problems. The same is true of those with a lifestyle like that of the American middle- and upper-income groups.

In adolescence such youngsters often blame their parents for removing them from their people; for the fact that the only people they can have close relationships with or date—if they date at all—are white; for the fact that blacks say, "You are not black." We have seen school failure, criminal behavior, extreme militant behavior, depression, and even outright mental breakdowns result from the identity confusion involved here. We have even seen black teens from caring families with good incomes become pimps, prostitutes, and drug addicts in an effort to be black or identify with the brothers and sisters. We have seen blacks blame whites and racism as a cause for all of their problems and get hung up on hating whitey at the expense of their own personal development.

Whites have similar problems. Is there a special problem here for blacks?

Yes, several. The uncertainty and confusion of adolescence usually decrease after young people test their abilities and find themselves adequate; after they find out what their past moral training, beliefs, and ideas will permit and not permit them to do or believe in; and after they have identified future roles that are acceptable to them and possible for them. Once feeling sufficiently independent and adequate, adolescents are able to identify with and use their parents as models for becoming their acceptable future selves. That is why, once past adolescence, most young people are not too unlike their parents in values and ways . . . although sometimes just the opposite results and specific differences do occur.

Parents secure in their own identities do not have to fight to control the adolescent, permitting the teen to concentrate on the fight rather than deal with the real issues of adolescence. Parents comfortable with their roles and identities as blacks, whites, doctors, lawyers, "African chiefs" . . . butchers, bakers and automobile-makers . . . are living proof to the adolescent that he or she too can find such comfort. But as black adults we are involved in at least two revolutions—a revolt against being singled out to be poor and against being oppressed on the basis of our race alone.

As a result, we are in the process of rejecting long-standing negative racial identities and limited and undesirable social roles and searching for positive and acceptable ones. This is similar to what is happening with young people and we, therefore, sometimes display the same confusion, fear, bravado and uncertainty around racial issues. We have seen adults seeking a positive black identity try on dashikis, particular hairstyles, and communal living. Some eventually return to modified previous styles but with a new and positive level of black awareness and pride.

The problem: during the period of redefining blackness—a

period that is still going on—some black parents and leaders can't convey a model of a way to be black without being self-defeating or consumed by antagonism toward whites and white-controlled America.

How does this affect black teens?

You help your adolescent best by understanding his or her feeling or problem but seeing the situation and calling it "like it is." Because we are so angry about conditions for blacks in America, so angry with whites, as an "out-group" it is sometimes possible for black teens to get black adults to go along with things that are said to be against the enemy even when it is not in the best interest of the youngsters. Blacks who won't compromise are called "Toms." It is a very real problem in a setting where guilty or manipulative whites will permit black teens to do whatever they want—even when it is clearly against their best interest.

In one predominantly white high school, the white staff put a jukebox in the black study hall "because they wanted it." We have seen black parents and teachers "use" black youngsters to express their own anger toward whites, only to find the youngsters antagonistic toward them unless they continued to go along with whatever they proposed, wise or otherwise. Where such relationships exist, adults can't be trusted and can't help young people deal with real issues in a realistic way.

We have seen a number of black youngsters hide behind race— back everybody away with attacks on "whitey" and "Toms"—only to have to face their real fears and problems later on, often too late.

How can I prevent my teen from using "race" to avoid his own problems?

Again, you aid best by helping your adolescent learn to "see it like it is." One eighteen-year-old freshman complained that he got a "D" because he was black. His roommate said, "Oh, I thought you got it because you had your behind in the sack during the man's class." If you acknowledged racial injustice—without seeing it where it didn't exist—and taught your youngster to keep moving toward his or her goals in spite of it, to fight it in an effective but non-self-destructive way, your adolescent is more likely to be the latter youngster.

You want to help your teen learn to spot people who talk "angry black" to cover up personal hostility, petty jealousy, and greed. Too many black youngsters have been led down the garden path by ego-trippers long on talk, short on commitment to blacks—and to the youth they get out on the limb. Several such "leaders" were called to pay the bail for teens they stirred to violence. They couldn't make it because they were off to hear "Little Johnny Somebody." However, it is important to recognize that many militants are deeply sincere in their commitment to blacks and not out to be exploitive.

How is the racial identity problem more difficult for black teens who have no or very little contact with whites? I would think that it would be easier.

The distortions of reality so common in adolescence are brought into line best by contact with reality. Many blacks have never had contact with a white person who was reasonably fair with all the strengths and weaknesses of all other human beings. Thus, it is possible to imagine whitey with strengths, weaknesses, and negative intents toward blacks which are not always there. It is easier to punch a stereotype to help establish one's own identity than it is to attack a real person, but positive blackness based on anti-whiteness is as hollow as the reverse. When the stereotype is all an adolescent has, he or she can get stuck at that level, reduce the problems of his or her life to whitey, and not move beyond this low level of identity and adaptation.

What is the cause of special identity problems for black youngsters out of what many consider the black community mainstream?

For different and complex reasons, whites and a few misled blacks have to date defined blackness in America as poverty, broken homes, troubled communities; ability in athletics; singing, dancing, pimping, and mugging; hating whites and being not too smart with little interest in learning academic subjects. If we were white racists trying to figure out how to keep blacks from moving into positions of power in order to improve their lot, we would try to convince them that to be true black you must meet the definition of blackness given above.

Often, unless you and your youngster fit this definition of blackness, you are said to be "white," "not black," or not black enough. It is the cause of some of the absolute terror and some of the psychosocial paralysis we see in black students from low-income families whose status as students means passage out of this definition of blackness. It is the cause of great conflict for black teens who would like to have friendships with blacks or whites, who enjoy Beethoven as much as Isaac Hayes' "Hot Buttered Soul," who prefer algebra to basketball, and so on.

Some black parents have mixed feelings about being black and can create severe identity problems for youngsters. We know of several youngsters who were reared in largely white communities by parents who preferred whites. But the youngsters reached dating age about the time their parents began to try to be black. They had encouraged their children to associate only with whites all their lives and then expressed strong disapproval of interracial dating. The youngsters, awkward with blacks, tried to repress interest in the opposite sex. But this caused them to have doubt about their sexual adequacy and in a couple of instances it led to serious psychological trouble. See our discussion under "Boy-Girl Relations" in this chapter.

What can I do as the white parent of a black youngster?

We have seen teens of interracial marriages or adoptions have no more than the ordinary racial identity problems. We have seen some have serious problems. If you have talked about the fact of your interracial relationship, the attitudes of others about it and the quality of black-white relationships in general in a comfortable way all along, your teen is less likely to have identity problems now. If overall development has taken place within a good family relationship, the likelihood of problems is less. Hopefully you have helped your youngster to be in contact with the full range of his or her black heritage. Hopefully you have not tried to compensate for your relationship and be blacker-than-blacks.

Children of mixed blood are considered black by society. Hopefully, you didn't ask your child to reject the black part of himself or herself nor encourage them to wear the white part as a badge to make up for being black. Your teen may accuse you of making him or her abnormal. Hear it for what it is—the adolescent attack-in-the-service-of-independence ploy. Guilt and fighting back make matters worse. Again, help them deal with the real fear, assure them that it's possible to be black and white and okay, and assure them of your continuing love whatever their future choice of friends, goals and causes.

Such attacks on you often come after rebuffs in mixed dating efforts or the like. That is why it is important for your child to understand his position as a black and society's response to blackness. It is also the reason that your teen should have had contact with blacks of similar style and interest—to appreciate the fact that he or she is not a racial nonperson, without a racial identity. If you have not talked out these issues before, now is late . . . but not too late.

How can I support a positive black identity during adolescence?

Your interest and care all along have given your youngsters a positive sense of themselves as people. This made it possible for them to achieve many things, view themselves as competent and good. You have talked about, had them read about, and exposed them to black culture and black achievement within the total culture. You have "shot down" negative and racist attitudes about blacks and you have given logical explanations for problems in the black community. Most of all, you have helped them understand that white racist attitudes and behavior are the problems of white racists and are no measure of your youngsters' value and worth as people, as black people. You will want to continue all of this.

As adolescents—idealistic, action-oriented, wanting to make their mark—they will want to do something about racial injustices. We must help them find constructive ways. The first and most important is their own personal development. We will discuss others. From all of this can come young adults, black, proud and able.

My son is about to graduate from high school and already has plenty of freedom, but talks often of his need for freedom. What does it mean?

Most teens are sick and tired of being in so obvious a dependent situation, even when they can make a number of responsible decisions. That is why it is best if they can be out of your house—in college, the military, other training programs—after high school. If your son appears obsessed by the notion of freedom, take a closer look and listen.

This is often the cry of a teen in conflict, unable to make a sound career decision or love choice or to make the break from the comfort of the parents' home. Recall that these and other issues are related to adequacy and identity concerns. You should try to avoid conflict around the "freedom" cry in order to help teens see what is really going on. Real freedom is an inner thing—an ability to observe, feel, and act in an independent fashion in line with personal needs, beliefs, and goals . . . as long as they are humane. A free person is free to live with his or her parents but doesn't *have* to; can wear jeans to church but doesn't *have* to; can disagree with a friend but doesn't *have* to; and so on. We sometimes help youngsters think about this by pointing out that some people would be "in chains" if they were naked in the park and others are free in chains.

It will probably help to point out that minor rules and restrictions for individuals protect the major rights and freedoms of all. You can point out how your household rules save you all a great deal of worry, confusion and general difficulty.

Values, Morals, and Attitudes

Do most black youths distrust whites?

According to some surveys, almost 50 percent of black high school students do not believe whites can be trusted. In contrast, a much smaller percentage of older blacks feel this way. Young blacks have been disillusioned by the rhetoric of democracy. Progress in solving racial problems in the past decade has been disappointing. The expectations of young blacks are high. They are more ready to face their anger and frustrations. These factors probably account for the differences.

Is it true that black youths are anti-Semitic?

No. Many black teen-agers are hostile toward whites because of the frequent encounters with merchants in the black urban community and many of these persons happen to be Jewish. However, a recent survey showed that black youths are less anti-Semitic than anti-white. This finding may be due to the fact that Jews are an integral part of life in the inner cities and thus more familiar to black teen-agers than other whites.

How can I help my teen-ager acquire a fair attitude toward whites? Would an integrated school help?

Positive experiences with whites—relationships of fairness and mutual respect—at an early age make it difficult, when one is functioning well, to hold a stereotyped attitude toward an entire group. However, black children in the inner city who are forced to attend segregated schools have little opportunity to positively interact with whites. It is not surprising then that many feel at odds with the entire white community. When discussing the matter with teens, you don't want to preach or try to make them admit that they are being unfair. Raise questions about charges they make about *all* whites which help them see they are generalizing unfairly. Be careful about your own generalizations. If you have a calm commitment to fairness, your youngster is likely to eventually develop the same.

Sending your youngster to an integrated school might help but not necessarily—particularly in a school with repeated racial conflict. In addition, adolescence is a rough time and a period when racial conflict is very likely to flare. Feelings of being adequate are so important that youngsters who don't feel good about themselves are very likely to try and put down members of another race in order to feel better. In some all-white middle-income areas where youngsters have been carefully taught not to openly put down blacks, they put down the most vulnerable white groups in their community.

The "new morality" confuses me. Sometimes I think our teens are in real trouble and at other times they are great. What do you think?

It is confusing. So much has changed so fast. Youngsters are unhappy with what adults have done with society—racism, immoral wars, irrational and arbitrary rules. They reject them but they don't have all the answers either. As a result this is a period of trial and error—from issues as minor as appropriate dress through trial marriage to relationship with authority.

The best approach for parents is to be open to new ideas and ways and not impose all the standards of our childhood on our children. *The test of a youthful idea, attitude or behavior is whether it is humane or not.* You may well want to stick with your standards and teens functioning well will respect them—if you respect theirs.

*Isn't it true that teen-agers take on the values
of their friends more than those of their parents?*

Only in some matters. Music and entertainment, fashion and clothes, and language styles are the areas in which peer group influence is the strongest. However, basic moral and social values that teen-agers hold are more likely to come from experiences at home. This has been absorbed all along, particularly in the late pre-teens, but what you say and do in early teens has great impact.

Teens are fairly "close-mouthed" about what's happening at school, on the team, in dancing class. But they raise a lot of questions to try and organize their thoughts about work, competition, race, class and so on. The pre-teens wanted to know why they lived in certain neighborhoods, why they couldn't vacation in Nigeria, why the houses are rundown in certain neighborhoods. The early teen may ask the same questions but is generally more philosophical—why is there war, why do some people have more money than others, etcetera.

Don't pooh-pooh the questions. They are serious and personal— "Who am I? What should I believe? stand for?" Your answers can help your youngster become fair or unfair in his assessment of people who are more or less fortunate, become satisfied or dissatisfied with his or her status. Your passing words of encouragement or comments on life can become powerful organizing forces, values, and attitudes: "Nothing beats a failure but a try," "A man's word is his bond," "The world loves a gracious winner," and on and on.

Thus, talks with your teens should be fun, but listen for the questions. Remember that your attitude and the expression of it can help him or her learn to "keep on keeping on" or give up, respect or abuse people, and so on. The basic attitudes, values and ways have been forming all along but they are being put together in a way now which is much the way that your youngster will carry them the rest of his or her life.

Coping with Your Teen-Ager

Are problems for teen-agers today greater than those
faced by young people a few decades ago?

Perhaps yes. The issues that confront today's teen-agers are profound—sexual emancipation, women's lib, rapidly expanding com-
munications, expanding technology, black rights, unpopular wars,
and confrontations with established authority. With a rapidly
changing society and family structure, the transition from youth to
adulthood is a more difficult stage.

Our children accuse us of not taking their ideas seriously.
But some of their opinions do seem silly.

That can be a problem. Some of the ideas teen-agers explore may
well appear foolish to adults. However, many adults have silly
ideas, too. Try to take your children's opinions seriously and try to
express your differences with the same tact you would use with an
adult with whom you differ. Remember they are exploring and will
reject many "far out" ideas themselves. Excessive teasing and
ridicule will sometimes cause them to hold on to an idea they
would otherwise reject.

My thirteen-year-old has become a real show-off, especially
around girls. How can I stop this behavior?

Many early adolescents go through a period of showing off. This is
a way of convincing themselves of their adequacy. It is also a first,
awkward attempt to be attractive to and to attract the attention of
girls. Anything more—holding hands or dating—is too threatening
at this stage for most youngsters. This period of showing off will
give way to more mature relationships in time. It does not naturally lead to a conceited adult. You can handle extremes with a
little good-natured bantering—"The manhood act again, huh?" or
whatever your quip—in a way so as not to put him down; and
don't use it too often. "Okay, that's enough," without great anger
or agitation, usually works with any excessive undesirable behavior—when your relationship is basically good.

*Our thirteen-year-old daughter seems to challenge
everything we say as if she wants to show us up.
How should I handle this?*

Banter can again be helpful with extremes—"Here comes the
Supreme Court again." A backdrop of good family feelings permits
you to do this. Stop if it bruises your child or brings more than a
smile and checking of extremes. Sometimes you can point out
directly that she doesn't have to challenge everything, that you are
glad she has her own opinion, that you respect it; but encourage
her to be objective and accurate in presenting challenging viewpoints. If you don't, you can contribute to the development of poor
thinking on her part. If she gets backed against a wall, caught
wrong and embarrassed, drop it. Who needs a victory at that
price?

*Our girl is fourteen and her feelings are easily hurt by
the slightest teasing. Is something wrong with her?*

As we indicated, teen-agers are trying on new identities and are
sometimes quite sensitive to critical remarks about their various
fads, fashions, and ways. Hostility and sarcasm should be avoided.
In addition, harsh teasing makes a teen-ager feel "like a baby."
Teasing, within limits, is normal and even healthy. Just don't go to
or permit extremes. For girls, an overemphasis has been placed on
their desirability, and often slight criticism or teasing about their
appearance may cause some girls to feel like failures as women.
You want to help your daughter learn to be attractive on the basis
of developing inner standards and not worry so much about pleas-
ing a boy. After you have been shown something and expressed
your approval, "How do *you* like it?" is a helpful comment.

*My boy is fourteen and used to be quiet and calm. Lately
he has begun to have temper outbursts at the slightest
provocation. Is this to be expected?*

Often teen-agers undergo many new frustrations because of sexual
and psychological changes and new social roles. It is not uncommon for teen-agers to go through periods of touchiness and
tantrums. Parents should try to understand this behavior but
should not permit abuse of other family members.

*My fourteen-year-old girl has recently become very
flirtatious with her father. Is that normal?*

It is not unusual for early adolescents to show a renewed interest
in the parent of the opposite sex during this period. Later the teen-
ager will transfer such feelings to a member of the opposite sex
outside the home. It is important that parents not respond to teen-
age interest with fear, rejection, or overseductiveness. Try to take
it in stride, but be sure *not* to encourage it.

*My fifteen-year-old son seems to develop crushes on older
women; last year it was my neighbor, and this year it is
another friend. Should this be considered a problem?*

Teen-age boys often develop crushes on older women. These
crushes are often short-lived and do not lead to anything, especially if the women don't encourage your son's attractions.

*My fifteen-year-old daughter objects to everything I say. At
times she says she hates me. How can a mother cope with this?*

Adolescents, in the process of asserting their independence, may
become quite angry at parents whom they view as too controlling.
Mothers and fathers should expect such outbursts from time to
time from their youngsters. Usually such hate feelings are short-
lived. Nonetheless, if conflict exists around particular issues between the two of you—try to work them out. Stop to listen and
talk with your daughter. Not everything is "just a teen-age stage."
Often we can make changes helpful to us and our teens, demonstrating a willingness to be fair without letting a teen do whatever
he or she wants to do.

*We have two teen-age girls who call us and older blacks
"Uncle Toms." How can we best handle this?*

Many young blacks lack a historical perspective. They view the
necessary adaptations of blacks during periods of great white
aggression as "selling out." The risk today in being outspoken
about racial matters is far less than it used to be. Your daughters'
reaction is like calling the plays for Sunday's game from an arm-
chair on Monday. The opinions of teens should be respected, but
they should be asked in return to respect the opinions and behavior

of older blacks who struggled in their own way to survive and bring about the improved conditions we now experience.

You might have them read about the dedicated work of black people of the past, doing the best they could as they understood it—in addition to the glib rhetoric of today. If they are clearly using "blacker than thou" to get by, point it out to them. If you are involved in civil rights efforts or contributing time or money to community improvement programs, your case will be stronger. But if you are sitting back enjoying your two cars, fine home, vacations, and furs without contributing anything to the betterment of the total black community—and rationalizing it with, "Them niggers ain't gonna do nothing no way"—your youngster has a good point.

Most important, don't take it too personally. We know militant leaders who have been called "Toms" by their teens. One father bantered very effectively with his taunting teen, "If you tell me that earning a good living is being a Tom, then call me Tom or Banana Boat, and I'll do a little shuffle too, because I'm going to keep doing just that!"—said in a friendly way.

Do black teen-agers generally have less respect for their parents than is shown by adolescents in other groups?

No. In fact, respect for authority and parents remains very strong among many black youngsters. Sometimes, however, depending on where they live and the social class of the family, black children may see their parents as helpless because of racist oppression in our society. Thus, a black child's sense of protection and security from his mother and father might be diminished. Nevertheless, parents who respect themselves are likely to gain the respect of their children.

Why don't teen-agers listen? I'm constantly saying, "I told you so!" But it doesn't sink in.

Adolescents often do it "their way" in a search for independence. It's not a good idea to say "I told you so!" to anyone. It usually makes a person resentful and more determined not to listen in the future. In fact your child may be making mistakes because he or she is doing the opposite of what you say rather than what makes sense to the child or you. You can sometimes raise questions which will help them see the logic—What would happen if you did . . . ?—rather than telling them what and how all the time.

Would it help me communicate better with my teen-agers if I used their "hip" language?

Usually teen-agers resent or are amused by parents' attempts to talk their talk. Their language style is part of their identity which is separate from adults and which they wish to preserve. It is better for the parent to be his or her self rather than awkwardly try to imitate adolescent colloquialisms. You have hip words and mannerisms from your own hip period which indicate that you are not an uptight square.

Is it right for a teen-ager to criticize his parents to their face?

Why not? Parents will never be perfect and should expect criticism from their children from time to time. Too many parents take criticism from their children as a sign of disrespect and become enraged. Such a reaction is uncalled for if the criticism is made *in good taste.* If they forget how to be respectfully critical—you taught them earlier, right?—remind them. Don't use their bad taste as an excuse to ignore the criticism. Don't accept the criticism just because it is "my baby being beautifully aggressive and assertive"! If it is just criticism, listen, learn, and grow. If it is unjust criticism, point out why and help "your baby" listen, learn, and grow. It is a valuable lesson in give-and-take which will be needed throughout life.

When is it right to beat a teen-ager?

Beating does little to aid your teen's development. When your teen is big, strong and impulsive, you can get hurt. However, parents are human beings and occasionally explode with hurt or rage. If this happens, you owe an apology to your teen-ager after you calm down. Teen-agers in particular react with extreme bitterness and indignation when they are physically whipped. Beatings make them feel immature and diminish their sense of autonomy and independence. Teen-agers often inwardly lose respect for parents who beat them, though outwardly they may appear compliant. It is best to try to reason with all persons rather than using brute force. See our discussion on spanking in Chapter 4.

What if my teen-ager hits me?

Make it strongly clear that such behavior is unacceptable and will not be tolerated. You should also physically defend yourself or obtain necessary help. If your child is repeatedly assaultive to you, you should seek counseling or professional help to try and eliminate the underlying problem and avoid future physical violence. But before a problem reaches this state you should have tried to develop a "new contract," which we described earlier in this chapter.

I am more experienced. Doesn't it make sense for me
to control my teen's thoughts and actions in order
to keep him from making mistakes?

Young people need the experience of making many decisions, having much success and making some mistakes. Paying the price for a mistake usually helps them learn to make a better decision next time. Certainly when the cost of a possible mistake is too high—in money, esteem, future opportunities—you will want to try and prevent it. The younger the teen, the more important your intervention. If you have permitted your youngsters to make many less important decisions on their own they are less likely to resent and resist you on the big ones.

The important thing to remember is that you are asking for trouble if you repeatedly try to control your teen-ager. Such parents often suffer permanent alienation from their children from mild to severe degrees. The more controlled and dependent your child, the more explosive the eventual break often is . . . and the more likely permanent alienation will be. Where the march toward self-assertion and independence has been gradual but continuous from infancy, your child will be able to use your help more easily, gain self confidence, and relate to you as an equal—or as a respectful superior—more quickly.

My friends tell me I shouldn't try to get my child to
do things by saying, "If you loved me, you'd do so-and-so."
Isn't it okay to make such an appeal?

No. Such comments sound like bribery to a child and may make your child feel unnecessarily guilty about not carrying out your every wish. You are controlling your child in the way that is most resented and most likely to cause explosive rebellion at some point. On the other hand, you don't want to let children neglect chores or do whatever they want to do. That would be permissiveness. Permissive parents neglect and hurt their children by not setting limits which give them a sense of direction and guidance.

Recently we have been trying to give our fifteen-year-old more freedom but he "goofs" every time. What can we do?

Youngsters who have not been encouraged to be independent, or do not have the knowledge, skill or confidence to handle freedom, sometimes play a funny little game called, "Free me, don't you dare." In this game they demand to be free and independent, "goof" in a way that forces you to step in and point to your stepping in as evidence that you don't want them to be free and independent.

What can you do? In a straightforward but friendly way, call the game; point out what is going on. Indicate your willingness to support freedom and independence when it is handled in a responsible way. Help them to develop the skills needed to handle a particular situation.

The question of curfew is a good specific example. It is best if you and your teen-agers work this out together. Ask them for their idea for a reasonable time or suggest your idea, giving reasonable choices, 10, 10:30 or 11 P.M., or whatever. Your suggestion should be based on what time they need to be in in order to function well the next day . . . and the time that is safe in your neighborhood. When your child's idea of a reasonable time is unreasonable, you should insist on your time. When you can come to an agreement and there are some infractions later, you can remind your youngster and hold him to his agreement. How do you pull away from "your boys" at a reasonable time?—"Later, man." How do you handle the teasing if any—"My old man is a mean dude." They know how. They may only need your matter-of-fact or bantering support to help them.

When a youngster breaks an agreement—like coming in at 2 A.M. when he agreed to 11 P.M.—you want to think about what he is saying to you rather than what he is doing to you. He may be angry and trying to hurt you, but he may be saying, "I'm on drugs, help me." Trying to get to and work out the problem is better than laying down the law—though you may have to do both.

How can you deal with, "But Roz is allowed to do it!"?

Your teen gains strength for his or her own independent position by listening to and watching you take an independent position. That position should be right and reasonable based on thoughtful consideration. You should be free to change if *good* reasons or changed conditions suggest you should. Your decision should be in keeping with your goals for yourself and your family. You must help your teens make decisions—to smoke or not to smoke, when to date, who to run with and so on—in this same way.

The formula (stated in a friendly way and in your own words): I am not Roz's father. Her parents may think or operate differently. This is what I want—for me, for you—and why.

Young people with a future goal and the confidence that they can reach it survive the perils of adolescence better than those without a goal. People with goals and confidence can make many decisions on the basis of whether the outcome will allow them to reach their goals or not. People without goals or fearful that they can't reach them frequently make decisions, often without being aware of it, which prevent them from being exposed to the danger of freedom, independence and failure. That's what many teen-age pregnancies, destructive marriages and even crime and delinquency are about.

The Question of Privileges

How much should we let our children talk on the telephone?

This depends on the other family members and their need for the phone, both to make and receive calls. As part of developing a sense of responsibility, teens should have some limits, preferably set by themselves. A family discussion should resolve most problems. If you can afford it and if you have a talkative teen-ager, it may ease family conflict if your child has a private phone. However, you should point out to him or her that it is important to share facilities and personal objects with other family members when appropriate.

*Is it all right for me to listen in on phone calls
occasionally to make sure my daughter is not up to
anything that will get her in trouble?*

It is never right to listen in on a teen-ager's calls without his or her permission. Adolescents usually become quite angry about such an invasion of privacy. They view it as a lack of trust and a lack of respect for their independence. Avoid reading children's mail or going through their belongings unless invited. A breakdown of trust resulting from such behavior may be disastrous to parent-teen-age relations.

Under extreme conditions (threatening letters, their own suicidal thoughts, and the like) children may leave mail out or diaries open hoping that you will read them and come to their aid. Even here, before reading you might point out that they appear to be asking for help and that you would like to do so. They will probably tell you their concerns. Press if they don't at this point.

At what age should teen-agers drive a car?

In most states teen-agers who are sixteen or over can drive a car and eighteen-year-olds can own one. We think this is a reasonable age. It is a good idea to have them maintain it out of their own earnings and take full responsibility for it, if possible. Generally it is better for your teen to take an approved driver education course than learn from you—powerful, competent parent who owns the car! This situation is "loaded."

*Even though the laws of some states permit sixteen-year-olds
to get a driver's license, what should a parent do if he
feels his child is not mature enough to drive?*

It is hard to tell whether a sixteen-year-old is mature enough to drive until he/she has the opportunity to show his or her sense of responsibility. Even youngsters who appear irresponsible will sometimes "straighten up and fly right" when responsible behavior is a requirement for driving. If your child is careless, negligent or takes unnecessary risks after using the family car for a trial period, car privileges should then be withdrawn until he or she demonstrates greater all-around maturity. Traffic fines and other violations should be paid by the teen-ager out of his or her own pocket if possible. More than one or two moving violations may be an indication of "not ready yet."

*My husband takes away car privileges from our boy
whenever he gets a poor grade in school. Is that a
good way to keep our son in line?*

Usually not. Car privileges and performance in school are separate matters. An awkward attempt to reward and punish your son in this way may backfire. It would be more helpful to investigate the real causes of his poor performance at school and provide help if needed.

*My husband has worked hard all of his life to buy a car
and simply refuses to let any of the children
drive it. Is this bad?*

Not necessarily. It sounds like a situation the family may just have to learn to live with. If the family's income is marginal, auto upkeep or accidents are a real consideration when deciding if children can use the family car.

Should teen-agers get an allowance?

Yes. But try to avoid their being completely dependent on you. When possible, they should try to earn their own spending money. If a teen-ager is away at school and unable to find a job, some money from the family should be forthcoming, if available. Whether there is an allowance or not, teen-agers should be expected to assume some responsibilities around the house.

How much allowance per week should teen-agers be given?

The amount should be based on the cost of routine and reasonable weekly activities such as movie costs, athletic events, snacks, and toiletries. It makes sense to pay for special events with extra money. Again, the value of an allowance is to help a youngster learn to manage money. Spend a little, save a little is as good a formula now as it was with your eight-year-old. Allowances should be adjusted upward depending upon the child's age.

*If a child works, should parents who can
afford it still give allowances?*

Sometimes. If a child works, you may want to reward his motivation by continuing his allowance. On the other hand, you may want to reward such an effort in other ways—a trip, special athletic equipment, a car or a contribution to his college or marriage savings. But, if the family needs money for other purposes, you may want to reduce or drop the allowance when your child works. If you explain your needs, your child will usually understand.

Should children who work be expected to give a part of their pay to the home?

Parents should not demand control of the child's earnings or even specify that a certain percentage of the earnings be turned over to the family. If you need the help, however, you should express the principle that the child has a responsibility to the family in the same manner as other workers in the family. Your teen-ager should be expected to purchase things for the home or supply the weekly allowance for a younger sibling. Parents should also encourage them to save some of their earnings. If you have not done so already, take your child to a bank and assist him/her in establishing a savings account. Even if you don't need the money but your teen-ager can't save, you might accept a share of his or her earnings and save it for the child. It is unwise, when you don't need the money, to use it for extras for yourself.

Should teen-agers have checking accounts?

Where banks and credit laws allow minors to have checking accounts, teens should be encouraged to learn to handle accounts early. Older teens with jobs should establish checking accounts because they help them plan their flow of money better. Checking accounts managed well also allow one to establish a good credit rating early in life. Poorly managed accounts can be trouble for you and your youngster. You want to help the teen form responsible habits—having a budget, knowing the balance, marking each withdrawal and deposit and avoiding spree check writing or credit card use. We have seen parents hurt each other by encouraging irresponsible checkbook and credit card handling by their teen. Be careful.

Should boys be given larger allowances than girls?

No, although there is the traditional notion that boys need more money than girls because they must pay for escorting girls. This belief is outdated. First, although girls may be taken out by their dates, girls require money for clothes, cosmetics, hair preparations and other beauty requirements. Secondly, more girls are "going dutch" and paying their share of the dates. We think it's a good idea that girls learn not to depend on boys, and learn to owe them nothing. In addition, many teen-age girls spend a good deal of their recreational time with female friends, and in these situations they must pay their own way. National estimates on teen-age expenditures indicate that girl/boy spending rates are about equal.

How much influence should parents have over what teen-agers buy with their allowances or personally owned money?

Little. Of course you have a right and responsibility to object to purchases of illegal items and goods. Hopefully, you have already helped your youngster learn to be reasonable and not a sucker for every gimmick going. You may want to raise questions which help your child learn to avoid being victimized. But for the most part the youngster's choices should be accepted. Again, part of the purpose of an allowance is to give your child an opportunity to learn how to use money. If he wastes it, he'll have to live with that. Parents should also avoid giving advances on allowance for this reason.

You should interfere as little as possible in the area of dress styles, a common point of contention between teens and parents. It is good, as a rule, to let your preferences and opinions be known but not insist that they be accepted. It is one way they express their individuality, although they are greatly influenced in styles by their friends. Unless the dress is extremely inappropriate or is injurious to health, it really can't hurt. Even when you must intervene, try to be helpful rather than critical.

What should we do if we don't have the money to give our children allowances?

Most families even on public assistance can afford to give the child some sort of token allowance. You should not feel bad about the amount. Your love and care are more important than the money you are able to give. You should never apologize for your income level. If you discuss your situation and what you are trying to do, most youngsters will understand and even want to help. In this case it is a good idea to strongly encourage both boys and girls to seek and find jobs. Employment is a constructive use of a teen-ager's time and provides needed income.

If there is a relative who has no children and earns a good

income, encourage him or her to "adopt" one of the children by supplying him or her with a weekly or monthly allowance. Don't be embarrassed to do this. Such relationships are in keeping with the extended family concept and should be encouraged among black families. This concept recognizes a number of adults as interested in and responsible for the child's development rather than one mother and one father. Your youngster should acknowledge his or her appreciation and be helpful in return where possible. The notion that "I deserve something for nothing . . . not even a thank you" should not be encouraged.

Personal Habits and Appearance

My fourteen-year-old is sloppy and never wants to bathe. Is this normal for teen-agers?

Often teen-agers are slow to accept responsibility for self-care. The reasons for this are often part of a wish to return to early childhood when mother and father watched over them. Don't nag your child about cleanliness, but do not permit him to offend other members of the family with filth and bad odors. Calm reminders and asking him to take care of himself without your help next time is the best approach. Usually pressure from friends and interest in the opposite sex will prod a teen-ager to cleaner habits. If the behavior is extreme, watch for signs of depression and seek help if other unusual symptoms develop.

Is it right for my adolescent daughter to walk around the house with bra and panties in front of her father or brothers?

If this has been an accepted practice in the family, it *may* be all right. However, if father or brothers are made uncomfortable, it should be discouraged. Generally, both teen-age boys and girls should be appropriately covered—so as to avoid unnecessary sexual teasing or enticement of others. This is even more reasonable if there are younger children. They can be overstimulated sexually in a way that can be harmful to their development.

My fifteen-year-old daughter is overweight. How can I help her reduce?

Obesity usually results from overeating, which *may* in turn be due to nervousness, depression, or just plain lack of discipline. Don't nag your daughter but find out how you might be of help if she wishes to lose weight. Try to keep meals and snack foods low-calorie. Health clinics and physicians can provide information about dieting. Teasing an overweight teen is cruel and can do more harm than good. Any reducing program should include a program of regular exercise which increases strength and muscle tone.

Is being obese sometimes a sign of fear of sex?

In some instances. Some teen-age girls and boys may wish to appear unattractive in order to avoid romantic-sexual approaches from the opposite sex. Occasionally, girls and boys who feel ugly may adopt a no-care attitude and overeat. Such youngsters need praise and support from their parents on their good points. Some children eat when tense or emotionally upset. This should be discouraged in a friendly but firm way.

My teen-age daughter is constantly teased by her friends because she wears glasses and braces on her teeth. How will this affect her?

She should let them know that she resents such teasing. After she has made her feeling clear, she should ignore them. Then it is no fun for the tormentors and the teasing usually stops. You should help her learn to see it as *their* problem and then it will do less damage to her good feeling about herself.

What should parents do about the hairstyles and personal grooming habits of teen-agers?

Usually nothing. You should encourage your children to be clean for reasons of good health. Unusual styles of dress popularized by youth are part of every generation. It is a way to say "I am unique and different from you but very much like my gang." You can buy grooming aides and make them available in the home but, as long as your youngster is neat and clean, you should not insist on their use or engage in constant nagging about his or her appearance. Today, nearly everything except bare feet is accepted in most places. Youngsters should be advised, however, of the risks of not abiding by dress requirements when they are looking for employment. The fact is that many people are denied jobs because of sloppy, untidy, or unusual appearance.

When should I allow my daughter to wear
lipstick and use eye makeup?

Wearing lipstick and eye makeup does not imply a girl is of loose morals as it did in the past. Getting into a battle over makeup is unnecessary. Try to help your daughter apply it tastefully and wear it at appropriate times. We think that in junior high school lipstick is okay and in senior high school eye makeup is all right.

Should I allow my daughter to straighten her hair?

Your daughter should be allowed to wear her hair in any way she chooses—*except* uncared for. Don't pressure her to wear an Afro if she doesn't want to. And don't push her to straighten her hair if she wants an Afro. Encourage your daughter to wear her hair in whatever way is most becoming and makes her feel comfortable. Even in Africa women arrange their hair in different ways. If your daughter is otherwise comfortable about being black, straightening her hair has little significance—it need not mean she's trying to be "white." If she isn't comfortable being black, making her wear an Afro won't help. You must discuss the reasons for her discomfort.

What if my son wants to get a "process"?

It's your son's choice. Among some young males, relaxing the hair with permanent straighteners is becoming the "in thing." However, most young men have adopted the Afro with their new black awareness. Both girls and boys are less likely to straighten their hair if they regularly receive approval and compliments from parents and others when it is *au naturel*. As we mentioned before, it is becoming increasingly clear that hairstyles are in fact hairstyles and not a true indication of one's blackness.

My young teen-age girls have long braids. They want to
cut their hair and wear Afros. I object. What should I do?

Long hair is one of the standards of beauty admired by blacks. Many black parents fear that cutting a girl's hair will keep it from growing. This is not true. On the contrary, hair well groomed, clean, and clipped grows well. There is no reason a girl's hair should not be cut if she desires a short style. The hair will grow back under normal circumstances. In the last analysis, adolescents should make their own decisions about hairstyles and grooming.

My daughter has recently bought some skin
bleaching cream. Should I say anything?

Perhaps she has some minor discolorations and blemishes which she hopes to clear up. However, if she is trying to lighten her skin because she is ashamed of being dark, she has a problem. Even when parents teach black pride in the home, youths often become unhappy about their skin color in school or through wider social contact. Talk to her about it. She should be assured that her skin color is perfectly fine. She should be helped to deal with her concern about being black . . . without scolding her for her lack of black pride. In any case, most commercial bleaching creams will not lighten the skin to any significant degree.

What if children in the neighborhood
have been calling her "black and ugly"?

It's a pity that some blacks still behave this way. Such remarks are vicious and cruel and are usually made by people who do not feel good about themselves. If your child develops self-respect at home at an early age, name-calling from children will be handled more easily. Racial slurs will have minimum effect. Your child might try talking directly to black children who make racist remarks, calling on them to respect her as she respects them, pointing out that they can't be black and proud and attack blacks for being black. You can sometimes help your child by contacting the parents of the name-calling children. But the parents of children who don't feel good about themselves often are not good parents and will not be interested. When nothing can be done, you want to help your child understand that it is *their* problem, not your child's.

My teen-agers won't go to the beach because
they're afraid of getting darker. What should I do?

They may have a problem about being black. On the other hand, they may just prefer a particular shade and be otherwise comfortable with their race. This is unfortunate because outdoor experiences are important for teen-agers. Avoiding the outdoors limits their total development and stifles their sense of harmony with nature, so important for the spirit. You should again discuss the matter of skin color with your youngsters and, if necessary, counter the forces which say it's bad to be black. You are not one of the forces, by any chance?

I have a very light-skinned daughter who feels ashamed she isn't darker. Sometimes she is teased by blacks in school about having too much "white blood." What do you advise?

Black people come in all shades. You should point out that "black is beautiful" means group and not only color. Brown, yellow, and white blacks are also beautiful. Blacks who attack other blacks on the basis of skin color are bad news. If she tells them just that, they may well stop. The fact that she is upset by the teasing can keep it going.

Profanity and the Teen-Ager

My teen-age girl uses a lot of dirty language around the house, like "fuck you" and "kiss my ass." What should I do about it?

If such language is being used by your daughter, it may be because you previously ignored it or did not make it clear which expletives should be deleted and which were acceptable. It is not too late to insist that she not use such language in your presence. Whether she feels it is all right to use profanity or not is irrelevant; she should respect your feelings. You can perhaps remind her of some habit that you have that annoys her and you therefore don't do out of respect for her feelings. However, if you yourself curse, it will be difficult for you to justify a demand that your daughter refrain from using profanity.

You should point out that excessive bad language is an immature way of handling an uncomfortable and disturbing situation. As previously mentioned, cursing directed at objects or perplexing situations is a form of emotional release that can be healthy. Again, you might remind your youngster that there is a time and place for everything; that unacceptable language in the wrong place is disrespectful and can bring them disrespect and a loss of opportunities. Swearing across a street or with strangers likely to disapprove are examples. (See Chapter 7 for more on profanity.)

What is the significance of black youth
using the word "motherfucker"?

In the past, the use of that term expressed great hostility and disrespect. It was a way of really putting a person down by suggesting that he was violating the universal incest taboo (mother-child sexual intercourse). Often the use of this term led to physical fights and sometimes killings because young blacks took this epithet as a profound assault on their honor and manhood, and on their mothers. Today the use of "motherfucker" has so changed that some young blacks use it as a term of endearment and respect. The terms "shit," "bitch," and "nigger" are all both epithets and expressions of endearment within sections of the black community. However, there are many black communities where very little of this language pattern is displayed.

What is the "dozens"?

The dozens is a game of words played by some young blacks in which they tease and provoke each other by using profane, often sexualized jingles. It's usually a put-down of "ya mamma" or other family members. An example: "I fucked ya mamma from roof to roof. She swore to God she was bullet-proof." Each person tries to one-up the other. It has been suggested that playing the dozens helps to toughen black youths for survival in a tough environment. We see it as an anger and tension discharge mechanism. The dozens sometimes leads to a physical fight as well.

Friendships and Social Relations

What should we do if our teen-ager starts
hanging out with people we don't approve of?

Teen-agers are particularly sensitive about picking their own friends. In learning about life, they will explore relationships with many different types of people. Parents should be concerned with the character and values of their teen-agers' friends, but should avoid rejection on the grounds of social class. It is important for blacks to feel a sense of brotherhood across class lines. You should take time and express interest in getting to know your child's friends.

It is best to allow your child's friends into your home. It will give you an opportunity to meet them and will avoid provoking your child into having to meet them in less favorable surroundings. You may want certain friends to visit only when adults are at home. Again, in cases where a friend may seem "undesirable," parents may sometimes exert positive influences on the friend and on their own child by expressing interest and understanding. If you have objections about friends, you should express them to your son or daughter. But here, as opposed to the pre-teens, it is important to actively discourage relationships with youngsters who persistently display undesirable behavior. Unlike pre-teens, troubled teen-agers can be trouble for you and your youngster. With a little help from a parent, a teen who is generally doing well will usually part company with one in trouble who abuses helpers and refuses help.

How should I help in this case?

You should intervene in a calm but determined way. Advise your boy or girl of the risks to his or her well-being and future. However, your child should not reject anyone merely because he was once in trouble with the law. Many black youths in the inner cities are unnecessarily arrested because of supervigilance by police officers and harassment from prejudiced white patrolmen. On the other hand, many teen-agers do commit criminal acts and you don't want your youngster involved. We realize that in some areas you must belong to a gang "or else." We can only urge you to do your best in this case.

Should we even allow our child to bring home a drug addict or a criminal?

Such situations must be evaluated individually. If an addict is being rehabilitated, friendships with "straight" people are important to him. But it is possible that some may abuse the family or steal. Your teen-ager should not expect his family to put up with any mistreatment from his friends.

The charge from your youngster may be, "You think we are better than him." You want to point out that black people who repeatedly exhibit criminal behavior in spite of efforts to help them are self-serving and anti-black. Your son or daughter should be encouraged to befriend persons who are trying to better themselves and the community. If someone steals from the family, it should be reported to the police. Such a "friend," after proven lack of trustworthiness, should be barred from your home—until he or she is successfully embarked on a rehabilitation program.

Some black boys at school criticized my son
because he has a few white friends. Is it wrong
these days for blacks to have white friends?

Our best hope for black survival in the long run is to support individual rights. You should support the right of your son to have friends of all races and religions. If your son wants only white friends and no black friends, however, he may have a problem. You will want to help him with his feelings about being black. Occasionally, some black youngsters may have racial self-hatred and reject friendships with other blacks. This is not likely to happen if they have been raised with a normal degree of racial pride and self-respect.

I have a sixteen-year-old who is very militant
against whites, but only dates white girls.
Isn't this hypocritical? What does it mean?

He "protesteth too much." Your son is probably deep down not really secure about his blackness and might be going to extremes of black militancy to cover negative feelings about blacks and personal feelings of racial self-hatred. His attraction to whiteness is evident in his compulsive pursuit of white girls and the exclusion of blacks. Such love-hatred reactions toward whites are not uncommon among blacks. You should try to help your son face his true feelings. He may well tell you that he is punishing Charlie (white male power structure). Something in the neighborhood of "bullshit" should lay that one to rest and make it possible to talk about real feelings. If he wants to date white girls, that's his business, but you don't want him to hide behind "stuff."

Teens and Leisure

How can parents influence teen-agers to be
more constructive with their time?

Adolescence is essentially a time of leisure in many respects. Many teen-agers are oriented greatly to things that are very close to their daily functioning. They are often very present-oriented. They are also very involved in an adolescent subculture, in which primary importance is given to interaction with their peers. They often become very preoccupied with concerns of their immediate friends, even more so than concerns of other family members. Much of the so-called idleness among teen-agers is a time of deep emotional experience for them, a time of heightened feeling and contemplation. Often these matters seem trivial to adults, but they are important issues for the young.

However if we give adolescents little responsibility and respect we encourage their idleness and self-isolation. Teen-agers require an environment where their serious participation in matters of the home and community makes a difference to that home and community. Such participation will deepen their sense of worth and personal value. Activities in which teen-agers can become involved are suggested later.

To what extent should teen-agers be allowed to plan their own time at home and away from home?

The more a young person thinks, plans, and takes responsibility for himself, the sooner he becomes self-reliant. In much the same way that adults plan their days, teen-agers should be allowed to do likewise. Yet it is important to coordinate plans in order to share rides, get errands done without a duplication of effort, and so on. This is good training in cooperation and coordination. You can help the young adolescent if you can raise questions and make suggestions which aid their planning without being critical or controlling.

Should teen-agers inform parents of their whereabouts at all times?

It is common courtesy for all family members to let someone at home know their whereabouts. Safety is the important factor here. If one plans to stay away longer than intended, he should telephone home to let other members of the family know that he is well. Often young people will become so wrapped up in their activities that they will fail to notify parents of their whereabouts. However, parents may complicate this problem by chastising the children when they call and probing too much into whom they are with and their whereabouts. Such nagging behavior often makes young people feel less adequate and less independent and discourages them from calling their parents; they would rather take the flack when they come home. If the child knows that your primary concern is his safety then it becomes easier for him to keep in touch.

It is reasonable to probe only when you feel that your youngster is in immediate danger. If you have concern about who he or she is with and what they are doing, it's better to take it up at another time . . . in a calm and constructive fashion.

*What are important points to consider
in teen-age recreation?*

Hopefully you have been exposing your youngsters to a wide range of activities and they have been finding plenty of their own. If a special talent or interest emerges, nurture it without developing unrealistic expectations. A fair piano player is not likely to be another Duke Ellington nor is a sandlot home run hitter likely to be a Hank Aaron. But fully developing the interest will be fun and will give your teen an area of mastery, a sense of competence. This is one of the reasons so many city youngsters spend so much time on the basketball courts.

Teens, like younger children, can fall into a rut—all music, all dances, all baseball, nothing. You want to help "nothing" get going again and try and help your teens expose themselves to a variety of recreational interests, although satisfaction and preoccupation with one should not cause great concern. For the most part, the older teen does his own thing.

Think safety without paralyzing your teen. Proper habits with the car, the batting helmet and so on should be called for in a calm way. You need not pry into every place they go but you should remind them that they must make sound judgments about whether the places they go and whether the people there and the ones they go with are safe. For safety's sake and not for control—particularly with young teens—you need to know roughly where to find them and when to expect them.

Is it valuable to send teen-agers away to summer camp?

It is especially helpful for young city people to get away to the country to enjoy activities that are not available in urban areas. Camp teaches new skills and gives children a chance to make friends from different backgrounds. It is an opportunity to learn how to relate without leaning on you and is good preparation for adjusting to college or the working world. Older teen-agers can find jobs as work-campers or counselors. Local churches, Girl Scouts, Boy Scouts and the YMCA, YWCA, and other social service agencies can give you information about summer camps. But don't send them away just to get rid of them. Don't feel that you have failed your child if you can't afford to do so or can't otherwise arrange it.

What should we do if we cannot find a summer camp
or if our children do not want to go?

Try to encourage your teen-agers to join local sports groups or clubs or find summer jobs so that they don't waste their summer hanging out on the corner . . . although corners, without drugs or dangerous gangs and guns, are not bad places if that's not the *only* thing your teen does. Libraries, museums, churches, and other service groups often have worthwhile free programs in which you should try to interest your teens.

Are teen-agers better off being left out of family outings?

Not at all. Teen-agers need to be part of the family. Trips to the beach, family vacations, and trips to relatives should include the teen-ager. The notion that adolescents are too "grown-up" to participate in family recreation is unfounded. However, refrain from forcing teen-agers to participate in family functions. Often encouraging them to bring friends along will increase their enthusiasm. They are more likely to want to go if they make some suggestions for outings.

Boy-Girl Relations

At what age should we allow our son
and daughter to go out on dates?

The age at which parents allow their children to date varies with standards in the community. Usually you can get a cue from what most of the other parents are allowing, although parents should not necessarily accept community standards for dating if they do not meet with their own personal attitudes. In some areas, parents permit their twelve-year-olds to date. In others, parents do not permit formal dating until sixteen or eighteen. The dating age should be based on the maturity of your teen-ager. When your child is capable of good judgment, and when he or she understands how to maintain respect in relationships, dating is reasonable. Many young teens prefer group dating in which they are not paired off. This protects them from going too far, too soon or simply getting "too close." This form of dating can take place early.

What if our daughter does not want to date interracially and the black boys are all dating white girls?

Most black boys are not dating white girls. Only a small percentage do. Thus, your daughter will probably meet someone she can date. It is important to boost your daughter's self-esteem without causing her to be intimidated by white girls or become excessively competitive with them. You may need to help her be attractive without compromising her rights or reputation. We have seen hostile, selfish, abusive people blame their dating problems on interracial dating.

Doesn't it have a damaging effect on black girls for black boys to pursue white girls?

It shouldn't. Blacks are slowly learning that black is beautiful and that they need not feel inferior. Parents should not condemn black men in general because some marry white women. All men and women have the right to date and marry whomever they choose. This right should be respected.

My thirteen-year-old daughter is not dating but has a crush on a white boy. She doesn't like the two black boys in school. How can I prepare her for the hurt possible here?

This is one of the very real problems of living in a predominantly white community. If this is the case and you want your child to be able to associate with blacks and whites, then long before adolescence you should arrange for natural contacts with other blacks. A good while before dating age it helps to discuss black and white attitudes toward interracial dating. You should let your own attitude be known but it is probably wise not to tell a youngster who he or she must or must not like or date. Adolescents often do the opposite of what parents say in this situation as a rebellious statement of their independence.

Most teens handle this situation by directing their interest toward people of their own race or religious groups. Some black parents in such situations have formed clubs for travel, study and general socialization so that widely scattered black youngsters can get together, experience themselves as blacks and form boy-girl relationships free of racial rebuff—although the usual aches of "I like him but he likes her and she likes somebody else" will and should be there.

If your youngster insists on interracial dating and the fellows criticize her white friend and he drops her, don't say "I told you so!" Again help her understand racial reality: that the problem is theirs and that she is a fine and worthy person; that she will find a steady. You will want to work a little bit harder to expose her to available blacks.

Suppose my teen-ager will date only light-skinned members of the opposite sex?

Teen-agers may harbor color prejudices which may be learned at home or outside. Black parents should be sure they do not instill such prejudices. For example, Kitty's parents rejected any dark-skinned boyfriend, regardless of his background or achievements. Her mother insisted that she date light-skinned boys because "You must think of your children. You're too brown and you don't need to marry any dark fellow." In Kitty's case, this caused her to dislike light-skinned men and see them all as arrogant, conceited, and selfish, even though she had discovered similar traits in her pre-ferred brown-skinned boyfriends. By reacting against her parents' prejudices, she lost her own ability to evaluate. There is some indication that the black consciousness movement has not elimi-nated this problem entirely, especially among the over-thirty generation.

I want my youngsters to date but I'm afraid that dating leads to sex too soon. How can I advise my youngsters?

In the past, before dates girls were told to "keep your dress down and your pants up" and boys were told, "Don't you bring nothing home." Not only was the advice often ignored, it created much discomfort and contributed to unhealthy attitudes about sex.

First, dating and boy-girl friendships are not all sex. They are mostly talking, laughing, thinking, going places together, and sharing experiences. Most early teens want no part of sex. We mentioned before that many prefer to date in groups to protect themselves from sex opportunities. Those who do get into sex early are often the ones who see no future, have no other way to feel "I'm okay; I'm somebody!" Even youngsters into heavy sex with many partners have sometimes changed the pattern when career or personal development opportunities came along.

You laid the groundwork for a helpful discussion of sex and dating when you told your eleven- or twelve-year-olds—when a question or incident gave you the opportunity—that when they are older, they might feel very strongly toward someone with whom they may want to have sex. At the same time, in all that you did with your youngsters, you helped them develop their self-respect. It helps to express confidence in your teens' ability to act in a way that will maintain that self-respect. It helps to remind them to allow themselves time to grow up and have the freedom to make choices that pregnancy and/or early marriage won't allow.

It is reasonable to express your attitude without imposing it. You want to explain the relationship of mutual respect and commitment that should be involved in a sexual affair. We think that it is not helpful to tell them that it is bad and they must or must not do it. Such warnings didn't work for many of us or, when they did, often made it hard for us to enjoy sex later on.

You should also explain that it's okay if they choose not to have sex until after marriage. Some will experiment—without a deep love attraction—out of curiosity or other need. This does not make them bad. The important thing is that they do so in a way that is not harmful to themselves. Teens given all the independence they could handle well from early childhood on—and your help to handle that which they did not handle well—are best able to handle the shifting and personal rules guiding today's behavior.

I have a teen-age boy who thinks of dark-skinned girls only as a "piece of pussy." How did he get such an attitude?

That's the wrong attitude for him to have toward any woman. Black boys who disrespect darker girls and see them as more sexual than girls with lighter skin are harboring racist attitudes. Perhaps your son is insecure and abuses girls to bolster a weak ego. Your boy sounds like a budding male chauvinist who should be helped to see girls as equals and not as objects for sexual exploitation. You also want to talk to him about his feelings about blacks.

How can we prevent our teen-ager from
confusing sexual attraction with love?

Because many Americans feel guilty about purely sexual attraction, they will call their sexual feelings "being in love." You can help your child by letting him or her know that sexual feelings are normal and acceptable, but that love develops over a period of time in a close relationship.

Should my teen-ager be allowed to take friends of the
opposite sex into his room alone?

Teen-agers occasionally desire to be alone out of the sight of adults or other siblings and these desires are not always sexually motivated. However, if you as a parent feel uncomfortable with this arrangement then you should not permit it, and you should explain your feelings to your teen-ager. He may not agree but if your relationship has been a good one he will probably respect your wishes.

I recently learned that my thirteen- and fourteen-year-olds
participated in a mixed skinny-dipping party at the beach.
How should a parent handle this kind of behavior?

Talk to your children about the nature of the party to ascertain whether it was merely swimming or if it also involved group sexual activity. Group sexual activity should be discouraged. It has risks and psychological dangers that even very mature adults are unable to handle. If nudity has too many sexual overtones for your family, you should certainly ask your children to avoid such activities with members of the opposite sex. Skinny-dipping, or nude swimming, is becoming acceptable in some communities in light of changing values toward nudity. In some communities, it is illegal and your children may be arrested and should be aware of the law.

I overheard a conversation among my fourteen-year-old son
and his friends regarding several boys having sexual relations
with one girl in the same incident. What should I do?

Your son should be counseled against such behavior. Participation in "gang bangs" is an undesirable act. It shows a lack of respect on the part of the boys—for themselves and the girl. This type of activity is not a healthy form of sexual expression. Often boys get pressured into these kinds of activities by peer influence. Such group sexual activity also runs the risk of rapidly spreading venereal disease. In addition, boys who participate in "gang bangs" often later experience a great deal of guilt which leads to feelings of low self-worth.

My sixteen-year-old son and his friends were overheard by another parent arranging a contest to see who could have intercourse with the largest number of girls during summer vacation. What should I say to my son?

Your son may be suffering from feelings of inadequacy or rebellion and it would help to talk to him about the meaning of his planned behavior. This type of sexual activity is unnecessary and a sign of complete lack of respect for females. Much of the unconventional sexual behavior or fantasies on the part of teen-agers, especially boys, often results from curiosity about sex and a lack of adequate sexual education available to them from parents and the schools. But don't be too alarmed. Boys fantasize about great female conquests but seldom carry out such acts. Often, it's male bravado to impress members of the group.

My seventeen-year-old son is shy and not very comfortable with girls. He can't dance or talk to girls on the phone, and when asked about girlfriends, he becomes very embarrassed. Should we be alarmed?

Fear of girls can often best be overcome for shy boys through participation in social activities, community work and other group projects in which girls participate. It would help, as in most instances, to talk to your son about any special concerns he may have in social situations with girls or women. Listen for fear of sex, and if it exists, help him understand that relationships with the opposite sex need not be sexual . . . but can be when both are ready. Don't become alarmed if your son shows a disinterest in girls during the high school and even early college years if there is no sign of a general social withdrawal. Boys become comfortable with girls at different stages.

*My nineteen-year-old daughter wants to live
with her boyfriend. What should I do?*

In the past, such living arrangements were frowned upon. Today, they are more socially acceptable. Living with someone is probably preferable to a too-early marriage. Sharing a home is much like a trial marriage and *may* help a person make a wiser choice of a permanent marriage partner. However, there is no proof that such couples make better marriages. It is helpful to discuss the pros and cons of her plans. Make your point of view known. But, ultimately, it is her decision. Condemn them? Are they humane people? In fact, some of us did in secret, with less commitment to each other, what they are doing in the open. Remember?

*Our daughter is coming home from college for a long
weekend with her boyfriend. The two of them share
an apartment in their college community. My husband
and I object to their sleeping in the same room in
our house. Is this objection unreasonable?*

We think your objection is perfectly reasonable. The key issue here is respect for parents' values in their own home. Young people can't always understand why parents value certain ways but the important fact remains that they *do* value certain ways. In the same manner that your daughter expects you to accept her college living arrangement (expecting you to continue sending allowances and tuition), she and her boyfriend should respect your wishes regarding sleeping arrangements in your home.

Does premarital sex lead to marriage problems?

Seldom. If a person should experience deep guilt because of premarital sex, then there is a potential for marital problems. In communities where female virginity before marriage is highly valued, premarital sex may lead to difficulties with a disapproving husband. Although sexual attitudes today are more liberal, many persons still have a double standard: premarital sex is bad for women but okay for men. Such attitudes have strong male chauvinistic origins. What is okay for the gander must be okay for the goose.

What is the best age for a young person to marry?

In recent decades, most people married in their late teens and early twenties. More recently, young people have been postponing marriage until later years. We believe that each person should develop fully before taking on the responsibilities of marriage and parenthood. A great number of early marriages end in social hardship and divorce. Mature adults are also likely to make better parents as well as have the necessary financial security to raise a family. Therefore, postponing marriage to the middle and late twenties would probably be of benefit to the black family and community.

Adolescents often have a problem with intimacy, with deep emotional closeness. This varies according to past upbringing. In general, the more secure and self-confident the teen-ager, the less fear there will be in being close to another individual. Young adults who have problems with identity and self-image may be unable to cope with the level of intimacy and give-and-take required in a marriage. Through their activities and associations with friends throughout adolescence, they slowly learn about the subtleties of close relationships—particularly male-female ones. This gives marriage a better chance. In addition, full educational development gives a teen a better shot on the job market and a better chance in marriage.

Sex Education

Have black families been too strict about sex in the past?

Frequently, yes. Because blacks have been accused of being sexually loose, many families have taken a strict puritanical approach in raising their children. Such an upbringing may cause excessive guilt and emotional conflict about normal sexual activity. Many people cannot fully enjoy sex for five or six years after marriage—if ever—because of such feelings.

How can we better help our teen-agers learn about sex?

As we have stressed from the start, sex education should begin early in life and should keep pace with a child's growing understanding. Adolescent boys and girls have many questions about sex because of their body changes—breasts, body hair, shape—

and strong sexual urges. Now those long-pent-up sexual urges have the possibility of going all the way to full expression—intercourse. Boys and girls are often anxious and full of questions—when, how, with whom? What will it be like? Will I be respected? Ashamed? Guilty? And so on. Your child may not feel comfortable discussing them with you. Books and other sources of information should be made available to them. You should be knowledgeable about sex. All of your talk about sex with your younger child was to pave the way for a smoother entrance into an adolescent and adult sex life. For a more detailed account of what you will want to discuss together see Chapter 7 and the information below.

How is sexual interest expressed in adolescence?

In early adolescence, you may still see some of the hitting, teasing, sexual jokes and jingles you see and hear among pre-teens. Much telephone gossip among thirteen- to fifteen-year-old girls is about boys and boys tease each other about interests in girls. Boys and girls masturbate, and there is some petting. Boys sometimes exhibit their pubic hairs and penises, usually in a small group and rarely more than a few times. In a few cases, there will be some physical contact—boy-boy and girl-girl. Sometimes there is boy-girl genital contact without intercourse.

Sexual intercourse takes place for many youngsters in late adolescence, although there are still young people who do not have intercourse until after twenty and after marriage. When it occurs in early adolescence, it may be too much for the youngster to comfortably handle. Sexual intercourse, for some, is a way to establish adulthood and end some of the confusion and anxiety of adolescence. Unfortunately, it usually doesn't do that because sexual intercourse involves other social relationship demands which young teens are not ready for, and guilt, confusion and anxiety result.

When they can't stand the intimate contact, they often ridicule, expose or put each other down in one way or another. One or both—but usually the girl—end up feeling used and guilty. We have also heard boys express guilt about using a girl although among many males, "making a girl" is still a badge of manhood. Some men never lose their adolescent need to prove their adequacy. Sex for them is not a warm, shared experience but a matter of domination and conquest.

*I know some black fathers who encourage their young sons at
ages as early as twelve and thirteen to go out and "get some"
to be a man. Is this good advice for young teen-agers?*

No. Young black boys should not be made to feel that masculinity
is derived from the number of times one has sexual intercourse
with different women. This can make sex a matter of domination
and conquest to the detriment of girls, women and men. It can
make satisfaction with married sex life or one partner more
difficult. There is much more to masculinity or femininity than
sexual performance. Again, it is not wise to push youngsters into
situations they may not be ready for. A youngster who is not ready
may be made to feel that he is an *inadequate* man. Fathers who do
this are using their sons to relive their own past while claiming
they are "schooling" them.

*What should I do if I walk in on my
fourteen-year-old son masturbating?*

If he is alone, it is best to excuse yourself and leave. You might
explain soon after that you understand that boys and girls masturbate and there is no reason for him to be embarrassed or guilty. If
he is with a friend or two, it is a different situation. This is a part
of the urge to show off or exhibit himself. There is still no cause for
alarm in that such sessions occur from time to time as teens experiment with their feelings, sexuality and ways to express them.

If it is a first occasion you might say, "Okay, boys, let's stop it
and get dressed. We know that you do that in private." Hopefully,
you have already discussed all the major aspects of sex, including
masturbation. A second time you would be more firm and at the
same time try and find out what gives—defiance, testing or an
inability to control the urge. Should group masturbation occur
again, you should seek professional help.

Threats are useless and cause unnecessary guilt and defiance. If
you didn't say anything, the likelihood of a repeated group
masturbation session is small. But it is better to comment because
then there is no confusion about where you stand and at the same
time it becomes clear that sexuality doesn't "scare your pants off."

What is a "wet dream"? Is it a bad sign?

A "wet dream" is an orgasm (sexual climax) with the discharge of
semen by a boy during sleep in response to sexual tension, often

caused by dreaming of a sexual encounter. It is a perfectly normal occurrence, especially in adolescence. A "wet dream" should not be confused with a pus-like discharge from the penis which may be due to a venereal infection. Girls have orgasms in their sleep, but there is no discharge of fluid. This is a normal pattern for many.

*Can you tell us more about the process
of discharging semen in the male?*

When a male discharges semen during sexual orgasm, it is called ejaculation. During climax, there are rhythmic contractions of the muscles of the penis which forces the sperm and other fluids from the male sex glands out of the opening of the penis. Sometimes the ejaculation is quite forceful, and young males will refer to it as "shooting" or "coming." Usually just before ejaculation a male can sense its onset and withdraw from the vagina during intercourse. This practice (coitus interruptus) has been used as one method of birth control but is greatly unreliable . . . an instant too long is possible at a time of pleasure.

Is oral-genital sex perverted?

It falls within the range of normal sexuality. Girls and boys should not be made to feel "dirty" if they ask questions about this activity. It becomes a sexual problem only when oral-genital sex is the only pattern of activity to the exclusion of sexual intercourse.

What are some of the old wives' tales about masturbation?

It is often said that acne (pimples) is caused by masturbation; that it can cause girls to walk crooked or become bow-legged; that it can cause hair to grow on the palm of your hand; that masturbation can make you go crazy or cause other mental problems; and so on. Any mental problem that might show up is likely to result from feelings of guilt about this normal human activity. No physical problems result from masturbation.

*Should we let our children bring sex magazines or
"girlie" magazines into the house? There's so much
pornography available on the newsstand these days.*

Teen-agers have ways of reading what they want. You should not buy girlie magazines for your youngsters. But we would not ban them. Interest in such magazines is a part of normal human curiosity about sex. It has not been shown that reading them is damaging to the normal sexual development of most teen-agers. However, such magazines are usually sexist and display derogatory and exploitative attitudes toward women—which may interfere with healthy boy-girl friendships. The cautions are that they not be flaunted in front of younger children or people who would be offended by them. If we make less of a fuss about sex, the attraction of the forbidden and the mystical quality will be removed. Sex will remain as an important, but not out of perspective, part of human relationships. Preoccupation (hour after hour) with girlie magazines may indicate a problem. In this case, you should seek help for your youngster.

Should teen-age boys not be kissed by their mother?
My son gets annoyed when I kiss him.

Many teen-age boys feel it's "sissyish" to be kissed by their mother. This is an unfortunate attitude probably related to a fear of developing sexual feelings toward their mother. It is okay to kiss your son, but don't be seductive or sexual in your display—and don't kiss him passionately. If he really objects to your kisses, don't force them on him.

Are black men sexual studs?

No. Some studies have reported an earlier age for sexual intercourse among some black teen-agers than among whites. For reasons not entirely clear, some young black boys and girls consider masturbation unnatural and, therefore, complete intercourse for sexual gratification. Some black teen-age boys have a particular need to show their manhood through sexual conquests. But overall the sexual patterns of blacks are healthy and not grossly unlike that of any other group. The stud image is a racist stereotype that is part of a myth that black people are "animalistic." Again, young black men should not be made to feel that they have to be super sexual performers. Such overcompensation is misdirected use of energy.

Is it true that black men have larger penises than white men?

No one knows for sure. However, the size of the penis has little to do with sexually satisfying a woman. Preoccupation among boys with the size of their penis is a waste of time.

*Does frequent and early sexual intercourse
develop a larger penis?*

No. The size of the penis is determined by biological factors and inheritance. Exercise of this organ will not make it larger.

Is there a high rate of homosexuality among blacks?

The exact rate of homosexuality among black men is unknown. It is probably similar to the white male rate. Kinsey estimates that approximately 4 percent of white males are exclusively homosexual. In this day of changing sexual patterns, nobody can be sure of the rate.

What about homosexuality among black females?

No one knows much about black female homosexuals. They do exist, but the numbers and causes for their behavior have not been well researched.

*Is it true that the absence of fathers from black homes
contributes to black boys becoming homosexual?*

Some social scientists believe that the absence of male role models may make it difficult for young boys to develop a masculine identity. However, most boys who grow up in fatherless homes do *not* become homosexual. At the same time, there are many homosexuals who grew up in homes with fathers. The reasons for homosexuality are complicated and depend on many different psychological and environmental factors.

*If a girl is a tomboy at age twelve and thirteen,
will she become a homosexual?*

Usually not. "Tomboy" is an inappropriate word to apply to girls who have an interest in sports and active adventure. Such labeling ("tomboy" or "sissy") restricts the potential of both girls and boys to have a broad choice of male and female role models. Vigorous girls can be as basically feminine as those who surround themselves with dolls and play house.

*If young boys or girls engage in homosexual acts,
does this mean that they will be homosexuals?*

No. Teen-agers satisfy many different curiosities with buddies and girlfriends and curiosity about homosexuality is no exception. Most do not engage in actual homosexual acts or do so in a disguised form and are not aware of it. Actual homosexual acts are infrequent and often exploratory. Usually the open interest in homosexual acts stops as a boy or girl commits himself or herself to an opposite-sex style. All of us maintain some level of same-sex interest. We should not be afraid of these feelings. They are more affectual (feeling) than sexual. Some of the anger and rage toward homosexuals is due to fear that their openness will weaken our control of our own feelings.

Teasing, rejecting or ridicule of a youngster displaying signs of homosexual interests can make matters worse. If a youngster is upset by his or her homosexual interests or behavior, parents should help the teen-ager arrange to consult with a psychiatrist, psychologist, or social worker. If there is no conflict, there is little that anyone can do about it. Our society seems to be adopting more liberal attitudes toward homosexuality. A majority of psychiatrists no longer consider it a "mental illness" but only a form of sexual dysfunction. We disapprove of social persecution and oppression of homosexuals. They have rights as well as any other citizen.

What is meant by the term bisexual?

This term is usually applied to a person who engages in sexual relations with persons of both sexes. It is still controversial whether such activity falls within the range of normal human sexuality. Some psychologists believe that so-called bisexuals deep down have a sexual preference that is basically homosexual.

Menstruation and Contraception

At what age does menstruation occur?

Menstruation usually occurs between the ages of nine and sixteen. If it has not begun by the time a girl is sixteen, a physician should be consulted. You should have your daughter see a doctor even before that time if in addition to no menstruation she does not develop any breasts or pubic or underarm hair.

It is important to explain to your daughter that each person is different; that some girls may start menstruation at a different time; that some may not be regular at first; and that some few women are never regular with their menstrual period. It should be pointed out that these differences do not mean one is a better woman than another. Differences simply mean that people are different . . . that's all!

Can playing around with boys bring menstruation on early?

No. The onset of menstruation varies from person to person. The variation has to do with each child's particular physical, hereditary, and environmental circumstances. A girl who menstruates early is not "fast" or "more woman."

What is the biological importance of menstruation?

Menstruation marks the biological beginning of womanhood. (It simply means that your daughter is capable of reproduction—of becoming pregnant.) The female begins bleeding from her uterus (womb) as a perfectly normal and healthy condition of growing up. Women counseling girls about menses must be careful not to impart negative attitudes or information that may cause them to fear and dislike everything associated with menstruation. For example, the problem of menstrual cramps and pain is not an unusual one. Some girls and women have very little pain while others have much more. Each woman is an individual with regard to her body.

When a girl starts her period, does that mean
she is also capable of having an orgasm?

The ability to have an orgasm has nothing to do with menstruation. Some girls may experience orgasm from masturbation before the onset of menstruation. Others may not experience their first orgasm until many years after the first menses.

Is a doctor's advice important at the time of the first period?

Hopefully your daugher is under regular medical care. At her next regular medical examination, be certain to report the onset of menstruation to the doctor. If she has not been seeing a doctor for a regular visit, she should start. It is important for him and her to develop a history of her physical condition. Females run a high risk of cancer of the breast and cervix. Your daughter should be taught from the beginning of menstruation to pay careful attention to her physical condition. The menstrual cycle and minor problems associated with it are often warnings of a serious health problem. As the teen-ager gets older, it is important that she develop the habit of visiting a doctor at least once a year for a quick and painless cancer-screening test of the cervix, commonly called the Pap test, and a breast examination.

What should parents tell their daughters about douching?

Frequently, young girls report that they see their mother's douche bag in the bathroom and don't know why it is used. Girls should be taught about douching, and told that it is unnecessary because the body has the ability to cleanse itself, particularly at their age. Older women generally douche to cleanse the vagina after sexual intercourse because it's faster than nature. If your daughter feels that she would like to douche anyway, she should be instructed to use plain, warm water, which is sufficient. Some doctors feel that using chemical preparations can eventually (particularly with frequent use) be harmful to the tissues of the vagina.

Is it okay for young teen-agers to use tampons or should they use sanitary napkins?

Tampons are perfectly acceptable for use by young teen-agers. In regard to another commonly raised question, most girls who are virgins are able to use tampons without difficulty.

Are girls weaker during menstruation and unable to participate in normal physical and athletic activity?

Menstruation is not a time of sickness. There is no reason for a girl to curtail any regular activities during menstruation. The major issue here is that teen-agers are often careless during this period and don't keep themselves as clean as possible or change sanitary devices often enough. If the hygienic precautions are taken, all regular activities are allowed. Of course, menstrual cramps, if they occur, *may* inhibit the physical activity of a woman. However, if a woman has any illness that might restrict her activity the advice of her physician should be followed.

Is bathing during the menstrual period harmful?

No. Bathing or showering is particularly necessary during menstruation. Tampons allow a woman to bathe without difficulty. If a sanitary pad is being used, it is simply removed before washing and bathing.

What about feminine hygiene sprays?

Feminine hygiene sprays are largely a perfumed powder. The spray is not medication and does not work as a substitute for soap and water. Doctors do not usually prescribe feminine hygiene sprays. They are a waste of money. Worse, they may cause irritation and rash because of sensitivity to the chemicals in them.

How exactly does the menstrual cycle relate to pregnancy?

Menstruation involves a cycle or process. The appearance of the blood is only one part of the total menstrual cycle. Some time between the eighth and twentieth day after the first day of bleeding is the time when a girl is most likely to become pregnant. This is the time when the ovum or "egg" becomes fertile within the girl's body and could become united with a sperm from the male if intercourse takes place. This uniting of egg and sperm produces conception and the development of a baby begins. Some people have sexual intercourse during the "safe" periods, the first to the eighth day after the start of the period or three or four days before the period. This is the so-called rhythm method of avoiding pregnancy but it is *highly risky*.

Can a girl become pregnant without sexual intercourse?

No. A girl may feel guilty and fear that she has become pregnant if she has petted with a boy or experienced an orgasm, or if the boy has fondled her in sensitive spots, or if she has touched male genitals. But pregnancy occurs only when the male sperm unites with a fertile egg and this happens usually when the male ejaculates ("comes") with his penis directly inside the female's vagina. It is possible, however, for a boy to ejaculate just outside the vagina and for sperm to enter the vagina and result in pregnancy.

When the opportunity arises or youngsters ask questions about artificial insemination, you can explain that in some few cases, with the consent of a husband and wife, a male donor can ejaculate into a tube and the sperm can later be inserted by a physician into the female's uterus or near the cervix or uterus opening.

*Can a girl only get pregnant if she has an
orgasm during intercourse?*

Orgasm is unrelated to becoming pregnant. If intercourse takes
place, a girl can become pregnant whether she had an orgasm or
not.

*Doesn't telling adolescent girls about contraception
give license to engage in sexual intercourse?*

No. Telling your daughter about contraceptive measures does not
mean that you are encouraging her to freely engage in sexual
intercourse. For many generations, parents have made the mistake
of thinking that sexual relations among adolescents could be
delayed by not telling them about sex. This is a dangerous myth.
There is no scientific basis for the belief that information about
matters relating to sexuality increases sexual activity. Remember
that sexual activity at this age is generally engaged in because of
strong pressures—sexual urges, curiosity, peer pressure, search for
companionship, a sense of adequacy—and it is unlikely that strong
threats of punishment will prevent it. On the contrary, they may
cause youngsters to "do it" to prove their independence or to fix
you. Even with the strongest indoctrination against sexual activity,
many girls and boys still engage in sex and some girls get pregnant. Again, it is best to try to give advice which will help your
child make wise decisions about sex and health matters but not to
forbid the act. (See our earlier discussion under the section "Boy-
Girl Relations" in this chapter.) Information about sex, contraception, venereal disease, and so on can cut down the existence of
myths and fears about pregnancy and disease.

*Can a girl become pregnant the first time
she has sexual intercourse?*

Yes, if she is fertile at the time. Unfortunately, many girls do
become pregnant the first time intercourse occurs. That is why it is
important that young women are informed about sex and contraception *before* initiation into sexual activity. Some women still
believe that only regular intercourse can make them pregnant. A
few girls believe that they can only get pregnant when they enjoy
the act. In fact, women can become pregnant after a horrible and
painful experience with a rapist.

What should I do if my daughter is raped?

Take her to a doctor immediately and report it to the police. Unfortunately, many police departments do not pursue the rapists of black women because of racist indifference. Black women should demand more protection in their communities. Your daughter will need a great deal of sympathetic emotional support during this time. She may develop fears of being alone or traveling alone or become generally distrustful of men. The important thing is to help her understand that the act does not make her a bad, tainted, worthless or doomed person. Your continued respect for her is more important than what you say.

Is there any way a girl can avoid being raped?

In general, girls should not pick up strange men and should avoid walking in dark, secluded places alone. However, once a rapist attacks, a girl's first concern should be to protect her life. If the rapist is armed and violent, it is probably best for her to give in and avoid physical injury. Afterward, she should immediately report the incident to the police. Women police officers who now handle rape cases have removed some of the embarrassment rape victims feel when filing a complaint in police headquarters.

*Is it all right for a girl to be sexually aggressive
with a boy if she is feeling excited?*

It's not a question of right or wrong. Young women today are much more aggressive in sex than a few decades ago. Females have as much right as males to express their sexual desires. Men and women must be aware of the attitudes and values of their mates in deciding how aggressive or passive they should be. As quiet as it is kept, men, likewise, have different degrees of passivity and aggression in sexual activity.

*If there is strong evidence that my daughter is engaging
in sexual intercourse or is on the verge of such activity,
should I encourage her to use the pill?*

Not necessarily. The overall effects of the pill on the female's system during her lifetime are not known. Oral contraceptives are readily available and simple to take, but they may not be the best method for the young, developing female. In addition, it is not likely that your daughter is engaging in sexual intercourse so frequently that a measure as dramatic as the pill is necessary. The diaphragm is effective and can be inserted before intercourse and taken out hours later. Many adults underestimate and place little confidence in the ability of young girls to properly use the diaphragm. It should not be overlooked as a method, since its effects on body functions are not as severe as those of the pill, IUD's (intrauterine devices), and related measures. Girls should also encourage their boyfriends to use condoms ("rubbers"). They are cheap and can easily be put in place when intercourse takes place at an inopportune time.

Suppose our religion forbids the use of contraceptives?

Many religions have concepts that pose dilemmas for those who have to adjust in a modern society. Each person must weigh religious beliefs against the possibility of pregnancy when deciding about contraception. It appears these days that most religious groups, unofficially at least, accept the practice of birth control.

Do women need to have children to feel fulfilled?

As more and more women find new opportunities for careers, they feel fulfilled without being mothers. Women should not feel forced to be mothers. For personal reasons, many may not wish to have children. No man or woman should have children out of a sense of obligation to relatives or society.

*What is the best number of children for a
married couple to have?*

That is hard to say. All things considered, the optimum number of children would be two or three for most couples. There is no particular virtue in having a great number of children who cannot be adequately cared for. The most important question parents should ask is how many children they can care for well with their energy level, social and psychological resources, and even financial resources—if you don't want outside help.

*If we think our daughter is pregnant but
she says she is not, what should we do?*

You must take your daughter's word. If she exhibits uncommon symptoms of minor illness, seems to be gaining a lot of weight and sleeps more than usual, parents should express concern about her health and suggest that an appointment with a doctor be made. If you make it clear that you want to help rather than criticize or ostracize her, she is less likely to resist.

*What should we do if our daughter does
get pregnant out of wedlock?*

An important consideration of families when a teen-age girl, still in high school and unmarried, gets pregnant should be an abortion. However, it is also important to keep in mind that there will be and should be many exceptions to this rule. If both the girl and the boy want to get married and are reasonably mature, and resources are available for this potential family to provide an environment for the healthy development of a child, then the pregnancy should be accepted and prenatal care immediately undertaken.

Occasionally, the girl's family may have the resources and desire to rear the daughter's child in an extended family situation. In coming to any arrangement, the welfare of the unborn child should be the most important consideration.

What if the teen-ager does not want an abortion?

If the girl does not want an abortion even though it appears to be the best solution, the parents should first make sure that her resistance is not caused by fear for her health or an effort to hurt her parents. A less emotionally involved professional person can help the family better examine these questions. Parents and/or others involved should talk with the teen-ager about the demands and responsibilities of rearing a child and indicate whether they will be able to give her financial as well as psychological support. If possible, the father of the unborn child should be brought in to clarify his intentions about providing for the mother and the child. Often when the boy's position is clear, it is easier for the girl to make decisions.

Traditionally, many girls have looked upon pregnancy as a means of identifying with the adult world. Some have used pregnancy as a way to get and keep the boy or man they love. These are not good reasons to have a baby.

What if abortion is forbidden by our religious teachings?

Many religious faiths are beginning to accept abortion and do not consider it murder or a sin. Each woman must weigh her beliefs and then make the best decision for her future well-being. We feel that neglect of an unwanted child once born is much more of a sin than abortion.

Which pills, laxatives, tonics, or concoctions work best to abort a baby in the first months of pregnancy?

None. For a healthy female pregnant under normal circumstances there are presently no generally prescribed oral means for abortion. Scientists are developing an abortion pill which can be used "the morning after" but it is still experimental. In many instances, girls, thinking they are pregnant, take laxatives or pills to bring on their period. If bleeding results from taking such pills, they were not pregnant. Parents can help their daughters avoid unnecessary sickness from such concoctions by explaining that they will not abort a fetus. Sometimes a miscarriage occurs. But miscarriages result from various weaknesses in the mother's system or the fetus and not from the pills. If one does take place the girl should be immediately attended by a doctor.

Will douching immediately following intercourse prevent pregnancy?

No. Douching is not a contraceptive method.

If we cannot afford to travel to a state where abortion is legal, should local illegal means be used?

No. Back-alley abortions may cause permanent sterility and even death. Social agencies in nearly every major city in this country will make arrangements for consenting pregnant teen-agers and their parents to go to states where abortion is legal and performed under sanitary medical arrangements in accredited hospitals. These agencies also give helpful educational information to pregnant women.

Will an abortion prevent a woman from having another child?

No. In the past, when abortions were done illegally under crude circumstances, complications resulted which sometimes permanently injured the reproductive organs. Usually an abortion performed by a doctor is safe and women can become pregnant again.

*Will an abortion cause you to have a
deformed child the next time?*

No. The probability of having a normal child after an uncomplicated abortion is as good as it was before.

What about guilt feelings following an abortion?

Any woman, regardless of age, should have proper counseling before undergoing an abortion if she has serious emotional discomfort about abortion. Parents and close friends can be especially supportive during these times. Doctors and nursing personnel can be helpful during the operation and hospital stay if they are sensitive, respectful and supportive. Now that abortion is legal, it is likely that women will carry less guilt about it as time goes on.

*There is a growing amount of literature on the
newsstands about the increase in the number of
vasectomies. What is a vasectomy?*

A vasectomy is a minor operation, taking only a few minutes, in which the vas deferens, the tube that carries sperm to the penis, is tied, thus causing the male to become sterile.

*Does a vasectomy cause impotency (inability
to have an erection)?*

No. The nature of the operation is not one that physiologically affects a man's capability to achieve an erection. Impotency after vasectomy, if and when it does occur, usually stems from psychological problems.

*Does impotency occur more or less among
black males than white males?*

There is no accurate or reliable data to suggest that there is any difference between white and black males in the number of cases of impotency.

Can vasectomies be reversed?

Not reliably at this time. It was once believed that vasectomies meant permanent sterility. Recent studies indicate that a small percentage of males who have successfully reversed the operation have been known to regain their fertility. There remains a serious lack of information on the effects of vasectomies.

*Should black male youths be encouraged to
consider vasectomy as a means of contraception?*

For many black males, manhood has been associated with fertility
because of racial oppression and denial of other rights, both social
and economic, enjoyed by white males in society. As long as there
is oppression of black males, these attitudes are likely to prevail
and it is most likely that many black males will object to vasectomies as a means of contraception. Young black men with no
children should not be encouraged to have such an operation even
if they feel strongly against having children or are asked to submit
to a vasectomy by their mate. Feelings about having children may
change; the chances of successfully reversing the operation remain too small at present.

*Why should a male consider such an operation with
all the contraceptives on the market for women
and the new legalization of abortion?*

Abortion as well as many of the contraceptives on the market,
including the pill, often cause hardships on women, both physical
and emotional. Vasectomy is a fairly minor procedure with little
hardship for males.

Venereal Disease

What about VD?

VD (venereal disease) is nearly always contracted through direct
sexual contact. Most doctors believe it cannot be gotten from bath-
tubs or toilet seats. The most common venereal infections are
gonorrhea and syphilis. Gonorrhea is generally easier to detect in
males than females. Usually three to five days after sexual contact
with an infected person, a pus-like discharge from the penis
appears and burning irritation occurs with urination (passing
water). Girls may develop a green or yellow-green discharge or
have lower abdominal pain. However, about 80 percent of infected
women show no symptoms. Gonorrhea infection can also occur in
the rectum or anus in men and women who have anal intercourse
with an infected partner. Gonorrhea should be treated immediately by a doctor because serious complications can develop, such
as sterility, fever, heart trouble and even death. Treatment is with

antibiotics and is painless. Today some physicians recommend that sexually active women should have a test for gonorrhea at least once a year, whether or not they have symptoms. The procedure for the test is simple and painless.

Syphilis is less common but more dangerous than gonorrhea. The first sign is usually a sore on the genitals, or on the lips or in the oral cavity (mouth, tongue) if oral-genital sex was involved, or in the anus through anal intercourse, about three to four weeks after contact, or as early as ten days or as long as three months after contact. It may later disappear with or without treatment and a skin rash will appear in the later or second stage. If syphilis is suspected, a physician should be seen. Often a simple blood test can reveal the infection. Treatment is with antibiotics. If syphilis goes untreated, extremely serious complications of the heart, brain, nervous system and other parts of the body can develop.

A man's use of a condom (rubber) is some protection against spreading VD but is not absolutely safe. Any person found to have VD should promptly seek treatment and inform his or her sexual partners so that they may seek medical attention immediately.

If a woman with VD gets pregnant, what effect does this have on the child?

If the woman goes untreated, her child can be born with syphilis and suffer serious medical consequences. Pregnant women who receive prenatal care are routinely tested for syphilis infection. If syphilis is discovered and treated early, the baby is not harmed.

Are there other venereal diseases besides gonorrhea and syphilis?

Yes, but they are rare. Information on these diseases can be found in most sex manuals. If a person has unusual itching, swelling, ulcers or sores or warts around or on the sex organs, he or she should consult a physician. One popular sex manual indicates that blacks have greater and inherited susceptibility to these diseases. There is no scientific evidence to support this claim.

What are "crabs"?

"Crabs" are tiny lice that invade the pubic hair. They can be caught from dirty linen and toilet seats as well as through sexual intercourse. They usually crawl about and cause itching. A doctor can prescribe medicine to be applied to the infected area that removes them in a day or so.

Is strong itching or an unusual
discharge a sign of VD in women?

Not necessarily and often not. Females sometimes have other infections in and around their vagina. They are caused by changes in body chemistry and minor illnesses of one type or another. Various forms of vaginitis (minor infections in the vagina) sometimes occur and recur. It is important for the female's mental assurance and physical good health that she consult a doctor whenever unusual discharge with an unpleasant odor, itching, or irritation occurs. The causes can usually be diagnosed, and medicine prescribed by the physician can quickly clear up minor infections. Advise your daughter not to delay getting medical attention when any discomfort in the vaginal area occurs.

Girls often avoid bringing such problems to the attention of their parents because they fear that the parents will think they have been engaging in intercourse. The parents' overriding concern for female adolescents during these trying years of sexual development should be the good physical and mental health of their child. Morality is an important issue, which most certainly must be considered. (See our earlier discussions under "Values, Morals, and Attitudes" and "Boy-Girl Relations" in this chapter.) Hopefully you have developed a way of responding which will permit your youngsters to come to you with any problem or issue.

Prostitution

Is a woman a prostitute if she has sexual relations
with several different men?

No. The key factor in prostitution is engaging in sexual intercourse for a fee or monetary payment, often with strangers on a one-time basis. Many girls and women who are not prostitutes have sexual intercourse frequently and with different partners.

Why do some teen-age girls, especially in
large urban areas, turn to prostitution?

There are numerous reasons young girls turn to prostitution, but the greatest reason for many is economic. Young girls learn from older sisters, mothers or friends that money can be earned through prostitution. If one comes from a poor home and has no skills for employment and jobs are unavailable, prostitution becomes a means to secure money to buy clothes and other things teen-agers desire. There are, however, some girls who become prostitutes because they are dependent or have a poor self-image or are rebelling against parents whom they wish to punish. We know girls from middle-class homes who work as prostitutes.

Prostitution can usually be prevented if parents provide sound sex education as well as an atmosphere of acceptance in the home that does not lead to rebellious, antisocial behavior in their children. Good preparation in dealing with "slicksters" and exploiters also helps. Trusting, idealistic girls who deny the realities of the world are sometimes led or pulled into prostitution. Sometimes, with the best parental guidance, a rare young woman may drift into prostitution because of deep emotional conflicts.

At what age are girls likely to turn to prostitution?

This varies with the emotional and physical development of the girl and the supply and demand for girls in a given low-income community. In recent years, with the increased economic and social deterioration of many inner-city communities, girls at younger and younger ages are turning to prostitution. Some girls can be seen on ghetto street corners at night who are clearly in their early teens.

Do female gangs encourage girls to practice prostitution?

Yes. In some instances, teen-age girls do get trapped into prostitution through association with girls who engage in this behavior. Often prostitutes are forced to recruit new girls by their pimps. However, in some cases, a young girl may have experienced sexual assault, feel guilty, and choose to engage in prostitution. She then may seek out others with similar aspirations. In numerous cases, it is not the influence of other girls, but attraction to a boy who aspires to be a pimp that gets the girl involved in this activity.

What about psychological functioning of prostitutes?

There are few good studies about the emotional and psychological development and functioning of girls who engage in prostitution. We do know that many move out of this kind of life, get jobs, marry, and have families. Others stay in prostitution into late adulthood, only stopping when they are no longer marketable. Women who don't want to be in prostitution but can't handle self-harmful psychological forces can often be helped by psychological treatment.

Is prostitution confined to the black ghetto and lower classes?

No. Prostitution is as old as civilization and occurs at all social and economic levels in white as well as black communities. Whether prostitution is recognized as a social problem is determined by the values of a given society. Prostitution is legal in some countries. In one respect, it is quasi-legal in this society: the male consumers are rarely prosecuted; it is the female who is arrested. Usually white prostitutes are found in the high paying call girl establishments in our large cities.

Contrary to popular belief, prostitution is not widespread within a ghetto area. Prostitutes usually operate in or near bars, and in commercial districts of cities where males from outside the black community congregate. Males (often white) come into the black community and "hunt" for young black girls on known prostitute streets or blocks. Traditionally, a smaller percentage of black men patronize prostitutes than whites.

Why do girls cooperate with pimps?

The two greatest reasons for the pimp-prostitute relationship are romantic attraction and protection and security. In many cases, the girls become very emotionally attached to the pimps. The pimp is then able to control the girl's behavior. In addition, as a male, the pimp often protects the prostitute from assaults by emotionally unbalanced consumers and from other hustlers on the street.

What is the relationship between pimps and prostitutes?

The pimp is usually the male upon whom girls depend for direction and protection in prostitution activities. Life in the streets is a competitive marketplace similar to business and industry. Prostitution is a business enterprise in the ghetto and the pimp is usually the manager. He determines when, where, and how the girls work. Usually all monies are turned over to him and he allots a given amount to the woman; he often manages all housing, health, purchasing, and other aspects of the girl's life. He also helps to keep her out of jail and provides for legal counsel if she's arrested.

Obviously the pimp–prostitute arrangement is a master–slave relationship—economic exploitation, physical abuse and psychological damage for the prostitute; material and social gain for the pimp. Pimps are *most* undesirable models for black youths.

Are certain types of males more likely
to become pimps than others?

Some young black men see pimping as a way of making big money and gaining status. Charm and charisma, ability to manipulate people, and attraction to a risky and promiscuous life are the characteristics of most pimps. Little is known about what makes one young man rather than others in the same neighborhood turn out to be a pimp, although many are known to have a deep dislike for women. We suspect that many of these young men would have done well in a legitimate business or government had they the models and opportunities to move in these directions.

What can parents or other adults do to help girls who
may be engaged in prostitution?

Parents who discover that a daughter is practicing prostitution are usually hurt, angry, and embarrassed. There is a tendency to despise or reject such girls. But many prostitutes get involved even when they don't want to do so and will need a parent's help to get out. At the same time they may well rebuff a parent who tries to help. They have often painted themselves into a corner by ignoring the advice of parents and are too embarrassed or guilty to openly admit a desire for help. In this case, it is best to offer assistance and maintain contact until a girl is able to take advantage of it.

There are a number of youth programs in large cities that aim at getting these girls, especially the younger teens, off the streets and into educational and recreational programs to redirect their interest and to train them for a variety of jobs. Too few of these educational and recreational programs for adolescents currently exist and there is need for more centers for youth where they can secure counseling, develop confidence, get education, and enjoy health recreation. Community-based residential centers are also needed.

Religion

*My children have been attending Sunday school and
church since they were very young. Recently, my
teen-agers have been resisting attending church.
Should they be forced to attend regularly?*

If they have been exposed to church as youngsters and are now
rejecting it, they should be allowed that right. On the other hand,
many teen-agers may continue to find church-going important, and
if so, this should be supported. The important issue is that
morality and teaching what is right must also take place outside
the church, in the home and in the community. As we mentioned
earlier, physical attendance at church doesn't necessarily make for
a good Christian.

*My teen-agers say that church is racist, dull, and irrelevant
to modern life. Can the church still offer opportunities
for healthy social activities for youth?*

Yes. In many communities, ministers are making the church relevant to today's issues among blacks. The church remains an
important institution for social action and social interaction—with
black awareness programs, clubs, dances, art, music, athletic programs and so on. It is still a place where many black youngsters
develop organizational and leadership skills. It is still an important
base or place of belonging which reduces the sense of alienation
and rejection for many black youths in the larger society. Rather
than attack this important black institution, help it, and challenge
your teen to help it become the more relevant force it needs to be.
It must also be kept in mind that the church has played a major
role in the civil rights movement under the leadership of Dr.
Martin Luther King, Reverend Jesse Jackson, and other fighters
for justice and equality.

*Our youngsters claim that belonging to a particular
religion tends to create animosity among people and
cite the Irish Catholic-Protestant and the Arab-Israeli
conflicts. How can a parent argue back?*

It is best to acknowledge the divisive nature of "our faith" carried
too far or "used" to justify exploitation and abuse of others who

believe or worship differently. Hopefully, you reject this misuse of religion. You can point out that humane people should recognize the brotherhood of all men and accept different religious forms without using difference for selfish political or economic ends.

Are young people today less religious?

It is difficult to ascertain whether youth today is less religious. The desire for spiritual enlightenment and devotion can take many forms. Many changes are taking place within organized religion; young people are joining new forms of religious activity ranging from types of silent meditation to other dramatic expressions of spiritual devotion. Some are involved in community service activities in order to find spiritual meaning.

My fourteen-year-old says she is an atheist even though we have a religious home. What could be wrong with her?

Nothing is wrong with her. Many young people question religious beliefs they earlier took for granted. Such questioning should be accepted. You should respect her atheistic views as she should respect your religious viewpoint. Adolescence is the period that teen-agers explore many new ideas. Many of their deep attachments to a particular ideology may come and go quickly. She is more likely to reconsider her views if her opinion is respected than if you try to force her to accept your views. Even if she doesn't there are modern "Godless" churches where fellowship and service to mankind is the same as the Christian mission.

With quieting civil rights activity there is evidence of an increase in church enrollment among young blacks in the traditional Christian religions. Is this a sign of regression back to accepting oppression?

Probably not. In fact it may be a sign of a stronger black community spirit. If the "new" black church addresses day-to-day economic, political, and social issues, it will become an important and greater force for justice and improved opportunities for blacks. The "new" minister can become an important model for black youth.

Mental Health

Are adolescents more likely to have an emotional breakdown than older people?

As mentioned before, adolescence is generally a period of great emotional turmoil and is fired by deep personal drives. The teen-ager experiences the onset of sexual interests and searches for independence. Some teen-agers may break down under such stress. However, most teens manage to channel these sexual urges and drives into constructive activities and learning behavior. Most youth are able to move through adolescence without serious emotional disturbance.

What is schizophrenia?

Schizophrenia often first appears during this age period. It is a mental disorder in which thinking is deranged. A schizophrenic person has strange ideas and may hear voices and see things that are not present in reality. He may imagine he is a famous person or that he has special magical abilities. Paranoid schizophrenics sometimes think people are plotting against them or trying to hurt them. Often schizophrenics are very withdrawn and have trouble making friends. (However, a teen-ager may be withdrawn and noncommunicative without being schizophrenic.) Some may get unruly. Occasionally, teen-agers may have extreme temporary upsets in which they act strange but are not schizophrenic. Unresolved questions about race, sex, and adequacy are often causes of upset. Hidden and open family conflict can also cause such upset. An upset youngster's behavior is often a cry for help for the entire family.

What should be done for a teen-ager who exhibits schizophrenia-like symptoms?

He or she should be helped to see a doctor privately or in a hospital clinic. Sometimes hospitalization is necessary. There are medications to help schizophrenics recover. With the additional help of psychotherapy, many lead useful and productive lives. Often it is important for the entire family to be involved in the treatment. Some people never become ill again. It is important not to reject or make fun of a child with mental problems.

Do other mental disorders affect teen-agers?

Yes, a few. The most common are severe nervousness, overactivity, and depression. If a teen-ager has prolonged periods of any of these, you should try to discuss his trouble with him. If this does not help, a doctor, social worker, local hospital, or mental health clinic should be consulted.

I hear that blacks don't commit suicide. Is that true?

No. Young black men in the cities have long had a high suicide rate and young black women are committing suicide in increasing numbers. Their suicide rate is becoming equal to the rate among young white males in the cities. Overall, the black suicide rate remains about one-half the white rate. About 1,000 black men and 300 black women commit suicide each year. Percent figures indicate that the suicide rate among unmarried teen-age girls (black and white) is ten times the national average. Thus, depression in a teen-ager should be taken seriously.

A person who is not eating well or sleeping well and is easily upset and tearful may be depressed . . . although he or she is not "dragging." Such symptoms should be reported to your doctor. In other cases, people in danger of committing suicide become argumentative and difficult in an effort to drive away family and friends and break all social contacts. Friends feel attacked, hit back, or desert without taking a look at the pattern. This pattern sometimes follows the loss of a boyfriend, close family members or so on. If you see youngsters breaking social ties like this, you should help them seek professional help. Pointing out that you think they are trying to drive you away because they are in trouble, upset, feeling bad or whatever is one way to raise the issue. Unfortunately in some cases, there is no warning nor is the victim always depressed.

Is drug overdosage (O.D.) a form of suicide?

Officially, O.D.'s are counted as accident statistics. However, we suspect that some of these accidents are suicides. But it is impossible to tell whether the overdosage is related to suicidal intentions. In some large cities, overdoses of heroin are becoming one of the leading causes of death among young black men.

Is daydreaming in teen-agers a sign of emotional trouble?

No. Everyone daydreams. It is normal to do so and it is normal for adolescents to daydream more than people of other ages. If their daydreaming leads to the neglect of personal responsibilities or withdrawal from social contacts, however, it deserves investigation. Excessive daydreaming may be an attempt to avoid dealing with the realities of daily life. If a teen-ager confuses his daydreams with reality, he needs professional help.

How do you get a teen who needs help to go for treatment?

You should be truthful and not use scare tactics or deception. When the area of difficulty is limited—school trouble, sadness, or depression—you can indicate that you see that they are doing okay in other areas but you are concerned about and want to get them help with their school problem or you want to help them become happier or whatever. Many teens struggling with urges and ideas often feel they are about to go crazy. For blacks this has usually meant hospitalization under bad conditions. The idea of talking to a mental health worker is still less available, less accepted and less expected. Thus when a youngster's problems are not extreme you can help by saying that you understand that he or she is not crazy before you explain the why, when and what will happen of treatment. It helps to discuss how to talk about coming for help with the mental health worker beforehand. With an older teen, it helps, after your initial contact and discussion with teen and helper, for the youngster to make his or her own appointment.

When the problem may require hospitalization, use basically the same approach but don't promise more than standing by or helping the youngster obtain whatever he or she needs to get better.

Drugs and Drug Abuse

Should teen-agers be allowed to smoke?

Cigarette smoking should be strongly discouraged. It has been proven to be very dangerous to health. It can cause lung cancer and contribute to heart and other lung diseases. The risks should be explained to the teen-ager. Unfortunately, despite many warnings, teen-agers continue to take up smoking in great numbers. After you have advised against it, the final choice will still remain with your child. But, if smoking irritates other members of the family, the smoker should not be allowed to impose his self-pollution on others. If you smoke, you provide a bad model. Stop, if you can, for yourself and your children.

Why are young people so quick to take up
smoking when they know it's dangerous?

They want to feel sophisticated and grown-up. It may also be a way of rebelling. It seems like a hip thing to do and may increase their feelings of belongingness with their group. Death from cancer of the lungs or other diseases at age fifty or sixty seems too remote to feel like a real danger to many young people. Cigarette advertising presents smokers as cool, attractive and masterful . . . one of the reasons we suggested that you help your child learn to "see through" the message of commercials at an early age.

Should we let our teen-agers smoke marijuana?

Smoking marijuana ("grass," "pot," "reefers") should not be encouraged. The legal risks should be explained. Remember that in all states it is officially illegal to smoke marijuana, although in some states the penalties are as minor as traffic tickets. Often young blacks are selectively arrested by racist police officers and receive stiff penalties. But if parents themselves smoke "pot" they would be hypocritical to insist that their children do not.

Should we allow our teen-age children to
smoke marijuana at home?

Some parents do allow their children to smoke marijuana at home because they feel that if they do smoke, home is a safer environment than the street or other unfavorable settings. But here you are involved in helping your child break the law. Besides, youngsters who smoke at home often smoke away from home anyway. We don't think it is a good idea but each family must set its own rules and take into consideration the effects on other family members, especially younger children present in the home.

How can we try to prevent our youngsters
from smoking marijuana or taking drugs?

Again, it is less what you say or do now than what you did in the past. Teen-agers who feel adequate, have ambitions and direction and can handle frustration are less likely to turn to drugs. Teens who are not under extreme neighborhood pressure to use drugs are also less likely to do so. In any case, discussion and knowledge about drugs can be helpful in the prevention of drug usage. The scare tactic is less useful than helping youngsters understand that drug usage can prevent their full enjoyment of life, limit opportunities, and cause them a number of personal and social problems.

In early teens or late pre-teens, it is helpful to discuss the issue of smoking marijuana and drugs in a calm fashion and at natural times. You should look over books on the subject and make the ones you consider most helpful available to your youngsters. Early in your discussion, without great emotion you should let it be known that you disapprove of the use of drugs. Youngsters sometimes point out that other youngsters are taking drugs or smoking "pot" and that they could do so without your knowledge. One helpful response is, "You could, but why would you *have* to smoke or take drugs?" Oddly enough, many youngsters have never asked themselves this question. This question often leads to other questions about what they want for themselves and whether drugs will or will not help them acquire it.

How does marijuana affect someone who smokes it?

Reactions vary with the individual. People generally say that they feel good and that experiences take on a greater intensity. Some claim to feel more sensual. Marijuana may enhance the pleasure of listening to music, tasting food, and sex. However, some people claim to feel no effects from marijuana and in others, severe paranoid reactions have occurred. Some studies claim no ill effects and others claim minor and serious effects. Some people who smoke marijuana daily in large amounts have been found to be withdrawn, lacking in ambition and neglectful of their personal responsibilities. There have also been some recent reports that heavy marijuana smoking may cause a decrease in sex hormones in males and loss of sexual interest.

Because the issue is so emotional and political, there will be no sure evidence for a while. When you discuss marijuana smoking with your youngster, it is best to admit that the effects are not fully understood. The issue is less whether it is harmful or not but that smoking pot or taking drugs is illegal . . . that there can be hard short-run and long-run consequences and *possible* harmful effects.

It is best not to get into what should be. Your youngster must deal with what *is* while finding acceptable ways of bringing about change . . . if it is that important. Help your youngster find constructive ways to establish adulthood . . . decreasing the need for rebellion and pot-smoking.

Can you get drunk from marijuana as you do from alcohol?

No, not exactly. Marijuana can make a person lightheaded and sleepy but usually not uncoordinated. Drunkenness from alcohol leads to uncoordination and staggering. Both alcohol and marijuana may make a person feel uninhibited. Usually judgment is impaired more with a "high" from alcohol than with one from marijuana. It is dangerous to drive an automobile or engage in other precision activities when under the heavy influence of either drug because they interfere with alertness and "reaction time."

*My seventeen-year-old boy smokes marijuana a lot
and has no motivation to do anything with
himself. How can I get him to stop?*

Marijuana smoking in excess may be a sign of deep emotional disturbance and serve as an "escape" from life's problems. Many teens having trouble making career choices, lifestyle choices and so on just "cop out" on drugs. If you cannot reach your son through discussion, the help of a mental health worker should be obtained.

*If my child smokes marijuana, is there
a chance that he might become a pusher?*

It is possible but does not always happen. The unfortunate problem is that although marijuana may be considered a less harmful drug, a pusher of marijuana usually is exposed to pressure and forced into pushing other drugs, namely, cocaine and heroin. Like many illegal activities in the black community, young people are attracted to them for the monetary gain. When education and jobs are not available, teen-agers turn to other ways of making money. When they feel that they have nothing to lose if they are caught, illegal activities become easier to engage in. If you can help your youngster think in terms of a future goal, this *may* help. Again, point out the risks he will take and the people he will hurt if he becomes a pusher of illegal drugs of any kind.

Doesn't smoking marijuana always lead to the use of hard drugs?

Not necessarily. Current medical knowledge indicates that it is not addicting and does not of itself lead to the use of hard drugs. Contact with the drug culture, where it is one of many drugs, might lead a person to harder drugs through social exposure.

What are "downers"? Are they dangerous?

"Downers" usually refer to sedative or sleeping medications. The most common "downers" are barbiturates, which are highly addicting. Overdoses can lead to death, particularly when mixed with alcohol. If one is addicted to barbiturates, withdrawal symptoms can include convulsions. Anyone addicted to barbiturates requires close medical supervision.

There is an increasing consumption of tranquilizing drugs such as Valium and Librium, particularly among girls and young women. Are these drugs dangerous?

These tranquilizers can cause dependency and addiction. When taken in heavy dosages over a consistent period of time, they can be as dangerous as the barbiturates. Although these drugs are only available through a doctor's prescription, there is an increasing amount being pushed on the illegal market.

What are tranquilizers?

They are a variety of calming drugs. The most common are Thorazine, Miltown, Valium, and Librium. It is now known that Miltown and, as mentioned above, Valium and Librium can be addicting when taken regularly in significant amounts.

Is it harmful to take tranquilizers with alcohol?

Both tranquilizers and alcohol are drugs. When taken together, they enhance each other's effects. It is not good to mix drugs and mixing of excessive amounts of any drugs can be fatal.

What is cocaine? Is it harmful?

Cocaine (often called "coke") is a stimulant drug that can sometimes cause a psychosis (loss of control over the mind). It is believed to be habit-forming but it is unclear how addicting it is. It should be classed with the dangerous drugs. If sniffed on a regular basis, it can damage mucous membranes in the nose and cause nosebleeds.

What is speed?

"Speed" (sometimes called "uppers") is the name given to a group of stimulant drugs like amphetamines. They can make one feel more alert and awake. Large quantities can produce extreme nervousness and rapid heart beat. "Speed" can also cause psychosis and is habit-forming. "Speed"-type ingredients are usually contained in ordinary diet pills.

What are LSD and mescaline?

LSD (lysergic acid diethylamide), "acid," and mescaline are hallucinogenic drugs. They can make you see things that are not there and can also cause trouble with thinking and can make a person psychotic. These drugs are extremely dangerous and should not be used.

Is heroin as dangerous as they say?

Yes. Heroin produces a feeling of great happiness and "being on top of the world" but it is strongly addicting. A person can quickly become dependent on heroin and must then devote his life to getting money to buy the drug. Much of the crime in the black community is committed by heroin addicts. Ten years ago the government estimated that there were 50,000 heroin addicts. Today, the estimate is 600,000. A disproportionate number are black youths.

Do methadone programs help heroin addicts?

They may help in some cases. Methadone is a drug chemically related to heroin that can be taken orally and reduces the desire for heroin. Clinics supply addicts with methadone under medical control. Eventually, through therapy programs an attempt is made to withdraw the addict from all drugs. The important aspect of methadone maintenance is the psychotherapy and related therapy which is required in these programs.

Why do some blacks oppose methadone programs?

Because the drug has not reduced the amount of drug addiction in the community. Methadone itself is addicting and addicts have sold it to others. Some addicts have died of methadone over-dosage. In addition, many black leaders fear that methadone is just a social control program to cut down crime and that unscrupulous politicians could use it to manipulate addicts by threatening to withhold their treatment.

What is the best way to treat the heroin addict?

No one knows for sure. But ex-addicts claim a high rate of success in rehabilitating other addicts. Groups such as Synanon in California and FIRST in Boston, which emphasize mutual self-help, claim great success. But many addicts refuse to enter self-help programs or drop out early. The most important factor in breaking the habit is the addict's own personal resolve to stop.

Is there much mixing of various drugs among teen-agers?

Unfortunately, reports indicate that teen-agers often mix several drugs such as marijuana and speed, or marijuana and various other pills. Reports are also coming in that addicts are mixing methadone with barbiturates. As mentioned earlier, all such practices of mixing drugs simply heighten the seriousness of the drug effects and increase the chances of overdosage and death.

What is the cause of the increased use of
drugs among black youths today?

There are a number of causes for drug use and abuse in our society, too numerous for discussion in this book. However, the widespread availability of drugs clearly creates a situation where young people have greater access to drugs and thus it is more likely that they will try and continue to use drugs. Also, black youths are more frustrated and victimized by poverty, joblessness, lack of recreation and other social problems. Such conditions are fertile soil for drug addiction. Unfortunately unless these conditions are attacked the wide use of drugs will not be greatly decreased.

Should teen-agers be permitted to drink?

There is no reason why teens should not drink wine and other alcoholic drinks on occasion. It is important for young people to learn how to drink in moderation. Young people who are denied opportunities to drink in moderation in a family often drink too much the first time they get away from home. The dangers to health from excessive and continual drinking should be explained. Not infrequently, a person will collapse and die after drinking great quantities of alcohol. People functioning well have their lives under control, including when and how much alcohol to drink . . . if any. You should not insist or tell your teen that it's cool or grown-up to drink alcohol if he or she doesn't want to do so.

Would serving wine or beer moderately with meals to the entire family as is practiced in some foreign countries encourage alcoholism in adolescents?

There is little scientific evidence to provide a factual answer to this question. However, light wines at meals are an added delight to dining and there is no reason that the entire family should not participate in such activity, even if younger children are merely given a few drops. Small amounts of wine or beer are not injurious to health and in themselves don't cause addiction.

Is it true that alcohol can damage the body?

Yes, every year many black men and women die from liver cirrhosis brought on by drinking too much alcohol too often. Chronic drinkers often develop brain damage and a psychosis (that is, they "go crazy"). Many lose their memory and judgment. In chronic alcoholics, there is a slow deterioration of the personality as well as the body.

Is it possible for an adolescent to become an alcoholic?

Yes, it is. Alcoholism often begins in adolescence. Alcohol is a highly addictive drug. Teen-agers who drink excessively have personal problems. A youngster with anxiety or depresson may use alcohol as a release. Parents should try to get to the bottom of the problem or seek professional help for such a child.

But can't drinking alcohol be a good release for a young person under pressure?

Yes, if indulged in in a mature way and not seen as the only means used to relieve pressure. However, many crimes of violence and fatal accidents in the black community occur when people are intoxicated. Frequently, family breakdown occurs because of alcoholic parents. In such situations, children are often abused and neglected.

Does alcoholism run in families?

Sometimes. It is felt that some persons may have a greater psychological or physiological tendency to become alcoholic, but this susceptibility is not likely to be strictly hereditary. Children of alcoholics are more likely to become alcoholics because of the breakdown and stress of the home due to an alcoholic parent. For complex reasons, many imitate their parent's life pattern.

What can we do to help a young alcoholic?

Alcoholics should be referred for medical help. There are many special programs for them at hospitals and clinics. Groups like Alcoholics Anonymous often are successful in treating alcoholics who want to break their habit and can provide information about other such programs. There are some youth-directed, self-help, anti-alcoholism programs emerging in many communities.

Violence and Crime

Is there any one thing that causes black youths to become juvenile delinquents?

The two most important factors associated with juvenile delinquency are a poverty environment and difficult family life. Because of racism, past and present, we have more than our share of both. However, the rate of juvenile delinquency among whites in disadvantaged environments is similar to the black rate.

What does "liberating" merchandise from a store mean?

"Liberating" is a black hip word for shoplifting. Some have the philosophy that it is the exploitive white store owner who steals from the people through high prices on poor merchandise. Thus, shoplifting is seen as a means of getting what belongs to the people. It doesn't work however. The shopowner merely raises his prices accordingly and shifts the cost to other customers in the community. It is important to impress on your child that shoplifting is a crime that can lead to serious difficulty with the law. In fact, young people may receive heavier sentences for their crimes than adults.

Is it true that black teen-agers shoplift more than whites?

We don't know. However, there are reports that many teen-age shoplifters are white youngsters from middle-class backgrounds, often with money to pay for what they steal. They steal for attention, as a form of rebellion against their parents and authority, and for other more personal and deeper emotional reasons. The problem for black teens, however, is that when they get caught they are prosecuted more often than white youths. Black youths are more likely to be sent to detention homes where they may begin a pattern of crime and antisocial behavior.

What is "boosting"?

"Boosting" is a form of organized shoplifting for profit, most popular among the street cultures and often related to the prostitution traffic. Many young men and women involved in prostitution activities also "boost" the clothes needed for the nighttime "business." In addition, they often take orders for specific articles from persons who are willing to buy stolen merchandise. Thus, the "booster" is not merely shoplifting for himself, but sells the stolen merchandise.

My daughter went shopping with several other girls; one girl was seen shoplifting, but they were all accused of shoplifting. What can a parent do in a case like this?

Store security agents are generally very hard on groups of teen-agers shopping together, whether they are black or white, but black youths often encounter more abuse. Guilt by association is a common cause of much teen-age difficulty with the law. Although teens usually prefer to shop in groups, as they derive most of their fun at this age in groups, your daughter should be encouraged not to shop with more than one girl unless it's a local store where she and her friends are known and trusted.

Is shoplifting widespread among teens generally?

No. As with most illegal activities, it's only a small percentage of teen-agers who engage in shoplifting. Most youths are trustworthy and spend their money to purchase goods. As a matter of fact, the teen-age consumer market amounts to billions of dollars, especially for such items as clothes, records, tapes, musical instruments, cosmetics, cars, and other items related to recreation and glamorizing.

Is it true that teen-agers are discriminated against by store personnel?

There are increasing complaints of discrimination and unprovoked abuse from store managers and salespersons toward teen-agers generally and black teen-agers feel these problems even more severely. For example, many of the musical tapes sold are defective; however, when teen-agers return them, they are treated discourteously and often not allowed returns in the same manner as adults. We know of several cases where a teen has been refused a return, but when the parent returned the same merchandise, it was accepted. Parents should serve as advocates for their children when such discrimination occurs.

What can be done about these shoplifting problems among teen-agers?

First, we must realize that much of the problem does not rest within the teen-age population but with the nature of our society. America is becoming more and more materialistic and youths who grow up under the influence of TV commercials and advertisements everywhere are encouraged to desire goods which often neither they nor their parents can afford. In addition, the motivation to have a range of materialistic symbols fits right into the adolescent's struggles for identity, social acceptance and a sense of security. Thus, teen-agers are very vulnerable to the advertising of goods.

If their parents can't provide them with many of the items they feel they must have, and they can't find employment (unemployment for white youths is three times the national average and for black youths is six times the national average), stealing becomes a real option for many young people, especially when parental guardianship is lax. Perhaps the problem of stealing cannot be really solved without a change in values and a deemphasis of the importance of material possessions. Again, if you prepared your child to understand that he or she can't have everything and that's okay . . . from an early age, a problem is less likely now.

It often upsets us that young blacks are so violent
with each other. How can we help prevent violence?

That is an important question. Murder is the second leading cause
of death among young black men. Malcolm X once warned, "My
experience has been that in many instances where you find Ne-
groes talking about nonviolence, they are not nonviolent with each
other, and they're not loving with each other, or forgiving with
each other." We cannot make excuses for the violence we inflict on
each other. Many homicides in the ghetto are related to the drug
addiction problem and competition among "pushers." Alleviation
of slums and poverty will help decrease the amount of violence.
Gun-control legislation would also be beneficial. Blacks should
actively enter the gun-control and drug-control campaigns. Blacks
should also support the establishment of homicide prevention
centers at clinics and other agencies in the community.

Building black pride will help. But the way we treat our
children *from the beginning* and the way we help them learn to
handle anger, conflict, and frustration will help most. If we punish
them violently and if they are encouraged to be violent when
others bother them—without first seeking a peaceful but honorable
solution—there is little reason to expect them to be anything else
but violent as teens and adults. See our previous discussions about
handling anger, confrontations, frustrations, and aggressions.

My eighteen-year-old son wants to keep a gun in the house
because he says he needs it for "protection." What should we do?

Some neighborhoods are tough, but keeping a gun in the home can
be dangerous. In a fit of anger, one family member may use it
against another. Many impulsive killings in the black community
occur in this way. Also your son with a gun at hand might be too
quick to settle a street argument by "shooting it out." Such an
episode may mean death or jail for your son and unnecessary
slayings of other blacks. Unless there is a clear and present danger,
no family member should be permitted to keep a gun in the house.
The legal possession of guns requires registration and a license in
most sections of the country.

If you must keep a gun, we hope that you established a helpful
practice long ago: nobody throws at, hits or otherwise attacks
anyone else while angry. Children who have learned to hit other

things, take a walk or run—*not a drive*—to relieve anger are less likely to turn to the gun immediately as teens. If you didn't start the practice before, now is the time.

My teens hate policemen. This can mean trouble.
How can I help them think about the police?

This is a very real problem. We all know that too many policemen are more respectful of whites than blacks, particularly of educated, middle-income whites than low-income blacks. Many blacks have been badly abused by police. At the same time, policemen are the symbols of authority. Their mistreatment of people says, "You are unimportant, of low value; you don't belong." Such abuse and rejection brings out anger and rage. (See our discussion of the black college youth in this chapter.) On the other hand, our communities have long suffered from poor police protection and we need better police-community relations.

We must organize and continue to press for improved police practices in our communities. At the same time we must encourage our youth to see policemen as individuals and to give respect to those who deserve it and to work through our organizations and the political system to remove or change the behavior of the abusive ones.

The black policeman is in a particularly difficult position. Some have risked promotions to fight racism in their departments and yet find themselves the targets of black anger. They are perhaps in the best position to limit abuse of blacks because they are on the inside. We hurt ourselves when we attack the very people who have the best chance of making police departments not only protect us, but treat us with respect. Help your sons and daughters think through such issues.

How should our children act if arrested?

Advise your children to never run from the police when they attempt to stop them. If pursued and stopped by the police, they should not accept abuse but they should not antagonize them. When asked questions, answer them directly. The police may search them for weapons. Again, this is not the time to fight police abuse. If it occurs a youngster should remember the details and gather all evidence possible. You should then enlist the aid of your church or civil and human rights groups to punish the offending officers.

If arrested, your child should ask to call you immediately and you should respond immediately. They should know that they should not answer any questions other than their name and address. A rapid response from you may help your child's case. You want to be supportive to your child at this critical time even though you may be feeling anger toward him or her. If you can afford it, you should obtain the services of a private lawyer immediately. If a private lawyer is beyond your means, contact your local Legal Aid Society for help. Usually if no outside lawyer can be retained, the court will appoint a lawyer for your child.

What can we do about teen-age crime? For example, should I turn in a teen who commits a crime against our family?

If it is more than a minor matter that can be settled between your family and the youngster's family, it is reasonable to seek police protection. On the other hand, it can be dangerous to act as a regular informer about matters which do not concern you. Teen-age crime is a very complicated problem. It is related to everything from neglecting or troubled parents through economic and racial exploitation to corruption and immoral behavior on the part of local and national public officials.

In some heavy crime areas, citizen groups have formed to look out for each other, work with police and, in some cases, to try and attack some of the problems which turn youth to crime. This is a helpful approach. It is unwise and dangerous to get into the business of actually trying to capture suspected criminals.

What is bail and how do we handle it?

Bail is money that must be paid in order for an arrested person to be released from jail while awaiting trial. On a minor charge, the police may authorize bail, on a major charge a judge decides. However, bail can be a discretionary matter. The judge is free to set bail at any amount he chooses or he may deny bail for serious crimes. The primary purpose of bail payments is to insure that the arrested person will appear for trial. Things which determine how great a risk you are include: length of time at your present residence, school or job status, family ties in the area, criminal record, etc. The bail system is unfair to the poor who do not have ready cash available. Bondsmen (the people who pay for the arrested person's release) are usually requested to put up a payment of about 5 to 10 percent of the court-determined bail amount. Bondsmen have wide latitude on what they can demand as security—jewelry, your bankbook, the title to your house—or they can refuse the case. If the defendant does not appear for trial, the total bail amount must be paid to the court.

What is probation?

Probation is a term used by the court to indicate that a person who is convicted of a crime can be released with certain restrictions on his behavior for a specified period of time. Probation is usually in place of a jail sentence. If probation is violated the person is usually imprisoned. Probation is seen as a form of rehabilitation. The probationer is allowed to function in the community while still under supervision of the prison system.

What is a pardon?

Official (usually by a governor, a committee appointed by the governor, or the President) release from or reduction of the legal penalties of an offense, or forgiveness for a criminal offense.

What is a parole?

Parole is the term used when a prisoner is released on good behavior before he has served his full sentence. Parole, like probation, places restrictions on the ex-inmate's activities. If parole is violated, the parolee may be returned to jail, generally for the full balance of the original sentence.

What is extradition?

The surrender of an alleged criminal by the state where he is apprehended to the state where the crime was allegedly committed, in order to stand trial.

*What can we do to help our child who
is sentenced to a term in jail?*

You should write and visit frequently. Contributing small amounts of money and gifts can go a long way to make a prisoner's time more tolerable. Books of various types, especially about problems and achievement in the black community, are often useful for persons in prison. Malcolm X and other leaders in the black community have used time confined in prison to increase their awareness through reading and writing.

You should encourage your adolescent to use the time and the programs, if available, for self-development. You should help your youngster understand that this is the most important contribution he can make toward solving some of the complex problems in the black community. By self-development, we mean work, school and social skills—including personal honesty, personal discipline, and realistic commitment to constructive goals. Some young people, more often with good family support, are able to use prison to turn their lives around.

What should we do when our youngster is released?

Ex-prisoners need a great deal of help to get back on their feet again. This includes both moral and financial support. Financial support, help in finding a place to live, and aid in obtaining a job are crucial. Have your son or daughter contact local rehabilitated ex-inmate groups; they can often give assistance and suggestions. Social rejection often makes it difficult for the ex-prisoner to be rehabilitated.

There is much talk about closing down detention homes and other prison systems that are used to incarcerate young people. Is it really a good form of rehabilitation to let the criminal back out into the community?

The issue of rehabilitation is very complex. Years of experience have shown that the so-called rehabilitation programs inside prison walls are largely ineffective, as proved by the high rate of repeated crimes and returns to prison. There is clearly something in the way a person relates to his family, community and outside environment that must be changed if criminal behavior is to be reduced. In addition, because so many criminals are victims of their life circumstances, it seems that the total community should take greater responsibility in helping youth adopt noncriminal behavior. Certainly careful screening of inmates for readiness is needed if such programs are to survive.

What is a halfway house?

A halfway house is a facility within the community that may be used by prisons or mental hospitals as the first step for returning inmates or the mentally ill to the community and normal routines. The halfway house is a step along the road to rehabilitation and is a progressive reform.

Education and the Teen-Ager

*You spoke in Chapter 6 about the importance of maintaining
close contact with our youngsters' schools. But what if
my teen-ager becomes embarrassed about parents visiting
the school and expresses the opinion that he doesn't
want his parents poking into school affairs?*

If you began visiting your child's school when he was in kinder-garten or elementary school, he learned early that your concern is for him to have the best possible learning experience. If your child nevertheless now indicates reluctance about your interest in school, point out to him that it's still part of your parental re-sponsibility and general concern that school be a good experi-ence. If he still objects, you might arrange to visit teachers while he is not in the class.

*Should teen-agers be encouraged by parents to participate
in school social and civic activities such as student councils,
clubs, and other competitive leadership activities?*

Yes. Leadership interests and skills are learned early. But you must keep in mind that not all people are leaders. Even if you are in a leadership position it does not always follow that your child will desire to be a leader. You must be very sensitive to each child's inclinations. If a child expresses leadership interests they should be supported and encouraged. If a child is not motivated toward leadership in school, don't push him or her. In some cases it develops later, if a child doesn't crush it because you are pushing him or her too hard. Perhaps in one family of several children only one of the children will have leadership characteris-tics; if so, try not to emphasize that child's accomplishments more than you do the activities of other children in the family. We know of black students who have criticized black youngsters for taking leadership roles in racially mixed schools and programs. As a group we need all the people that we can beg, borrow, or steal who are interested in and able to hold executive and leadership positions among blacks and in racially mixed settings. Some black youths criticize because they are jealous, afraid of competition with whites, or just plain alienated. You should help your youngster understand the feeling but "keep on keeping on" . . . everywhere.

What is the best form of parental encouragement for leadership?

Take an active interest in what your child does in school activities. Ask questions, express support to your child if he/she wants to get involved by talking about your own involvement in school or close friends that you remember who were leaders. Explain to your child how the process of leadership is learned from experiences. Suggest that your child read biographies and autobiographies of great black and white leaders in which their childhood is described. Many of these personality profiles record early leadership activity in school and church.

If there is no student participation or mechanism for participation in leadership activities in the operation of the school, should the parents object?

Yes, student participation in school gives early opportunity for leadership experiences, especially for black children who have fewer opportunities for activities that prepare them for leadership roles in society. Student participation is needed at various levels in the operation of the school including classroom activities, curriculum selection and development, school personnel training and sensitivity, and student government. If the opportunity to participate in school policies and programs is not available in your children's school, find out why. Try to get it going. If there is no democracy in their school life, they may well grow up without an understanding of how democracy should work in the larger society.

What should we do if our boy reports racist remarks made by the teacher to individual students or to the class?

You should report such remarks to the principal and ask for his help and intervention. It would also help to bring up racial problems of this nature at parent-teacher association meetings. Often race relations workshops for the teachers may be of some help. See our discussion in Chapter 6.

*What is the talk of student rights in
junior and senior high school?*

From the disruptions that have occurred in junior and senior high schools over the past several years, school officials and educators have come to realize that there must be basic codes indicating student rights and responsibilities in schools. Student rights policies teach students social responsibilities and many organizations such as the American Bar Association and the White House Conference on Youth advise that educational institutions develop codes that spell out student rights and responsibilities and mechanisms for such codes to be carried out in the schools.

*What can parents do about junior and senior high school
students who don't apply themselves to studying or
other activities that develop their intellect, but merely
goof off hours and days at a time?*

One of the major problems is not obvious and is difficult to correct even when known. Work habits, comfort and pleasure in getting a job done, become a pattern most easily in the seven-to-twelve-year-old age range. The planning, organizing and discipline to get things done is developed in this early period and leads to achievement and that achievement feeds on itself until one is almost addicted to doing it—work or mastery of a task—math, English, carrying out the garbage, or perfecting the hook shot. Praise, approval and respect or admiration from parents or peers leads to the development of inner standards and determination which remain with us more or less all of our lives.

If the above does not happen, for any reason, goofing off at work or play can become the rule. Little parental support, poor teaching, a school where few children are interested in learning, a specific learning problem or an undetected health problem such as poor vision can lead to failure, efforts to cover up failure which lead to more failure, frustration and a turning off of academic work. If other work areas are not available—athletics, the arts—a youngster may miss the opportunity to develop mastery or work skills and develop a goof off style. Even though the child may want to do well at some point, he or she may have difficulty.

*Wouldn't a more flexible, relevant school
program help such youngsters?*

It has been said that relevant social issues and a school that does
not require active teens to stay pent-up would help. Where this is
the problem such an approach is useful. Some schools are too rigid
and irrelevant in their programming. But it has been demonstrated
that the most disciplined students benefit most from less structured, more "on your own" programs. It is also true that many
undisciplined students can't concentrate on black studies, social
issues, and other matters which should be of relevance. Many
floundering high school students do well after experiencing the
discipline of military life.

What can be done for such teens?

Parents, teachers, or counselors should talk with them. Point out
what you see as the problem. One approach is to encourage them
to get into programs which require hard physical work, routine,
determination, planning, organizing and even token punishment
for less than the best effort. You can then help them transfer the
skills learned and the pride experienced to academic areas. We
have seen youngsters develop the needed discipline and drive
after getting involved in demanding athletic and wilderness programs but also demanding, well organized choral groups and other
activities. Sometimes you can help a youngster achieve, complete
or master very simple tasks and move to more complex tasks after
some success and eventually get them "back on the achievement
track."

*My fourteen-year-old is very bright but won't work
because others call him odd. What can I do?*

Occasionally, some black teen-agers are made to feel guilty by
friends because they are "too smart." In some neighborhoods,
blacks have an anti-intellectual attitude and persecute and hassle
students who take their studies seriously. They are called "square"
and worse. Such pressure may cause a black teen-ager to fear
success and try to fit in with his group. If this happens, he will
resist doing homework and other academic chores. In this case,
you should actively support your child's academic interests and
help introduce him or her to other youngsters with similar goals

. . . or successful adults. Seek out church, school, YMCA, and other programs for gifted or talented youngsters.

You must stress the importance of independent thinking. If he or she has been allowed to be an independent thinker at home, your teen is less likely to be badly influenced by peers. You should not encourage your youngster to isolate himself or herself from friends of his or her choice. This often requires that such a child play more roles, but bright students have the capacity to do this. We have seen youngsters be "one of the boys" or "one of the girls" and still do their thing with the books and participate in helpful extracurricular activities. When the pressures are severe and this can't be done, if possible, it can be helpful to send your youngster away to school or to another community. Many schools have scholarship aid for such students.

Are there other causes of poor performance even though a youngster "has it" intellectually?

Yes. Struggles with parents can be one. "You want me to make all A's; therefore, in the name of independence, I will make all C's." "You want me to make good grades, go to college and become a banker and live like you; therefore, in the name of independence I will strum a guitar in the park and live a life of genteel poverty . . . but with love." That may be okay but have him understand what he is asking for . . . for himself . . . not you!

Comfort in high school and fear of failure in the large world is another. Some black teens, particularly from low income backgrounds have mixed feelings and guilt about "leaving my people" or "joining the Establishment." Such feelings may lead a black teenager to purposely fail in high school to escape facing these issues. For some, there are just too many confusing issues, too many choices. Do nothing is their answer. Personal emotional conflicts may be the cause as well as many other factors.

How can parents help?

The tendency is to see a lazy kid . . . "with more opportunities than I had." If there is a struggle with you, move back. We discussed the method earlier. You want to indicate that you see he or she is having trouble. Ask how you can be helpful. Assure youngsters that you want to help them achieve what they want for themselves. They may gradually reveal their confusion or fear, often in indirect ways, off the cuff comments, "Who wants to go to college anyway?" (Fear of failure?) You can reassure them. Help them realize that they don't have to answer all the questions and issues right away. Help your teen understand that he can help black people whenever and however he develops a talent and uses it in a humane way. Help them understand that they don't have to be Martin Luther King, Jr., or Thurgood Marshall to have done their part; that they don't have to make a giant footprint on the sand . . . just work up to their ability in algebra and be a just, caring person.

Where there is a serious emotional problem, don't deny it because you think it will make you look bad. Seek help if it is available to avoid a greater problem later.

My teen is not having study problems.
How should I avoid trouble?

You should continue (as you have been doing from an early age) to expect your youngster to study, to do homework and to learn outside of the school setting . . . for himself and herself more than the fact that it will please you. Strict setting of hours each night for such pursuits may be good for one child and not so good for others. It is a fact that many teen-agers spend the required hours in their rooms each evening, but do more daydreaming than studying. You should ask them to work out a plan to get their work, play, etc., done in a way that is convenient and right for them. Even teen-agers getting along fine often need help in developing good activity plans and study habits, particularly as their workload increases. You may be able to help your child plan his study routines or he can be referred to a study skills counselor associated with the school.

If a child is doing very poorly in a subject shouldn't he be
required to spend more time studying the subject?

Maybe, but in most cases, not alone. If a boy is doing poorly in math, requiring that he go to his room and study his math is probably further frustration for him. Homework on subjects in which the child is doing poorly often requires that the child work with someone who can help him find specific learning blocks. Very simple common-sense tests can be applied to some of the difficulties youngsters have with certain subjects. If your son has trouble with math each year, there is often good indication that he never learned the basics to start with; therefore, each year gets more difficult. If your child continues to have difficulty in a particular subject and especially math and English, it is important that several types of approaches be tried to help the child. Sometimes remedial courses and tutorial instruction are necessary.

What should a parent do when a child comes home with a poor report card in conduct and schoolwork?

The report card in many ways is not an adequate measure of a child's educational progress and it does not necessarily explain the true educational needs of a pupil. Bad report cards should be looked upon as signals that something is wrong in the child's school relationships. You must take the time to have a three-way conference with the teacher(s) and your child concerning his or her progress in school. You should not just chastise your youngster and sign a bad report card.

Our girl has dropped out of high school. What can I do?

Try to get to the underlying problem and get help for her. It can be for any of the reasons above and many more. Try to help her return to school—the same or elsewhere. Some private schools for such students provide scholarships. If nothing works, don't condemn her. Help her plan for the future. A year or two of work and she may well want to return to school.

If parents desire to send their children to schools outside of the community, should the children be consulted before such a decision is made?

Yes. Furthermore, the reasons for such changes should be explained to them and parental expectations clearly expressed. Too often children are arbitrarily sent away without clear discussion among parents and children of the importance of quality education to the child's development, and as a result, these students' performance in the new school often does not improve. When you send youngsters from a predominantly black school to a predominantly white school, you want to help them understand the social and economic reasons for some of the differences they will observe. You want to prepare them for possible racial difficulties. See our discussion in this chapter about preparing black teens to go to predominantly white colleges.

*How should parents handle a black child who goes
to a predominantly white school and soon begins to
disrespect his family and his parents because he considers
them deprived, unqualified, uneducated, and inferior?*

Several reports from parents indicate that this type of behavior may be on the increase among black youth, especially as such educational opportunities open up. Parents must be prepared to counter such impressions with convincing historical information about blacks, with the confident expression of pride in black people. In addition, it is important that your youngster participate in enough positive black experiences so that he can deduce for himself that there are strengths in the black community. A parent with strong negative feelings about being black can serve to further convince the youth that he is right. When the problem is extreme, it may be necessary to send the child to a "community school" where he can see blacks functioning in responsible positions of authority and settings that refute his negative impressions. It is probably not good, however, to take a child out of a predominantly white school environment and place him in a predominantly black school if he objects. Under these conditions, he will see what he wants to see.

*My son wants to become a famous athlete and doesn't put
enough time into his studies in high school. Is that okay?*

No, your son's academic studies should come first. Classroom work should not be neglected in favor of sports. Many black folk heroes have been athletes and many black youths try to emulate them. (The same is true of music and musicians and, unfortunately, pimps and prostitutes.) You want to remind your son that very few people earn a living as athletes or in other highly visible and popular professions. It is fine to develop any skill he has and channel it into a legitimate area. But you want to remind young black men and women that most people "make it" as teachers, lawyers, electricians, technicians, and so on. Thus it is important for him or her to strike a balance—enough basketball, music, etc., and enough attention to academic studies. You want to help him or her seek excellence everywhere—more than fame anywhere.

With this approach fame is possible but you are left with good skills elsewhere—and less disappointment—if you don't make it to the top in basketball or whatever.

My girl goes to her room to study and turns on her
radio full blast. Can she really learn anything that way?

Surprisingly, some people can study effectively under such conditions. If she is getting her work done, fine. However, if the loud radio playing is disturbing others, she should be asked to reduce the volume. The volume of music is often a problem between black and white teens at college or wherever they live together. The same rules should hold away as hold at home. If racial animosities are at play they should be discussed directly and separately, and not played out around a radio which is too loud to allow concentration, work or sleep.

In the early 1960's there was much talk about the school dropout
problem. Are there many black teen-agers still out of school?

Yes. According to the U.S. Department of Labor Statistics, in 1971, about half of all black teen-agers were not in school. The dropout rate of black teens in college was also high. Of those not in school, over one-third were also unemployed.

Should we encourage all of our children to go to college?

Only if they appear interested in going. People who are forced to go to college are often unhappy, drop out, and waste money. Some students are better suited to careers in nonacademic occupations. Youngsters might wish to be auto mechanics, plumbers, electricians, truck drivers or construction workers, for example—none of which require a college degree. There are now many openings for blacks in the technological fields which only require one or two years of college or other training. These jobs pay very good salaries. You should help your teen seek the necessary training for these occupations. Nonetheless, you should encourage him or her to at least complete high school.

A number of black youngsters have trouble at
predominantly white colleges. What is the problem?

The adjustment to college is often difficult for youngsters, black or white, rich or poor. It often means a move from a situation in which you were comfortable socially, good academically and known by many students and adults to a community of strangers as good as or better than you academically. The move is at a time when teens are throwing off parental and societal values and ways and attempting to find who they are and what values and ways they can live with.

In addition to the above, black youths are throwing off a negative societal attitude and often a negative personal attitude about blacks; in search of a positive black identity. There is a need to be active and to make blackness and the world okay, right now, yesterday. Because of past racism there are too few black authority figures with too little power; thus it is sometimes hard to trust them and use them as models and "evidence" that they can make it.

Again, because of racism, past and present, many black students are from modest to "little competition" backgrounds and many white students have been in highly competitive situations since nursery school. Many whites are from families where parents are decision-makers and community leaders—some with money and "contacts."

Outright and subtle racist acts cause much difficulty. A security guard yelled at a black student to get off the grass in a way that he ordinarily addressed "town blacks" but not students. He changed his tone when he discovered he was a student. Situation: rude white authority figure; emerging black determined to be a man; some guilt over different status to town blacks; and a probable penalty for a violent response. Outcome: rage and anger which he handled by smashing a plate glass window and injuring his arm.

All of these things affect a person's confidence, sense of "right to be here," right to be future leaders and, in turn, his or her ability to perform socially and academically. For these reasons, many equally bright black youngsters do not perform as well as some whites. Many catch up late in college, professional school, or on the job after they experience enough success to feel "I am and I can."

What has been the black student response?

Attack and withdrawal, some healthy and some not so healthy. Attack has ranged from militant strong arm tactics to disciplined academic and social action. Withdrawal has been designed to create social comfort and has ranged from black living quarters to individual apathy and paralysis. Black studies programs, black cultural and social programs have been a useful middle ground and necessary awareness approaches; although even here, in some cases, you see protective withdrawal and attacks—"no whites in our black history course." The most troublesome outcome has been the destructive black on black attacks—on black peers of different color, income and style; on black faculty (and vice versa) and sometimes even on black townspeople. We have seen too many bright black youngsters—with unhealthy responses—drop out or barely make it, without the grades or the growth to go on to professional schools. Black on black conflict is tragic but understandable. Oppressed people in a competitive system usually fight each other as much as or more than they fight the oppressor.

How can we help?

Parents, teachers, and community leaders must be more understanding. We must help black youngsters, before and during college, think through the maze of complex issues they face. We have heard too many black leaders condemn the youngsters and talk about "the hard times we had"—less money, *no* black faculty, blatant discrimination, and so on. What our generation did not have was the five to ten years of sensitization to the severity of racism during our growing social awareness period of eight to eighteen years old. In addition we had less charge to do something about it, other than learn and graduate.

As individuals and as a black community we must fight racism in colleges, universities and everywhere else. But to achieve the numbers to do this, we must get more black students through, achieving well, in spite of racism. If we are open with our teens rather than put down their concerns and feelings, we can be helpful.

You want to encourage your youngster to participate in black campus affairs and legitimate causes. But you should stress that good academic performance comes *first*. Well trained professionals will have more power to effect change than students . . . although students can help keep us all honest. Every social problem your youngster is concerned about now will be there, in some form, four, eight years from now. Again, you want to remind students that they must determine who (peer, black or white faculty) is for real—what he or she *does* rather than how much noise they make.

Without putting students down, you might ask them if they don't have to experience the system before they can understand how to effectively change it; whether they don't have to follow before they can lead. You might also suggest to them that they can aid the black cause through service. In some college towns with many black students, it is difficult to find tutors, scout leaders, big brothers, etcetera, for younger students. Some black students, because of limited previous exposure, attempt to make appointments with busy people on short notice, show up late or fail to show up without notice, fail to acknowledge unusual assistance and so on. Parents and teachers in charge of pre-college programs should help students develop such skills.

Black on black attacks: We must all help each other look at what we are doing to each other.

"Black men have been kept down and black women should now take a back seat and allow the men to take the leadership positions in college and in careers after college." Expletive deleted! We need all the best people we can produce and don't let your daughter buy that jive.

Many black students have none or few of these hangups. With continued help, fewer will develop them.

Should we encourage our children to attend a predominantly white college?

You should help your children think about what they want in a college—academic, social, prestige, etcetera—but urge them to make their own choice. There is no reason that they *must* attend a predominantly white school. Some black students feel more comfortable in a predominantly black atmosphere. Black colleges have played an important role in developing black leaders. The quality of academic offerings in black colleges is being strengthened by the increased number of well-trained blacks on these faculties. On the other hand, nowadays many "white" colleges have enough black students to prevent your children from feeling isolated. Predominantly white colleges should not be avoided because of fear of competing with whites. Students should select a college where they will receive a good education in line with their career goals.

My daughter wants to major in black studies in college.
Isn't that a waste of time?

Black studies should be seen as any other major field of study, no less or no more. We need competent and knowledgeable blacks in the field of black studies as in all other fields. But it should not be selected to resolve identity problems or to prove one's blackness. At the same time, black studies programs are important in enhancing a student's understanding of white racism and black consciousness. She should not select black studies because she heard it is "easy." That attitude in itself may indicate she is a victim of tactics used by some to discredit black studies programs. She might wish to select a backup major in another field to maximize her future job opportunities.

Careers and Employment

How can we help our teen-ager select a career?

First, help your child to explore the many career possibilities available. Parents sometimes try to fulfill their own dreams through the careers of their children. It is unwise for you to try to force your teen-ager into a career primarily because of your desires. Youngsters should be encouraged to make their own career decisions with parental help and guidance. You should discuss issues such as satisfaction, income, employment conditions and opportunities a particular career will bring. This will help your youngster determine whether that field is "him" or "her" or not. Have your teen-agers arrange to talk to people in fields in which they have interest.

School guidance counselors should be the best source of career information but this is not always the case. Many community organizations have educational counseling services. Check with the Urban League, NAACP, the United Negro College Fund, and other national or local education action groups for advice or referral to the appropriate program. In most urban areas there are counseling programs at Model Cities, Neighborhood Youth Corps, and Youth Opportunity Centers. Local community colleges are increasing their counseling services and many colleges and universities have transitional counseling and tutorial services for high school youth.

*You spoke earlier of the high unemployment rate among
black teen-agers. What are some of the causes for this?*

First, it must be clearly understood that the desire for employment
is high among black teen-agers. But jobs and training programs are
just not sufficiently available. Many black teen-agers who are high
school dropouts often lack the skills required for white collar jobs.
Discrimination by unions also keeps young blacks out of appren-
ticeship programs and high paying blue collar jobs. Many available jobs are far from the areas where many black youths live, with
poor transportation to and from the jobs.

*Should black teen-agers be encouraged to take jobs
even though they're still in school?*

Yes, as long as the hours are not so demanding that they interfere
with school performance. A job can serve important purposes for
teen-agers. In addition to supplying them with money, jobs help
them learn new skills, job requirements and responsibilities.
Through job experience young people also get practice in scheduling their time and accepting just authority. On the job, they may
also gain practical experience in race-related problems with which
they will have to cope in the future.

What is the best way for a black teen-ager to get a job?

Check your local youth employment center for jobs. Often the
city's Chamber of Commerce, or Mayor's Office, or Model Cities
will have special listings for young people. Particularly in large
urban areas, there will be a number of community groups which
specialize in job placement. Newspapers and radio broadcasts are
often helpful. It is probably best to aid a more timid youngster in
his/her job seeking. It is also important for you to express an
interest in the type of work and the kind of pay and treatment
your child is receiving on the job. If your teen-ager seeks a summer job, it is important that job hunting is done well in advance.

Some youngsters are not aware that appearance, personality,
and style are important with regard to securing or holding a job. A
youngster who has been taught to make a "good show" all along
has an advantage. One who has good work habits—on time, takes
care of business, and is cordial with others—has the best chance of
holding a job. Of course this does not mean take anything. Even

when one must stop abuse, there is a way to do it that will increase the respect one gets, when dealing with reasonable people, rather than cost one the job. Parents, teachers, counselors, and others should have given a youngster these skills, but if not, better now than after a few work failures.

We know of work programs where liberal whites could not tell poorly groomed black youngsters that they were in trouble job-wise. If you can't say, "Look man [or however you say it], you are not going to make it like that" and tell him how he can, you should not be in that job.

*Is it true that black children are less motivated
to achieve on jobs than youths from other groups?*

No. The level of motivation among black youths ranges from high to low as it does with other racial groups. A child's aspirations are largely determined by his environment. A child assesses his life chance in reference to the people with whom he identifies. The motivation to achieve is directly related to his past encouragement and support for work efforts, and to his belief that he has opportunities or access to satisfying work experiences.

*Should we allow our boy to drop out of
school to join the Armed Services?*

You should encourage your children to remain in school. If your son decides to join the Armed Services later, his chances for advancement will be greater if he has a high school or college education. If he decides to join anyway, urge him to take advantage of the education and training programs in these services. Follow up even if he has no initial interest. The discipline developed in the service sometimes makes it possible for a youngster who could not previously work in school to pursue educational or training programs later on.

What if our boy wants to join the volunteer Army?

Black men should join the Army if they really desire to do so. It is important that blacks attain positions of authority within all the branches of the Armed Services. In addition, the Army can help many young men develop discipline, a sense of responsibility and maturity. There are several negative aspects to the volunteer Army, especially the fact that the Army is often the only place to secure employment for certain groups of men.

Is there still racial discrimination in the Armed Services?

Yes. Black military personnel indicate that there is still discrimination, but it is more subtle than the open bigotry of the past. There have been racial clashes between white and black American troops in many parts of the world. However, there is now more opportunity for training and advancement for blacks than ever before. Some black men feel there is more racial equality in the Navy, Army, and Air Force than in civilian life.

Should girls enlist in the military? Doesn't it offer educational opportunities and a chance to travel?

As girls and young women look favorably to careers before marriage, the military is a reasonable option. It does offer valuable educational and travel opportunities. Other programs such as the Peace Corps, Africa Travel Groups, and so on also offer training and travel programs that aid in providing services to nations developing economically and educationally. It should be kept in mind that the primary mission of the military is war-related. You want to make certain that your youngster has considered this fact before making a decision.

Should black youths be advised to join the police forces of this nation, including the FBI?

Yes, if they have an interest in doing so. There is a need for black input and control of the social organizations and institutions that affect the black community. Crime rates among black people are high, in part, because indifferent and/or hostile white policemen have not shown proper respect for nor enforced the laws in the black community. Hopefully, black officers would have a different attitude and a greater commitment to and understanding of black community problems.

What careers do you think will be important for black youths to consider in the future?

Blacks have traditionally been involved in the service areas—teaching, medical care, social work, and so on. These are important areas but we need blacks in all fields, eventually obtaining our fair share of leadership positions. The employment areas most promising for blacks in the future include: business and economic development, technological fields, politics and government—at the local, state and federal level—foreign affairs, especially focused around Africa and the Caribbean, and social planning.

Aren't there enough blacks now going into professions?

No, although the number of black college graduates is increasing. We still have a long way to go for proportional representation. Black men represent about 8.5 percent of all employed males in the United States but only about 2 to 3 percent of all doctors and dentists and only about 1.5 percent of all engineers.

Community Involvement and Political Action

How can we involve our teens in building a
stronger black community?

Hopefully you have exposed your youngsters all along through your own involvement in community activities. At adolescence youngsters begin to look beyond their own needs. They identify with community ideas, ideals and causes as a way of establishing their own identity. Service to others and the community helps them to establish their humanity. Teen-agers should become involved in community self-help activities and particularly programs helping younger children. We have too few black college youngsters involved in community service activities because the idea of service and the opportunities to serve or help others are not introduced at the elementary school age. They should also participate in programs which will teach them about the nature of racism and provide them with realistic humanistic strategies to reduce this problem in our society. The attitudes and awareness gained during adolescence are carried into adulthood.

What clubs or organizations should we
encourage our teen-age children to join?

Teen-agers can become involved in activities of the major civil rights groups as well as in local community groups. The NAACP, the National Urban League, the Southern Christian Leadership Conference, the Congress of Racial Equality, and Operation

PUSH (People United to Save Humanity) welcome the active participation of black youth. Sororities and fraternities are also working on community projects and offer social opportunities.

Are there other groups?

Yes. There are church organizations, Muslim youth groups, and many emerging community-based youth organizations. In most large cities there are agencies that have programs for youth or referral services. The YMCA and YWCA's now have branches based in the community with special programming for young people and there are local community action agencies under the Economic Opportunity Program. Teen-agers and young adults should be encouraged and aided in establishing their own organizations around special programs in the community such as anti-drug and anti-crime projects, clean-up campaigns, educational tutoring programs, big sister/brother programs with preschoolers and various other education, recreation, and community development projects.

*Should we permit our children to join
groups which advocate violence?*

Many such groups are involved in constructive programs such as economic and community development, free food programs, free medical clinics and political involvement. Most have advocated violence only in self-defense. However, because of police attacks there *is* a danger to your youngsters' well-being as a member of any such group. You should discuss *all* the pros and cons of joining such a group with your teen-ager. If you feel that it is dangerous, unnecessary and you don't want your child to join, you should say so in a calm, rational manner. But it is unwise to tell a teen that he or she cannot and must not join. That can be the stimulus to join secretly, even when he or she really doesn't want to, and you may never know.

Should we encourage our eighteen-year-old to vote?

By all means. But again, teen-agers learn by example. If you want your eighteen-year-old to vote, you should vote. If she went to the polls with you when she was nine or ten, she is more likely to want to vote now. The black community needs to exercise its political strength through the ballot box. Presently, just over one-half of eligible black adults are registered to vote. Often far fewer actually vote.

My son recently turned eighteen years old; however, he refuses to register to vote. He says voting won't make a difference for black people. What can I say?

This is a very unfortunate point of view held by some young people. You should help your son understand changes come about through many kinds of strategies and the ballot is an important one. Malcolm X had the correct point of view when he said that we must work to liberate black people through any means necessary, and voting is clearly an important means. There is a give and take in the political process that doesn't pay off on a large scale every day. On the other hand, if you don't stay involved at every opportunity, it rarely or never pays off. When you have something powerful which people need, you are more powerful and they must pay attention to you and your needs. If we don't vote and remain interested and involved in the overall political process, our needs will be ignored because we will not be the margin of victory in an election or a force to be reckoned with at the city council hearing.

Complicated political and economic shifts are taking place right now which will leave cities unable to educate black children, provide recreational services and so on. Yet black public officials point out that even blacks who vote go home and leave them without visible support in the week to week battles against resistent police departments, city councils and other powerful public and private officials.

We can dream of dramatic actions which will bring about rapid change. But, all things considered, the only thing we can really count on is a day to day effort in the political and economic arenas. You should help your youngster think about the role he or she is or isn't playing, can or can't play. Is your child in groups which have ties with decision-makers—unions, political clubs, etcetera? Again, we love the art or aesthetic side of black culture, but if we don't encourage our youngsters to pay more attention to the political and economic side, our communities are going to be in even deeper trouble in a few years.

Because too few blacks vote and it is so important to the welfare of our young, we want to respond to a few questions which many of you will consider "elementary." But some of these issues keep people away from the polls and away from general participation in the larger society. We hope you will consider such "minor" issues and discuss them with your youngsters and others you work with. School and other programs at every level should develop ways to make participation in the larger political process less foreign.

How does a teen-ager register to vote?

In most cities, there is a voter registration section in City Hall where a person can register anytime during the week. In some large cities, there are community-based "Little City Halls" where residents can register in their own neighborhood. During major local and national election periods special voter registration times and places are established and there is publicity about where and when to vote in the news media. Voter registration is often closed several weeks before major elections, so it is not good to wait until a major election year to register to vote. Young people should register on their eighteenth birthday, or soon after.

What should a black youth do if denied registration at City Hall?

Often people are denied the opportunity to register because they go to register without proof of birth date and residency. Be certain that your youngster has written proof of these two things when going to register. There should be no other reason to prevent an American citizen from voting. Race, literacy tests, voting fees, and other devices are now *illegal*.

Is it true that if a youth has been in trouble
with the law, she/he cannot register to vote?

Juvenile delinquency and other misdemeanor offenses such as traffic offenses do not disqualify a youth from voting privileges. The only crimes that prevent an eighteen-year-old from voting are felonies.

If an eighteen-year-old plans to go away to college
for four years, what address should she/he
use as residency, home or college?

Students in general should maintain residency in their hometown in order to vote in elections of local importance. It is not difficult for them to obtain an absentee ballot.

What does voter education entail?

Voter education can take many forms from basic instruction on how to use voting machines to information on complex taxation issues. Few city governments in America provide adequate non-partisan voter education and the citizen has to rely on private sources or political campaigns for necessary information. Unfortunately, when people go to register to vote in most cities of this nation they are not even instructed on how to use the complex voting machines. The schools or community groups in your area should make it their business to conduct voter education courses where children, beginning in their pre-teens, can go through demonstrations using voting booths.

Often, persons running for political office will hold meetings, all-day conferences, "meet the candidates night" and related activities to inform voters of the key issues. Local chapters of the NAACP and the League of Women Voters are usually good sources for voter education. Young black women should be encouraged to join the League of Women Voters, or to organize their own voter education groups within the black community.

What should a registered young voter do if he goes to
the polls on voting day and is told he's not registered?

Don't just walk away. If you know you are registered, ask the clerk at the polls to check further. If nothing results, go to the main City Hall or place where you originally registered. Many communities also give voter registration identification cards. If this is the procedure in your community, each voter is responsible for presenting such identification at the polls. Encourage a youngster to clear up what are usually bureaucratic misunderstandings so that he or she can at least be sure to vote in the next election. You should urge and assist them in contacting a civil rights group if they are denied either registration or the vote.

What if a young voter gets confused in the voting
booth and doesn't know what to do or can't find
his candidate's name on the ballot?

Often if a person feels pressured, she/he will panic. Instruct the young voter to take his or her time and read the ballot carefully. Even though there may be a long line of people waiting, there is usually no time limit on staying in the voting booth. If young voters have problems with the levers, they should call the booth attendant for assistance. Don't be embarrassed. Many people are sometimes confused.

What is bloc voting?

Bloc voting usually refers to a special interest group supporting one candidate or issue. For instance, the entire black community might only vote for black candidates on the ballot. Many political critics discourage bloc voting, but it has been used effectively by ethnic groups for decades to get their candidates in office. We believe that it is important to vote for the candidate who will best meet your needs and the needs of your community, black or white.

CHAPTER 9

A Final Word

You have now read many questions and answers with some general and specific discussion on rearing the black child. We hope that our responses have been helpful to you, whether you are a parent, teacher, social worker, or friend. We realize that we have not answered all of your questions—a book of this short length can only begin to discuss the issues that relate to black child development. But we have tried to provide general approaches to child rearing that you can apply to your specific problems in helping black children in your home and community.

This book then should be a basic guide to you and a source of important information. But you, the parent or caretaker, still remain the best judge—the final "expert"—on how to rear your child. We urge you to continue to rely on your basic, good common sense in coping with the everyday issues with your youngsters. Respect your children as individuals and they will respect you. Remember that your task is to develop your skills to be an effective child-developer and that your goal is to produce a healthy, strong, and mature black adult who is able to cope, achieve, and constructively bring about change in America.

We want to stress once again that some of the information you want to provide your children with and some of the ideas you want to help them think through are complicated and sometimes threatening. Thus, you must always play it by ear. You want to use words and give explanations suitable to your child's age. You don't want to jam information or ideas down your child's throat when he or she is not ready (can't tolerate it) to hear it. You don't have to explain anything all at once. If you are able to talk about anger, race, sex, drugs, and other charged areas, your youngster will open the topic, or make it known that it is okay for you to open the topic, for discussion.

But sometimes we all get tired and emotionally taxed in caring for our young. We adults too are only human and cannot expect perfection in ourselves. We will make mistakes. But that is part of life. No single mistake, usually not even many, will "break" or hurt your child as long as you genuinely care and you are doing your best. Even your best is not enough in some situations, but that is all you can do.

There are times when we all need support and guidance. This is a fact for which we need not feel ashamed. Stand ready to consult the books suggested on the following pages that deal with specific issues in child rearing and we urge you to seek help in assisting your youngster whenever situations arise that overwhelm you. Talk to your friends, speak to your clergyman, teacher, and social worker, and don't be afraid to consult with a psychologist or psychiatrist when the need arises. Don't be embarrassed to ask questions and seek advice—none of us has the luxury of knowing all the answers. Many persons both professional and nonprofessional can be an important resource to you as you struggle in this often harsh world to raise a healthy black child.

Social problems of poverty and racism continue to affect a great bulk of the black community. But, today blacks are attempting to look beyond the basic struggle for survival and want to participate fully in the dreams and opportunities shared by all citizens. Building strong black children will help these dreams to come true. While your job is important, it does not help to get uptight. Relax and enjoy your children.

If this book contributes just a small bit to these goals, our efforts in writing this volume will be time well spent. We are satisfied that there will be a brighter future for all our sons and daughters.

Suggested Readings

1. The Black Child

The Black Child, Special Issue, *Ebony* Magazine, August 1974.
The Black Child: A Parent's Guide, Phyllis Harrison-Ross and Barbara Wyden (Wyden).
Getting It Together, Phyllis Anne Harrison, M.D. (Globe).
The Psychology of Black Language, Jim Haskins and Hugh F. Butts, M.D. (Barnes & Noble).

2. General Child Rearing

Baby and Child Care, Benjamin Spock (Pocket Books).
Baby Learning Through Baby Play: A Parent's Guide for the First Two Years, Ira J. Gordon (St. Martin's).
Between Parent and Child, Haim G. Ginott (Avon).
Between Parent and Teenager, Haim G. Ginott (Avon).
How to Father, Fitzhugh Dodson (Nash).
How to Parent, Fitzhugh Dodson (Nash; New American Library paperback).

3. Books on Child Discipline

Living with Children: New Methods for Parents and Teachers, Gerald R. Patterson and M. Elizabeth Gullion (Research Press).
New Ways in Discipline, Dorothy Baruch (McGraw-Hill).
Parent Effectiveness Training, Thomas Gordon (Wyden).

4. Books Which Help Parents Understand the World from the Child's Point of View

The Complete Book of Children's Play, Ruth E. Hartley and Robert M. Goldenson (Crowell).
Your Child's Sensory World, Lise Liepmann (Dial).
Your Inner Child of the Past, Hugh Missildine (Simon and Schuster).

5. Books on the Education of Your Children

Give Your Child a Superior Mind, Siegfried and Therese Engelmann (Simon and Schuster).
The Open Classroom: A Practical Guide to a New Way of Teaching, Herbert R. Kohl (Random House).
A Parent's Guide to Children's Education, Nancy Larrick (Trident; Pocket Books).

6. Guides for Children's Reading

Best Books for Children, Patricia Allen (Bowker paperback).
A Parent's Guide to Children's Reading, Nancy Larrick (Pocket Books).

7. When Your Child Is Ill

When Your Child Is Ill: A Guide to Infectious Diseases in Childhood, Samuel Karelitz (Random House).
Young Children in Hospitals, James Robertson (Barnes & Noble).

8. A Guide to Baby-Sitters

A Parent's Guide to Baby-Sitting, Faye Cobb (Pocket Books).

9. Sex Education

Boys and Sex, Wardell B. Pomeroy (Delacorte).
Facts About Sex, Sol Gordon (John Day).
Girls and Sex, Wardell B. Pomeroy (Delacorte).
New Ways in Sex Education: A Guide for Parents and Teachers, Dorothy Baruch (McGraw-Hill).

10. The Handicapped Child

Caring for Your Disabled Child, Benjamin M. Spock and M. O. Lerrigo (Macmillan; Fawcett paperback).
Child in the Shadows: A Manual for Parents of Retarded Children, Edward French and Clifford Scott (Lippincott).
The Directory for Exceptional Children: Education and Training Facilities, Porter Sargent (Porter Sargent).

11. The Adopted Child

Adoption and After, Louise Raymond (Harper & Row).
If You Adopt a Child, Carol and Helen Doss (Holt, Rinehart and Winston).

12. Understanding Drugs

Marijuana, A Signal of Misunderstanding: The Official Report of the National Commission on Marijuana and Drug Abuse (New American Library paperback).
A Parent's Guide to the Prevention and Control of Drug Abuse, Paul M. Goldhill (Regnery).
You, Your Child, and Drugs, Child Study Association of America (Child Study Press).

13. Divorce

Explaining Divorce to Children, Earl A. Grollman, ed. (Beacon).
Parents Without Partners: A Guide for Divorced, Widowed, or Separated Parents, Jim Egleson and Janet Egelson (Dutton).

14. Crises of Childhood

What to Tell Your Child about Birth, Death, Illness, Divorce and Other Family Crises, Helene Arnstein (Bobbs-Merrill).

15. Safety

The Mother's Guide to Child Safety, Bryson Kalt and Ralph Bass (Grosset & Dunlap).

16. Careers

The Guide to Career Education, Muriel Lederer (Quadrangle/New York Times Book Co.).
Lovejoy's College Guide, Clarence E. Lovejoy (Simon and Schuster).

17. Child Development

Child Care and Development, Louise B. Ames (Lippincott).
Child Care, Who Cares? Foreign and Domestic Infant and Early Childhood Development Policies, Pamela Roby, ed. (Basic Books).
The Child Under Six, Jesild Hymes, Jr. (Prentice-Hall).
Childhood and Adolescence: A Psychology of the Growing Person, L. Joseph Stone and Joseph Church (Random House).
Childhood and Society, Erik H. Erikson (Norton).
Children: Behavior and Development, B. R. McCandless (Holt, Rinehart and Winston).
Clinical Aspects of Child Development, Melvin Lewis (Lea & Febiger).
Current Issues in Adolescent Psychiatry, Joseph Schoolar, ed. (Brunner/Mazel).
Disadvantaged Children: Health, Nutrition and School Failure, Herbert G. Birch and Joan D. Gussow (Harcourt Brace Jovanovich).
Early Child Care: The New Perspectives, Caroline A. Chandler, Reginald Lourie, Ann Peters; Laura L. Dittmann, ed. (Aldine-Atherton).
Infants in Institutions, Sally Provence and Rose C. Lipton (International Universities Press).
The Learning Child, Dorothy H. Cohen (Pantheon).
The Magic Years, Selma Fraiberg (Scribner's).
Sympathetic Understanding of the Child: Six to Sixteen, David Elkind (Allyn & Bacon).
Theories of Child Development, A. L. Baldwin (Wiley).

18. Children's Rights

Beyond the Best Interests of the Child, Joseph Goldstein, Anna Freud and Albert J. Solnit (Free Press).
Children's Rights: Toward the Liberation of the Child, Paul Adams et al. (Praeger).
Crisis in Child Mental Health: Challenge for the 1970's, Report of the Joint Commission on Mental Health of Children (Harper & Row).

The Rights of Children, Special Issue, *Harvard Educational Review;* Parts I & II, November 1973 and February 1974.
Violence Against Children: Physical Child Abuse in the United States, David G. Gil (Harvard University Press).
When Parents Fail: The Law's Response to Family Breakdown, Sanford N. Katz (Beacon).

19. The Family

Black Families in White America, Andrew Billingsley (Prentice-Hall, Inc.).
The Black Family: Essays and Studies, Robert Staples, ed. (Wadsworth).
The Black Family in Modern Society, John H. Scanzoni, ed. (Allyn & Bacon).
The Child in His Family: The Impact of Disease and Death, Volume 2, E. James Anthony and Cyrille Koupernik, eds. (Wiley).
Children of the Storm: Black Children and American Child Welfare, Andrew Billingsley and Jeanne M. Giovannoni (Harcourt Brace Jovanovich).
The Family Life of Black People, Charles V. Willie (Merrill).
The Future of the Family, Louise K. Howe, ed. (Simon and Schuster).
The Social Context of Marriage, J. Richard Udry, ed. (Lippincott).
The Strengths of Black Families, Robert B. Hill (Emerson Hall).

20. Women's Rights

Changing Women in a Changing Society, Joan Huber, ed. (University of Chicago Press).
The Female Eunuch, Germaine Greer (McGraw-Hill).
Vaginal Politics, Ellen Frankfort (Quadrangle).
Women and Child Care in China, Ruth Sidel (Hill & Wang).
Women's Liberation: Blueprint for the Future, Sookie Stambler (Ace).

21. Children in History

Centuries of Childhood: A Social History of Family Life, Phillippe Aries (Vintage).
The Child and the Republic: The Dawn of Modern American Child Nurture, Bernard Wishy (University of Pennsylvania Press).

Children and Youth in America: A Documentary History, Volumes I & II, Robert H. Bremner et al., eds. (Harvard University Press).
Parents and Children in History: The Psychology of Family Life in Early Modern France, David Hunt (Basic Books).

22. Racial Issues

The Autobiography of Malcolm X, Alex Haley, ed. (Grove).
Beyond Black and White, James P. Comer (Quadrangle).
Black Child, White Child: The Development of Racial Attitudes, Judith D. Porter (Harvard University Press).
Black Power: The Politics of Liberation in America, Stokely S. Carmichael and Charles V. Hamilton (Random House).
The Black Power Revolt: A Collection of Essays, Floyd B. Barbour, ed. (Porter Sargent).
Black Psychology, Reginald L. Jones, ed. (Harper & Row).
Black Rage, William H. Grier and Price M. Cobbs (Basic Books).
Black Skin, White Masks, Frantz Fanon (Grove).
Blaming the Victim, William Ryan (Vintage).
Children of Crisis, Volumes 1–3, Robert Coles (Little, Brown).
Dark Ghetto: Dilemmas of Social Power, Kenneth B. Clark (Harper & Row).
How to Get Along with Black People: A Handbook for White Folks (& Some Black Folks Too!), Chris Clark and Sheila Rush (Third Press—Joseph Okpaku).
Invisible Man, Ralph Ellison (Signet).
The Mark of Oppression, Abraham Kardiner and Lionel Ovesey (Norton).
The Moynihan Report and the Politics of Controversy, Lee Rainwater and William L. Yancey (M.I.T. Press).
Nature of Prejudice, Gordon W. Allport (Addison—Wesley).
The Negro American, Talcott Parsons and Kenneth B. Clark, eds. (Houghton Mifflin).
Nobody Knows My Name, James Baldwin (Dial).
Prejudice and Your Child, Kenneth B. Clark (Beacon).
A Profile of the Negro American, Thomas Pettigrew (Van Nostrand Reinhold).
Racism and Mental Health, Charles V. Willie, Bernard M. Kramer, Bertram S. Brown, eds. (University of Pittsburgh Press).
Racism and Psychiatry, Alexander Thomas and Samuel Sillen (Brunner/Mazel).
Sexual Life Between Blacks and Whites, Beth Day (World).
The Souls of Black Folk, W. E. B. Du Bois (New American Library).

White Over Black: American Attitudes Toward the Negro, Winthrop D. Jordan (Penguin).
White Racism: A Psychohistory, Joel Kovel (Pantheon).
Why Blacks Kill Blacks, Alvin F. Poussaint (Emerson Hall).
The Wretched of the Earth, Frantz Fanon (Grove).

23. Education

Black Self-Concept: Implications for Education and Social Science, J. A. Banks and J. D. Grambs (McGraw-Hill).
Day Care and Preschool Services: Trends and Issues, Ronald K. Parker and Jane Knitzer (Avatar Press).
Democracy and Education, John Dewey (Free Press).
Illusions of Equality: The Effect of Education on Opportunity, Inequality, and Social Conflict, Murray Milner (Jossey–Bass).
Inequality in Education, published in two issues by the Center for Law and Education, Harvard University: *Perspectives on Child Care,* December 1972, and *Citizen Voice in the Public Schools,* November 1973.
Learning for Tomorrow, Alvin Toffler, ed. (Vintage).

24. Love and Sex

Human Sexual Response, William H. Masters and Virginia E. Johnson (Little, Brown).
The Menstrual Cycle, Katharina Dalton (Pantheon).
The New Sex Therapy, Helen Singer Kaplan (Brunner/Mazel).
The Sex Book: A Modern Pictorial Encyclopedia, Martin Goldstein and Erwin J. Haeberle (Seabury).
Sex Education and the New Morality: A Search for a Meaningful Social Ethnic, Child Study Association of America (Child Study Press).
Sex, Gender, and Society, Anne Oakley (Harper & Row).
The Sexual Adolescent: Communicating with Teenagers About Sex, Sol Gordon (Duxbury).
A Teenager's Guide to Life and Love, Benjamin Spock (Pocket Books).

25. Television

Children and Television—Lessons from Sesame Street, Gerald S. Lesser (Random House).
The Early Window: Effects of Television on Children and Youth, R. M. Liebert, John M. Neale and Emily S. Davidson (Pergamon Press).

26. Poverty

Culture and Poverty: Critique and Counter-Proposals, Charles A. Valentine (University of Chicago Press).

The Other America: Poverty in the United States, Michael Harrington (Penguin).

A Relevant War Against Poverty: A Study of Community Action Programs and Observable Social Change, Kenneth B. Clark and Jeannette Hopkins (Harper & Row).

Tomorrow's Tomorrow: The Black Woman, Joyce A. Ladner (Doubleday).

27. Violence

Report of the National Advisory Commission on Civil Disorders (Bantam).

Violence in America: Historical and Comparative Perspectives, Hugh D. Graham and Ted R. Gurr (New American Library).

Violence in the Family, Suzanne K. Steinmetz and Murray A. Straus, eds. (Dodd, Mead).

28. Youth, Attitudes and Problems

The Changing Values on Campus: Political and Personal Attitudes of Today's College Students, Daniel Yankelovich (Washington Square Press).

Manual on Alcoholism (American Medical Association, Chicago).

The Uncommitted: Alienated Youth in American Society, Kenneth Keniston (Dell).

Youth and Dissent: The Rise of a New Opposition, Kenneth Keniston (Harcourt Brace Jovanovich).

Index

parent-teacher relationships, 180–
184
parole, in criminal cases, 360
passiveness
vs. aggression, 63
dangers of, 12
patience, teaching of, 41
Peace Corps, 377
peek-a-boo games, 40
peer pressure, coping with, 270–
271
penis
child's interest in, 69
in sexual intercourse, 254, 323–
325, 329
washing and handling of, 53
period, *see* menstruation
permissiveness in infancy, 53–58
personal development in baby,
30–31, 43–44
pets, mistreatment of, 205
photography hobby, 259–61
piano lessons, 259
pictures, drawing of, 35, 38, 75–77
pimps, 339–41
planning and organizing problems,
163–64
play
anger and frustration in, 74
"best" kind of, 76–77
body control through, 77
"favorite friends" in, 85
importance of, 75–81
indoor and outdoor, 34–35
language development in, 77–78
learning through, 40–41
parents' role in, 160
rejected child in, 85–86
for school-age child, 129
social development and, 83–84
supervision in, 84–85
Pledge of Allegiance, 12, 117–19
policemen, dislike for, 224–27,
358
pornography, 323–24
postnatal depression, 27

power struggles in childhood, 47
praise, as discipline, 237
pregnancy
abortion and, 333–34
douching and, 334
explaining of, 252–53
health during, 26–27
intercourse and, 329–30
malnutrition in, 17
marriage and, 332–33
mechanism of, 252–53
miscarriage and, 334
out of wedlock, 333
preschool child and, 100
premarital sex, 319–20
preschool child (ages 2–4), 59–
114
adopted, 103–07
books for, 79
dancing by, 77
death and, 112–13
disciplining of, 70–75
divorce and, 110–11
drawings by, 76–77
fairness and sharing in, 88
"favorite" in, 99–100
guilt in, 90–91
hospitalization of, 109–10
immoral conditions and, 89
lying by, 92–93
morality of, 87–95
mother's energy and, 102–03
mother's later pregnancy and,
100–101
parent's illness and, 108–09
play of, 75–81
punishment of, 70–75
race issue and, 65–69
reading to, 78–79
sex and, 69–70
sexual intercourse in presence
of, 91–92
sharing by, 88–89
society and, 83–87
stealing by, 89, 93–94
striking at or by, 73

T